CHINA-YELLOW

China-Yellow

Robin Hutcheon

The Chinese University Press

ISBN 962–201–725–8

THE CHINESE UNIVERSITY PRESS
The Chinese University of Hong Kong
SHA TIN, N. T., HONG KONG
Fax: +852 2603 6692
E-mail: cup@cuhk.edu.hk
Web-site: http://www.cuhk.edu.hk/cupress/w1.htm

Printed in Hong Kong

Contents

Introduction:
A Sea Change

For many hundreds of years China all but turned its back on the sea. It was of little interest to anyone but fishermen and pirates and their families. Its 14,000 kilometres of coastline was a natural buffer to the unknown, and what the eye could not see over the horizon did not matter. No enemies threatened from the east; the sea was not used for recreation nor admired for its beauty. It was where marauders and typhoons lurked and while marine life of all kinds found its way into markets of coastal towns, fish from inland lakes and rivers supplied most of the people's needs.

Chinese painters virtually ignored it and poets found little inspiration in the many moods of the seas, the tumbling waves, the rise and fall of the tides and the denizens of the deep. There was little in the way of waterfront development; minority and aboriginal groups were left to build huts or live on boats, afloat or ashore. For many centuries maritime marauders had lean pickings because of the poverty of the coastal rim.

Excavated beach settlements of earliest times show that life was spartan — a few bowls, fish cages, arrow heads, cooking pots and fish hooks. In the summer months many parts of the coast were battered by storms and typhoons; a strong gust could wipe out a rice crop, strip banana palms and batter lychee trees while a storm surge at high tide could inundate whole villages taking hundreds of lives. Apart from fishing, the big industry on the coast was the production of sea salt on tidal fields.

The coastline had none of the allure of the wine-dark Adriatic or Aegean Sea, and the myths and legends that abound in Chinese literature lack the nautical flavour that flows through European folklore. This is not to suggest a hydrophobic streak in Chinese people, for their civilization, rooted firmly in the alluvial plains of the northwest, is richly endowed with the element of water. Rivers, streams, lakes, reservoirs and canals are a common feature of the Chinese landscape; for the ever practical Chinese, water has to be useful and productive and kept under firm control. Five thousand of its rivers debouch into drainage basins of more than 100 square kilometres, one-third of that number extending to 1,000 square kilometres, equivalent to the total area of Kowloon, the New Territories and all the islands that make up Hong Kong.

The rivers of China, moreover, have a total navigable distance of more than 160,000 kilometres. Thus water is an ever present reality in the lives of most of the 1.2 billion people and becomes severely threatening in times of flood. The Chinese were among the earliest to devise flood control and prevention measures; as intuitive hydraulic engineers they were quick to discover ways and means of harnessing water to irrigate their fields to ensure regular crops of rice and vegetables.

In later years the Chinese developed maritime skills and built ships to sail the oceans and the seas to nearby islands such as Taiwan, Japan, the Philippines and, by skilful navigation, to the southern shores of Asia. In time, they sailed to the Indian subcontinent, Arabia and Africa — daunting journeys for all but hardened and experienced seamen relying on little more than the sun, the stars, and the prevailing winds and currents. The maritime trade was not, however, the lifeblood of China which prided itself on almost total self-sufficiency, materially and morally. What voyages it undertook in the dawn of the dynastic era appeared to have been occasional ventures in search of the exotic; for the most part, tribute missions from neighbouring states brought with them the trifles and trivia coveted by the rich — the elephant tusks, rhino horns, pearls, bird's nests, shark's fins, *bêche-de-mer*, tropical delicacies and spices.

Shifting boundaries within China caused by local rebellions and usurping strongmen, and violent incursions from aggressive border tribesmen tended to keep the focus of national attention towards the West; in times of peace, camel trains plodded across the barren sandy wastes of Turkestan and the snowy passes of the border states to bring the produce of Arabia, Africa and even Europe to China in exchange for silks and porcelain. This was China's front door to the outside world through which also moved the teachings of Indian Buddhism, Islam and even in a small way, Christianity and Judaism. Confucian China, however, had its own codes to bind the people and build a civilization as enduring and as unchangeable as any in history — until the new philosophies and ideas of the nineteenth and twentieth centuries supplanted them.

These changes were long in gestation and they arrived not in the books of itinerant monks or at the point of swords or spears of invading tribesmen but by sailing ships catching the monsoon winds blowing up the China seas, carrying silver and opium, and manned by sailors, soldiers, adventurers, revolutionaries, missionaries, diplomats and merchants from the West.

The main point of impact was the southern province of Guangdong though in earliest times, neighbouring Fujian was equally prominent both in receiving and initiating overseas contacts whether with Southeast Asian communities or further afield.

Much has been written about Hong Kong and Shanghai and the trade and investment both these cities have attracted. Of Guangzhou, less has been written except for the period immediately prior to, and during the Opium War. It is once again prominent as China's southern provinces swing on the coat-tails of a massive investment and development boom originating in Hong Kong and from a number of leading industrial nations anxious to make the most of China's huge force of workers and their increasing skills, versatility and adaptability.

Extravagant predictions are being made about how this region of China, particularly, will develop in the future and the extent to which the flow-on will benefit other parts of the country, many of which have been designated as Special Economic Zones. There is frequent speculation about the political impact on China as a whole, as increasing prosperity stimulates consumer demand and ushers in a higher quality of life which in turn impacts on the policies of the administration.

This book deals with the past and present and speculates on how China may grapple with the future; its concern is mainly with the economy and the way of life of the people. As with all economic change, sooner or later it stimulates political forces to work out the best ways of managing and controlling this process in the interests of the people. The influences that arrived through China's two main seas — the China and the Yellow — and their impact on the people, are the subject of this book.

Acknowledgements

There are many people who helped in bringing all the material in this book together: the Public Records Office at Kew, the PRO in Hong Kong, the Royal Society in London, the State Library of NSW, the staff of the South China Morning Post library and the librarian, Ms Judy Young, the Director of the Royal Botanic Gardens of NSW, Dr Carrick Chambers, Professor Brian Harrison, Mr G. R. Ross, Dr Solomon Bard, Dr Dachin Yih, Dr John Y. Wong, Mr Eric Cumine, Mr Neil Cumine, the late Mr Frank Doyle, the late Mr Noel Croucher, numerous friends in London, Hong Kong and Sydney, my wife, Bea, daughter, Jane, sons, Stephen (in Beijing) and Andrew (in London), daughters-in-law, and my late parents with whom I spent the first twelve years of my life in many parts of China. They contributed in many valuable ways. I thank them all for their help, advice, support and encouragement.

The insights on Chinese traditions, practices and attitudes offered by my wife were of immense assistance. The critical reading of my manuscript by Ms Olivia Wong and Professor Alice N. H. Lun Ng of The Chinese University of Hong Kong was particularly appreciated and her many suggestions were most helpful, as were conversations with Hong Kong friends, particularly Sir David Akers-Jones, Sir Piers Jacobs, Sir Jack Cater and Denis Bray. I also have to thank Ruthanne Lum McCunn for permission to describe events from the life of Lalu Nathoy in her biographical novel *Thousand Pieces of Gold* published by Design Enterprises of San Francisco. The ideas and insights of several other authors and lecturers, notably Professor Brian Harrison, have also contributed to the structure and detail of the story. To them, also, many thanks.

Illustrations have come from a number of sources; those by Auguste Borget from *La Chine Ouverte* by P. E. Forgues, published by H. Fournier, Paris, 1845, and republished in the author's biography of Borget; those by William Alexander, from *Views of 18th Century China*, published by Studio Editions Ltd; those of George Chinnery, from the author's biography of the artist, published by Form Asia. The photographs similarly are from several sources: the late Noel Croucher, who passed his collection to me; Mr K. A. Watson of Hong Kong; my late father, from his collection of photographs of Shanghai, and from *Shanghai of Today*, a collection of Vandyke prints taken in the 1920s, published by Kelly & Walsh, Shanghai. The New China News supplied two photographs in the final chapters. The cover photograph was provided by The Hong Kong Museum of History, Urban Council.

Personal reminiscences, experiences, interviews and chance encounters also helped to provide detail otherwise unobtainable. A cruise to China, arranged months previously, landed my wife and I in Beijing on the night of 4 June 1989, where at the British Embassy with Sir Alan and Lady Donald, we experienced the tense build-up to the coming storm and its bitter aftermath, without however witnessing the violence other than through the lenses of CNN. The Cultural Revolution was an experience remembered by all in Hong Kong in 1967. Bombings, piracies, air raids, floods, typhoons, evacuations, were all part of the life of old — and young — China Hands. However, this is a historical survey, not personal reminiscence, and it relies on the contributions of many.

CHAPTER 1

The Age of Discovery

A gang of workmen hauled two long planks from the muddy river bank to the side of a large squat junk. A thick central mast with a furled rattan sail pierced the main deck amidst benches for oarsmen, with heavy wooden oars stowed into the bulwarks. Labourers hammered wedges into the base of the gangways and tied the tops securely to the bollard on the junk's deck. A light rain fell as a few hundred people formed a corridor to the water's edge. A crew of weather-stained men lined the decks, hanging on to rigging as the surging tide ripped past the ship's side. Soon a line of chair-bearers came into view and stopped to allow the passengers to alight. A gong sounded. Smoking incense sticks were plunged into bronze braziers, the smoke spiralling into the moist air. Burning bamboo sticks crackled as the procession of 100 young men and women walked silently to the ship's side; they turned briefly to the assembly of officials and relations and bowed. Then two by two they mounted the gangways and disappeared into the lower deck of the junk. Large crates of treasure had been loaded into the holds hours before under heavily armed guards.

The fore and aft anchor stones were hauled aboard by sweating seamen chanting as they strained at a creaking capstan. As the junk cast off, oarsmen thrust long poles into the river to check its swing as the tide carried it into midstream. The crowd of watchers on the bank surged forward to the river's edge to catch a last glimpse as the oars were slipped into rowlocks to control its headway. It gathered speed until the tall mast of the junk disappeared downstream behind the fringe of trees on the bend of the river.

The mission of the young men and women — all well educated and from good families — was to search for an elixir for an Emperor craving immortality but ever fearful that his life would be cut short by illness or an assassin's knife. It was a land where hatred and terror reigned despite his boast that under his rule "the black haired people enjoy calm and repose." This rule he now wished to extend to "the four ends of the earth."

The truth was otherwise. The Qin Emperor Shihuangdi had endeared himself to few in unifying the feuding Chinese states. Apart from pacifying the northern tribes and extending the Great Wall he had thrust his despotic rule westwards and southwards to scoop in vast areas of land headed by feudal warlords. His aim

Figure 1.1 The Great Wall as sketched by Auguste Borget, following his return from China.

was to keep out the ever restless central Asian marauders bent on plundering the rich fertile croplands of the Yellow River, and to extend the boundaries of the late Zhou dynasty to embrace the barbarian lands of what are today Yunnan, Guangxi, Guangdong, Fujian and Tonkin.

In twelve hectic years (221–209 BC) this dynamic Emperor not only redrew the boundaries of the Chinese state but strengthened his grip on the south by forcing thousands of labourers to dig a 50-km canal to Xijiang or the West River. He then rounded up criminals, vagabonds and destitutes and ordered them to farm the lands of the south, whipping the recalcitrant locals into line at the same time. Through his henchmen, he instilled iron discipline among his people, "eating up its neighbours as a silkworm devours a leaf," as the great first century historian Sima Qian wrote.

Confucianism with its humanity, dignity and magnanimity was dumped; legalism and realism were introduced in their place. The classical writings were burnt, stubborn scholars tortured or executed and by a process of machiavellian intrigues coupled with decisive military strikes, the Qin ruler stitched together the fabric of the present Chinese nation, albeit tenuously. One of his greatest reforms was the standardization of the writing system throughout the empire which did more to bring about a national identity than any draconian edict, giving diverse people speaking different dialects the ability to communicate.

The young people who set out to search for the elixirs to prolong his life — the third such mission — never returned. Were they and their treasure ship seized by pirates, tipped off about their mission? Were they overtaken by a typhoon or shipwreck? Or were they, as some believe, washed up on the shores of the Japanese islands to enrich the emerging Iron Age tribal people with the pearls of Chinese culture, language and civilization?

The Qin Emperor, warned by fortune tellers of his dynasty's approaching nemesis, became a reclusive figure, moving from palace to palace and leaving affairs of state to a fearsome deputy, until death finally cornered and conquered him. The frantic activity of his last thirty years is today visible for all to see in the tumulus uncovered in 1974 by archaeologists in Xi'an. There, 700,000 artisans and workmen set to work to sculpture an army of more than 7,500 terracotta life-size soldiers and servants to accompany him on his last march to the underworld.

The Great Wall, the Grand Army, the network of canals and the wealth of jade, ceramic and bronze artefacts demonstrate that not only was the Qin Emperor a bold, innovative and dynamic tyrant but that China was already well endowed with unlimited manpower of high intellectual and artistic abilities, a powerful civilization needing little help from the outside world.

The extension of Qin rule to Guangdong and Guangxi did not bring prosperity in its wake but opened the eyes of newcomers to the potential of the south as a rice granary and an abundant source of diverse marine life and pearling which could do much to enrich those willing to toil and trade.

Following the collapse of the short-lived Qin rule, Guangdong and Guangxi moved into a new political orbit dominated by a military governor, Zhao Tuo, who established himself as King of Nan Yue and thus held sway for almost a century by judiciously offering regular tribute to the Qin successors. Aboriginal Yue people were still the dominant group in this area, but no longer a distinct element they merged more and more with new immigrants from north and south, attracted by its mild climate, fertile fields and relative security from the warring factions in the west and northwest. Han people found themselves mixing with aliens who in the words of one immigrant, "cut their hair short, tattooed the body, lived in bamboo groves with neither towns nor villages, possessing neither bows and arrows, nor horses or chariots."

While the local aboriginals were unskilled at raising crops they were expert fishermen but each resented the presence of the other. The newcomers were seen as intruders who brought with them disease and in turn fell victim to local infections. Military garrisons, moreover, showed little patience with aboriginals who resisted the influx, driving them to the coastal extremities or to highland areas where they became scavengers and outcasts, creating tribal and clan enclaves that persist to this day.

Among those who settled in the southern provinces were traders and shopkeepers who made contacts with seamen and tribute-bearing visitors from neighbouring states bringing new and exotic merchandise such as fruit, spices, pearl shell, even new strains of high yielding fast-growing rice, first cultivated in India 3,000 years before Christ and which gradually spread west and east, finding particularly fertile soil in the tropical wetlands of Southeast Asia. Similarly the breeding and cultivation of water buffaloes, pigs, ducks and chickens developed through contact with people from southern Asia as well as a rudimentary silk industry, though this was well established in other parts of China.

The southern Chinese showed a streak of resourcefulness in creating their own economy. Many of the delicacies, now a standard part of a Cantonese banquet, were introduced from neighbouring tropical countries as trade contacts widened and deepened and as Chinese communities took root in Southeast Asia. They were keen to improvise and experiment and quick to adopt new ideas and influences.

Not only were Chinese traders, venturing south along the coast, able to bring back spices such as cardamom, cloves, cashews, coconut, chilli, pepper, *bêche de mer*, and abalone but also preservation techniques enabling them to dry fish and pickle foods. They also learnt how to adorn the body with the iridescent blue feathers of kingfishers and precious stones. From the hill people of Cambodia they learnt how to carve elephant tusks and the horns of rhinos; for while elephants were also known in south China they had been steadily forced southwards with other animals, such as tigers, following the inevitable destruction of forests and habitat that accompanied the movement of people under the Qin clearances.

One of the more unusual curiosities favoured by the Chinese

was ambergris, used both in cookery and in perfumes but also prized for its medicinal value and as a tonic. This was a secretion produced in the stomach of the whale where the beak of a squid, eaten as food, had become embedded in the lining. It was collected by islanders off the Gulf of Aden and on beaches in Eastern Africa, often by luring sperm whales with a trail of tunny fat impregnated with opium, causing it to fall into a stupor. It was then seized, spiked with a harpoon, towed ashore and dismembered as much for its bones (to form the frames of habitations) as for its oil and the ambergris found in its stomach.

The more exotic additions to the Chinese culinary catalogue came later; this was a process of slow evolution and earnest, enterprising evaluation which resulted in a unique and distinct cuisine for the Cantonese palate, markedly different from that favoured in other parts of the country. In the case of ginseng, revered as a tonic or for the spur it gives to the libido, the Cantonese relished the roots found in the forests of Manchuria and Korea. As innovative traders and inveterate go-getters they shaped not only their own lifestyle but pioneered their own dietary preferences and contributed extensively to the medicinal pharmacopoeia of Chinese herbal practitioners, a process that continues to this day through their extensive contacts with the western world.

If it was not Chinese genius that devised the first wind-powered vessel,[1] no nation has had greater access to water throughout its history than the Chinese. Yet it was not the sea that beckoned them but their own extensive internal waterways. Unlike the ancient Egyptians whose civilization revolved around one deeply mystical life-giving river, the Chinese were literally inundated with water which trickled from melting ice and snow in distant mountains, gurgled through mountain streams, gushed

---

1. Bjorn Landstrom, the nautical artist-historian, records a picture of sailing craft in Egypt more than 3,000 years before Christ.

down waterfalls, surged through rivers, filled vast lakes, spilled into ricefields and emptied into huge estuaries staining the sea with its brown silt for many kilometres off the coast. The network of rivers, canals, lakes and streams gave the people the world's first natural roadways, largely maintenance-free, and a resourceful people were quick to take advantage of what nature had so abundantly bestowed. Over thousands of years, Chinese farmers became highly skilled in irrigation and conservation in devising ingeniously simple water wheels and hydraulic systems and basic means of transport and conveyance.

The Chinese sampan — familiar all over China — grew out of what were essentially three planks or logs lashed together — a type of craft still in use in rivers and lakes, notably at Guilin. Primitive it is, but manned by a single pole or oar at the stern it serves as cheap personal transport, freight carrier or fishing vessel. With a canopy over the rear and a few more planks around the sides it becomes a home for whole families who spend their lives afloat. For a country so prone to flooding the value of such a simple means of transport must have emerged even before the first wheel rolled mankind into a higher quality of life.

While there is a major technological gap between a three-plank or three-log sampan, and a vessel capable of making long voyages at sea, Chinese shipwrights were fully able to match what others had achieved elsewhere. Where the Egyptians were able to sail the Nile and the Mediterranean Sea 3,000 years ago, other coastal dwellers were quick to realize the power of the wind and apply it to travelling on the surface of the sea.[2] The speed with which technical innovation moved was the price of progress, not only of individuals but entire communities. It remains true to this day.

If China neglected its coasts for many years, relying on its

---

2. Even used to assist wheel barrows on land!

western approaches for trade and foreign contacts, its own vast river system encouraged the growth of water transport, and this existed for many hundreds of years before the Qin emperor sent his first youthful trade missions overseas to search for his life-extending elixir. They were oared, poled, towed or sailed — often a combination of all four testifying to a high standard of marine architecture.

Southern China's developing economy in Han times, following the downfall of the Qin rulers, was the incentive for incoming traders as well as for tribute bearers to set up markets for goods they carried. As sail-power developed, prevailing winds and weather conditions dictated the trade and tribute season. For southern China this meant arriving in November with the winter monsoon and sailing again with the onset of the south-west monsoon in March.

Of the vessels known in later times to frequent the ports of southern China, these had to be navigable in shallow river estuaries as well as deep seas, and the builders of the day put their faith in vessels with flat bottoms and broad beams, giving greater all-round stability in the roughest of seas, as well as a secure base for ballast and cargo, though lacking manoeuvrability until the perfection of stern rudders about 1,000 years ago. Nor were these rudders limited to steering but acted like the centre-board of modern yachts and helped the junk hold its course with the wind abeam.

Later, naval architects would design junks with masts raked in different directions to prevent gybing in a following wind; they also devised a high poop to protect the vessel from heavy following seas and to provide sheltered space for the crew. Many carried leeboards, lashed to the sides, to stop them drifting sideways. The sails were another remarkable feature for they could be raised and lowered swiftly on a windlass or more laboriously by men on deck; and, made of stiffened matting or jute, they could be swung easily on the masts to enable them to sail close to the wind. Many of the features found in early Chinese junks, including a primitive

Figure 1.2 Coastal junks seen by William Alexander in China as he travelled
north with the mission led by Lord Macartney in 1793.

spinnaker, later became standard fittings for modern racing
yachts.

The genius of the Chinese architect was to be seen in the
variety of boats designed for different seas, rivers, lakes, as well
as for different cargoes. The old elongated salt carriers, with a
length-to-beam ratio of twenty to one and used mainly on inland
waterways, looked like the grain carriers which sailed the Great

Lakes of Canada in the early years of this century. The salt-carriers were equipped with a long oblong sail and many oars to help when the wind dropped, and would carry seventy tons of salt.

An even more curious river craft was the shallow-draught, crooked-stern junk which sailed the Wu River in western Zhejiang. This had a curious upward twist in one corner of the stern from which a giant oar was worked by a team of men standing on top of the deckhouse. The 15-metre oar was designed to give it greater manoeuvrability as it navigated around rocky outcrops in the fast flowing river. Other junks were designed to be towed by teams of labourers, hauling them upstream through the rapids. These had a long, slim design with a shallow draught and were towed on paths so precarious that many who lost their footing were thrown into the swirling stream and never seen again.

While the maritime provinces of south-east China had been experiencing steady growth during the early years of the Han dynasty they were not then major export zones, the early trade flows occurring through the western borderlands. The Emperor, Han Wudi (140–86 BC), sent an emissary to negotiate peace with the nomadic tribes who lived in what is today Xinjiang Province. Tribesmen detained the man and held him for thirteen years before releasing him and agreeing to form an alliance with the Han rulers; they then joined forces in striking at the even more hostile tribes in the north-west known as Xiongnu, and after defeating them, China opened trade routes to central Asia and beyond with such highly prized products as silk, tea and hand-crafts, some of the silk finding its way to Rome to adorn the glitterati of what was then Europe's greatest civilization.

Not satisfied with securing the Western gateway for trade, Han Wudi pushed south to consolidate China's hold on Yunnan and Guizhou, but in doing so, exhausted his treasury, denuded his army and left the economy almost bankrupt, disrupting trade and causing widespread social upheaval, merchants and traders suffering in the process, and severing contacts with Southeast Asia in the process.

But while trade and the economy may have been stifled in Han China's early years, the seafaring community survived in the southern provinces and in later years sailings as far south as Java were well known. If the claim of one scholar is to be believed, Chinese sailing ships "discovered" the west coast of America more than 1,000 years before Columbus. Professor Lian Yunshan, a research fellow from the China Pacific Historical Society in Beijing, says that a Chinese monk travelling with 200 people in a fleet of three ships, landed near the present site of Los Angeles in the year 412.

The monk and well-known traveller, Faxian, recorded the voyage in his autobiography after the fleet had drifted for 105 days. How it was possible to determine that the community he visited, and which he named as "Yepoti," was in fact on the American continent, is not clear; others assert that "Yepoti" was the island of Java though if so, the monk encountered no Buddhists on an island that had come under their influence more than three centuries earlier. This all seems tenuous speculation but regardless of where the fleet landed, Chinese sailors, merchants, monks and even migrants were on the move across the waters of the China Sea long before the Western discovery of the sea approaches to Asia in the sixteenth century. They were also well aware of the existence of other civilizations even if the Chinese rulers were inclined to belittle their rich culture and intellectual attainments and were ignorant of the extent of their power and influence.

The centre of the world was China, on the fringes of which lived minor barbarian people who could only be regarded as tributaries. Suffice it to say that Chinese provincial officials as well as seamen and traders were well aware of the diversity of people and cultures and recognized the potential for a flourishing trade in the area. Furthermore Chinese families were beginning to settle in what is today northern Vietnam. The influence of

Buddhism, emanating from India before Shihuangdi (221–209 BC) had unified China, was also known to Chinese travellers and envoys who had encountered the new religion in various parts of Southeast Asia.

Figure 1.3
Presenting tribute to the Emperor, a scene by the French artist, Auguste Borget, who visited South China in 1839.

Moreover, foreign embassies bearing official titles arrived in China by sea in the early years of the Han dynasty. The visitors from what may have been outlying provinces of Roman-occupied Asia minor, also travelled to other parts of Southeast Asia. Roman coins and other goods thought to have been circulating in areas controlled by Rome have been found in Vietnam, Thailand and northern Malaya. All these could have reached these areas by means other than direct visits, but the Chinese capital with its growing contacts should have been aware of a vastly bigger and more enlightened world than it ever recognized officially. Cambodia, particularly, was known as an advanced civilization even if the people were dismissed as "black and ugly."

Chinese rulers had accepted the teachings of Buddha in the first century after Christ, and thereafter the new religion spread throughout Chinese domains without however displacing or disrupting Confucian teachings with the emphasis on ethics and personal conduct. The introduction of Buddhism led to both pilgrimages by Chinese monks and missionaries to spread the religion. Once again the sea lanes from the southern provinces were favoured as an alternative to the perilous land routes through Tibet and the south-western border regions, recurrently harassed by hostile tribes bent on plunder and booty.

The monk, Faxian, returning from a mission to collect scriptures in India and Sri Lanka in the fifth century, travelled on a Chinese ship from Sumatra to Guangzhou. It carried 200 people and had provisions for fifty days. His fellow passengers included many Chinese merchants who may have lived in Sumatra for part of the year and returned regularly to their home port, possibly having families in both places.

Faxian's ship was thrown off course by a violent storm which drove it hundreds of miles up the East China Sea to the coast of Shandong. How the ship's captain carried out his navigation is not made clear; possibly he used astronomy and solar observations though later he was able to find his way home by heading west and tracking southwards down the coast.

Another long sea voyage took place in the late seventh century when the monk, Yijing, sailed from Guangzhou and visited India by way of Southeast Asia, spending time in parts of the Malayan Peninsula and Sumatra, notably Palembang, on both the outward and homeward journey — proof again of the strong and growing maritime links between China and Southeast Asia and the Subcontinent beyond.

It was also a time when southern China prospered under the more settled and cohesive conditions of the Tang dynasty (AD 618–907) which also saw an increasing influx of people moving to the southern extremities of Guangdong and the Hong Kong region. So closely did the local people identify with the Tang administration that they described themselves as people of the Tang, speaking the language of the Tang in the land of the Tang.

The one major blight on the Tang record in the deep south was the Huangchao rebellion of AD 875 which fell on Guangzhou at the height of its maritime power. A revolt against incompetent rulers, exacerbated by severe drought, led to an uprising in Hunan which resulted in the fall of southern Guangdong including the capital. Residing there were hundreds of foreign traders; Arab reports claim the death toll among these visitors was "horrific." Why they were singled out for butchery is uncertain though the south got its revenge when an outbreak of malaria wiped out a third of the rebels. However, Guangzhou as a trading port was slow to recover from the massacre.

China's Tang rulers also considered the area of Vietnam to be a province, though this was the last period of direct Chinese rule. During that time it became thoroughly indoctrinated with Chinese characteristics; the Chinese influence also spread to other non-Han areas and Guangzhou became an important centre for the outreach of Chinese culture, traditions and teachings.

With the fall of the Tang in AD 907, northern Vietnam shook off Chinese rule and became independent, and while the new Song rulers tried to reinforce their hold this was unsuccessful. They were more successful in the Malayan Peninsula and Sumatra, however, in gaining recognition as a friendly maritime power and as a trading partner. The famous Song celadon porcelain found its way south to places like Borneo and Sumatra and Chinese people also settled either permanently or seasonally in these places where they were said to be peaceful, industrious and well liked. Increasingly a two-way trade developed, carried almost entirely by the growing fleets of Chinese junks using maritime compasses to pinpoint their destination with increasing accuracy.

The compass was indeed the greatest advance in navigational aids since sailors ventured over the horizon. For while oars and rudders of one kind or another could help to achieve direction and while the passage of the sun by day and the position of the stars — particularly the Pole Star — together with seasonal winds were invaluable celestial signposts, the sky is never so obliging as to ensure they are visibile throughout the day or night.

Not so the compass which made its debut in European writings at the end of the twelfth century and such a revolutionary innovation could hardly remain secret for long. However, the magnetic needle was known much earlier in China, and a scholar in the eleventh century told how Taoist geomancers "rub the point of a needle with a lodestone so that it acquires the property of pointing south — but it always declines slightly to the east and is not due south." The writer then suggested that it should be hung by a fine silk thread and held in a place where there was no wind — admittedly a difficult task at sea; alternatively the magnetized needle was placed on a straw in a bowl of water. The effect would then be for the needle to point south and if true south could be established, the other end of the needle was due north. And so "in dark weather (the mariner) looks at the south-pointing needle."

If seamen were the main beneficiaries of this discovery, the credit goes to geomancers for what in China was the far more important need — to ensure auspicious, favourable or benevolent influences which are part of the ancient lore of *fengshui*. Essential to determining the ideal set of circumstances for the design and outlook of a building, the location for a grave, the alignment of a road, the date on which to start a journey, the geomancer was the first to be consulted; an important part of his equipment was the simple compass with its elaborate chart of positive and negative influences.

That eminent Victorian expert on "things Chinese," J. Dyer Ball, recalls how difficult it was to lay the telegraph line between Guangzhou (known as the "the City of Rams") via the Pearl River estuary (known as the "Tiger's Mouth" or Bocca Tigris) to Hong Kong, via Kowloon (which means "Nine Dragons"). A telegraph line leading sheep through a tiger's mouth to the lair of nine dragons was surely a recipe for disaster, self-evident to any well-educated Chinese gentleman of the nineteenth century, and a bewildering hurdle to the Western telegraph company looking for the most direct route between the two cities.

Self-sufficient though Chinese rulers, officials and scholars imagined themselves to be, there was much to learn about other countries and Chinese travellers equipped with the compass and sturdy multi-sailed vessels, were keen to record their impressions of what they saw: whales which managed to strand themselves on beaches; great birds which could "mask the sun" in their flight and "swallow live camels"; artistic ways of decorating elephant tusks and rhino horns; the dress habits (or lack of them) of African people; precious stones, fragrant woods, spices, birds, feathers, rare metals, not to mention the extraordinary animals that were to be found, including a white elephant (in Sri Lanka) with seven rubies "the size of hen's eggs" on its forehead.

One writer told of a "camel-crane" in Africa two metres tall — "it has wings and can fly but not to any great height." Then there was an animal, striped like a tiger and the size of an ox with front legs one and a half metres high and hind legs only a metre, "its head is held high and turned upwards." The same writer also describes a mule with red, black and white stripes "wound as girdles around the body."

These were occasionally hunted with poisoned arrows, and just occasionally caught alive and sent overseas as tribute gifts. On more than one occasion, ostriches, rhinos, giraffes and zebras found their way to China's imperial courts for exhibition in a local zoo. Not all these remarkable animals would have been shipped on Chinese vessels. Transshipment was common but apart from the obvious difficulty of caging these large creatures and keeping them alive in heat and cold, calm and storm, for hundreds of days, the size of the ships was more than adequate for the task. Marco Polo told of the Grand Khan possessing lions, leopards and lynxes (non-indigenous to China) to hunt boars, bears and deer.

Ships of up to 200 tons were recorded in Tang times with smaller "ox-head" vessels for the coastal trade and still smaller ones for use on rivers. The largest could be away on long international journeys lasting two years, with the passage time from Iran to China taking almost five months and with the China–Sumatra leg lasting from one to three months depending on winds and ports of call. Generally, the China junks would set sail in the eleventh or twelfth month with the onset of the strong northerly monsoons and return with the south-west monsoons in early summer.

In the Song dynasty, not only was there a flourishing merchant marine but an increasing Chinese naval fleet in the East China Sea — with some authorities recording the number of seamen at 50,000. If this figure seems high the value of the annual trade with the East Indies, India, Sri Lanka, Arabia and Africa was rising rapidly and Chinese vessels were displacing Arabian vessels not only from Southeast Asia but parts of the Indian Ocean as well.

At leading ports in Guangdong and Fujian, many Arab and Indian traders resided and the volume of international trade was not only making local pirates bolder but enticing Japanese freebooters to chase down the slow-moving junks. Proof of the popularity of Chinese exports has come to light in the discoveries of Song porcelain in Java, south India and East Africa. Silks, silver, gold and copper cash also found their way overseas. Moreover a flourishing entrepot trade developed between Saphardic Jewish traders in the eastern Mediterranean and India and Indonesia; exotic Oriental exports would take the same route back to Europe.

In the thirteenth century, when Marco Polo visited China, the shipbuilding industry was preparing ocean-going ships for journeys to India and the Persian Gulf. The sea route was said to be "as safe as the land route," though storms, pirates and navigation errors would have been as calamitous as brigands, sandstorms or lack of water in the desert.

Polo reported on the southern Chinese port of Zayton, famous for its shipping, its seamen and navigation skills; it was the destination for spices imported from India and the East Indies, and was prized as an international market for pepper and pearls. It was at the port of Zayton where many of the 4,000 ships used in Kublai Khan's ill-fated invasion of Japan were built. The invasion of 1281 was a failure because of a providential (for Japan) "divine wind," or *kamikaze*, which battered the Chinese fleet causing serious losses and supply problems.

There was nothing wrong, however, with either the construction of the ships or their navigation, and they carried a reported 100,000 Chinese, Korean and Mongol troops who succeeded in establishing beachheads but were then surrounded by samurai warriors and finally cut to pieces by the Japanese army as the cyclonic winds disrupted their supply lines. The port from which some of the fleet set out, Zayton, cannot be located today but was thought to be on the Fujian coast, possibly Zhangzhou, west of Xiamen. At one time a revenue collector was stationed there to tax foreign shipping, and a mosque existed with the date of 1403, thought to have been built on the site of an earlier mosque erected by Arab traders.

The vessels that Polo saw at Zayton were described as bigger and more commodious than any known in Europe. Made of fir planks these vessels had more than fifty cabins below the main deck to accommodate merchants. The ships were fitted with watertight compartments so that a gash from a submerged rock or reef or a passing whale would not imperil its buoyancy. Whale bumps were not uncommon in those days before the intensive whale hunting of the nineteenth and twentieth centuries decimated their numbers.

Polo's descriptions might strain credulity were it not for corroboration from several other western travellers in that era. Crews of 200 and 300 as well as 100 or so merchants and passengers, sometimes accompanied by wives and children — with an all-up complement of 700 people per ship — embarked on these voyages with holds crammed with merchandise. The hulls were double (at times, triple or quadruple) planked, nailed and caulked. Rotten boards infested with seaworms were not replaced but had new planks superimposed. Some of these vessels were four-masted with additional masts and sails carried to replace those damaged during passage, though they could also be used as auxiliary masts to make the most of prevailing winds; all were armed with cannon to fight off pirates; they also had oars for entry to, or departure from ports, rudders, two anchors, compasses, lifeboats and auxiliary craft which they lowered to catch fish, or which could in turn tow a becalmed ship at certain stages of the voyage. Vegetables were grown on board in pots, a vital defence against the illness of scurvy and well in advance of western navigators and travellers who were unaware of the value of fresh food and citrus fruit until well into the eighteenth century. On such a ship Polo travelled to India. Similar descriptions survive from other Western and Chinese travellers.

The ever superstitious Chinese sailors had one unusual custom which has not survived to the present. To test the omens for a long voyage, a member of the crew — usually the eldest — was given a generous portion of rice wine, trussed to a large kite and flown aloft. A good flight was considered a favourable omen and was the last formality before weighing anchor, but if lift-off was unsuccessful and the luckless sailor plunged into the sea, the heavy stone anchors remained on the seabed until a successful flight could be launched — and another volunteer found to take his place on the kite.

Chinese vessels invariably had large eyes painted on their bows — a custom that continued until this century. The logic was simple; in years when the compass could only give a rough idea of direction, a vessel needed a good pair of eyes, as much to reassure consignees, as crew and passengers.

Marco Polo, his father and uncle were staggered by the wealth and size of Chinese cities during their prolonged stay. Following the expulsion of the Song emperors in 1278, there was a temporary eclipse of international trade, though it was quick to revive under Kublai Khan, as Polo records in his narrative. The river traffic, particularly, astounded him, the numbers running into tens of thousands. In China, not only was there great wealth but circulating among traders was paper money based on the inner lining of the bark of the mulberry tree, sealed and signed by various officials and produced in different units.

Kublai's "stately pleasure dome" at Xanadu was far more than an opium-induced fantasy of the English poet, Samuel Taylor Coleridge. Polo tells of the "huge palace of marble and other ornamental stones ... marvellously embellished and richly adorned" in which Kublai lived during the three summer months. Moreover it was only one of several.[3]

The extensive travels of Marco Polo not only made the Pope aware of the existence of China and its enlightened civilization but confirmed what others from Europe and Arabia have recorded, that there was a vigorous trading economy in many parts of Asia. In maritime terms this was far more extensive than in Europe and the Mediterranean.

The Atlantic Ocean, however, was a formidable physical and psychological barrier which European explorers did not succeed in breaching until the sixteenth century when Columbus made the first east–west crossing and Prince Henry the Navigator

---

3. Today it survives only as a scattering of stones at a hilly site near Shangdu, about 150 kilometres north-west of Beijing.

bullied, cajoled, bribed and threatened his crews to sail south down the African coast, with all the horrors this called up among navigators and explorers not yet certain of what lay beyond "the edge of the world." But they found it was an ever-receding edge.

Moreover, while European nations may have gained equality in some aspects of their civilization, the Chinese with inventions such as the compass, the stern rudder, printing, the iron plough, floating reservoirs and gunpowder proved they were technologically more advanced. However, with their conservative rote-based Confucian education system they failed at the next stage to make the quantum leap into scientific and industrial progress.

Marco Polo's carefully restrained reports on China were read in Europe with a mixture of incredulity, bewilderment and disbelief, but contributed to the eventual break-out of Spanish, Portuguese, Dutch and British explorers in the sixteenth century, driven by a fear of encirclement by the growing power and might of Islam in a golden crescent running from Constantinople to the Straits of Gibraltar.

One of the most remarkable series of journeys undertaken by a Chinese official was made by a court eunuch, a Muslim from Yunnan, named Zheng He. This occurred in the Ming dynasty (1368–1644) when he was given charge of a huge fleet of more than sixty vessels and 36,000 men ostensibly to search for an absconding heir to the throne, though he carried with him a shopping list for the ladies of the court.

He took part in at least seven missions between 1405 and 1433 to thirty countries in the Indian subcontinent and islands in the Indian Ocean, the East Indies, the Persian Gulf, Hormuz, Aden, Mecca and parts of the East African coast. But because rivals at court were jealous of his royal patronage and despised extravagance, trade and contact with foreigners, the official records of Zheng He's voyages no longer exist.

However, although they proved unprofitable, official tolerance was extended generously for twenty-eight years and did help Chinese people to accept that if they wanted to promote trade and communication with the people of Asia, they had to learn their languages. A foreign language school was said to have been founded following the return of the first expedition though its fate is unknown.

An inscription found in a temple in Fujian in 1935 gives (in part) this account of Zheng He's travels: "The Emperor [Xuande, 1425–1435] has ordered us and others at the head of several tens of thousands of officers and flag troops to ascend more than a hundred large ships to go and confer presents in order to make manifest the transforming power of the Imperial Virtue and to treat distant people with kindness. From the third year of Yongle (1405) till now we have several times received the commission of ambassadors to the countries of the Western Ocean.[4]

"We have traversed more than one hundred thousand *li* of immense water spaces and have beheld in the ocean huge waves like mountains rising sky-high, and we have set eyes on barbarian regions far away while our sails, loftily unfurled like clouds, day and night continued their course, rapid like that of a star, traversing the savage waves, as if we were treading a public thoroughfare. Truly this was due to the majesty and good fortune of the court and moreover we owe it to the protecting virtue of the Celestial Spouse." (Guanyin, the Goddess of Mercy)

The inscription went on to report that at the height of storms "there suddenly appeared a divine lantern shining in the mast; as soon as this miraculous light appeared the danger was appeased, so that even when in peril of capsizing one felt reassured that there was no cause for fear." The light was presumably the phenomenon known to many seamen as "St Elmo's Fire." The inscription went on to name the seven expeditions carried out

---

4. The inscription then listed countries such as Cambodia, Java, Palembang, Siam, Sri Lanka, India, Cochin, Hormuz, Aden, Mogadishu — thirty locations in all.

between 1405 and 1433, one of the most remarkable seafaring journeys recorded in history.

While somewhat sketchy accounts survive, greater detail came in books written by others who were either captains of one or more of Zheng He's fleet of junks or were passengers. Moreover, also surviving were some of Zheng He's maps which contained compass directions and some of the nautical information collected by the fleet. These demonstrate that China was a significant maritime nation capable of mounting fleets to the furthest points of the Indian Ocean.

This growth of maritime power, moreover, was maintained for several hundred years from the thirteenth to the sixteenth century. It only began to decline when the Ming dynasty turned its attention from south to north as the Manchu tribes became aggressive and threatening. But in the early years of the dynasty, as much to preserve Pax Sinica in the South China seas, as to safeguard trade and frustrate piracy, China's naval and merchant fleet was by far the biggest in the region. As Chinese sailors moved west, however, a new political force in Europe began its push to the east, heralding a collision of cultures and civilizations that would reverberate through the next five centuries.

CHAPTER 2

Western Approaches

People of the Mediterranean proved to be the most intrepid and innovative in the Middle Ages. Locked into a lake with a known landfall at every point of the compass they longed to break the mould that encased them, to discover the wider world. Sailing north to the ports of France and Britain to trade and to fight was a common experience. Venturing out into the unknown Atlantic beyond the Cape Verde Islands was another matter. The first honour went to an Italian but it was the Iberian court which sent him across the great ocean. The Portuguese and the British explorer, John Cabot, were swift to follow, the latter reaching Newfoundland only five years after.

"After Jesus Christ, no individual has made a bigger impact on the Western world than Christopher Columbus," a recent biography of the sailor-explorer declared.[1] Columbus, sponsored by Spain and armed with maps from Italian scholars, was assured that by sailing west from Europe he would reach China; when he discovered America instead, he thought it was India, but when it proved to be neither, others had to pioneer the sea route to Asia. Cabot also thought Canada was Asia.

Meanwhile, Bartolomao Diaz had rounded the Cape of Good

---

1. John Dyson, *Columbus, for Gold, God and Glory* (London: Hodder & Stoughton, 1991).

Hope in 1488 — as momentous in its way as Columbus's voyage. Ten years later Vasco da Gama, sailing with 160 men in three ships, under that inspired navigator, Pedro Alenquer, reached the west coast of India. Previously all trade between Asia and Europe went via the Red Sea and thence through territory controlled by aggressive Arabs or Turks, or prowling Mongols.

A word should be said at this point about maritime rivalry between Spain and Portugal, not helped by Portugal's failure to commission Columbus to cross the Atlantic in 1484. The two neighbours were perpetually squabbling for ascendancy on the Iberian peninsula and for the upper hand in Europe, always keen moreover to catch the Pope's eye and win his approval. The Treaty of Toledo in 1480, decreeing the division of the Atlantic, proved contentious. Tired of their intrigues Pope Alexander VI made a ruling in 1493, dividing the lands discovered by the two countries. Even that did not resolve the issue and the two had to wait another year for another treaty (of Tordesillas) to be signed. This recognized a north–south line west of the Cape Verde Islands, with land discovered to the west belonging to Spain and to the east, Portugal. At that stage there was no telling which side had come off best, but Portugal was determined to exploit its sphere of influence and discover what else Asia had to offer.

They were helped by a number of innovations which made it possible for mariners to sail out from home ports with greater confidence. These included more seaworthy ships, navigation by the stars, progress in map-making with the introduction of scales of latitude, the construction of celestial globes or sky maps by astronomers such as Nicolaus Copernicus of Poland and Tycho Brahe of Denmark in the sixteenth century, and greater knowledge of ocean currents and weather.

Of particular importance to mariners was the device known as the marine astrolabe (derived from the Greek word for star) which in the Middle Ages helped sailors to find their latitude. Later navigators made greater use of the sun, but it was not until the advent of the marine sextant, in general use until recent times, that accurate instrumental navigation was possible. While navigation on an east–west track in "closed seas" such as the Baltic or Mediterranean posed few problems, the great oceans with their strong winds and currents were best tackled by hugging the coastline. And what no measuring instrument would tell the early Portuguese navigators was the length of the African coast; this they had to discover the hard way — sailing its full distance to 35 degrees south before "turning the corner" at the Cape of Good Hope.

The consolation was that along the length of the African coast were slave markets and gold deposits. Always, however, the great temptation was to find out where it ended. Then, having passed Cape Agulhas (the Portuguese word for needles, because the reef-strewn, rocky coast had caused many wrecks) 100 miles further on, and turned east, the Portuguese were fired by hopes of new and exciting discoveries. Here, however, the Portuguese struck a new phenomenon — some of the wildest seas in the world where the great Agulhas current sweeps south at up to sixty centimetres a second, and where tides and winds create sudden "holes" in the sea, claiming many victims, even in the twentieth century. Having mastered this, they headed north–east and their voyages culminated in landfalls on the west coast of India, Sri Lanka and later, Malaya. This was truly courageous sailing.

The pivot for East–West trade at that time was Malacca to which all goods from Arabia, Africa and India were consigned; similarly, to that port went all the spices from the East Indies and the China produce. Malacca was not just a thriving entrepot but a major centre of shipping, commerce and warehousing; it had an international community of traders and merchants living there for at least part of the year, with a reputation built up over centuries.

The coming of the Europeans would change this dramatically, not because they could offer superior services or more profitable means of trade — for even goods from the Mediterranean reached Malacca through Arabia. Having crossed several seas and oceans with their wares, however, they had no intention of returning in ballast. The Portuguese, under the command of Diego Lopes de Sequeira, saw the dimensions of the trade and with their versatile ships and superior firepower they were determined to muscle in.

Sailing with Sequeira was another intrepid sailor, Fernao Magalhaes, but when he failed to win promotion and the recognition of the Portuguese court, he not only switched allegiance but nationality. Henceforth his triumphs would redound to Spain and he is remembered in history as the great Ferdinand Magellan, gaining a commission to search for the Spice Islands of the Moluccas in a five-ship fleet passing south of Cape Horn and into the Pacific Ocean. In one of the greatest maritime voyages ever undertaken in 1520, and with his crew wracked with scurvy, down to its last few rat-nibbled biscuits and lacking fresh water, he reached Guam, the Philippines (where he met his death), and eventually the Spice Islands, all of which were claimed for Spain and Christianity. His companion and second in command, Elcano, on returning to Spain with a full load of spice, was given the right to carry on his coat of arms, a globe with the words "First to circle me." What Magellan's fleet did was sail more than four times the distance of Columbus, crossing not one ocean but three, and also achieved what he failed to do in finding the western route to Asia. He is remembered today by the Strait of Magellan through which he passed from the Atlantic, on a day so calm that he christened the sea on the other side, the Peaceful Ocean. Truly, a great Portuguese navigator who met an untimely end at the age of forty-one.

Nor did it end there. Having forced back the Islamic tide in their own land the Portuguese were in no mood to leave the lucrative Asian trade monopoly in their hands. A passage to India and the riches of Asia became the first priority. Columbus having taken the wrong turning after leaving the Spanish port of Palos, passes out of our story. Even Vasco da Gama rates only a passing mention, for in 1511 the Portuguese adventurers under Alfonso de Albuquerque dropped anchor in Malacca and took possession of the port; the ruins of the castle he built overlooking the beach, and the graves of his sailors and soldiers remain to this day.

Eight years later a fleet laden with pepper, headed by Fernao Peres de Andrade, visited Guangzhou. His reception in the city was encouraging and after a first meeting with the mandarins he was escorted to the Chinese capital to be scrutinized by a curious Emperor, Zhengde of the Ming dynasty (1505–1521). In a series of bureaucratic muddles, however, Peres reached the Chinese capital as the Emperor left on an extended tour of the south. The next year the Emperor died and Peres was bundled back to Guangzhou and placed in custody.

His brother, Simao, was of a different ilk; dismayed by Peres's treatment, he began aggressively and blotted Portugal's reputation by his buccaneering behaviour. At first the Chinese allowed the Portuguese to establish a settlement on the outskirts of Ningbo; according to one historian an "irregular kind of smuggling-trade" was conducted along the coast of Guangdong, Fujian and Zhejiang.[2] But Simao's behaviour, and that of his successors, led to bitter complaints from the populace. The Chinese decided these roistering men had to be taught a lesson and after a pitched sea battle, involving a force of 60,000 Chinese marines, the Portuguese were sent packing. Thereafter, foreigners were outlawed from the coast for the next thirty years.

This marked a reversal of the cordial welcome extended to overseas traders in Song times when Arabs were allowed to settle in Guangzhou and even take Chinese wives; they were also given enough freedom to settle disputes among themselves without reference to Chinese courts. Some were allowed to hold official positions in China; such was the tolerance and trust of foreigners.

---

2. Charles Boxer, *Fidalgos in the Far East* (Hong Kong: Oxford-in-Asia, 1968).

In Tang times, Indian and Persian traders operated out of Zayton and Guangzhou and there was an official Commissioner of Shipping appointed by Beijing to supervise the collection of customs revenue; so great was the maritime trade and so serious the menace of piracy that China set up a convoy escort service and a coast guard.

From Tang times, moreover, the Board of Rites (Libu) in the Chinese capital, handled the reception of foreign dignitaries, though this was mainly protocol and ceremonial rather than diplomatic — indicative, in any case, of the arrival and departure of high-level visitors for whatever reasons. So long as they conformed to stipulated procedures, implicitly recognizing the supremacy of the dragon throne, and paying due obeisance, they were welcome to visit and unroll their mats to display items of trade.

The Portuguese fidalgos (literally, *filho d'algo* or someone's son; once used to describe a nobleman, but in a republican age is rarely used except mockingly) were however a bunch of tough soldiers of fortune bent on smashing the Arab stranglehold on trade and stamping their own authority from the Persian Gulf and India to China and seizing as much territory as they could defend and rule. They had bought Chinese products in India and had sniffed the heady potion of Eastern herbs and Oriental spices. They set up a string of fourteen forts on the east and west coasts of India and Sri Lanka and at Malacca, Chinese junkmen and traders opened their eyes to the riches of Cathay just up the South China Sea.

They succeeded so well that the Pope bestowed upon Portugal's King the title of "Lord of the Navigation, Conquest and Commerce of Ethiopia, Arabia, Persia and India." Since all these countries were well beyond the pale of the Roman Catholic Church — in fact, one was in the province of the rival Coptic Church — the title was meaningless, but nevertheless pleased his client state, Portugal.

Great as Portugal's maritime triumphs were, the detail of its record was less glorious and the depredations of "dwarf pirates" (Japanese marauders) and the arrival of foreigners provoked very different reactions in China. The first thing the Ming dynasty did was to tighten its defences and put teeth into the "Tiger's Mouth" at the entrance of the Pearl River.

Figure 2.1 A Chinese fortification on the river as seen by William Alexander when accompanying the Macartney mission.

From antiquity, Guangzhou, also known as the City of Rams, had lived within the enclosure of a thick wall, and in the 2,500 years prior to the coming of the Westerners these walls had been extended to accommodate the influx of migrants attracted by its growing wealth. It had been the first city of the province from the time of Emperor Shihuangdi and was later capital of its successor, the breakaway Nan Yue state. It reverted to being a provincial capital when the Han rulers annexed it and brought it back within the boundaries of China. Under the Tang, riches and religion made their mark and temples and pagodas were built as well as dwellings for expatriate traders, causing the walls to be extended again to take in two neighbouring hill sites.

The urban sprawl continued under the Song and Yuan rulers (960–1368) with more walls being built. Then a new surge of people occurred as the Mongols squeezed out the last of the Song rulers from their refuge on the Kowloon peninsula, in a sea battle off the island of Lantau island. Once again Guangdong boomed and the wall-builders were again busy with extensions and reinforcements. By the Ming dynasty (1368–1644 AD) the city had grown unrecognizably. The Pan and Yu hills were flattened and the outlying areas were joined up with the city. The Qing successors added a further flourish when it became the capital of the vice-royalty of Guangdong and Guangxi (the two Guangs). No Chinese camelot, it was nevertheless busy, populous and thriving.

Guangzhou was at its most prosperous when the Portuguese sailed to the mouth of the river in the early sixteenth century. Some of Peres's crew had distant visions of blue, stylized temple tops, tall pagodas and crenellated towers in the city situated on the north banks of the Pearl River. This was itself a branch of Xijiang or the West River and part of a maze of channels and islands which make up the estuary, brown with swirling mud carried from the hills and mountains of western Guangdong and Guangxi.

The Portuguese, unlike the Persians and Arabs before them, were not invited into the city proper. The Chinese were quick to decide that these roughnecks would be a divisive, turbulent and troublesome influence in the city. Their small lateen-sailed caravels may have looked insignificant compared with the huge 200-ton trading junks of the Chinese but their brass cannon were deadly and given a choice between Japanese dwarf pirates and

Portuguese fidalgos the Chinese decided that if anyone was to camp at their doorstep, the lesser evil came from the West. But let them be confined to the extremities.

At first, the Portuguese were restricted to the island of St John or Sanchuan, about 100 kilometres southwest of Macau where they conducted an annual exchange of goods. This was later transferred to another island known as Lampacao which was nearer Macau. Within a couple of years, the Portuguese were grudgingly allowed to settle on an outlying spit of land noted only for its seafarers' temple dedicated to the goddess A Ma.

An intriguing question is why did the Portuguese settle for the peninsula of Macau when just thirty kilometres to the north were three large islands offering deep water harbours and shelter from cyclonic winds. The Portuguese have frequently been taunted with being short-sighted in ignoring Hong Kong or Lantau. At that time, however, and for the next 350 years, a deep-water harbour offered no advantage to ships of such shallow draught and was a day's journey away. Macau's small silted harbour was ample for its time and the Portuguese wanted a site close to the mouth of the river leading to Guangzhou. In short, Macau was ideal.

The Portuguese brought not just a prospect of new trade but a spark of moral rectitude as well. For while the rough and ready sailors were accused of abducting Chinese children into slavery and seducing the women, the missionaries who followed soon after were the most civilized newcomers to reach China since the Indian Buddhists 1,700 years earlier — men of piety, learning, and armed with a Bible and a crucifix.

The ever curious Chinese were familiar enough with books, but the radically different Roman alphabet indicating consonants and vowels, intrigued the local scholars; also the words ran horizontally from left to right across the page unlike the Chinese script which ran from top to bottom and from right to left. Most baffling was the crucifix — a replica of an instrument of execution with the victim nailed to it, who was worshipped as a triumphant redeemer ... it made no sense to the logical Chinese mind; Chinese people would take a long time to accept the notion of the Crucifixion and Resurrection of the Son of God, and make that leap of faith. But the books they brought, their scientific notions, the mathematics they demonstrated, the artistry they employed and their scholarship in a whole field of knowledge was of great interest to the erudite Chinese. Not the least of their early successes was to correct discrepancies in the all important Chinese calendar.

The Portuguese were not the first Christians to penetrate China. Nestorian missionaries had travelled across the deserts of Turkestan in the sixth or seventh century and survived in western parts until about the tenth century. But they were never a threat to Buddhism and when the Franciscan, Giovanni de Montecorvino, reached the court of Kublai Khan's successor, Timur, the Nestorians were extinct.

The first Roman Catholics hardly survived the Mongol occupation and when foreigners were ejected by the incoming Ming emperors, China was without a Christian presence for almost 300 years. The next group of missionaries were the Jesuits who travelled with the explorers partly to serve the spiritual needs of Portuguese sailors but later to bring Christian teaching to the people of Asia. Father (later Saint) Francis Xavier, who travelled up the South China Sea from Goa and Malacca, was the first to pitch his tent within sight of the Chinese mainland. He was determined to land in China, if necessary to bribe his way there, and he landed in 1552 on the island of Sanchuan. After four months in the torrid heat of a South China summer, however, his promised visit to the mainland was vetoed by the local mandarin, and he died two weeks later.

The honour of being the first to reach Guangzhou went to Fr Melchior Nunez Barretto three years later; he did little more than plead (successfully) for the release of a few captured Portuguese sailors. Others followed in Barretto's footsteps. All tried to stay in the city as teachers or students of the language but the Chinese were adamant; no permanent residents would be allowed. Macau had become the tolerated beachhead of the Portuguese invasion and that was where the missionaries had to reside for at least the next twenty-five years, until in 1578 the priests succeeded, where the traders failed, to get a foot in the door and set up permanently on Chinese soil, thanks to their ability by that time to speak the language and conform to Chinese etiquette.

The efforts of Fr Matteo Ricci in the first years of the seventeenth century to convert the court at Beijing, make fascinating reading. The Portuguese not only secured the first permanent foothold on the coast of China but their missionaries brought the

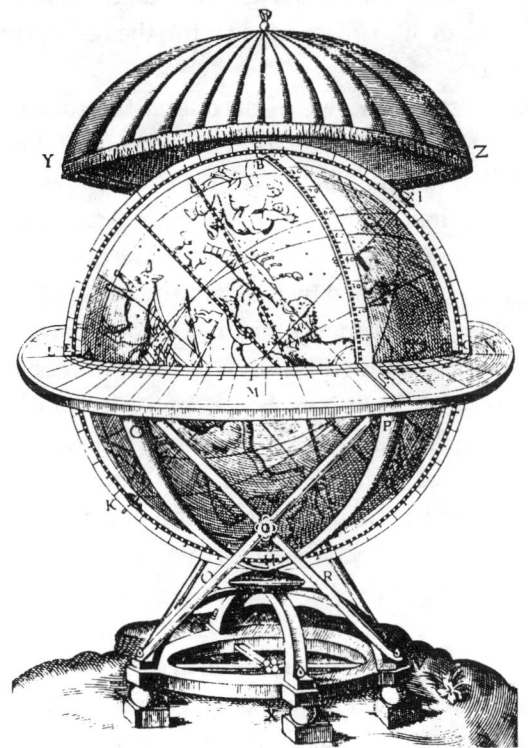

Figure 2.2 The Globus Magnus of Tycho Brahe, 1584, which helped navigators to make epic voyages of discovery.

light of European learning to the Orient and were the most potent influence in the introduction of the new science of Renaissance Europe. The Chinese court scholars were politely interested when the missionaries were able to display their knowledge of astronomy and mathematics; they also helped to revise the calendar and to make cannon, to exhibit new printing techniques, new styles of painting and to propound a new religious doctrine.

Impressive as their erudition might be, the behaviour of Portuguese traders and secular administrators in Macau convinced China that Western civilization posed no threat to the ancient Confucian society and had little of lasting value to offer. Moreover Portugal which had led the charge into Asia, was itself being overtaken by the even more boisterous Dutch, French and British. It would soon fade into obscurity leaving the field to more aggressive competitors.

The Dutch stood in awe of no one at the turn of the seventeenth century. Helped by the navigational breakthrough achieved by Gerardus Mercator (1512–1594) with his famous "projection," their ships had been sailing to Asia since early in the sixteenth century when still a province of the Spanish Hapsburgs. Though at first constrained by the Papal division of the world into two rival spheres of influence, the Dutch breakaway from Spain in 1579 gave their seamen a free hand to plunder the lucrative spice markets in the Moluccas. For them the terrors of the Inquisition and excommunication were a thing of the past.

The Dutch East India Company was founded in 1602, a joint venture between the States-General and six private companies. Self-interest dictated the merger, partly to avoid internal competition and partly to enlist the help of the Government in the inevitable showdown with Portugal. The Dutch, who by then had largely embraced the protestant faith, argued that in any case, the Papal decree to King Manuel of Portugal making him "Lord of the Navigation, Conquest and Commerce" covered only Ethiopia, Arabia, Persia and India. East of the Subcontinent was no-man's-land and therefore fair game for Dutch traders.

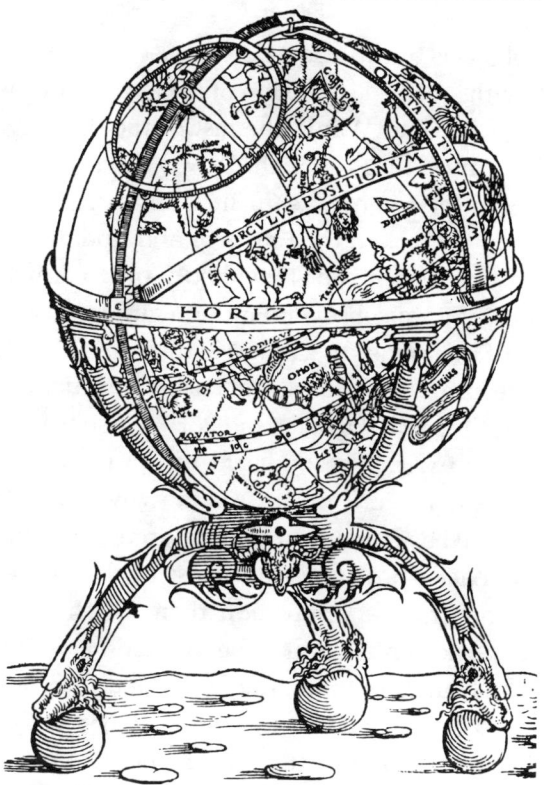

Figure 2.3 Schöner's Celestial Globe, 1533, was a vital aid to seamen charting new routes to the Far East.

By plotting straight lines on maps with Mercator's epoch-making atlas, the Dutch were quick to spot an inviting slice of the market in spice-rich Batavia. When competition intensified they imposed colonial rule on Java, Sumatra and the Moluccas, at the same time expelling the Portuguese not only from the East Indies but also Malacca on the Malayan Peninsula, Formosa (or Taiwan, for many years known by its Portuguese name of "beautiful"), and Japan where they would remain for more than 200 years.

The Dutch eyed the China trade enviously and, with the help of Chinese merchants settled in the Indies, managed to get a small share during their regular trading visits to Japan. One of their early triumphs was to capture a Portuguese carrack off Macau in 1602, laden with a prized collection of Ming blue-and-white ware with the reign mark of Wanli, the last of the dynasty, probably poisoned by a tyrannical eunuch. It was the same year that Fr Matteo Ricci, after twenty years in China, reached Beijing to present a striking clock to the Emperor and update the calendar. Down south, the Dutch sent their booty off to Amsterdam. To their amazement it raised several million guilders.[3] With the congratulations of their masters ringing in their ears, the Dutch knew they had to secure a China base and corner this lucrative trade.

However, they failed to eject the Portuguese from Macau and had to be content with a secondary role opting for a base in the Pescadores Islands near Taiwan. Again, why the Dutch did not seek an alternate base on one of the hundreds of offshore islands on the China coast is not known and possibly has more to do with the strength of Chinese opposition than Dutch hesitancy. The Dutch were quick to realize that they would have to direct their appeals to the Chinese capital; they mounted three embassies in the seventeenth century between 1656 and 1686 but gained only minor trading concessions from the Qing emperor, Kangxi.

An even greater menace to the Portuguese was a huge pirate fleet under the command of a Ming supporter, Zheng Zhilong, who held the coast of southern China to ransom for fifteen years, controlling the trade with India and its principal exponents, the Spanish, Portuguese and Dutch. Zheng wanted a fair share of the proceeds. The Manchu rulers tried to bribe him into submission with the offer of the title of Admiral of the Sea, but with a powerful fleet under his command he called the shots. For a long time he resisted but was later foolish enough to pay a visit to Beijing to hold discussions with officials and spent the rest of his life under house arrest. His son, the celebrated Koxinga, inherited his

---

3. It would also come to be known as *kraak porselein* and would be copied by Dutch potters at Delft, with much less charm and grace.

mantle and was happy enough to see his father remain a guest of the Manchus.

The Qing — the name adopted by the new rulers in Beijing (1644–1911) — knew little of geography and less of the Western barbarians now milling around Guangzhou; nor did they realize that the new wave of traders had leapfrogged Africa, India and Malaya to reach their shores. It was not until a Jesuit cartographer drew up an accurate globular map of the world that the Beijing court was able to understand the significance of the European initiative. A lesson in geography was not enough, however. A lesson in history and contemporary affairs on the other side of the world was about to follow.

One of the major prizes in Guangzhou was the silk trade, and Macau rapidly became the centre for exports both to the Spanish in Manila and to the Japanese. There would be as many as fifty or sixty sailings a year in either direction, with the Dutch continually at loggerheads with the Portuguese over their share of the trade; this led to an attempt to invade Macau in 1622, repulsed by Portuguese priests manning cannon, with heavy Dutch losses. Moreover, there were times when Lisbon cracked down on exports to Manila, in which case Chinese middlemen were quick to step in. Whoever carried the silk knew there was a good market. Galleons carrying half a million silver dollars crossed the Pacific Ocean and sales with profits of between 50 and 100 per cent were recorded.

Macau in those years was a city of 20,000 Chinese, a few thousand slaves and people of mixed race and a tiny minority of mainland Portuguese. At one time, only one Portuguese woman lived there, the rest being Eurasians. But it was a feisty, prickly city, proud of its origins and traditions, with church and senate wrangling frequently over precedence and protocol.

The travel writer-artist, Peter Mundy, who accompanied the Englishman Capt John Weddell on his visit to China, described the scene in the seventeenth century: "Macau standeth at one end of a greatt Iland built on rising hills, some gardeins and trees

Figure 2.4 An old Chinese woodblock of Macau.

among their houses making a pretty prospecte somewhatt resem-
bling Goa, though not as bigge; their houses double tyled, and
thatt plaistred over againe, for prevention of hurracanes or
violent wyndes that happen some yeares, called by the Chinois
Tuffaones. Before Macau are many islands, some greater some
lesse, some inhabited, most part nott; high uneven land, no trees,
much grasse and plenty of water springs; very stony." These
islands were used by the Portuguese for picnics which lasted
"eight or ten daies, more or less according to their pleasures,
under the tentts they carry with them in some fine little vally by a
running water."

The Chinese refused them permission to cross to any part of
the mainland so that the Portuguese provided all their own
amusements. Mundy found their sari-clad wives and children
"ritche in jewells and apparell," and well endowed with slaves,
the male variety being African ("curled-head Caphers") and the
female, Chinese. They enjoyed frequent "feastings and rejoycings
att their weddings, Christnings and Holidaies (which are often)".

Mundy however felt the official wrath of the local Captain General when he went to pay him a visit, all over Weddell's ship taking a number of Macau residents to Goa[4] when they should have taken Portuguese ships. Unaware of the incident, Mundy walked into Government House, and "before I could gett uppe staires hee mett mee, and before I could beegin to speake, hee fell a rayling in most violent manner with uncivill and discourteous language." Having delivered this broadside, he ordered Mundy back to "our shippes and (said) thatt whomsoever hee found ashoare in the morning, he could cause him to bee hangued and confiscate all the goods found in the towne; and soe hee left mee without suffring mee to speake one word."

Weddell was the first Englishman to join the China queue. He arrived just before the Qing came to power. As usual the British were late-comers; in an era when the country was convulsed by post-Reformation religious strife and internal bickering its foreign policy was dominated by its immediate continental neighbours — France, Spain and the Low Countries. Not the least of England's worries was a civil war which brought an end to the monarchy; for the next ten years it became a de facto republic under a Lord Protector named Oliver Cromwell. Two British companies had been granted charters as early as 1600 to trade between the Cape of Good Hope and the Strait of Malacca, and despite his distractions at home Cromwell handed out more rights to the Asian trade in 1657.

The visit to India and China by Weddell was a bit of a gamble, literally. The East India Company, one of the two chartered trading ventures, had been granted a royal monopoly to exploit the trade to India and all points east, but was slow to return dividends; a rival trader with a close link to Charles I — perhaps a tennis partner — suggested another venture. Charles agreed

---

4. They did so to avoid capture by the Dutch and paying duty on their cargo.

and Captain Weddell with four ships was authorized to test the waters at Macau. He arrived in June 1637, officially a merchant but in reality a privateer.

Naively, Weddell began what would turn out to be a three-year voyage, with little more than royal letters of authorization and pleas of assistance to the Portuguese. Not surprisingly, all were ignored. The Chinese were not impressed with the arrival of yet another Western barbarian flag begging for a share of the spoils; furthermore it was a potential source of friction with competitors already on the scene. As for the Portuguese they were not about to give up any part of their hard-won trade to rivals known only too well for their bumptious and aggressive behaviour in Europe, not to mention their repudiation of the one true faith and the authority of the Holy Father in Rome. Little wonder Peter Mundy received such short shrift from the Captain General in Macau.

Captain Weddell did not take kindly to being kept waiting outside the Pearl River estuary, and decided to find out the reasons; he sent a pinnace to within fifty kilometres of the city, but his two lieutenants were stopped and told that if they wanted to trade they had to lodge a petition with the Chinese mandarin in Macau. Weddell saw his plight immediately — a catch-22 situation, with the Portuguese unwilling to help and the Chinese capable of endless prevarication.

Weddell, like all seamen of his day faced with such an impasse, took matters into his own hands. He again tried to force the river but this time was stopped by forty junks and an official who ordered him to come no closer. The Chinese forts on either side of the river were reinforced with cannon and seeing Weddell as a pirate, the Chinese gunners fired warning shots to impress upon the Englishman that he was not wanted.

In those years there was little to distinguish merchantmen from warships other than flag. Weddell carried both. Sailing in hostile waters, encountering King's enemies and pirates everywhere the captain of a merchantman went to sea well armed with cannon, swords and muskets; Weddell may have seemed piratical to the Chinese but he was a trader seeking profits as his warrant stipulated. When the Chinese guns opened up Weddell bared his own teeth, and his broadsides raked the Chinese forts with shot. Not satisfied with shelling, Weddell sent a landing party ashore, seized the fort and tore down its flag. He hoisted the King's flag and removed thirty-five Chinese cannon. Thus British commercial intercourse with China began violently, a precursor of what would occur often in future.

Weddell's second encounter with the Chinese also resulted in bloodshed when his men went ashore to obtain supplies of food and encountered 350 swordsmen; a fight followed and several were killed on both sides. The entire expedition was marked with duplicity, hostility, bribery, prevarication, treachery and stupidity and after several months of bartering, bombardment and bullying, Weddell was lucky to escape having purchased 20 tons of silk and a few sets of porcelain, 50 tons of ginger and 750 tons of sugar. He also managed to save most of his money as well as the lives of three men he had foolishly sent disguised to Guangzhou, only to be cornered, isolated and imprisoned by Chinese officials.

After reducing the Chinese fort on the Bocca Tigris to rubble, Weddell was eventually persuaded to leave and told never to return. It must have been a strong Chinese curse that sent him on his way for in the Indian Ocean homeward bound his ship was lost with all hands. Only one of his four ships returned to England after a 36,000-mile journey lasting thirty-two months with only part of the cargo and the trading silver. Despite this discouraging start the growing fortunes of the Dutch kept alive hopes that the East India Company could establish a profitable trade with China. Meanwhile, King Charles had other things on his mind — a war with the Scots, a rebellion in Ireland and a growing row with Parliament. His chief antagonist, however, was Cromwell who later performed a service for China, a favour that went unknown and unacknowledged — the beheading of the king.

During the era of Cromwell's Commonwealth that followed Britain concentrated on subjugating Ireland and quarrelling with the Dutch while disenchanted and disillusioned Englishmen and their families began leaving in droves to settle on the shores of the New World of Columbus and Cabot across the Atlantic. Little wonder that China enjoyed a long respite.

A last word about Weddell. Misguided he may have been but he was no fool; he knew trade with China was a high risk venture; but there were also great prizes — including seizure of Spanish treasure ships which Weddell surprisingly resisted off Macau. Not only was he a former East India Company captain well used to sailing and trading in unchartered waters, but the Dutch had clearly outlined the problems in a memorandum in 1627. It said: "Concerning the trade to China, three things are made especially known unto the world. The one is the abundant trade it affordeth. The second is that they admit no stranger into their country. The third is that trade is as life unto the vulgar, which in remote parts they will seek to accommodate with hazard of all they have." With the promise of a brighter future, England decided the likely gains outweighed the risks and renewed its trade.

It may be wondered how England would have reacted if the roles had been reversed; how might the Government of the day have responded if four large Chinese junks, bristling with cannon, had sailed up the Thames with the demand to carry on trade, and had blown up the Tower of London or some other national landmark when the merchants were slow to spread out their wares. English arrogance in assuming that China would crumble at the first sign of pressure and agree to unfettered trade was typical of the high-handed presumption of the time. In the wake of the English came the first French ship to Guangzhou in 1698, followed by the Danes in 1731, the Swedes in 1732 and the Russians in 1753, with no more spectacular results.

China's wealth was legendary but so was its aloofness, its inaccessibility and its self-centredness. Its international outlook, however, had been conditioned by centuries of self-contemplation. China was not the imperial bully or the aggressive superpower to the Asian region that France, Spain, and Britain were to Europe. The wars that China fought were mainly internal and defensive. The 6,000-km Great Wall was a barrier to keep marauding tribes out. China's stability for hundreds of years ensured the peace of eastern Asia. Its neighbours wanted nothing more than to placate the giant to the north, to recognize the greatness of its culture and civilization, as well as its influence in the region, to offer tribute and trade and carry on their own lives without interference. Not so the pushy and acquisitive Europeans.

Barring the way to intercourse with the Middle Kingdom were more than language, customs, laws and means of exchange; barbarian traders unversed in the subtleties of diplomacy might well have decided that the only way to make an impact was to play the part of the wild bull in the China shop. Both the British and Dutch had expected the Portuguese in Macau to help as intermediaries, to provide letters of introduction and stand guarantor for good behaviour. However, the Portuguese were under the thumb of China and had no independent bargaining power even if they had wanted to help a serious and powerful rival to become established on their doorstep. True, a coalition of three European nations might have succeeded where one had failed, but there was no wish to join forces and the Portuguese wanted the China cake for itself.

England was thus seriously flawed in believing it held the key to Guangzhou and its trade. Greed and the glory of being first prevailed. The Chinese were contemptuous. Even the Jesuits, peaceful, patient and long-suffering (in that part of the world at least), offering a wealth of learning and scholarship, felt the brunt of Chinese apathy and disdain. How could the justifiably suspicious Chinese know there was any difference between turbulent traders and proselytizing priests? Both had something to sell, both wanted something in return, both sought a foothold within their borders.

The East India Company hesitated briefly before resuming the China initiative; then in 1644, seven years after the Weddell visit, it despatched *Hinde* on a new trading venture. As with Weddell's fleet, the first encounter with officialdom resulted in demands for huge measurage fees. Carrying silver reals of eight as trading currency her captain was forced to hand over 3,500 (about four times more than the specified figure) before she was allowed near the river entrance, only to find that there was little to buy in the city where administration had all but broken down following the suicide of the last Ming Emperor. As the Manchu conquerors approached the capital, piracy was rife, and the bureaucrats were trying to buy them off with bribes; even the Portuguese in Macau were up in arms against their own viceroy in Goa.

Nor did things improve with the coming of the Manchus (or Qing). A ship's captain wrote of Guangzhou that there was "no certainty of trade in any part of China under ye Tartars. There is soe many great vessells of rogues yt lie about ye mouth of ye river yt it muste be a lusty ship and double-manned to go thither." And although the Manchus appointed their own administrators in Guangzhou in 1653 and at the same time set up a customs house under a mandarin in Macau, it was another thirty years before they were able to pacify the province.

A couple of English private ships poked their bows through the Bogue but came away empty-handed and absconded without paying measurage demands — "and this caused ye Mandarines to lay heavy tax upon ye city of Macau"; which in turn was passed on to the next EIC ship to show itself in the river.

The new Manchu administration seems to have taken the view that if visiting trading ships could not be forcibly deterred, the next best was to make them pay heavily for the privilege of trading with China. The measurage charges then imposed were the beginning of a deep-seated vexation that would persist up to the outbreak of the first Anglo-Chinese war in 1841. Nor was it the only charge to be inflicted upon visiting ships. As the trade grew, so did the bureaucracy in Guangzhou, each official ready to apply his own exaction or to take a cut of the charges. Moreover Beijing itself often made heavy demands on the trade for contributions for "flood relief" in various parts of the country, and the local mandarins were expected to recoup this somehow — how better than to sting the barbarians clamouring for trade?

The Hoppo (from Hubu, a corruption and abbreviation of the mandarin title for Commissioner of Customs) was quick to present his demands and the Governor and the Viceroy also had their hands out waiting to be greased. Under these extortionate regulations trade was sanctioned and foreign vessels admitted to Guangzhou — and nowhere else.

Over the centuries Guangzhou had built up an elaborate mandarinate ranging from the first to the ninth class. Under the Governor General of the two Guangs was the Provincial Governor, the Superintendent of Finance, the Provincial Judge, the Collector of the Salt Gabel, the Grain Collector, the Intendant of Circuit, the Departmental Prefect, the Inferior Departmental Prefect and the Independent Sub-Prefect as well as the Sub-Prefect and his deputy, the District Magistrate, his two assistants, two Township Magistrates, the Inspector of Police, the Inspector of River Police, two Secretaries, the Treasurer, the Prison Master and the all important Superintendent of Customs who was addressed as "Your Excellency" and was a class 3 blue button mandarin.

Their annual salaries were by any standards abysmal ranging from $20 to a high of $110, but on top of that they all received very large anti-extortion allowances amounting, in the case of the Governor General, to almost $15,000, with the Governor receiving $7,500 and the Superintendent of Finance $4,000 while the Superintendent of Customs commanded no more than $1,500. Why he did so badly compared with the others is not clear, though Beijing realized he would never retire poor.

This elaborate hierarchy, complete with ten ranks of judges, existed in both the Ming and the Qing dynasty years but with the growth in foreign trade the financial kickbacks to the top two dozen in the administration were enormous and to win appointment to the lucrative southern provinces was a veritable licence to print money.

When the mandarins in the mid-seventeenth century became too greedy and oppressive, the foreign traders boycotted Guangzhou and tried their luck in Japan, Taiwan, Cambodia or Tonkin (in what is now Vietnam). But the King of Tonkin enforced even more stringent demands on the foreigners who found that "now we are within the King's power, we must be obedient thereto." The list of bribes, exactions, gifts and perks levied by Tonkin applied even to Chinese junk masters, and kept the court in clover until the end of the century for that city was the only source of supply for Chinese silks. The English tried bartering their prickly woollens but wool was unpopular in a tropical climate and sales were dismal. It was like offering sows' ears for silk purses.

The Chinese had been making silk for at least 1,000 years before the birth of Christ and exporting it for almost as long. Not satisfied with growing it they also wove it to the highest possible standards, so much so that when a sample was snipped and burnt it left no residue of ash — an age-old Chinese test of purity. The result was that China sold by weight rather than length and refused to bargain, declaring "we cheat neither old nor young."

Taiwan was another alternative outlet to the Western traders. The Dutch occupied the island for forty years and beat off all challengers. It proved a useful stopover en route to Japan. Later the Ming loyalist named Zheng Chenggong (better known as Koxinga, whose father was held under house arrest in Beijing) ruled the island with a rod of iron. The traders found his impositions no less exacting than those of the Guangzhou mandarins, particularly after he lost control of the mainland port of Amoy (Xiamen) in Fujian Province which was also a promising alternative to Guangzhou.

After a series of running battles between Koxinga and the

Manchu navy, the East India Company was again able to return to the Pearl River — this time with greater rewards and less angst. Persistence would lead Britain and other European traders into a highly lucrative and mutually profitable trade that made fortunes for many and filtered down to a wide range of industries. These ranged from shipbuilders, sail and rope makers, crate-makers, carpenters, timber workers, clock-makers, furriers, spinners and garment-makers (woollens in England and silk in China), tea growers and processors and a vast array of middle-men who acted as bankers, lawyers, insurers, clerks, forwarders, carters, customs agents, wharf labourers, seamen, interpreters, missionaries, soldiers, revenue collectors, as well as the extensive commercial network of salesmen, shopkeepers and compradores who bought, sold and traded the goods.

The other side of the coin — the social impact on people — was less attractive and the political impact, though long in gestation, would usher in profound changes not just for Asia but the world, with reverberations and repercussions echoing through the ether to this day.

One of the most immediate and devastating consequences was the arrival of new strains of disease, brought by crews from Europe, diseases which were either rare or unknown in Asia; no less was the export of Asian calamities, chief of which was the Black Death which in the course of four years in the middle of the fourteenth century wiped out between 17 and 28 million people, or between a quarter and a half of the populace. It was brought to Europe by a Genoese fleet entering the port of Messina in Sicily where virtually every member of the crew was dying of a disease picked up "somewhere in the Orient."

The disease, a bacteria which lives in the digestive tract of fleas carried by rats and humans, was one of the most virulent known to mankind and permanent reservoirs existed in China, central Asia, Siberia, the Arabian peninsula, Iran, Libya and East Africa. It is uncertain how the contamination spread in the fourteenth century. One expert believes that the overland route through north China and central Asia was the most crucial; but the new born spice trade from south Asia was also suspected, for goods were transshipped to Red Sea ports and then taken overland to the Nile delta. The infected rats followed the trade.

Not only was the Black Death a terrible calamity, it struck repeatedly with further outbreaks in the late fifteenth century wiping out about a quarter of the population of England, the Netherlands and France. It was described by one authority as "the greatest biological-environmental event in history," comparable to the two world wars in the twentieth century, and one of the major turning-points of Western civilization.[5]

Another "imported" disease was syphilis, though suggestions that Columbus and his crews brought it back from the New World must be viewed with scepticism. Only a year after Columbus left on his voyage it was sufficiently rife in southern Italy to infect a whole army — a French mercenary army consisting of Germans, Swiss, Scots and Irishmen — who took the "Italian pox" back to their homelands. Its origin is uncertain and while Asia cannot be stigmatized there is no doubt it and other diseases such as smallpox, cholera, beri-beri, measles, leprosy, dysentery, influenza and typhus, spread significantly throughout the world, travelling via the East–West trade routes and carried as much by European sailors as by Asian villagers.

Another disease, cholera, was not known in western Europe until a Portuguese Jewish physician, Garcia d'Orta, travelled as personal physician on one of the first fleets to the Far East; among his achievements was to print the first Western medical treatise in India. He described Asiatic cholera as one of the most potent killers of the Subcontinent. It is still largely confined to the Third World and periodically shows up on the China coast.

Another eminent physician to record descriptions of endemic

---

5. Robert Gottfried, *The Black Death* (London: Robert Hale, 1984).

illnesses in Asia was the Dutchman, Jacobus Bontius, who brought to light the existence of beri-beri (from the Singhalese word meaning weakness), endemic in India and other parts of Asia. The victims were invariably people suffering severe deficiencies in diets for which there was no known cure until the improvement of living standards and the development of vitamins, particularly thiamin, many centuries later. Smallpox was another ancient scourge, long known in China and first described in the third century as "Hun pox" and thought to have spread with the invading Huns.

While Western records were able to catalogue the impact of various diseases introduced from abroad, the interest in statistical records, particularly on a national basis, was almost non-existent in Asia. Consequently, the extent and duration of epidemics and the identification of the viruses responsible are largely absent from local chronicles until modern times.

The devastation wrought by Western intruders into the island society of the south Pacific, however, is recorded by many writers, brought about by disease, drink and general unruliness. Sir Joseph Banks wrote that in 1789 the population of one island in the Tahiti group had been reduced by 90 per cent compared with what it was in 1769 when visited by Captain Cook's *Endeavour*. This tragedy was repeated at many points along the European trade routes through Asia and the China seas. As Alan Moorehead wrote of the South Pacific: "With the protection of its isolation gone and its whole way of life turned upside down, it was at the mercy of any intruder."[6]

Contributing to the spread of depravity and disease was a combination of rising urban populations in both Europe and Asia living in densely crowded, unsanitary conditions. Batavia, where the Dutch were colonial masters, was described as "one of the

---

6. Alan Moorehead, *The Fatal Impact* (London: Hamish Hamilton, 1966).

most unhealthy places in the world" with open sewers running alongside virtually every main street in the hot, humid and often flooded conditions; following a tropical downpour the city was a breeding ground for myriad germs and viruses. Sir Joseph Banks on Cook's expedition to the south Pacific, reported that of every 100 soldiers sent out by Holland, 50 of those who survived the sea voyage would be dead at the end of the year, 25 more would be in hospital and only 10 would be fit for duty.

Nor was this a Dutch problem alone. The British up to the middle of the nineteenth century had not managed to improve or control hygiene in its colony of Hong Kong where in certain Chinese areas people lived side by side with pigs, cows, goats and chickens, with no piped water supply. British soldiers as much as local residents, suffered appallingly from the swift spread of disease, many carried by rats, fleas, flies and mosquitoes which flourished in the unsanitary conditions, producing a death rate of one in four.

Conditions were no better on board the merchant or naval ships involved in the trade. A lack of fresh fruit, vegetables and meat and an unrelieved diet of dried meat and weevilly biscuits decimated the crews and left the men walking skeletons after long sea voyages. Mortality rates were high, the Portuguese reporting losses of between a quarter and a half of the crew on journeys to India. A ship's surgeon in the time of Elizabeth I had discovered that fresh fruit juice would help to prevent scurvy but it was a century later before James Lind published his paper and it took an enlightened and considerate captain such as James Cook, to put these ideas into practice in his transit of the Pacific.

As if the diet was not bad enough, discipline was barbaric and the lives of those who populated the lower decks were "nasty, brutish and short." Tardiness or displays of reluctance to perform duty by seamen led to a few hefty whacks with the butt of a musket or a flogging with a rope's end to the point where they collapsed on their knees and begged for mercy. Other innovative forms of punishment included something like bungie-jumping, only the victim was thrown from a yard-arm, his feet tied to a rope long enough to ensure that he would end up in the sea and be subjected to continual ducking as he was dragged along the barnacle-coated ship's side. At other times offending seamen would be keel-hauled (dragged under the ship's hull three times) and then flogged.

The Dutch had no qualms about putting anyone who complained about food into irons for ten days, and serving them with bread and water. For picking a fight, a seaman would have a knife plunged into his open hand and "slit to the fingers," virtually rendering him useless for any further service. For those who were found guilty of arson they would be thrown into a fire, while a convicted killer was bound to his victim and thrown overboard. Blasphemy or insolence to the admiral was punished by keel-hauling, once, twice or thrice, depending on the degree of seriousness. In the case of mutiny, the ring leaders would have their hands chopped off before hanging.

The men-of-war of those times, though splendid to contemplate from the dockside or at sea, were four to five-deckers, displacing about 1,000 tons and requiring the timber of about 1,000 oak trees. No environmental protectionists were around in those days to thwart the rape of forests. Their ten main canvas sails had an area of about 1,200 square metres and they carried 64 guns. Their 150 crewmen included everything from a sea captain, a priest, a barber-surgeon (a profession combining the surgical skills of hair dressing and amputation), a master-at-arms (who wielded the cat-o'-nine-tails), a trumpeter, several carpenters, two helmsmen, twenty gunners and ninety seamen. Additionally they would carry up to 300 marines, as much to maintain order aboard as to fight off boarders from enemy ships.

Sailing anywhere could often be agonizingly slow, with contrary winds buffeting departing ships for a week or more before clearing port. Not all were good seaships in days when naval architects, striving for size and grandeur, often relied on guesswork, sometimes disastrously, as in the case of the Swedish warship *Vasa*, which keeled over on her sea trials and sank in Stockholm harbour (but now salvaged and restored.)

Life on board was spartan, for the Dutch fleet was manned by conscription, with one man in ten being taken for active service, and aged from fifteen to sixty. He could be a seaman which at least ensured him the freedom of the deck, or a marine which would see him cooped up in the battery deck, maintaining cannon when he was not engaged in musket drill. His food would consist of grain porridge, dried beans or peas, salt beef and pork, dried or salt fish, dried biscuits and stale bread. Fresh food was rare until he got ashore, but the biggest danger was the outbreak of dysentery, malaria or diphtheria which decimated the crews of the early years of the seventeenth century. Constant companions to the men were rats, lice, cockroaches, flies, mosquitoes and a catalogue of verminous camp-followers, winged, multi-legged, tentacled, stingers, biters and blood-suckers — a mini-ecosystem of creeping, crawling misery — brought aboard at ports of call.

But if life at sea was pretty hellish, it was no bed of roses ashore. Recalcitrant soldiers, guilty of insubordination or dis-obedience, would be yoked with ball and chain and consigned to do road work, or if considered beyond redemption, dumped on an uninhabited island and left there. The amazing thing is that the trade was able to survive at all, dependent as it was on ships where the crews were systematically beaten senseless for trifling misdemeanours and subjected to the full rigours of blistering sunshine, howling storms and beating rain for long hours of the day. The only attraction in going to sea was the prospect of a better, more lucrative existence somewhere over the horizon, for at home urban squalor and poverty were worse than that in a Third World village today.

CHAPTER 3

A Foot in the China Door

For England, the closing years of the seventeenth century were rich in scientific discovery. The Royal Society was founded in London in 1660 with interests in trade, agriculture, shipbuilding, meteorology, history and navigation. It was the age of Isaac Newton, Robert Boyle, Edmund Halley and Robert Hooke, when the nation's pre-eminence in scientific, mathematical, astronomical and philosophical inquiry led the world. A breakthrough in contacts with China at this time might have transformed the complacent self-sufficiency of this ancient Confucian civilization steeped in, and obsessed with the classics. But it saw no need for change. With the revival of the monarchy, Charles II may have been enjoying golden days at home but his East India Company had a hard time penetrating the bamboo curtain that China had pulled around itself. British ships reaching the Pearl River estuary were able to do small amounts of business with freelance trading junks which slipped through the cordon of "Tartar war boats," with goods intended for export to Japan. But Chinese officials made it known that under no circumstances would they consent to foreign merchants coming ashore to trade, nor would they be allowed to found a settlement.

British ships in those days carried a team of four supercargoes who acted as an independent committee of salesmen/buyers despatched by, and answerable to the East India Company. At the head was the "eldest of the council" who was simply the most experienced and mediated when differences arose. With Guangzhou in a truculent mood, the China traders sometimes had more luck in Xiamen and often a bribe not accepted in Guangzhou worked a minor miracle further north, even to the extent of allowing British and Dutch ships to unload their goods in a warehouse ashore.

But the pickings were anything but rich and on a cargo valued at 10,000 pounds, as much as one-fifth could go in "presents to the Emperor" in Xiamen, or as measurage dues and other charges, and gratuities to customs staff in Guangzhou. Either way, the Western traders paid dearly for the privilege of doing business.

The supercargoes had the unenviable task of deciding how much squeeze to pay before the venture was aborted. For while the English ships carried cargo which included lead ("as good as money"), woollen goods (made in England and hard to sell) and sometimes pepper picked up in the East Indies, 90 per cent of the business was settled in cash; these were silver coins, mainly Carolus dollars,[1] and made in Seville's Royal Mint from silver mined in the newly discovered deposits at Potosi, Peru, and Zacatecas in Mexico. Silver was as highly prized in China as in Europe and these coins were the basis of the trade for three centuries; there were also Mexican-minted dollars (nicknamed the "eagle"), duccatoons minted in Venice and to a lesser extent French crowns and German or Scandinavian rixdollars.

These coins were never counted but weighed, and the weight became important in later years when Chinese dealers "chopped" out a fragment to test its quality, for the touch (or fineness) of the silver was also taken into the reckoning. Each type of dollar was given a "touch value" depending on its origin. In addition, it was found that certain coins bearing the head of a particular monarch

---

1. Named after the Spanish Hapsburg monarch, King Charles IV, but better known on the coast as the Pillar dollar because of the "pillars of Hercules" in its design.

were more highly esteemed because of the head featured on the coin. The dollar of Carolus IV, nicknamed "old heads" by the Cantonese, commanded a premium of 30 to 40 per cent for more than eighty years.

Figure 3.1 A money-changer in the eighteenth-century scrutinizes a copper coin. A sketch by William Alexander.

English silver coins, incidentally, never featured in the trade as they were a forbidden export. Besides, the Chinese were stubbornly loyal to the first Western coins they encountered and on which they built their trust. Little wonder that the Western trading ships attracted pirates, when each ship to sail over the horizon was a floating bank — nor were the pirates too particular whose face was on the coin.

Another function of the supercargo was translation and the trade patois of the day was mainly Portuguese. If they were lucky, a Chinese-speaking missionary helped out, repaying small favours shown by the traders. Mostly, the intermediary was a semi-literate Chinese who had his own pocket to line. With the proceeds of the lead and woollen goods, the English in the earliest missions bought cheap gold,[2] silk, a beverage called "thea" (of which more will be heard later), rhubarb, musk, sugar, copper, zinc, quicksilver, vermilion and China root (a thick fleshy root-stock like sarsaparilla); and there were fine judgments to be made on the quality of each item. The supercargo's council thus had to determine the level of profit at the end of each voyage.

The chief or eldest supercargo could earn a salary of 100 pounds (apart from commission or a percentage on his own trading) while his deputies would earn about half. In terms of the Indian trade, ships could show 100 per cent profits, but not all of this went to the East India Company as the captain and the officers had their private trade proceeds to come out of the final figure as well — as much as 25 per cent. However, any losses were also their responsibility; as to the profits, the company wanted a net 20 per cent and "the rest of the gain justly, whatever it proves to be, shall be yours and immediately returned you in dollars by the first ship after the sale of such Chyna goods (in London)."[3]

That rule held good in peace time, but if war with the Dutch should break out the court of the East India Company wanted 40

---

2. At about 65 per cent of the European price, until the Chinese woke up to the higher value it commanded overseas.
3. H. B. Morse, *The East India Company Trading to China*, vol. 1 (1929; reprint, Taipei: Ch'eng-wen Publishing Co., 1975).

per cent "for running the risk & c." As for the ships, some were EIC-owned, others chartered. Nevertheless the captains were hard-nosed businessmen as well as expert mariners and juggled the fate of the ship and crew and the mood of the wind and sea dexterously with the whims of a fickle home market.

These vessels were away often for years at a time; they sailed from Europe heading south down the Atlantic to Cape Town, which became a major port of call from the time of the earliest Portuguese voyages. There they would take on water and provisions and refit with spare parts carried on board.

Earlier the Dutch had taken an interest in a small island in the south Atlantic which the Portuguese had discovered in 1502 — St Helena, 122 square kilometres in area — but while it had its attractions as a port of call on the way to the Indies, the British East India Company squeezed them out and took it over for themselves. The Dutch had to look elsewhere and won a far more desirable prize.

Thanks to a shipwreck in Table Bay in 1647 the Dutch East India Company were alerted to the possibility that it might be settled as a permanent supply station. Within five years the Dutch had begun to build a fort and plant vegetable gardens. From there it was a short step to colonization, increasing settlement, and the introduction of slaves to serve the settlers. The British could keep their mountainous, volcanic island nearly 2,000 kilometres to the west.

From Cape Town the Indiamen would then transit due east to Batavia, with the Portuguese, British, French and Danes making side trips to Goa in India, Sri Lanka, Madras, Malacca, and then passing south of Singapore, they would sail up the South China Sea to Guangzhou (or Canton, as it was known in those days). For survival these ships carried not only trade goods earmarked for various destinations, but cannon and muskets for close-quarter encounters at sea.

With their mixed crews, drawn from every port in Europe, peace could break down at any time; a ship which sailed with

Dutchmen as allies, could, in the course of a two-year journey, find friendships turn sour long before the homeward run — for it would have to run the gauntlet of the Dutch-controlled Strait of Malacca or the Sunda Strait. Moreover, running fights with the Chinese mandarins in Guangzhou were not uncommon — sometimes to recover masts, sails, guns or powder pledged as sureties at the outset of trade — and more than one ship had to take flight leaving behind supercargoes and sailors, often to a cruel fate in captivity.

At other times the Englishmen were at odds with the French who because of their diplomatic courting of the Qing Emperor Kangxi (1662–1722) enjoyed greater favours in building up their trade and contacts with China. The French were late-comers to the China scene after setting up a trading station on India's east coast at Pondicherry in 1674. To claim their share of the trade both the British and the French skirmished ashore and afloat, and if a profitable trade meant slashing or shooting a few of their rivals that was just part of life at the sharp end.

Long-term, however, neither the Dutch nor the French gained any major benefits from diplomacy — the Chinese treated the Europeans as one, occasionally to be played off against each other — and it was the pushy, aggressive British traders, who were ready to take their ships as far north as Ningbo and the Zhoushan islands, who grabbed the lion's share. The English East India Company was not yet a monopoly; others vied for the trade, including Englishmen operating under the Austrian flag. With all this jostling it was a case of first in, first served. Not satisfied with just a place to store their goods the East India Company was, at the turn of the seventeenth century, looking for a "permanent factory" or island base for the China trade. Ideally they would establish themselves on the island of Zhoushan — much favoured by the British — but an attempt to build a trading station with a permanent representative received short shrift from the Emperor, and they were ejected. While some British traders used Bencoolen in Sumatra as a base, others operated from Banjarmassin on the southern coast of Borneo, where they took on pepper, a popular commodity for the Chinese. But much nearer to Guangzhou was the island of Pulo Condore off the southern coast of Cochin China, and the EIC established its China Council at Condore with a fort and garrison of soldiers; it was a regular port of call at which all China-bound EIC vessels were given their final orders on what goods to buy. It suffered a brutal and tragic fate when the entire population was murdered and the factory destroyed by pirates.

As the Ming court declined, piracies multiplied and trading became hazardous. Nor was it a matter of finding safety in friendly ports such as Macau for at that time the Portuguese were rebelling against the Viceroy in Goa. An East India sea captain reported that the Portuguese had murdered their own Captain-General in Macau and were "soe distracted amongst themselves that they are daily spilling one another's blood." While this was going on "the Tartars overrun and waste all the inland country, without settling any government, and soe some of their great men rob and spoil all the sea coasts." As for Guangzhou "there is soe many great vessells of rogues yt lye about ye mouth of ye river yet it muste be a lusty ship and doubled-maned to goe thither; & as times now run, under ye Tartar's government (there is) little security of persons, any trade or dispatch there, nor is there any certainty of trade in any pt of China under ye Tartar." (sic)

This persisted for several years until the incoming Manchus began restoring order. And having endured the foreigners for more than a century, the Chinese then decided to soften their rigid stance. The Manchu (or Qing) Emperor Kangxi began by appointing official merchants to monopolize the trade in Guangzhou. A self-styled "Emperor's" merchant set himself up with a licence bought from the court in Beijing, but British traders found there were rivals in the city prepared to undercut him whenever possible.

A more workable solution appeared in Xiamen where a

collective of Chinese merchants was set up to deal with the tricky, evasive, hard-bargaining trigger-happy barbarians. This was later copied by Guangzhou. Lording it over the merchants, however, was the Hoppo. He was able to collect 4 per cent of the business done, whether by the private merchants or the Emperor's man. However, as the latter had no private capital he rapidly lost the respect of the trade and was replaced by the collective body.

In this way, the new Manchu regime found it easier and more lucrative to foster foreign trade rather than frustrate it. Besides, the Portuguese at Macau were neither active shippers nor effective brokers; their trade was paltry, their concerns domestic and their relations with the Dutch, French and British prickly and irritable. Still dubious of the aggressive British and not yet trusting the wily and ever fractious Cantonese — "who would sell their grandmothers, or someone else's, if a market developed" — the Manchu rulers wanted a more durable arrangement, with fixed and stable measurage charges yielding a fair income for the Emperor (up to 10 per cent) with no arguments.

In the early eighteenth century Guangzhou was a city of 900,000 "and there is no day in the year but shews 5,000 sail of trading jonks, besides small boats for other services, lying before the city," according to one of the East Indiamen captains. The French had stolen a march on other Europeans by gaining agreement to station a trader in Guangzhou in 1699, an arrangement which persisted for twenty-five years; it would take the East India Company several years to gain the same privilege, though premises of some kind were available for the storage of cargoes.

Captain Charles Lockyer in 1711, reported: "you must expect to be visited by the greatest sharpers in China. A great many will drop into your Chamber one after another, under pretence of selling the commoditys they bring with them, and seem to quarrel who shall shew first, while others of their comrades pilfer and steal in the mean time. Their long coats favour this design; nor want they cunning or boldness to attempt the most hazardous and daring enterprises."[4]

Slowly a row of foreign-designed houses would make their appearance outside the city walls, complete with national flags, on the Guangzhou river-front. These were the so-called foreign "factories" which made a picturesque scene on the riverfront, much favoured in later years by Western and Chinese artists as souvenir paintings. Hundreds of such views were executed in a variety of media and are today a common sight at art galleries and specialist exhibitions.

The word "factory" may suggest that some manufacturing process occurred there; this was not so. They were buildings to house the Western factors or commission agents who conducted the trade, and the buildings usually consisted of a warehouse and offices on the ground floor and living accommodation and dining areas above. They were occupied for five or six months of the year during the trading season. This began when the prevailing winds enabled sailing ships to cover the last leg of their long journey from England or Europe up the South China Sea to Guangzhou. This was usually in October. The ships spent the next four or five months trading, unloading and loading cargo before catching the last of the northerly monsoons in late February on their journey home.

In the summer months there was no business in Guangzhou and the traders moved to Macau where they built or rented summer homes. Strict rules of residence applied in Guangzhou which were tightened and refined as the years went by. These homes were comfortable without being palatial and the residents had no right of access to the city; local produce was brought by vendors to their doors or to the common land on the waterfront which was also their only area for exercise and recreation.

---

4. H. B. Morse, *The East Indian Company Trading to China*, vol. 1.

The buildings were not owned by the traders but built and rented by Chinese merchants, based on a design common to various parts of Asia inhabited by foreigners. Thus they were drawn up on European lines with large windows, high ceilings, cool dark passageways and shady courtyards, each one differing slightly from its neighbour. This so-called "compradoric" style remained a feature of local architecture until well into the twentieth century. Another building in the same style in old Guangzhou, also owned by the Hong merchants, was the "Consoo House." This became a council chamber (hence "Consoo") for the factories at the top of Old China Street and survived as a prominent landmark until the early years of the twentieth century.

The Chinese made two demands on all foreign traders; no opium was to be imported on pain of death and confiscation of the vessel — this was also endorsed by the Council of the East India Company at Madras, but did not stop it coming in — and all ships entering the river must surrender all powder, cannon and small arms before starting to talk business. Memories of Captain Weddell's first expedition were deeply etched in the official Chinese memory.

With more than half the ships entering the river British, the Chinese officials found one other deficiency exasperating — their inability to comprehend the "hung-mo lo," or red-haired barbarians. No longer could they rely on Portuguese go-betweens; the British treated Macau as an irrelevance and insisted on going up-river to do business. No Briton of that day understood Chinese and in any case learning Chinese was forbidden, though the Jesuit priests found a way around it.

The British traders, employing hand signals, speaking slowly, occasionally shouting and throwing in the odd word of Portuguese, Indian or Malay, insisted on speaking in their own tongue; how the Chinese comprehended it and what they were able to make of a Highland Scot, a Yorkshireman, a Jordie (from Newcastle), a Welshman or a Dubliner, beggars imagination. But to their credit the Chinese established a small core of so-called linguists who had enough contact with foreign languages to devise a lingua franca; this persisted for more than 100 years and was still in use in many parts of China to the middle of the twentieth century.

Not until the arrival of the missionary, Dr Robert Morrison in 1807, were the British able to communicate with Chinese officials in their own language. That millions of dollars of trade were transacted each year with increasingly complex financial arrangements as silver dollars were phased out, and as exacting regulations were imposed by the Chinese, is a tribute to the tolerance, persistence, patience and good sense of all involved.

The language was a caricature of colonial ways and reflected the manner in which British traders conducted their business in many parts of the world; but at a very basic level it was geared to do business, and succeeded. The word "pidgin" (or pigeon) was a corruption of the word "business," so while numbers were all important, the connecting words only needed to describe the nature of the transaction, the price and delivery date. Grammar, syntax, tense and spelling were superfluous and the language, while mainly English, with a vocabulary of about 700 words, included Portuguese, Malay and Indian words which were all part of the patois of the times.

The word "mandarin" came from the Portuguese word meaning "to order"; "compradore" came from the word "to buy"; "joss" from the word for God — "deos"; "maskey" from masque, or never mind. India contributed words like bazaar, shroff, tiffin, lac (100,000), coolie, bungalow, chit and kaarle (curry). This was almost the staple diet of all foreigners in those days, as much to flavour the food and as to disguise its less endearing qualities.

Then there were composite words like "chow chow" which either indicated food, a variety of goods, or something worthless. Anything good was "No. 1" and the possessive case always entailed use of the word "belong." Chinese words also crept into the language. Foreigners, today more politely described as "sai yun," were invariably "fan-kwai lo" or "kwai lo" meaning foreign devil people or devil people. The Dutch were "Ho-lan yun," the French "Fat-lan-see" and later, the Americans were "Fa-kei kwai" or the "flowery flag devils," while their country was "Gum San," or the Gold Mountain.

To be able to toss in words of this complexity required a familiarity and dexterity indicative of long experience. A simple observation by a Chinese merchant that "Fan-kwae lo no likee Chinee chow chow. My chow chow belong No. 1, all time gip he come my house," would signify to the cogniscenti that foreigners were not keen on Chinese food even though the host only served the best quality when they visited his home. If the merchant were a little less diplomatic he might utter "Fan-kwae chin-te-le-mun too muchee foolo" which would mean that foreign gentlemen were excessively foolish. But more graciously he might add: "Maskee, he belong olo flen. My likee he," to indicate that nevertheless he remained an old and admired friend. As he shook hands with a departing guest he might add a farewell very similar to that used today "See you tomollo," regardless of when their next appointment was. "Tomollo" thus also signified the future tense, while "alledy" (already) indicated a completed action and hence past tense.

The stranger to the Chinese scene might well recoil in horror at the bastardization of the language but the old hands slipped into the vernacular with ease and invariably conducted long and detailed conversations. But it was left to the linguist to translate the mass of words into intelligible Chinese for the Manchu officials who would invariably be Mandarin speakers with barely a working knowledge of Cantonese. Moreover, the Chinese bargained for everything, rolling up the long silken sleeves of their garments and displaying fingers to indicate price; and compromise was an art form practised in every part of life. The foreigners were quick to discover that and adapted to it, rather than resort to anger and exasperation which only amused the Chinese.

In addition to the ban on opium and weapons, no foreign women were admitted to the factories; they had to stay in Macau. In any case few came to China until the nineteenth century. When they did, they were mobbed by gaping crowds. Furthermore, no foreigner was allowed to use a sedan chair for this implied equality with officialdom. Foreigners were not permitted to roam the countryside. No diplomatic envoys were allowed to live in the country and any diplomat who was admitted to Beijing must perform the kow-tow to the Emperor, signifying a subservient status. There was also a ban on exporting Chinese silver; Chinese merchants should not become indebted to foreigners by contracting excessive loans — though this happened with increasing frequency as the trade grew. Chinese people should not leave the country without permission; those who did were regarded as deserters, rebels or pirates and risked death if they returned — unless as successful businessmen, when they would be honoured with imperial awards.

Emigration in the early years of the Qing dynasty was forbidden, though it had been happening unofficially for hundreds of years, and like most official Chinese edicts would be honoured more in the breach than in the observance. China, being self-sufficient, needed nothing from the world, though barbarian traders could buy the products of China provided they conformed to Chinese rules, regulations and practices. They could not learn to speak or write the language; they could not intermarry (but liaisons were common) and they were at all times to be subject to Chinese law while in the country.

As with all rules, however, the Chinese and the Europeans found ways around some of them, some of the time, but after a century of prodding and probing the frustration, friction and ferment they provoked led to a fateful breakdown between the two countries. But the evolution was gradual and painful and the first step was the creation of a body corporate of Chinese merchants capable of handling the growing Sino-Western trade. The mandarins were unable and unwilling to become involved save to cream off the 10 per cent profits and any other small or large cashflow they could get their hands on. This included, in addition to the duty, payment for the officials, linguists and weighers, boat and coolie hire, the purchase of silver and even the difference in weights — "the emperor's being 18 per mille larger than others."

There had to be a better way of doing trade with just a small handful of Chinese merchants for when one died in 1720, the English traders were left dealing with a monopoly. However, the merchants of Guangzhou themselves took the initiative to form a guild and in that year made an agreement "in the most sacred manner — by going before one of their idols, and there swearing and sacrificing a cock, and drinking the blood."[5] The agreement resulted in a charter of thirteen "laudable aims" including equality of treatment, punishment for fraudulent behaviour by either side, malpractice and evasion, avoidance of monopoly and a fair distribution of trade among the merchants. This became the Hong merchants' code of practice, a self-imposed regulatory system which was observed at most times.

Eventually, the Chinese merchants became established as the Co-Hong, thirteen in all, mutually supportive in theory but in practice all out to corner as much of the trade for themselves as they could. Several would fall by the wayside but those who managed to keep afloat made fortunes by supporting the most dependable traders and by conducting their business with sagacity and scrupulous honesty.

The Co-Hong became virtually the Chinese overseas trade co-operative and in many cases individual merchants passed on their business to sons or nephews using trade names as famous in their day as the giants of the China trade today. The Co-Hong survived from 1720 until the outbreak of the Opium War and they

---

5. H. B. Morse, *The East Indian Company Trading to China*, vol. 1.

were officially licensed and recognized, having attained their positions by the volume and continuity of their trade, as well as by paying heavily for the permit.

With the licence came other signs of imperial favour, notably a coloured button of rank on their caps, and a title, much like a knighthood or peerage in England, though nothing came free in this society. Membership of the Co-Hong had its obligations and regular demands were made upon them to contribute to all sorts of worthy causes. All this would be built into the prices of the commodities sold to the traders.

In theory and in practice they held the monopoly of the trade and were answerable to the Hoppo, who received his appointment from the Emperor. This was proof that while trade may have been regarded somewhat contemptuously by the hierarchy, and the Europeans as troublesome and uncivilized, yet the pickings were rich. As long as the foreigners continued to buy the produce of the country in increasing quantity without creating shortages of any essential commodity, the view was that the trade should be encouraged so long as it was conducted within the strict limits of the laws and decrees of the land.

The Hong merchants were virtually the counterpart of the East India Companies established by the Netherlands, Sweden (whose first ship arrived in 1731) and England. For China it simplified control of the export trade and ensured not only the payment of all duties on imports and exports but also control of the foreigners based in Guangzhou. This also saved the foreign merchants from becoming enmeshed in the red tape of Chinese bureaucracy and as the trade involved many millions of dollars a year this gave the Chinese Government a close insight into what was coming into and going out of the country, as well as who was involved in the export trade.

Behind the Co-Hong was a vast army of subsidiary or "outside" merchants providing everything from silk and tea, which constituted the bulk of the shipments, to floor matting, rhubarb, umbrellas, fans and minerals of various kinds; all were taxed or

Figure 3.2 A disgraced mandarin takes his leave, as sketched by Auguste Borget.

tithed as their goods filtered through the canal systems of various Chinese provinces to the south coast.

If the Hong merchants made millions out of this privilege, quite a few went bankrupt by speculation and indebtedness to foreign traders. This became such a serious problem that in 1779, a "Consoo Fund" was set up to support Hong merchants who became bankrupt. Who paid for this fund? The foreign merchants who were levied with a 3–6 per cent tax on all goods they dealt in. Needless to say, little remained in the fund. Both the Hong merchants and the mandarins raided it repeatedly and when a crisis occurred fifty years later the larder was bare. This certainly aggravated relations between China and the West prior to the Opium War.

The successful merchants built large estates, lived lavishly and entertained splendidly, some like Tinqua, supporting five wives. They all formed close friendships with many of the foreign traders and a deep sense of mutual respect grew up. When things went wrong and when the Viceroy or the Hoppo went on the warpath after an incident involving a breach of the rules or a commotion in which foreign seamen were involved, the Hong merchants took the brunt of the official ire.

Not once but often they would be threatened with the bastinado (or beating with a long bamboo pole) and the Hoppo would think nothing of chaining up a Hong merchant and sending him under escort by a jailer to the factories of the foreign merchants to demand redress for some incident, the hint being that unless compliance was obtained the Hong merchant would be tortured and jailed and his possessions confiscated; the ultimate threat was one of deportation to the wilds of Xinjiang, which was as far west as one could go in the empire and from which rarely would they return alive.

Many thought this was an elaborate charade staged by the mandarins to impress the European merchants and often it may have been just that, but the threat of punitive sanctions was always present. W. C. Hunter, the American trader living in Guangzhou in the early nineteenth century, recalls the case of the Hong merchant Man Ho, a great favourite with the foreign community with his courteous manners and old-world charm. He had been accorded the privilege of wearing a blue button on his cap. Nothing could save him, however, when he was judged bankrupt and the Hoppo sentenced him to transportation for life to the north-west frontier regions — as the Cantonese described it, "a colo country" — where he was made a sweeper in a temple. By virtue of bribes to the right authority, and thanks to a generous farewell present subscribed by other Hong merchants and European friends, he was able to afford the minimum comforts of life. He only returned to Guangzhou in his coffin, however, when the rigours of the climate and the privations of existence sapped his health.

The snakes-and-ladders lifestyle of the Chinese people affected the rich and famous as well as the humble worker. The Chinese system allowed the poorest student to climb the ladders through a benevolent classics-based education system culminating in the imperial examinations (from which the judges and officials were selected) but the prospect of failure hung like a sword of Damocles over all and the highest in the land could find himself reduced to ignominy and poverty through neglect of duty.

Some European sea captains found it more convenient to trade with smugglers but for the big trades, such as silk and tea, it was not possible to buy the quantity or quality demanded in the markets of Britain and Europe. The goods had to be ordered several months in advance, with cash down payments for delivery at specific dates. To be caught buying from smugglers meant instant eviction and neither the captain nor the ship would be re-admitted. As for the smugglers, the Chinese judicial system assumed guilt at the outset and few escaped decapitation after a summary trial.

Smuggling thrived when internal order broke down and when the rewards of contraband were so great (as with opium) as to overcome fear of punishment; this was usually conducted by people who were bandits or brigands anyway and who faced death by a thousand cuts whenever they were caught. Living on offshore islands and recruiting impecunious fishermen, they roamed the estuaries in search of victims but the foreign traders for many years avoided them.

To get a foot in the China door in the early eighteenth century meant playing the game by the rules; broadsides and bluster had not paid off and tempting as it was for the Westerners to play off one Chinese merchant against another they found that they did best by linking up with a dependable Hong merchant who could guarantee price, delivery and quality. Moreover, the goods ordered were shipped from inland suppliers directly to the warehouses of the Hong merchants where they were stored, weighed, bundled and marked before being moved directly to the anchorage at nearby Whampoa and from thence to the ships.

Writing of the days of the Co-Hong, W. C. Hunter said that "as a body we found them honourable and reliable in all their dealings, faithful to their contracts and large-minded." Their private homes were "on a vast scale comprising gardens, grottoes and lakes crossed by several stone bridges, joined by pathways neatly paved with mosaic designs of fish, flowers or birds";[6] one of the most beautiful was that of Pwankeiqua who had a large retinue of servants to maintain him and his family in a state of vice-regal opulence.

At the Chinese dinners he attended, Hunter would be served delicacies such as *bêche-de-mer* and bird's nest soup with plover's eggs, shark's fins and roasted snails. The bird's nests were imported from Java at thirty Spanish silver dollars a pound. Another merchant grandee was Howqua, if anything more generous and more gracious than Pwankeiqua, who also had the distinction of becoming a brand name for a blend of China tea and who in 1834 was estimated to be worth $26 million, today equivalent to several billion American dollars.

Associated with the East India Company and its successors in the private trade, Howqua commanded widespread affection among the foreign community and was held in the highest esteem for the way in which he waived or postponed debts and contributed to the recovery of other Hong merchants who fell on hard times. These Cantonese gentlemen, displaying the highest business ethics, and impeccably honourable, represented the golden age of the China trade which lasted for about a century.

---

6. W. C. Hunter, *The Fan Kwai at Canton* (1882; reprint, London: Kegan Paul, Trench, 1965).

George Chinnery's much-copied paintings of the slim, spare almost emaciated Howqua with his droopy eyes and whispy beard, and his more affable, portly, smiling colleague Mowqua, capture the essence of this age of dignity and decorum in the annals of Sino-Western relations. There were incidentally several generations of Howqua, all members of the Wu family, the first obtaining his licence in 1731 and thus one of the longest serving members of the Co-Hong, which continued until the outbreak of the Opium War in 1839.

As for the mandarins in Guangzhou they often proved tricky, arrogant, dictatorial and grasping, and relations with the foreign merchants were, more often than not, severely strained; the foreigners constantly sparred with them over port charges, measurage dues and extortionate demands with no clear justification. In 1739, one small but significant advance was recorded: the Chinese authorities agreed to three classes of measurage for ships, and fixed charges accordingly.

Measurements were taken from the centre of the foremast to the centre of the mizzen mast and for breadth, from side to side just behind the mainmast. First-rate ships then paid 7.77 taels (approximately an ounce of silver — the name possibly coming from the Hindi word *tola*) per unit; second-rate ships 7.14 taels and third-rate, 5 taels. On top of that the ships had to pay 1,950 taels as presents, 1,600 going to the Emperor, part on the ship's arrival and part on departure. French ships paid 2,050 taels and ships from India, 1,850 taels. A ship of about 500 tons thus paid a total of 3,274 taels in charges for her right to enter port and trade. In that year, fifteen ships visited Guangzhou, seven being British, the rest, French, Danish, Dutch and Swedish. British ships were rarely bigger than 500 tons incidentally; for those above that displacement were obliged to carry a chaplain regardless of crew numbers — an unjustified extravagance, in their view.

But if the mandarins at Guangzhou were imperious and autocratic no less was one British admiral at that time. He was Commodore Anson who (in 1742) sailed into Macau in HMS

Centurion, promptly requesting permission to careen and refit and to reprovision after a long passage around Cape Horn. The Chinese ordered him not to pass the Bogue forts at the mouth of the river. Anson spluttered with rage and delivered an ultimatum to admit him or face a broadside. The Captain Weddell incident left the Chinese in no doubt he meant business, so he was admitted and obtained permission to careen and refit. Having completed that task he set sail only to run into a Spanish galleon bringing in 1.5 million pounds worth of silver from Acapulco to Manila. As Britain was at war with Spain he seized the Spanish ship as a prize.

He then returned to Guangzhou to pick up more stores and when the Chinese were once again slow to comply he demanded an audience with the Viceroy. Once again the Chinese kept him waiting and while standing off the city, *Centurion*'s crew saw a fire break out (which destroyed 100 shops and eleven streets). Without waiting to be invited, Anson's men raced ashore and helped quell the flames.

Once again the British commodore called for an interview; this time, as an act of gratitude the Viceroy yielded, and Anson then proceeded to lecture the official on the delays he experienced in having stores delivered, and on the hardships endured by the foreign merchants in Guangzhou, hoping this would be rectified as soon as possible. The Viceroy heard him in silence and closed the meeting with the wish that he would enjoy a prosperous voyage home, and ignoring the impertinence of a mere naval commodore who presumed to lecture the Emperor's representative.

If the commodore had no hesitation in throwing his weight around, the traders were more circumspect, living as they did almost on a full-time basis in Guangzhou and having no defence against any Chinese display of displeasure. Moreover, there were about 3,000 foreign seamen of all nationalities at any one time who were ready to join in a free-for-all whenever they felt cheated or short-changed by a shopkeeper. After long months at sea, the taste of sly grog distilled ashore by local vendors led to arguments, fights and riots among the visiting sailors, not to mention horrible hangovers. Restoring order fell to the ship's officers and marines (if any) rather than local officials who scurried for cover when hooliganism broke out.

No European country could boast about the behaviour of its crews and the prospect of shore leave fired the blood of every ship-weary mariner. Going ashore in Guangzhou called for special skills of timing for the officers of all ships. To let British and Lascar seamen ashore when the Dutch or French were enjoying terra firma — even when the countries were not at war — was playing with fire.

The Chinese ultimately designated separate islands in the estuary for shore leave, with Dane's Island for the English seamen (originally set aside for Danes) and French Island for the French. Even then segregation was necessary, for crews were rarely of one nationality and the sampan owners ran a continuous water taxi service between the islands each of which had their own grog shops, shopping bazaars and floating brothels. When countries were at war, the hazards of shore leave were multiplied considerably.

While Chinese traders and shopkeepers were ready to sell anything and offer any service, one of the most lucrative was to brew moonshine liquor and the Dutch and British matelots would vie to see who could achieve oblivion first; the Dutch had the better record and in 1685 they established their reputation. In that year the officers invited the Manchu grandees aboard their vessel to exchange toasts at New Year. Things got out of hand, however, when the ratings mixed sugar, eggs and rice wine and freely quaffing this potent egg nog "they began leaping and dancing until they collapsed like drunken swine" — a rare spectacle for the mandarins who no doubt considered it spontaneous entertainment in their honour, though not comparable with their own Cantonese acrobats.

So good was the egg nog recipe that it was circulated to other

Figure 3.3 An examining magistrate questions a woman charged with prostitution, punishable by several strokes of the long bamboo. A sketch by William Alexander.

Figure 3.4 Punishment by the imposition of the cangue was common in imperial China where minor misdemeanours could earn the accused person confinement for a period of days or weeks in such a device. The nineteenth century painting is by William Alexander.

ships in port, including the East India Company ships, and the crew lashed casks of the concoction to the ship's side to help them through the doldrums on their homeward voyage. Many more sailors fell victim to the noxious brews of the Chinese shop-keepers and several of the drunken brawls resulted in the death and injury of Chinese by-standers.

As one Select Committee report observed: "the horrid liquor to which they have such easy access and which the Chinese mix with ingredients of irritating and stupefying qualities causes a state of inebriety more maddening and ferocious than that oc-casioned by any other liquor or spirits." That particular brew came from an illegal still erected by Chinese shopkeepers on Dane's Island. The report concluded: "It is disgusting to par-ticularise the scenes we witnessed (and) it is only a matter of surprise to us that they do not occur more frequently and fatally."[7]

One of the most daunting aspects of life in China in those days was the arbitrary and draconian Chinese legal system where the accused was invariably presumed guilty, and confirmed in most cases by confessions obtained through torture. This broad generalization must be qualified by the existence of various checks and balances within the system which allowed cases to be passed from one authority to another for reconsideration. In some cases they were transmitted to the throne before a final decision and the confirmation of a sentence. In theory, and occasionally in practice, accused people could be exonerated and in some cases, judges could be overruled and punished for excessive sentencing.

The Chinese system recognized the Confucian stress on the need for just treatment and the exercise of mercy, but in practice, and at the lowest level of society, it was rare to escape punish-ment; the Chinese prosecutor might be bought off in a case in-volving injury but where death occurred the law demanded a life

7. H. B. Morse, *The East India Company Trading to China*, vol. 2.

Figure 3.5 Jesuit priests in Beijing wrote to the Royal Society in London, giving explanations of the origin of Chinese characters.

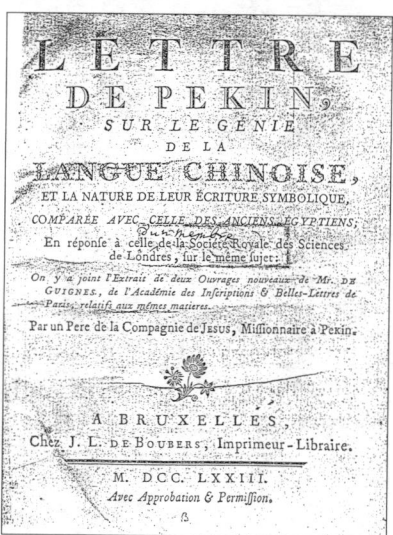

(a) This letter was written by Father Joseph de Guignes.

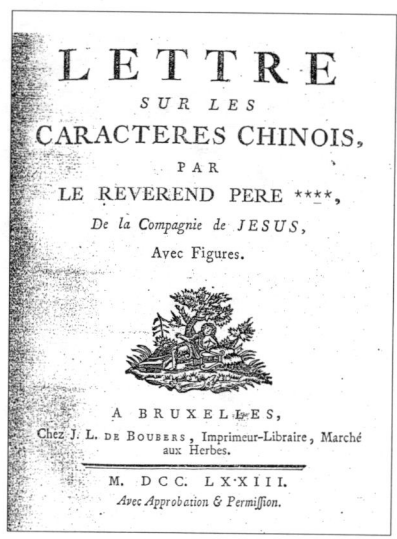

(b) This letter with two sample pages was written by Pierre Cibot.

(c) Sample pages of Pierre Cibot's letter on the origin of Chinese characters.

for a life. The substitution of proxy victims was not uncommon. On many occasions during the 300 years of Sino-Western contacts prior to the Opium War, foreign seamen were accused of murder following an accident or a fracas in which Chinese people were killed. In each case the life of the accused was demanded at the risk of a total disruption of trade.

Incidents like these served to create a minefield of uncertainty and fear between the Europeans and Chinese who demanded a high and sometimes impossible price for the survival of the trade. Cultural differences contributed considerably to the misunderstandings, and differing concepts of justice exacerbated attempts to bridge the gulf. The inability to overcome the language barrier served only to perpetuate frustration. How could Chinese and foreigners interact without the ability to understand or be understood in a common language?

So bewildered were the British with the Chinese language, written and spoken, that in 1764 the Secretary of the Royal Society, Dr Charles Morton, found himself in the middle of an academic argument in England as to whether Chinese and Egyptian forms of writing were the same. The debate spread to Europe. Many of the European literati strongly disagreed.

To resolve the matter Dr Morton wrote to the East India Company to ask for "one or two good dictionaries of the Chinese tongue and characters with a literal explanation annexed thereto, and also some other capital books of the Chinese, both with and without translations. The books most desired are history, civil and natural, laws, geography and the fundamentals of their religion."[8]

After soliciting the help of Portuguese Jesuit missionaries in Beijing, the EIC committee in Guangzhou sent off fifty volumes including books of Chinese verse, an explanation of characters, a 26-volume dictionary and a shorter one of fourteen volumes.

---

8. Royal Society records, 1764.

The whereabouts of the books today is a mystery. The Royal Society's Deputy Librarian, Mr Alan Clark, was unable to find any evidence that any volumes were received from the East India Company. In those days material sent to the secretary was "sometimes treated as their personal property." On the other hand they may have been lost en route to England. However, the Royal Society Secretary, in the course of giving his opinions in a learned paper, did have access to a Chinese dictionary.

Moreover, there is no doubt that some correspondence did take place between the Royal Society and the Jesuits. In the journal of the Royal Society on 23 June 1768, Dr Morton stated that a letter had been received that was twenty-eight pages long and was bound in a cloth folio, with forty-four pages of notes annexed and twenty-seven pages of drawings.

The Jesuits, to their credit, went to considerable trouble to show that Chinese writing, while it may not have been as ancient,[9] had a long, proud history of its own, needing no help from the pharaohs of antiquity. Morton agrees that Chinese is one of "the most ancient of languages" but concludes that while both began from simple pictograms and symbols, "any connection between the two modes of writing, is hardly discernible at this day."[10]

It was clearly time for the British to start learning the language themselves as an essential step towards understanding the civilization of China. Not that that contributed to harmony and enlightenment, as the following chapters show.

---

9. Even that is hotly debated by experts who in some cases give a prehistoric Chinese tribe in Shaanxi a 2,000-year lead on the Middle Eastern Sumerians.
10. Royal Society records, 1764.

CHAPTER 4

Home Away from Home

Chinese people have been on the move southwards from earliest times, first to what is now central and southern China, later to parts of Southeast Asia. The flow has been continuous though it has quickened and multiplied to the point where it is today the largest movement of people anywhere on earth.

As any sailor in the South China Sea will confirm, not a day passes without encountering at least one small junk or a fleet of them under sail, some with nets spread like butterfly wings, others just sailing aimlessly, in the best of weather and the worst, sometimes with a woman squatting on the deck, a baby strapped to her back, fanning a stove or doing the washing, the man tending a net, reeling in a line, adjusting a sail or often lying in the stern, one foot on the tiller, smoking in contemplation, oblivious of the sea, the winds, the time of day, or the precarious state of his boat in a wind-swept, foam-flecked ocean. Is it Sunday, Wednesday or Friday? Where is he going? Are there fish in his nets? What is the weather going to be like tomorrow? Does he know? Does he care?

It is a timeless scene and from the deck of a passing steamer a tossing junk in full sail in the China Sea is as unremarkable as the flight of a twitchy-winged seagull, the gliding swoop of an unblinking albatross or the frantic leap of a school of flying fish. Today, sail has all but given way to diesel and the fishing boats are bigger and sturdier. They still pitch and toss precariously, but increasingly they are using modern aids of sonar to spot schools of fish, satellite navigation to fix their location, ship-to-shore radio to keep contact with home base, radios to receive latest weather forecasts, and even television to entertain them at sea.

This history is about the China and Yellow Seas and the many movements that occur on them, and while Western traders discovered them only in the twelfth century and began using them regularly as a trade highway in the sixteenth, the Chinese have been sailing on them since the dawn of civilization. Whether fishing, buccaneering or trading there have been junks on these seas for thousands of years.

Moving away from familiar to unfamiliar shores has likewise been a common trend. With little more than a name and a native village as identification, the search for a better, more peaceful and prosperous life has been a constant spur to move on and over the horizon. Needing neither passport nor visa, people have crossed hills, valleys, rivers and seas in their quest, and over hundreds of years have merged themselves into the landscape, taking familiar totems with them, exporting their culture and way of life.

The boat people, so familiar in recent years, landing on alien and often hostile shores and travelling on weather-beaten craft, are part of this same process. The more affluent fly out from Hong Kong or Singapore or Taiwan every day of the week. The southern Chinese are a restless, almost nomadic people and are scattered all over Southeast Asia, but mainly along the coasts of the China Sea. Under the threat of invasion or revolt or famine or flood in their own county, or simply in search of a better way of life, people moved to the Philippines, Borneo, Java, Sumatra, Singapore, Malaya, Thailand, Cochin China, Cambodia and Tonkin in ones and twos, and tens and twentys, settling, populating, building, farming, fishing, buying, selling, mining, planting, pruning, tapping, harvesting, importing, exporting, marketing, always active, always one jump ahead of the more laid-back local, always with that extra flair and insight. Multiply that by more than a thousand years and fifty generations and it is no wonder they are such a force in the economies of the regions.

The colonial era in Asia gave that a major boost and emigrants multiplied rapidly. With them went that spirit of enterprise and an urge to make a fortune they could never have made at home. As a result, the dynamism of today's overseas Chinese, the *huaqiao*, is legendary. As Professor C. P. Fitzgerald says: "The motive of the southward expansion has not been cultural colonisation or commercial domination. It just happened because the Chinese people are what they are, and because they refused to assume the hammock-under-the-coconut-tree lifestyle of the people they adopted as neighbours."

This was bound to have repercussions. If the Chinese did not themselves overwhelm the local economy, "the threat of it forced local governments to goad their own people into action." The results were often painful and much Chinese blood was spilt, as we continue to see in our own times, notably in Indonesia, Malaysia and Vietnam.

It was the overthrow of the Ming dynasty in China by the Manchu conquerors and the settlement of Taiwan by the Dutch which gave Taiwan a significant influx of mainlanders from Fujian Province — only 150 kilometres across the strait but in a small junk, about a two-day trip, depending on wind and weather. The Dutch had built small trading posts on the island to bolster their position in Japan where they were making and manning cannon and mortars during the Tokugawa Shogun's battle for internal ascendancy.

That all came to an end in 1641 when the Dutch found themselves inadequately garrisoned and were thrown out by the Ming patriot, Koxinga (the anglicised name taken from Guoxingye, in the Fujian dialect) who had himself been ejected from the mainland by the Manchu invaders. His move to Taiwan was much like that of the defeated Guomindang under Chiang Kai-shek in 1949 who fled to the island when the communists overran the mainland.

The Manchus took swift measures to isolate him. They banned all sea travel and closed the coastal areas of the eastern seaboard following harrasing raids by Koxinga in 1650. At the same time mainland trading ports were closed to Western merchants and the Manchus thereafter restricted visits to one port, Guangzhou, and this was strictly policed by the local coastguard. For more than forty years Koxinga and his son held out until the Dutch helped the Manchus to recover the island, leading to the re-opening of four ports on the mainland coast. Slowly the tide of migration began to rise again.

The Philippines had been another favoured destination for Chinese boat people from before Song times, drawn by its lush, fertile, tropical climate, and they both traded across the South China Sea and settled there. But it was the coming of the Spanish colonists in the late sixteenth century that led to an influx of skilled Chinese tradesmen needed to build the barracks, forts, churches and habitations of the new society. Unfortunately the Spanish never quite rid themselves of the fear that the Chinese wanted to take over the islands and there followed a succession of edicts and restrictions by Spain which led to protests and demonstrations. The resulting crackdown in 1603 turned into a massacre and accounted for 44,000 men, women and children. There was a repetition of this thirty-six years later. This brought a temporary halt to Chinese settlement. But without the Chinese, the Spanish were helpless and they had to lift the ban and begin again.

When Koxinga became master of Taiwan just across the Bashi Channel, and only a few miles from the Philippines, the Spanish once again trained their muskets on the Chinese, terrified of an uprising and conquest from the north. This time, thanks to mediation by the Archbishop of Manila and the subsequent death of Koxinga, the Chinese were spared. Today the Chinese community, more than 400,000 strong, has merged with the Filipinos and is a potent force in business, banking and industry. As Professor C. P. Fitzgerald has said: "Perhaps no other overseas Chinese community suffered so much from the oppression of the colonial rulers, nor occupied such a key position in the economy of the country to which they had migrated."

In British, Portuguese and Dutch colonial outposts — the East Indies, Singapore, Borneo, Malaya, Sarawak — the Chinese again followed the Western flags, though in each case their track record of trading and residence began hundreds of years earlier. Chinese Buddhists were among the earliest to touch base with the island of Sumatra in the years when the new religion was fanning out from India. This long exposure to Chinese residence led to greater acceptance by local people and as their economic prosperity grew the numbers of settlers ran into hundreds of thousands as word got back to China that their skills and entrepreneurial expertise were needed. Great clan and family dynasties were formed in each of these territories. So powerful did the Chinese become that the colonial powers were able to exploit local resentments by targeting Chinese settlers as the basis of discontent, and what happened in the Philippines was repeated in the East Indies on several occasions.

One of the worst was the massacre of 1740 when Chinese immigrants rose in revolt against an increasingly harsh and corrupt Dutch administration in Java; estimates of the slaughter ran to 10,000. Many of those killed were Chinese boat people who by island-hopping through Borneo, or hugging the coast of Cochin China and Malaya, had slipped into the island of Batavia. The threat to Dutch rule was so serious that it was feared that if the native Indonesians had joined the Chinese, the Dutch East India Company could have been expelled — for this came at a time of decline of Dutch power in Europe and a flagging interest in the Indies trade. In spite of this, and by cleverly playing off Chinese against Indonesians, the Dutch hung on for another 200 years.

At the end of the nineteenth century, Professor Clive Day of Yale University, estimated that the Chinese made up about 1 per cent of the population of Java and were "the natural middlemen of the East" with very few labourers or farmers, and the majority "living by their brains not by their hands."[1] At the same time they formed a link between the natives and the Europeans. He recalled that in earlier years the Dutch had used them as political agents, particularly "tax farmers," and as such they inflicted "horrible oppressions" on the people, but in the eighteenth century they were considered "indispensable in their capacity of manufacturers, traders and money-lenders." All internal trade in Java was in their hands and "they were the life and soul of commerce." Clive Day concluded that either the European merchants did business with them or not at all — such was their power in the commercial sphere. In 1897, there were as many Chinese as native depositors in local banks. As for Chinese shops, customers found better stock at cheaper prices and were served more quickly.

On the other hand the Chinese had a bad reputation among natives, cheating in trade, advancing money at usurious interest rates and exploiting them "sometimes mercilessly." Clive Day concluded that "the Chinese take much the same position in modern Java that the Jews took in mediaeval Europe; they are giving the natives some primary economic education, and they are hated for it just as the Jews were hated.... The Chinese trader is to the native consumer the missionary of the modern economic organisation. The Chinese have been disliked in Java not because they were Chinese, but because they were tax-gatherers, money lenders and traders.... Their competitors, the Indo-Arabs, of the same religion as the natives, are even more disliked. The Javanese have a saying by which they contrast the two races. 'They both bleed us, but the Moor hurts.'" Today the Chinese have merged into the local community and number more than three million.

By the middle of the eighteenth century Western empire builders had set up outposts throughout Southeast Asia and the Chinese were flocking in on every tide. While the Malayan

---

1. Clive Day, *The Policy and Administration of the Dutch in Java* (1904; reprint, London: Oxford University Press, 1966).

Peninsula and Singapore had largely escaped foreign scrutiny, there had been skirmishing between the Portuguese and Dutch over the entrepot trade in Malacca. With the arrival of the British and the search for a jump-off point for the China traders it was Malaya's turn to experience occupation.

In 1785, Colonel Light took over the lease of the island of Penang from the Sultan of Kedah and it swiftly became a magnet for Chinese immigrants though neither Penang nor Malacca, which also came under British rule, lived up to Britain's early hopes as trading outlets. Easily the most significant acquisition was Stamford Raffles's purchase of a small island on the tip of the Malayan Peninsula, following Britain's move from Bencoolen in Sumatra. There he swiftly built up the thriving city of Singapore.

One of the prime needs was people and Raffles did much to encourage the arrival of Chinese immigrants when Singapore, Malacca and Penang needed labour to work the tin deposits, the rubber, coffee and pepper plantations and to build the commercial sinews of the new settlements. It led to widespread abuses in the traffic of coolies from China who were carried down in huge junks estimated to weigh 600 to 700 tons. As many as fifty anchored in Singapore harbour each year and would remain in port between March and April to catch the prevailing monsoon back to China. The junks were essentially slavers. How they collected their human cargo of up to 600 men from various parts of the China coast may be guessed; a bit of bribery, chain gangs and plausible salesmanship filled the holds for each voyage, for which the migrant paid nothing but was made to pledge several years of wages in return for bare subsistence.

Conditions on the junks were appalling. They could decently accommodate 300; however, most were grossly overloaded and the mortality rate high, in one case 250 out of 600 died and were tossed overboard at sea. Most of the wretched survivors were held aboard ship in harbour until the owner bargained a price for their services with local pepper and gambier (a root used in tanning) growers. The men were then spirited away to the jungle interior to be put to work clearing and planting; few were ever heard of again, falling victim to malaria, malnutrition or roaming tigers.

In the middle of the last century, of Singapore's 90,000 people, two-thirds were Chinese, the balance Malays and Indians, whereas Penang with 130,000 was predominantly Malay, with about a third Chinese, while Malacaa was 80 per cent Malay and only 20 per cent Chinese. Males were by far the major element, most Chinese migrants either supporting wives in China or intending to return to marry one or more. Two-thirds of the successful ones returned to China. Meanwhile the traffic in women — particularly young teenagers — was an evil that persisted for years. No less a problem were the secret societies which sprang up and exacted strict obedience on all their clansmen in return for protection and support in times of need. The more benevolent *hui* or communal group, dominated by a "Captain China," built links between home and their adopted society, and were more positive in impact.

In Singapore, the Chinese moved into everything where trade was concerned and comprised 90 per cent of the urban commercial community, prominent in such fields as warehousemen, tailors, carpenters, blacksmiths, grocers, butchers, tinsmiths, blacksmiths, opium vendors and barbers. In one occupation the Chinese held the monopoly — as cashiers at local banks — and a visitor recalled that "the everlasting chink of dollars to be heard on passing these establishments is almost deafening ... (for they) count, and at the same time test the genuineness of dollars with remarkable exactitude and rapidity, by pouring them from one hand to the other ... (and) they are never known to be incorrect."[2]

As the Chinese in Singapore were drawn from various parts of the China coast, the island's population became a melting-pot

---

2. John Cameron, *Our Tropical Possessions in Malayan India* (1865; reprint, Hong Kong: Oxford-in-Asia, 1965).

for a variety of clans and dialects who ruffled each other's feathers interminably, with serious riots breaking out when a chopper or a knife failed to gain redress. In one of the two worst incidents in the 1850s, an argument broke out between two groups — the Hokiens and the Teochews — over something as trivial as the ownership of some bananas, ultimately involving hundreds of fighters and resulting in the complete closure of the business district lasting more than a fortnight. On another occasion, the Chinese community as a whole rebelled against a new law imposing maximum fines of 500 rupees, and effectively closed down the city until an official explanation was forthcoming. It was a chilling demonstration to the British of the key part played by Chinese in the life of the commercial community.

Yet the Chinese have succeeded economically in Southeast Asia in spite of the fact that they have never until recent times sought a part in the political process. Their origins are as diverse as their choice of destinations. They came from many parts of Fujian as well as northern and southern Guangdong and their dialects emphasize that diversity. Today all remain distinctively and proudly Chinese — descendants of people who were either abducted, bribed or took their chances on coastal vessels which sailed from port to port down the coasts of Cochin China, Thailand and Malaya.

There are exceptions. Today's Vietnamese Chinese are mainly the descendants of emigrants who moved south on foot under the impact of Chinese rebellions and invasions through the centuries, as well as to make money by helping colonial powers exploit forests and mines. In Thailand, under pressure from a strong independent monarchy, the Chinese immigrants were forced to assimilate and take on Thai names and the culture of the country if they were to be accepted.

Burma and Cambodia took in fewer Chinese; the reason is not hard to find. In moving, the Chinese followed the dollar and went where report said the pickings were richest. Moreover Chinese men were apt to marry within their own race; the need to return home to take a wife and have children — even if he later abandoned them in his native village — lies at the heart of every emigrant. Both countries were remote, and while rich in teak wood and jade, the road to Mandalay was not strewn with the same promise as Southeast Asia. As for Cambodia and Laos the prospects there were as dark and gloomy as their impenetrable forests and inhospitable people.

The economic growth that Chinese immigration would bring to Southeast Asia was immense, but Britain's concern in the eighteenth century was with China. If Penang and Malacca were unsuitable as bases for the China trade because they were on the wrong side of the Malay Peninsula, Singapore was a bit too far south to be of much help in days when a sailing ship could take six to eight weeks to beat north up the China Sea to Guangzhou. However, each British possession in Malaya was also a guarantee of protection for British shipping en route to China, and also served to counter Dutch influence on the other side of the Strait of Malacca. It was like a giant chessboard with Britain building a defensive strategy to secure what it saw as the ultimate prize. But it also served to stress the need for a port somewhere in the China Sea itself — Pulo Condore at first and finally Hong Kong — where the opening to China would be made.

Meanwhile the East India Company continued its relatively modest trade with China, not yet convinced it had found a pot of gold but well worth cultivating in the hope that the Portuguese, Spanish, French, Dutch and Danes (with a trading post in Serampore, India) would weary of their colonial attachments and leave the scene to the British. No such luck. Each knew there was a fortune to be made in the East. The British had not invested a substantial eight million pounds in 200 sailing ventures (between 1635 and 1753) for nothing. Yet considering the content of its trade, mainly tea and silk, neither could be classed as essential commodities. Some might question why increasing numbers of British ships could sail half way around the world, with all the dangers this involved, to pick up ever increasing quantities of the dried and smoked leaf of a camellia bush. But what was then a delicate refreshment for the top 5 to 10 per cent of the population would in time become a national obsession. As for the silk imports, they appealed to a tiny minority of society ladies and the rhubarb to fewer still — more a medicine for the constipated than an addition to the diet. Yet the trade made money and though its practitioners did not know it, would soon make very big money.

By the middle of the eighteenth century, Britain was one of the strongest powers in Europe, spreading its domains to North America, India and South Africa; it was also on the verge of several scientific discoveries that would sweep it into a far-reaching industrial revolution, based intially on steam and later on electricity. A rising middle class and a prosperous mercantile community wielded increasing power, once the sole right of kings.

Like the Chinese who were migrating in increasing numbers to greener fields on other shores, Europeans, tired of religious bigotry, squalor, poverty and scarce opportunities at home, saw better prospects over the horizon. A growing purchasing power and clear signs of demand and supply were all the incentives the merchant-seafarers needed to become involved in the luxury-led surge that was galvanizing the economies of Europe.

It was the age when London alone boasted more than 500 coffee shops and when the new drugs of coffee, tea, tobacco, brandy, gin, and whisky were nibbling at the budgets of a rising middle class of artisans, traders, shopkeepers and professionals, while for their wives, silks, soap cakes, perfumes and whale bone corsets were enhancing feminine charms; at the same time, the wickedly wealthy were indulging in gambling sprees, spending thousands of pounds a night at cards and other amusements in gaming houses.

Trade itself was a big enough gamble though by now it was paying good dividends in China. But it was to the gaming salons of the capital that the wealthy flocked, wagering money in sums that even in this reckless age seem prodigal. The Liberal politician, Charles James Fox once gambled at the rate of ten pounds a minute for twenty-four hours — if true, a sum of 14,400 pounds — but even that paled into insignificance by comparison with the 32,000-pound splash in one night by a wealthy MP bored with proceedings in the House of Commons.

Drinking was also a national pastime enjoyed by the wealthy (who drank "abominably," according to one observer) and the impoverished (for whom gin was a cheap escape from reality). Part of this wealth came from the proceeds of the China trade but there were lucrative markets in other parts of the world, and the accompanying industrial revolution put Britain into the driving seat of Europe, ahead of its rivals in almost every department of science, astronomy and technology. With it came prohibitions against the export of machinery, skilled workers and manufacturing techniques, in a fit of national greed and selfishness to ensure these talents stayed at home. Militarily, Britain was master of India, thanks to the victory of Clive at Plassey in 1751, and though shortly to lose its colonies in North America it held its place in Canada after evicting its old rival, France. With its clear leadership in industry and world trade Britain was anxious to seal its ascendancy in China; thus it turned its thoughts not to a new military base — perish the thought! — but an equally ominous euphemism, "an insular possession," where it would rule under its own jurisdiction without having to worry about Chinese bureaucratic extortion or judicial barbarism.

Unfortunately, on the opposite side of the world, the Manchu (or Qing) rulers, having won the mandate of heaven and having consolidated their rule were not inclined to tamper with ancient customs which treated all outsiders as barbarians who visited China only as tribute-bearing, homage-paying, kow-towing guests. The ancient rules on how to show reverence to the Emperor were confirmed, and diplomacy's only function was to proffer gifts that would be most pleasing to the Son of Heaven. The early Qing emperors were long-lived and powerful and under them China appeared in no danger of losing its ascendancy in

Asia. Nor was its Confucianist society threatened by the new dynamism of the West.

The Portuguese and Italian Jesuit missionaries made little headway in gaining converts to the faith and while as astronomers they had proved themselves to be more accurate than Chinese practitioners, and while their cannon had helped in the rout of the Ming armies, yet China had no conception of the changes occurring in other parts of the world. Nor did they realize how quickly their country was slipping behind in the emerging technological and scientific age, and how crucially these would dictate the pace of change in the nineteenth and twentieth centuries.

What the imperial eye did not see, the body politic of China did not grieve. The eunuchs and scholars surrounding the throne were as blind and as unconcerned about the acrimonious foreigners on their southern extremities as the Imperial Dragon himself. China had no foreign diplomats, no Foreign Office, and now not even a navy, and its network of antiquated coastal forts and its coastguard were considered sufficient to keep any seaborn aggressor at bay.

The court in Beijing, moreover, was not greatly troubled about happenings in Guangzhou. An issue of major concern to the Select Committee of the East India Company was that several traders had money owing to them by Chinese merchants amounting to almost one million pounds. They were pressing for repayment or liquidation of debts dating back eleven years, with interest rates of 18 or 20 per cent inflating the figures enormously.

The Select Committee blamed the Chinese for their extravagant way of life and also for extortion by officials. Several Chinese merchants were said to be "hopelessly bankrupt" and could only agree to try to repay over a period of ten years to "avoid the utter ruin of all the merchants in Guangzhou." So concerned were British suppliers in India that two warships were sent to Guangzhou to present a petition to the Viceroy and Hoppo.

The problem arose because of the increasing sophistication of the trade. Where in the early days China sold goods on a simple cash basis, the growth in volume now required making contracts for delivery 300 days hence, with part payment in advance. Added to that, British traders were compounding the problem by becoming unofficial bankers and extending loans at high interest; and to make matters worse when Spain declared war on England in 1779 British traders began to run short of the Spanish trade dollars, which the Chinese merchants tried to exploit to claw back some of their indebtedness.

In the meantime the mandarins in Guangzhou reacted to news of the huge debts with yet another decree — or rather the reinforcement of an old one — prohibiting the offering or acceptance of loans at interest under threat of transportation to a distant province and the forfeiture of the loan; also merchants were reminded that accumulated interest must not exceed the original principal of the loan (at that time it was running at three times the principal). Strangely the edict, which also banned the employment of Chinese servants by the European traders, was unknown to the EIC's Select Committee, which however now employed a British translator more skilled in the Chinese language. What they discovered horrified them and spurred them to action at the highest official level.

When the Emperor was eventually confronted with the debt problem he reacted by banishing two bankrupt Chinese merchants, coupled with the enforced sale of their assets. However, the first call on the proceeds went to settle the Emperor's dues with the residue to defray their commercial debts; the balance was to be paid in ten annual instalments without further interest. What was even worse for the British and foreign merchants was that the Hoppo was to be given increased powers to fix prices of goods sold to them. This amounted to a Government takeover of the independent Chinese trading system.

At the same time a further demonstration of Chinese impatience came in the public strangling of a French sailor from an

English ship who killed a Portuguese sailor in a period of heightened tension and "boisterous patriotism" when seamen mixed ashore. The Chinese carried out the execution without trial which the EIC considered to be "a dangerous precedent." The council argued that "foreigners are not allowed the benefit of the Chinese laws though in this instance one of them suffers by the rigor of them and they are governed by such rules as the Mandareans declare to be their will."

In answer to protests from the EIC, the Governor of Guangzhou replied that if the foreigners could not control drunken, riotous and quarrelsome sailors from their ships, as he was responsible for good order in the city he would take the action that should be enforced by the foreigners. Nor did he sweeten matters by issuing a statement later that "You English are a lying and troublesome people ... (and) if any of you English in future shall do wrong, whether supercargoes or individuals, he shall be punished to the full measure of his crime."[3]

Part of the problem was that while the EIC was responsible for its own ships visiting China (eleven a year) increasing numbers of so-called "country ships" (owned by private traders in India) were appearing and refusing to answer to EIC authority. One such vessel, while lying in the river estuary, had followed a Spanish ship sailing from Macau to Manila, and seized it. The English captain on return to Macau with his prize was arrested and thrown into prison and in the meantime the vessel he had taken was blown ashore and wrecked. The captain was held in prison for two months and ordered to pay $70,000 for the wrecked ship. The Chinese assembled 2,000 troops to ensure he paid up.

There was also a forcible attempt by an EIC surgeon to recover a $11,000 debt from a bankrupt Chinese merchant. Incidents like this, as well as the importation of opium by country

---

3. H. B. Morse, *The East India Company Trading to China*, vol. 2.

ships, embarrassed the EIC and played into the hands of the Viceroy and Hoppo who wanted tighter controls on the dominant British element in the foreign traders in China. There were other irritating rulings by the Hoppo which only served to exacerbate feelings between the British and the Chinese; by contrast, at the height of the commotion, the King of Siam sent his annual tribute through a team of docile envoys carrying a large consignment of timber, 3,000 piculs (the Chinese hundredweight, equivalent to about 50 kilograms) of pepper, 300 piculs of tin, 100 elephant tusks, three elephants, several peacocks and peahens, as well as "sundry presents" to minor officials. Why couldn't the British behave like the Siamese, asked the mandarins, and why were the truculent barbarians so incapable of complying with this age-old custom which others found so easy to follow?

The Hoppo determined there was to be no softening of the rules. When the foreign traders made a joint protest on the "shameful exactions" on movements of cargo between Guang-zhou and Macau, the Hoppo called in all the Chinese com-pradores of the foreign merchants and gave each twenty strokes of the bamboo because it was "their roguery" that was the cause of the complaint "not his just demands." To cap it all came the affair of the British country ship *Lady Hughes* which on entering Chinese waters, fired a salute from one of her guns. A Chinese barge nearby took the full brunt of the shot, resulting in the death of two people aboard.

Immediately came demands from the provincial judge for the gunner to be surrendered and when the captain refused on the (truthful) grounds that the man had absconded, the Chinese lured the charterer into their power and imprisoned him until the wanted man (now on the high seas in another ship) was produced. At the same time, something akin to martial law was declared ashore to demonstrate China's determination to exact obedience.

Protracted negotiations followed, the Chinese giving the British to understand that the wanted man was needed only to answer routine inquiries. Assurances were sought by the British and other foreign representatives for his safety and when at last the Chinese appeared genuinely to launch only a formal inquiry into the accidental death of the two bargemen, the captain of *Lady Hughes* produced an old seaman from his crew. He was offered as a substitute in view of the Chinese insistence on having someone to answer questions.

The man was immediately thrown into jail and two months later the Chinese blandly announced that even though two Chinese had been killed the demand for retribution would be satisfied by only one execution — and the poor old proxy was tied to an execution post and strangled in another part of town. Further provocations followed when British seamen invaded French Island and beat up a group of French seamen as their contribution to the Anglo-French hostilities taking place elsewhere in the world. As a sign of their displeasure at the inability of the British to control their men the Chinese suspended trade for sixteen days at the peak of the season.

It was thus apparent that while Chinese officials strongly and reasonably complained about the indiscipline of British crews and the repeated failure of the EIC to deal with them — except when a mutiny occurred on one of its own ships — they proved uncompromising in the way they sought to regulate trade and impose their laws and decrees. Moreover the extortionate demands their officials made over and above official charges and duties were vexatious and provocative. Not that corruption was unknown to the British, but when it fell on a trade that involved spending months at sea, separated from families, out of touch with investors and agents, and unaware of market fluctuations at home, as well as having to contend with enemy fighting ships, pirates, harsh discipline and a terrible diet, every additional irritation and hurdle assumed almost explosive proportions.

In a bid to resolve matters it was decided to address complaints to the Emperor himself, and in 1787 Britain nominated a distinguished soldier to take the Chinese bull by the horns. He was Lt Col Charles Cathcart, MP, who was Quartermaster-General of the Army of Bengal. No mere emissary of the EIC, he was to be a royal ambassador of the King of Great Britain and he was to sail to China in HMS *Vestal* and buy suitable presents up to a value of 4,000 pounds for members of the court, and to carry a gold box containing a letter from the King.

There was controversy from the outset. The EIC saw itself overshadowed and the possibility of its monopoly being jeopardized while the creditors were at sixes and sevens as to how Cathcart should represent their concerns. But the even bigger sticking point was the suggestion in his instructions that he should land at the port of Tianjin, south-east of Beijing, without warning, this to avoid any chance of premature refusal. With one foot in the door and a letter from King George III in a gold box to hand direct to the Emperor, who could refuse? After all he was King of England, Scotland, Ireland and Wales.

As for his demands, Cathcart was to negotiate the cession to the British Crown of a depot where British merchants might be able to meet with their Chinese counterparts and do trade deals. For while "our views are commercial, having not even a wish for territory, we desire … only the protection of the Chinese Government for our merchants … and to secure us against the encroachment of other powers."[4] As for the location of this depot, one suggestion was Macau. Whether Britain had ever floated this notion to Lisbon is not known. But if the Chinese were not inclined to remove the Portuguese, the British would prefer a site near Xiamen (Amoy) which was in fact closer to the tea and silk growing districts.

The British proposal would allow Chinese people living on the site to remain under Chinese jurisdiction, but the British traders and their staff would be subject to British law. And if the

---

4. H. B. Morse, *The East India Company Trading to China*, vol. 2.

Chinese were unhappy about ceding territory, Cathcart was
expected to get the best possible terms for regulating the trade.
The mission sailed from England on 21 December 1787, but HMS
Vestal was back within a year after the sudden death at sea of
Cathcart.

Perhaps it was just as well, for he was expected, once having
set foot on Chinese soil, to encounter "some intelligent Portuguese, Spanish or Italian missionary who may be free from any
national attachment or prejudice" to be employed as a translator/
advisor, if there was no alternative. It is not hard to imagine the
mirth at court in Beijing when the Emperor Qianlong was confronted with this motley band of uniformed officials from an
island no greater in area than Guangdong Province, half a world
away, gold box in hand, asking for a small stretch of Chinese real
estate to carry on trade. The effrontery and presumption was
almost breathtaking.

By a fortunate coincidence, shortly after Cathcart's death and
the aborting of the mission, the British were presented with an
unprecedented opportunity to go to Beijing at the invitation of the
Chinese. The Chief of the Select Committee of the EIC in
Guangzhou was summoned by the Hoppo to call on him to hear
his proposal. As the Emperor was soon to turn eighty it was
proposed that two representatives from each trading nation
should visit Beijing to pay their respects.

So dumbfounded were the British by the idea that they saw it
as a trap — once in never to return — and in any case it was sure
to lead to demands to perform the kowtow to the old emperor.
The idea was that of the Viceroy of the two Guangs who was
seeking ways and means of gaining the court's favour and the
Hoppo was now trying to solicit reaction. The interview between
the Hoppo and the EIC Chief ended in a grudging "in principle"
agreement, but the British remained wary.

The EIC court in London were furious when they heard of the
hesitant attitude of its committee in Guangzhou and told them so
in no uncertain manner. Nothing more was heard of the idea,

however, and it was thought that the Viceroy had had an attack of cold feet and that the idea had been dropped. The British, however, were determined to proceed with a new mission and this time selected an eminent Irishman, George Macartney, who had proved an able colonial administrator and diplomat. At the age of twenty-seven he had been sent to the court of St Petersburg as ambassador, having previously held office in Dublin as Chief Secretary, and in Grenada and Madras as Governor.

Macartney was either wiser or better advised than Cathcart and certainly enjoyed better health. Rejecting the idea of a surprise visit he stressed that due notice should be given, and he wanted it made known in advance that this was not a mission to redress past grievances but to congratulate the Emperor on his eightieth birthday. Incidentally he proposed discussing arrangements for conducting trade in future "to the mutual advantage of the two countries." Macartney also felt it would help if he sailed in a naval ship and had a military retinue for parade purposes. Also he wanted men of scientific and artistic attainments to accompany the embassy to stress the high degree of civilization in England. He nominated his former deputy in Madras, Sir George Staunton, as his deputy.

Macartney was to be paid a salary of 10,000 pounds a year plus an allowance of 5,000 pounds and he was to take gifts valued at 13,000 pounds, the total cost of his 95-man mission in the 64-gun HMS *Lion* to be defrayed by the East India Company. His primary objectives were sixfold: to lift the restraints and extortions on trade in Guangzhou; to bring down the cost of Chinese exports by opening up trade in places nearer the growing areas of tea and silk; to lighten the burden of Chinese duties, particularly those recently increased to liquidate the debts of Chinese merchants; to give British traders equality with the Portuguese by providing an island or depot where merchants, ships' crews and merchandise could be given temporary residence; to have the laws changed whereby innocent people could be substituted for those accused of serious crimes, and for judicial responsibility to be transferred to the EIC; and finally to bolster British exports to China in order to redress the growing imbalance in trade stemming from the rapidly rising cost of imports of tea and silk.

Again it was to be stressed by Macartney that Britain's desire for a small tract of ground or an island was purely commercial and in no sense to be seen as territorial. And of course if there was any chance of a treaty of friendship and alliance, followed by the appointment of a "perpetual minister" from Great Britain, that was to be pursued. But there was still no mention of any

Figure 4.1   The Emperor Daoguang of the Qing Dynasty, as the French artist, Auguste Borget, saw him in his mind's eye. The two never met.

reciprocity for China, such as a Chinese trade depot in the River Thames, nor was it foreseen that Beijing would ask for any — and in the event it did not.

Macartney sailed from Portsmouth on 26 September 1792, and reached the approaches to Guangzhou on 20 June 1793. He avoided all contact and communication with Chinese officials and sent his despatches by his own transport to Tianjin to be forwarded to the Emperor, thus avoiding any risk of interception and frustration by local mandarins anxious to stop it dead in its tracks.

Surprisingly the mission met no hurdles of any kind. Macartney was treated honourably in all ceremonials and it moved with remarkable smoothness from the time the mission arrived in Dagu (Taku), off Tianjin, on 5 August, to the time of his first audience with the Emperor in Rehe on 14 September, to the presentation of letters on 3 October, to his departure and arrival in Guangzhou on 19 December.

Commentators have described the mission as "from first to last, little more than prisoners in silken bonds." Qianlong was the generous, affable host throughout, stressing the gracious and courtly manners of a highly civilized and ancient country dealing with a distant and irrelevant embassy which had come to pay tribute. He had seen it all before; what was so special about the King of England, Scotland, Wales and Ireland that the pattern of reception should be changed?

But what should be done about the royal letter and requests? Qianlong waved them aside. Let the officials reply in the usual manner, putting the impertinent newcomer in his place. Why should the Chinese change? Did they desire trade with the foreigners? Did they need the goods they brought, including the woollen underwear so beloved of the red-haired barbarians? Were not the foreigners the ones who sought tea, silk, rhubarb and other Chinese trivia, so much so that they sent ships half way round the world, fighting their enemies en route and facing all kinds of perils, to reach China first? What good would an ambassador achieve? If there were wrongs to redress why could not officials on the spot in Guangzhou deal with them, with far greater chance of success than the mandarins in Beijing?

Qianlong graciously praised the choice of Macartney as ambassador; he had been received honourably but it was obvious that the King "dwelling afar cannot be well acquainted with Chinese manners and institutions." The imperial reply then went on to demolish Macartney's proposals one by one: no, to the opening of Ningbo, Zhoushan (Chusan), Tianjin and Beijing to trade; no, to the ceding of an island at Zhoushan or a depot or islet anywhere else; no, to a change in the trading arrangements at Guangzhou; no, to a change in the duties charged or measurage applied to British shipping; no, to the propagation of the Christian religion (not one of Macartney's demands). In short, the Emperor told the King of England where to get off and to "act conformably to my intentions" if he wanted to preserve peace and amity on each side.

The basis of Qianlong's reply was this: "How can our dynasty alter its whole procedure and system of etiquette, established for more than a century, in order to meet your individual views?" He added: "I have but one aim in view, namely to maintain a perfect governance and to fulfil the duties of the state; strange and costly objects do not interest me, and I have no use for your country's manufactures." There was a final warning that if after receiving the decree Britain allowed its merchants to proceed to Tianjin and Zhejiang to trade, they would not be allowed to land or live there but would instantly be expelled. "Do not say that you were not warned in due time! Tremblingly obey and show no negligence. A special mandate!"[5]

Thus Macartney was sent packing, with gifts for the King and for the crew of *Lion*. There were tasty morsels to eat, happy

---

5. H. B. Morse, *The East India Company Trading to China*, vol. 2.

memories of a magnificent cavalcade through one of the world's oldest and proudest civilizations — much of which was charmingly captured by the official artist, William Alexander, in a series of paintings. But it amounted to a bitter rebuff to the British requests which could only hasten a showdown. By coincidence a Dutch embassy under the distinguished administrator, Isaac Titsingh, arrived in Guangzhou in 1795 and travelled on to Beijing, gaining great favour by performing the kowtow but returning as empty-handed as Macartney. No more successful were three Portuguese missions to Beijing in the seventeenth and eighteenth centuries in a bid to remove the irksome presence of the Chinese mandarin and customs house from Macau. Qianlong was the last great imperial ruler of China; thereafter would come the decline of the Qing dynasty, gathering pace as a war, begun more by accident, stupidity, greed and miscalculation, escalated to bring about a succession of rebellions, civil wars and finally the rarest of happenings in China — a revolution. But first, it's time for a cup of tea, today the world's most popular beverage.

CHAPTER 5

A Tale of Two Plants

Britain's "discovery" of tea fuelled the China trade for more than 200 years. Hundreds of thousands of tons of what was known as *cha*, *thea* or *the*, was transported in British, American and European ships to slake this extraordinary thirst of people at all social levels.

The Chinese had been drinking the beverage for thousands of years unaware that anyone else could form the same attachment to this quintessentially Chinese refreshment. That it had marvellously restorative qualities, was relaxing and the outstanding accompaniment to any meal the Chinese of course fully understood; but with its self-sufficient economy and having never indulged in the export trade, China saw no need to try to foist it on others. Like all products of Chinese genius, it had a long and ancient history and an almost accidental origin.

Legend had it that thousands of years ago, a Chinese emperor visiting his far-flung domains sat down to rest under a camellia bush. He fell asleep in the hot sun and an attentive courtier placed a bowl of boiling water beside him to refresh him after his nap. A wind blew a few leaves of the bush into his bowl of steaming water and when the Emperor awoke he discovered the bowl, took his first sip and declared it delightfully refreshing which won compliments and promotion for the surprised courtier. He was clever enough to identify the bush and repeat the practice of dropping a few leaves into hot water whenever the Emperor called for refreshment.

Figure 5.1 Carrying loads of tea with bamboo harness and shoulder pole.

An institution began, and with royal patronage spread swiftly to all corners of the empire. Curiously tea did not make the same impact on visiting merchants as silk which was a major item of trade almost 2,000 years ago. Europeans were comparatively late in calling on the Middle Kingdom and slower still to appreciate and adopt its culture, cuisine and civilization. Even Marco Polo

failed to realize its potential though he is credited with introducing noodles to the Italian diet.

Columbus exploited the gold and silver of the New World
and Francis Drake its tobacco, but it took a British or Dutch or
Portuguese trader of the seventeenth century to realize that this
simple Chinese brew might have a future in the coffee houses of
Europe then opening in increasing numbers. Why tea made such
a deep impression on the British (today far more is consumed in
Britain than in other European countries) is not clear. But virtually
from its first importation — possibly by a sea captain bringing
home an unusual gift — it proved to be a success. After that it was
on the cargo manifest of every ship returning from China — not
only British but European. By the 1650s it was being advertised
and sold in London coffee houses; public sales of the leaf began
soon after. Samuel Pepys, the British diarist, tells how he first
tried a cup in September 1660 which he enjoyed. Like coffee,
which had been introduced from Arabia or Africa shortly before,
its popularity spread quickly.

East India Company ships thereafter made regular purchases,
their sailings increasing from one or two a year to four, five and
six. The imposition of high duties by the British Government did
nothing to discourage the practice even though tea was selling for
between one and three pounds sterling a pound. The fall in the
landed price in the early to middle eighteenth century was largely
because the East India Company's monopoly was undermined by
French, Dutch, Danish and Swedish imports, which were then
smuggled from the Continent to Britain.

Figures taken from the records of the East India Company
show that from 1769 to 1772 English ships imported more than
10.6 million pounds of tea from China, with Continental ships
bringing in a further 20 million pounds — equivalent to about a
pound for each person in the population. As a result the EIC
warehouses were heavily overstocked and the smuggled product
from Europe, which avoided duties, sent prices crashing.

To relieve this situation the British cabinet asked Parliament to give a drawback for the entire amount of duty held in England but made the fatal mistake of imposing a three-pence duty on each pound landed in the colonies. The cries of outrage were loudest in the port of Boston in the colony of Massachusetts. Tea was indeed the trigger which fired the first shots in the American War of Independence and Bostonians vented their anger by dumping consignments of China tea into their harbour on the night of 16 December 1773.

In the next two years, British imports fell to less than a third of the previous three-year period, while those carried by continental ships rose. Ten years later, with the threat of bankruptcy averted, the EIC regulated their imports to the point where the reimposition of duties hoisted the price back to two pounds ten shillings a pound, when the average weekly earnings of a worker were less than a tenth of that figure. It took another fifty years to bring tea within the range of the average worker and gradually the price fell to fifteen pence a pound.

In 1985, tea was selling in Britain about ten times cheaper, relative to average workmen's wages. Little wonder that outside of China and India, Britain's tea consumption today tops the world. It is also the beverage British people consume most each day — 45 per cent drink tea, 21 per cent coffee, 19 per cent beer and 12 per cent soft drinks.

How does one account for this extraordinary obsession? Clearly there were big profits to be made by the East India Company, as well as the shippers and the brokers of Mincing Lane in London who distributed the leaf. But this national interest developed long before the age of mass media advertising, when its appeal could only have been spread by word of mouth.

In the eighteenth century, however, social conventions were changing and the institution of tea drinking was gaining adherents at a very high level. Anna, the seventh Duchess of Bedford, had begun to popularize what came to be known genteelly as "afternoon tea" and there is a delightful painting of her seated at table with her guests sipping tea from bowls, served from a silver teapot.

By the middle of the nineteenth century, tea played a minor part in the plot of many English novels as it was sipped, swallowed or slurped (rarely, except by the vulgar) and crept into the poetry of Kipling, Brooke and Wordsworth. The eighteenth-century novelist Henry Fielding considered that "love and scandal are the best sweeteners of tea," while Alexander Pope in his *Rape of the Lock* proclaimed: "Here though, great Anna! Whom three realms obey, does sometimes counsel take — and sometimes tea." Samuel Johnson recalled in 1757 the ecstasy of "a hardened and shameless tea-drinker who has for 20 years diluted his meals with only the infusion of this fascinating plant; whose kettle has scarcely time to cool, who with tea amuses the evening, with tea solaces the midnight, and with tea welcomes the morning." William Congreve (1670–1729) has two characters retiring "to their tea and scandal according to their ancient custom." Thomas Babington Macaulay, a century later, tells of the old philospher "drumming with his fingers, tearing his meat like a tiger and swallowing his tea in oceans." As for William Makepeace Thackeray, he lamented: "Why do they always put mud into coffee on board steamers? Why does the tea generally taste of boiled boots?" And who has not heard the song, attributed to Charles Dickens: "Polly put the kettle on, we'll all have tea"?

Ever inventive, however, English society ladies decided that delightful as tea was, it needed an accompaniment. At about that time, another hungry aristocrat, the Earl of Sandwich, found that by putting a filling between two slices of bread he had created his namesake. He made his remarkable discovery during a 24-hour session at a casino with no time to take a proper meal. He added little to his reputation when as First Lord of the Admiralty he presided over the loss of the American colonies (keeping his ships at home to watch the French) though Captain James Cook redeemed him by naming the Hawaiian Islands after him, a name

Figure 5.2 Transporting tea from plantations in eastern China to waiting
clippers at the treaty ports.

they retained until they came under United States protection a
century later.

Thanks to the patronage of the aristocracy, swiftly followed
by the Royal Family, afternoon tea could be sure of a permanent
place in the British way of life. Indeed it soon became a national
pastime. It was also by far the biggest element in the China trade,
with silk exports valued at a quarter of tea. The one problem was
that the Chinese always demanded payment in Spanish silver
dollars, with the result that over the years the net outflow of silver
coins by British traders became substantial. In times of war with
Spain, when the supply of coins dried up, Britain even considered
minting the highly favoured Spanish dollars in India using imported silver, though this was never put into practice. But it was
because of the drain on silver that Britain became desperate to
find exports needed in China.

There were few. By far the largest (after opium) was Bombay and Bengal cotton, accounting for one-third of imports. The EIC tried on one occasion a consignment of coal which was rejected by the Chinese (who used firewood or charcoal) and the consignment had to be burnt in the British factory's fireplace in Guangzhou instead of wood. Woollen garments and underwear were unpopular though "long ells" and "camlets" (garments made of mixed fibres including wool, silk, angora and other exotic animal hair) were more popular though most of these originated from outside the UK. Britain tried linens, stationery and swordblades — none was wanted. However rabbit, otter and seal skins and furs were in demand in China, some of which came from Russia through ancient overland trade routes. Britain had to import many of the furs from Canada, a trade which the Americans developed when they began sending their own clippers to China after 1780. Also the Americans discovered a Chinese liking for ginseng, a root which grew in north American forests, as well as salt fish from New Providence. None of this really helped the British pay for their indulgence of tea, however.

So great was the demand that often other products ordered from China were packed inside the tin-lined tea chests. A striking example of this came to light in recent years with the salvage of the cargo of a Dutch East Indiamen, *Geldermalsen*, which ran aground on a notorious reef off the island of Bintan, east of Singapore in January 1752. Packed inside the hundreds of tea boxes (valued at around 400,000 guilders) was a large consignment of blue-and-white porcelain, valued at about one-tenth of the tea. Almost 250 years later, the tea was of course worthless, but the porcelain, made in the famous kilns of Jingdezhen, all of which was salvaged from the sea bed, was worth a fortune when sold at auction in Amsterdam as the so-called "Nanking Cargo."

Many were complete dinner services, and their placement inside the tea chests was typical of the ingenious way the Chinese packed a fragile cargo. None was high quality porcelain but was nevertheless attractive and would have found buyers in many parts of Europe. Curiously many of the items recovered retained indelible brown tea stains resulting from their long immersion in the tea chests, though this in no way detracted from their charm and was seen by many buyers as proof of their remarkable history.

An earlier discovery of a sunken junk carrying a cargo of Ming porcelain (packed in rice husks on this occasion and dated about 100 years earlier) demonstrated a thriving export trade by China to its overseas compatriots. When sold in Amsterdam in the mid-1980s, these raised almost 2 million pounds sterling, or about a fifth of the total of the Nanking Cargo. Of the junk cargo, it was speculated that while most was destined for Chinese shops in the East Indies, at least part was intended for onward shipping to Europe, with motifs that might appeal to non-Chinese buyers. These latter items were called "kraakware," named after the porcelain taken to Europe by Portuguese carracks in the first flush of East–West trade. However, porcelain was a minor export item compared with the big ticket items of tea and silk.

Moreover, there was no likelihood of building up a trade to rival the value of tea, and Britain faced the invidious choice of curbing its thirst for the beverage or finding some other way of redressing the trade imbalance. Hence the urgency of the representations by Lord Macartney's embassy to Beijing and the need to reduce Chinese duties.

Overall, the tea boom had been highly beneficial to the British economy, then in the throes of an industrial revolution that pitched it into leadership of the commercial world. While twenty sailings a year to China was not remarkable compared with its overall international maritime activity, yet the growing volume of trade required the design and building of ever faster and bigger ships to sail the oceans of the world.

This in turn led to demands for safer and more reliable navigation, crews with higher skills, as well as bigger wharves and warehouses, more stevedores and clerks and road transport to move goods about the country; likewise the insurance industry, as well as catering and retail outlets, received a boost. Names such as Twining and Lipton became prominent and British tastes led to the broadening of the market for new blends and varieties. From China the great black teas of the eighteenth and nineteenth centuries were Keemun, Bohea and Lapsang Soochong, while the green variety included Singlo, Twankay, Hyson and Oolong. If many of these varieties have disappeared from our supermarket shelves it is because tea is no longer the monopoly of one country as it was 200 years ago.

Tea is grown in many central and southern provinces of China and the camellia bush thrives on well-drained slopes in soil which is not too acidic and prefers fairly warm, humid conditions without the risk of prolonged frigid temperatures. Where in India and Sri Lanka the tea growing areas are fairly concentrated in Assam, Darjeeling and East Bengal, in China they are widely dispersed and each area produces a variety that offers its own special flavours.

Figure 5.3 Cultivating tea in China for the export trade, one of the biggest earners in the eighteenth and nineteenth centuries.

Today, tea is grown in twenty-five countries around the world and there are about 1,500 blends though the average supermarket range contains no more than fifteen to forty different types of tea. China tea today has a specialist following and has been largely displaced by Indian and Sri Lankan varieties. However, because of China's vast population, all of whom are avid tea drinkers, production is still greater in that country than anywhere else.

The move away from dependence on China tea began in the late nineteenth century largely due to the efforts of a British botanist in the middle of the last century. He was Robert Fortune who was commissioned by the East India Company to visit China and collect tea plants and seeds of the *Camellia sinensis* to be grown in India.

Fortune has told his story in two books following his travels in China, disguised as a Chinese. For months, speaking only a little of the language he visited the Chinese tea-growing districts at a time of deep hostility to all Europeans only a few years after the Opium War in 1839. He travelled hundreds of miles by boat, sedan-chair, and on foot to collect the choicest seeds and specimens, enduring considerable hardship in the process and surviving attacks by brigands and strikes by chair-bearers. His knowledge of the terrain, based on rudimentary maps and local intelligence, was amazingly accurate in locating the prime tea-growing districts — a practice rarely attempted by the tea-buyers in Guangzhou or Shanghai who for the most part bought what their Chinese clients offered them.

Fortune claims his disguise was effective and that although most realized he was not Chinese he passed himself off as a merchant from an outlying province on the north-west frontier. In some ways his trek through China resembled the epic travels of the Arabist, Sir Richard Francis Burton between 1850 and 1870, through parts of the Middle and Near East. Fortune was accompanied by Chinese assistants and engaged others to help transport the more than 20,000 tea plants, thousands of seeds, a large supply of implements as well as considerable know-how on the manufacture of tea, to the Himalayas of India and the hills of Assam. If anyone can be credited with the development and growth of the Indian tea industry, it was Robert Fortune.

Not satisfied with just collecting the raw material, Fortune persuaded eight Chinese experts to accompany him to India to set up the industry there. Fortune's endeavours were initially under-taken to benefit the people of India and to reduce the price of tea there from four to six shillings a pound to four to sixpence a pound. But it was also done to reduce Britain's dependence on the China product and to reduce its drain of silver. India is today a major consumer but also one of the world's biggest exporters of tea and its dark colour and stronger taste are of greater appeal to the European palate.

In launching the Indian tea industry, Fortune achieved for that country what another British botanist, H. A. Wickham, did for Malaya in introducing the rubber tree from Brazil by collecting 70,000 seeds from the Amazon. Two other eminent botanists living in Malaya, Hugh Low and Henry Ridley, were responsible for getting the rubber industry started. It was typical of British policy of the nineteenth century to turn its colonial territories into fertile productive regions capable of employing people and providing enterprise and industry where it did not previously exist.

Fortune did not ask the Chinese Government for permission to remove tea plants and seedlings. He went there with money in his pockets and bought them with the approval of those who grew them; his intentions must have been obvious. Along with the tea plants went many other botanical species of plants and trees which adorn English parks and gardens today. This was an age of horticultural experimentation and the extension and ex-pansion of the English country garden. Plants were introduced from all parts of the world as Victorian travellers returned with seeds and cuttings carefully preserved during their long sea voyages home.

Fortune was not the first botanist or horticulturist to collect plants with a commercial potential. He was one of more than fifty significant collectors from several European countries — Russia, Germany, France, the United States, Britain — who tramped the hills of China between the seventeenth century and the communist "liberation" in 1949. Among the Britons involved were the two John Reeves, father and son, who as tea inspectors in Guangzhou during the years of the East India Company, collected plants such as azaleas, camellias, peonies, chrysanthemum and ornamental garden plants which they transferred to the Royal Horticultural Society. Even earlier was James Cunningham who visited China in 1698 in the service of the EIC and was stationed at Xiamen and Zhoushan and collected dried plants.

During their mission to China both Lord Macartney and Sir George Staunton spent part of their time collecting dried specimens and Clarke Abel, physician with the Amherst expedition, spent some of his leisure hours walking the hills of Beijing and Nanjing collecting specimens. Many collectors were Roman Catholic priests living in outlying provinces. Diplomats, generals and civil servants were among others who fell under the spell of Chinese flora and sublimated their nostalgia for their gardens at home by picking the best and brightest from the hillsides and valleys of China.

The big names of British and Continental horticulture such as George Forrest (1873–1932), E. H. "Chinese" Wilson, Jean Marie Delavay, Jean Pierre David, Francis Kingdom Ward, William Kerr, Frank Ludlow, Joseph Rock and Sir Henry Veitch are credited with collecting thousands of species of Chinese flowering plants and sending them back to the great herbaria and botanical museums of Britain, the United States and Europe for identification, naming, cultivating and hybridizing. These ranged from roses, a number of bulbs including iris and lily, hydrangea, clematis, jasmine, rhododendron, magnolia, peony, and "Lady Slipper" orchids, to the intriguing pendulous vine, *Actinidia chinensis*, or Chinese gooseberry, which Wilson collected from

Figure 5.4 At any time of the year, Chinese families admired flowers, grown naturally or carved in semi-precious stones. Here a Chinese artist shows a hawker carrying porcelain pots of flowering trees in Guangdong in the nineteenth century.

Hubei in 1900 and introduced for cultivation; from it emerged the widely popular kiwi fruit, today grown in many parts of the world and consumed universally.

Perhaps no species more than that most widely admired of all garden plants — the rose — benefited from China imports. The Banksian roses, named after Captain Cook's botanist Sir Joseph Banks, have introduced white, cream and yellow clusters of climbers, while from southern China came the *Rosa chinensis* — a double crimson first imported in 1792.

One of the most unusual was the so-called Bourbon rose found early in the nineteenth century on the bleak windswept French island of Reunion in the Indian Ocean, a natural hybrid of the Autumn Damask and Old Blush China rose. From this chance hybrid, seed was sent to Paris where it was grown in the garden of Napoleon's wife, Josephine, at Malmaison, and was later sent to England. Experts acknowledge that these and other roses have become a part of the ancestry of the modern garden rose.

This floral flood led to the transformation of not just the traditional English garden, but of gardens great and small all over Europe, the Americas, Australia and wherever people have the love and luxury to grow the colourful profusion of plants and trees nature offers. Thousands of new varieties and new species found a favoured place, challenging not only the commercial developer but the botanist to devise hybrids giving variations in colour and shape. At the same time, major cities all over the world found space and money to extend parks and gardens and to build plant houses in which to reproduce the more fastidious species in conditions approximating those in which they thrive in nature.

The result is that Chinese and Japanese gardens are today a commonplace feature of cities around the world. In the depths of a Northern winter, the tropics have been recreated to house delicate orchids or humidity-loving ferns or desert-dry cacti, each with its own climatic needs. The intrepid collectors of the last century, amateur and professional, several of whom were murdered or were killed in accidents during their expeditions, have done much to enrich our appreciation and admiration of the intricacy, detail and diversity of our planet's plant life. To Fortune, however, goes the credit of extending the tea industry to new areas of cultivation and for the variety of blends available today.

There were gains for the Chinese economy as well. In spite of China's insistence over the years that it had no need to trade with the foreigners, the tea industry reaped a fortune over two centuries, the revenue running into millions of pounds for growers, blenders, curers, packers, carriers and of course the merchants who sold it, as well as the government which taxed it, to say nothing of the officials who milked the trade with their extortionate demands on the industry. It may be regretted that Fortune was not alive 100 years earlier, for had he undertaken then what he did in the 1840s, India might have made tea its export cash crop instead of opium, which forms the next part of our story.

For thousands of years mankind has been held in thrall by the sap of the plant *Papaver somniferum*, better known as the poppy. The sap which oozes from incisions on the ripening seed pod is the stupefying attraction, and for this the poppy is still widely cultivated, as it has been for thousands of years. Who first discovered opium — was it the Sumerians, the Egyptians, the Greeks, or a Stone Age clan somewhere in the lake district of Switzerland — is unknown. But the tall red distinctive flower — from a family of twenty-eight genera and 250 species — possessed not only beauty, and grew freely and easily in temperate and subtropical climates, but its seedpod was found to contain a substance which induced a sense of well-being, freedom from pain, anxiety and fear, and if taken in large enough quantities induced sleep and a deep sense of tranquility — and even death in highly concentrated doses.

In colour, opium's white juice when extracted from the pod turns reddish-brown and is ingested or smoked or swallowed. It was known to the ancient Greeks and to the Romans, and may have been given to Greek soldiers before battle and was certainly used as a poison in imperial Rome to guarantee the succession of Nero after the death of the Emperor Claudius. But it was used selectively and specifically and did not become a substance of mass use or abuse until many centuries later. Medicinally it was always in demand and the Arabs found a growing market for it around the coast of the Indian Ocean during the middle ages, from where it probably reached China to supplement whatever supplies were grown within its own borders.

The Arabs had a weakness for it in the early years of the Islamic awakening, for while the Koran strictly forbad alcoholic beverages, opium escaped notice, and for those seeking a release from reality or a stepladder to more profound meditation or inspirational enlightenment, the poppy found favour without offending against the word of the Prophet. The Mohammedans named it "afyun" and it was known to the Chinese a "afuyong" or "yapian." There were no official strictures against its import in the years of the Song and Yuan dynasties because it had a limited following and caused no social disruption.

Poets, painters and writers seeking inspiration could transport themselves with a pipe or two. It was no more a vice than drinking, and some of China's best poets were also well-known tipplers. Chinese herbalists valued it as an addition to their medical pharmacopoeia and the Arabs were keen to acquaint their clients with its properties and applications.

The Indians decided that it was well within their own ability to cultivate the flower and they turned it into a major cash crop for which there was a growing market at home and overseas. It was exported in the form of bricks, cakes or balls and proved a valuable boost to the colonial economy in years when it was respected rather than despised, helping to balance the budget and pay for a growing army of civil servants and soldiers needed to maintain the British Raj. It was the opium exported from India, largely by British traders, that ultimately reversed the imbalance in the China trade and also gave a hefty shove to war between Britain and China.

The opium poppy had been grown for centuries in outlying provinces of China, and supplies had also travelled from Thailand, Burma and Cambodia through various land corridors. The level of consumption, however, was small and of no great concern to the Government. Little if anything was heard of it before the Tang dynasty and at that time it was largely confined to medicinal uses.

Writers of that era could wax eloquent over its properties notably, "when boiled (the seeds) become a drink fit for Buddha. Old men whose powers have decayed ... should take this drink." Use of the drug, however, gained a significant boost when another narcotic was introduced to China from the Philippines, notably tobacco.

The biggest colonial power at that time was Spain and having imported tobacco from its domains in South America, it then set about creating new markets in Taiwan and Fujian Province in the late sixteenth century. Chinese traders in both Manila and Xiamen found a profitable market for the leaf, a plant then grown only in Mexico, the West Indies and parts of South America. Spain either allowed the re-export of the cured leaf to other parts of Asia or planted seeds in the Philippines. Chinese traders were quick to discover it and established thriving markets in Java, China and other parts of Southeast Asia for the cured leaf and for plants.

To their credit, not everyone in China welcomed the leaf and in the reign of the last Ming emperor an edict of prohibition was issued and this was endorsed by his Qing successor. But just as King Charles I and King James I of England had thrown their weight against it unsuccessfully, the Chinese emperors had no greater success and in Taiwan, seriously plagued by malaria, the practice evolved of smoking tobacco with opium to neutralize the fever's effects. A similar mixture was used in Java and an early Dutch doctor declared: "Unless we had opium to use in these hot countries, in cases of dysentery, cholera, burning fever and various billious affections, we should practise medicine in vain."

The Chinese obviously relished the mixture and Sir George Staunton, deputy to Lord Macartney who visited Beijing in 1793, said that many of the higher mandarins took opium and that "they smoke tobacco mixed with other oderous substances, and sometimes a little opium." This persisted in spite of an edict proclaimed by Yongzheng (the third Qing emperor, 1723–1735) in 1729, imposing severe penalties on the sale of opium and the operation of opium divans. Within the precincts of the Forbidden City, however, the court attendants lived in a privileged sanctuary of their own making.

In this situation, the Qing emperors suffered from the same blind eye syndrome as Admiral Horatio Nelson who at the battle of Copenhagen ignored the signal he did not wish to see. At that time, imports of Indian opium amounted to 200 chests a year and the ships concerned were Portuguese which obtained their cargoes from Goa. The British were not far behind and in 1773 they succeeded in pushing up exports to 1,000 chests a year when the East India Company decided to join in. It reached such serious proportions (4,000 chests in 1790) that the first major ban took place and official exports were prohibited.

From 1800 the trade went underground and the EIC was forced to relinquish its involvement — that is its transportation, but not of course its production. Private British traders, aided and abetted by the EIC in India, were happy to find a way around the ban; while Englishmen brought in Bengal or Patna opium, and Portuguese a variety grown near Goa, the Americans, following the revolution in 1774, specialized in Malwa and Turkish opium.

But of all the opium imported, the Chinese preference was for the Bengal cake which could be turned into a smokeable extract. This was processed in the factories of Ghazipur (near Benares) and Patna, and until the time of auction was the exclusive property of the Government of India (at that time, the East India Company). Once sold, of course, the EIC was happy to disown it even though it knew perfectly well who was buying it and its destination. In 1835, opium accounted for half the total value of imports to China. How much more was smuggled can only be guessed.

For the next thirty-eight years the trade proved lucrative to the Western merchants and venal Chinese officials who closed their eyes and opened their hands to local smugglers; they operated from waters just out of reach of Chinese coastguards, though eventually the trade centred on Lingding (Lintin) Island, in the Pearl River estuary. This was well within reach of the authorities yet enjoyed the charmed environment of an unofficial sanctuary. The smugglers and sailing ships used it as a rendez-vous, their imports held in closely guarded floating hulks to comply with the prohibition against landing the noxious drug on Chinese soil; transactions were conducted in silver specie.

China now experienced the same difficulties as Britain in the drain of silver, for the cost of the contraband trade was put at 10 million taels a year (a tael was equivalent to 575 grains of silver). The figure may have been exaggerated but because smugglers are not in the habit of extending credit, and demanded cash on the nail, and because India itself imported little from China (the tea and silk shipped from Guangzhou went mainly to England), there was an obvious outflow of specie, a new experience for China and one it was determined to halt.

The debilitating effect of the drug was equally pernicious and the massive scale of the imports meant that it penetrated deep into the central provinces of China and to people at many levels of society, some of whom could ill-afford the indulgence.

The trade grew to such an extent that special shallow-draught "crab" or "centipede" boats, manned by up to sixty oarsmen, were built by the Chinese smugglers to negotiate the narrow estuary inlets. These were not only very fast but the crew were also well trained in beating off challengers with spikes fitted at the ends of their long oars. Boarding parties found that they resembled a porcupine and were virtually impregnable, though the more zealous mandarins found ways to trap them whenever they wished to demonstrate their obedience to Beijing's edicts.

The Qing court, already in decline, saw the impact of the opium influx and the silver drain as a double blow and con-sidered it part of a conspiracy by Western traders to undermine Chinese morale and soften up the country for a major trade offen-sive, coupled with the seizure of territory. Colonial subdivision of the country might well follow as other nations, encouraged by British pressure, joined in demands for trade concessions and the relaxation of controls, taxes and duties on their shipments. Lord Macartney's failure to gain the ear of the Chinese court was not the last word to be heard on the subject. Nor were the pesky barbarians likely to be content until they squeezed China into submission. Beijing might try to tough it out and turn up the heat against opium imports, but the Western demands to ease trade restrictions would continue.

The court in Beijing may have believed that the superiority of

Chinese civilization would prove the winner in the long run but far-sighted Chinese in other parts of the country knew that no wall was high enough to keep out a technologically superior enemy. The Yuan and Qing invaders had broken through Chinese isolation with swords, spears and horses. The Jesuit priests had shown China that the West was now more advanced in industry and science and that it was moving into an era of dynamic technology.

Until the eighteenth century China had held the literary ascendancy, with more than half the world's books — novels, poetry, essays, histories, philosophical discourses and legal and administrative treatises — written in Chinese. Now the tide was running out. However insistent China was that it needed nothing from the outside world, it was powerless to prevent the China Sea barbarians from probing and plundering its coastline and rivers, its ports and its people, sapping their stamina and undermining their morale.

All China knew of this outside world was what it saw in the fifty or so semi-permanent residents living in thirteen terraced houses on the Guangzhou waterfront, and the crews of as many as seventy foreign vessels which visited the city each year. Its experience with these visitors and the occasional high-powered missions that visited Beijing convinced it that while Western nations could be troublesome and awkward they were no more a long-term threat to China than the Arabian traders centuries earlier. They should be tolerated, their orders for tea, silk and rhubarb fulfilled, but kept in their places in the far south; their silver dollars were welcome to the individuals concerned and the throne took its share of the profits as the tea and silk industries prospered. The Hoppo and the Viceroy could claim some success in limiting their inroads into China and achieving a fair return to the public (and private) purse. The opium problem could be resolved given a resolute administrator and this became the throne's chief concern.

But the impatience of the British, in particular, was beginning to make itself felt. In 1801, Napoleon Bonaparte ordered French forces to invade Portugal in an attempt to squeeze out the small British army led by Sir John Moore and the Duke of Wellington. The British Admiralty feared that as Napoleon's forces floundered in the Peninsular War, French men-of-war might try to score an easy victory by landing in Macau. A well-named and strongly armed British warship, HMS *Arrogant*, arrived off Macau, heading a convoy armed with a company of infantry and artillery. Later, two more frigates arrived, intending to land British forces in Macau, apparently to forstall any French action.

The Chinese became alarmed and strongly denounced the British intention; the Governor of Macau did his best to plead ignorance, aware that he was not master of his own house and unwilling to provoke a crisis with the Chinese. With the British standing by at Lingding, all sides watched anxiously for signs of a French strike, but nothing happened and when word arrived that France and England had concluded peace talks, the British convoy sailed off amidst a peel of indignant denials that they had any ulterior motives in seeking to occupy Macau.

This was, however, the age of Bonaparte, desperate to exclude British trade; seven years later France was again showing its teeth in a new threat to Europe. Another British admiral turned up in the Pearl River estuary, this time accompanied by 300 troops from Madras, intending to land in Macau to frustrate any attempt by Napoleon's forces in the Far East from moving in. Without authority from the Portuguese in Goa or permission from the Chinese, and with many misgivings on the part of the East India Company supercargoes, Rear-Admiral William O'Brien Drury put his men ashore. He assured them all that Britain and Portugal were allies fighting a common enemy, that the move was entirely defensive and precautionary, and that they would depart as soon as the danger was over. There was no ulterior motive.

The Chinese were not about to swallow that and reacted swiftly and with determination. The Viceroy stopped all trade; the Portuguese objected; and the English traders wrung their hands in exasperation at this ham-handed manoeuvre by the Royal Navy. The Viceroy of Guangdong was not prepared to tolerate any defiance and began a series of threats, some direct, some by rumour, all of which threatened to destroy the EIC's trading position in Guangzhou. Faced with this kind of confrontation, Drury blinked and ordered the re-embarkation of his troops, sailing off in a Gilbertian huff. Trade in the river was reopened and thus one more crisis passed, but not before the Viceroy and the Governor were demoted for allowing the British to land on Chinese soil.

Another alarm was a local rebellion which threatened Guangzhou and which prompted the EIC to offer whatever forces it could to defend the city. The Viceroy would have none of it and told the Select Committee he did not need foreign assistance and indeed succeeded in crushing the rebels, the leaders of whom had assumed imperial insignia and titles. The rebels were immediately executed and cut into thirty-two pieces.

This was followed by a surprising suicide when the Viceroy heard that the Governor of the province, his subordinate in fact, had forwarded a critical report to the Emperor on his attempts to put down the rebels. So distraught was the Viceroy that he snatched the snuff-bottle from the Governor's girdle and stuffed it down his own throat — an act calculated to achieve revenge and self-justification. For in Chinese eyes, to take one's life in the presence of one's accuser was to turn the tables against one's antagonist. The Viceroy's death was widely lamented by the foreigners who considered him a mandarin of incorruptible integrity and noteworthy humanity. Not so the Hoppo who continued to raise duties to repay the debts of bankrupt Hong merchants, and he also admitted new Hong merchants into the Co-Hong at $70,000 each.

Signs of increasing restiveness in Guangdong Province — reflecting the decline of the dynasty — came in increasing acts of piracy, not just involving single vessels but huge fleets said to number 400 junks with 70,000 to 80,000 men aboard. Fortunately with the on-off war against France, British ships travelled in heavily armed convoys capable of taking on French marauders, led by a line-of-battle ship with 64 guns; thus they were not seriously threatened by the pirates. Yet pirate fleets so large could intimidate any smaller vessel and if pressed, bring the cities of Guangzhou or Macau to their knees. The Governor maintained a fleet of twenty boats to repel the pirates and while adequate to police the relatively safe waters of the estuary, they were no match for the fleet at sea, nor could they challenge them in their lairs up and down the coast.

Though unloved and unwanted, British naval vessels now appeared off the river with increasing frequency ready to offer help if needed, the EIC pointing out the "enormous value of the trade at stake — not less than 20 million taels, import and export, the magnitude of the merchant fleet endangered valued at 30 million taels, and the Chinese revenue of not less than 1.3 million taels a year, which would be lost if the trade came to an end."[1]

If the Chinese mandarins shared these concerns there was no sign and they refused to concede anything likely to give the foreigners (and particularly the British) a second foot in the door. They were also adamant that contact between Chinese and Europeans should be limited to the minimum. When it was brought to their notice that British ships were making up losses in their crews, caused by death or desertion, with Chinese seamen recruited ashore, there were indignant protests. Did the British not know that it was forbidden for Chinese people to travel abroad, asked the mandarins.

By a coincidence, visiting Guangzhou at that time was Tiqua, the "Captain China" at Penang, who had travelled there fifteen years earlier to take up work for the East India Company. He was now anxious to recruit more Cantonese to live and work in that

---

1. H. B. Morse, *The East India Company Trading to China*, vol. 2.

city, a request endorsed by the British Lieutenant Governor, Mr R. T. Farquhar. Despite the ban on emigration, however, no obstacles were placed in Tiqua's way, as he was a man "of very considerable property and large funds." The EIC, however, refused to carry the emigrants, out of respect for the Chinese prohibition. Chinese people seeking a new life in Asia were not deterred, and were able to take passage on a foreign sailing ship, in most cases financed by contractors, rather than risk themselves in junks. Their destinations in the nineteenth century were to range far beyond the China coast.

The iniquitous coolie traffic will be discussed in a later chapter, but it was yet another sign of heaven withdrawing its mandate from the Qing dynasty when local people voted with their feet in large numbers to seek a better way of life in defiance of the official prohibition. Not always did this eventuate. Some jumped from the frying pan of China's domestic decline into the fire of colonial slavery and serfdom overseas.

Hundreds of thousands perished, in many cases long before reaching the shores of the promised land, in conditions even more horrific than the trans-Atlantic slave traffic, the Highland clearances in Scotland following the rising of Bonnie Prince Charlie, and the Australian convict ships. When it came to mass transportation in the eighteenth and nineteenth centuries, Britain was a brutally efficient pioneer with a mortality rate that won its perpetrators the supreme accolade of shame.

CHAPTER 6

Infectious Distempers

At the turn of the nineteenth century Britain had dug itself into a deep hole — not just with recalcitrant colonies shaking off the paternal yoke in America and the French posing a challenge in Quebec, but out of the bloody mire of the French Revolution emerged a man who was to galvanize the attention of Europe for more than twenty years — the Little Corsican, Napoleon Bonaparte.

Writing of those times, Winston Churchill vividly set the scene: "Machinery, the rise of population and extensive changes in employment all presented a formidable social problem. Napoleon had closed the Continent to British commerce, and the answering British blockade had made things worse for industry at home. There was much unemployment. Smashing of machinery during the Luddite riots of 1812 and 1813 had exposed the complete absence of means of preserving public order. Bad harvests added to the prevailing distress. Extremist radical leaders kept up a perpetual and growing agitation.... Not only was there grinding poverty among the working population, but also a deep-rooted conflict between the manufacturing and agricultural classes. The economy of the country was dangerously out of balance."[1]

---

1. Winston Churchill, *The Island Race* (London: Cassell, 1964).

On the financial front, Britain had run up an astronomical debt of 250 million pounds and the great challenge facing the Prime Minister, William Pitt, in his first ministry was to stabilize and reverse that trend. Britain too had its times of internal tension when the Royal Navy rose in mutiny at the Nore and Spithead; a few years earlier a British admiral, John Byng, had been executed on the quarter deck of his ship for not displaying the zeal expected of a senior officer of the Royal Navy in turning back the French tide in the Mediterranean.[2]

The Nore mutiny was a stark sign of the times when British seamen were still treated abominably despite winning her battles. Nor was morale in the army much higher, with the shambles of Yorktown not far behind. William Pitt the Younger undoubtedly enjoyed the solace of a cup of China tea (but preferred something stronger) during these tense days. However, it is hard to believe the choice of an "insular possession" in the South China Sea figured prominently on his cabinet agenda, with many more worrying issues clamouring for attention.

Following on from the mutiny, Pitt's first task was naval reform, both in improving conditions for seamen and choosing effective leaders. One other reform would take longer to achieve — the design of ships able to play an effective part on the world scene. For while it is still possible to admire the classic lines of Nelson's flagship, HMS *Victory*, in her drydock at Portsmouth, the naval ships of its day were about forty years old (and those used by the EIC even older). They were designed in an era of hidebound regulations which saw English shipbuilders stagnate and fall behind the innovative Spanish, French and American designers.

Only its seamen and admirals were able to preserve the advantage with their tactical brilliance and raw courage. Too often

---

2. Voltaire would quip that Britain from time to time found it necessary to shoot an admiral *"pour encourager les autres."*

ships were designed for action in particular seas, though in an age of imperial expansion there was no excuse for the decline of British shipbuilding with its need to sail anywhere in the world. One of the biggest hindrances was the bureaucracy that ensarled the Admiralty, ensuring that ship design was always years behind the times.

These ships, some displacing 2,200 tons and carrying up to 100 guns, were huge and cumbersome. They carried up to twenty-one sails exceeding 8,000 square metres in area and weighing ten tons, and they needed a large crew to man them. But in the close encounter fighting of their day, a broadside from their three-tiered gun decks would cripple an enemy ship within 200 metres or demolish a fort of the thickest stone.

It took the Americans to show the way with what one writer described as "small, handy fast ships commanded by sailors of exceptional alertness of mind and body"[3] and another who said they were the first ever built with speed, instead of carrying capacity, as their chief requirement.[4] These were flush-decked brigs and schooners, long and low in profile, and known as "Baltimore Clippers." They began to emerge from American dockyards at the time of the revolutionary war, many as privateers and later slavers; they harassed the slow, ponderous craft of the Royal Navy and took a steady toll of the enemy. Variations of these ships, built to master the huge seas of the north and south Atlantic Oceans, the southern Indian Ocean, the Roaring Forties, and the stormy South China Seas, would soon make their debut off the coast of China as opium clippers, tea clippers and whalers.

The opium clippers were a smaller ship with streamlined keels and racing sails, built on the lines of the private yachts then

3. H. B. Morse, *The East India Company Trading to China*, vol. 2.
4. Basil Lubbock, *The China Clippers* (1914; reprint, London: Century Publishing, 1966).

appearing in the English Channel and the Mediterranean. The Americans knew that if they were to wrest any part of the China trade from the EIC they would have to sail their ships from ports such as New York, Salem and Boston in Massachusetts, all the way across the Atlantic Ocean, under the Cape of Good Hope, beat their way up to India to collect their opium, then sail south to the East Indies before driving up the South China Sea. This would mean battling with north-east monsoons, with heavy head seas and strong currents if they were to steal a march on their rivals. This would enable them to discharge their cargo of thick dark cakes of Patna opium and the balls of Benares opium into the receiving hulks at Lingding or Namoa, without waiting for the change of seasonal winds.

These hulks were usually old East Indiamen, owned by firms engaged in the trade, all manned by large fighting crews and big cannon to ward off the pirates who would swoop in and out of a misty spring sea to take their chance plundering ships loaded with hundreds of thousands of pounds worth of stock imported from India, Persia and Turkey. These receiving ships were few in the early years of the nineteenth century but as the trade surged in the late 1820s and 1830s they were stationed at Lingding, Namoa, Xiamen, Fuzhou, and Hong Kong's Kap Shui Mun.

Another class of small clipper would then carry them up and down the coast, pulling into the windless shallows of small inlets and creeks before handing over their consignment for cash up front. Here the danger of attack or treachery from mandarins in-the-know was greatest and the speed of turnround most important and it was a case of all hands being armed with cutlasses and loaded pistols to deter any opium buyer planning a quick snatch of the entire ship.

Retribution would be swift in that event, for the opium traders were hard men with deadly weapons who settled scores without trial or inquests, using teams of enforcers led by ex-naval crews who would burn down a village or small port from which the pirates or brigands had operated. Another way of settling scores would be to tip off the mandarins in Guangzhou where to find a big opium haul.

These opium-carriers found one useful ally — Christian missionaries needing to distribute tracts and bibles up the coast. Several spoke fluent Chinese and one — the German missionary Charles Gutzlaff, managed to serve Mammon and God, negotiating opium sales as well as preaching the gospel. He could not have been in any doubt about the immorality of the trade and in his memoirs wrote that he pondered the dilemma for many hours before deciding to take ship and head north. It was one of Jardine's vessels, the *Sylph*, on which he travelled and he not only spoke fluent Chinese but, dressed in native garb, he could have easily been mistaken for a local.

The main concern of British traders was the way in which the Americans had moved into the China trade with their fast, smart, well-run clippers. In the year 1809, there were forty British ships on the coast and thirty-seven American; the year before the Yankees had contributed only eight out of sixty-two. The English ships were sluggish in build, sail power and manoeuvrability and

Figure 6.2   Charles Gutzlaff in native dress, by George Chinnery.

ranged from 1,000 to 1,200 tons in the case of Indiamen to 700 tons for the country ships running from India. The Americans were rarely more than 500 tons.

Carrying up to 1.5 million pounds sterling in cargo or coin, the EIC ships would make an outward voyage in four to five months, spend six months in Guangzhou awaiting tea shipments and a change in the monsoon, and then take another five months on the homeward leg. The Americans would take 100 days and did the round trip in little more than a year. Moreover the Yankee clippers could outsail the pirates, always on the lookout for a slow or becalmed vessel or the victim of a typhoon. But as the pirate fleets grew, a lone Indiaman would have to be swift to the cannon to deter the small multi-oared boats coming at her from all quarters.

The other problem was that British sailors, many press-ganged into service, were deserting to sail on American ships with their higher pay and better conditions, though the discipline if anything was harsher with bosuns and masters wielding clubs to make sure the decks were scrubbed white, twice daily, and clear of sails, rope and tackle.

On the whole, reports filtering back to England told of a far more competitive and seamanlike ship flying what the Chinese described as the "flowery banner." The EIC ships, flying the "rice character" flag (because of its resemblance to the Chinese character for rice, *mi*) were respected by the Chinese for the business they brought, their regularity in the trading season, as well as for their good record in meeting obligations and settling accounts. At least half the China trade (imports and exports) was on British account, not including the opium, 75 per cent of which was carried in British or Parsee-owned ships.

While there was little chance of American ships stealing this trade from the British it was an age when profits came before principles. If the EIC ships declined to carry the drug there were any number of Indian country ships willing to take part; and with fortunes being made on each shipment by the private firms, the old monopoly practices of the EIC melted under the blowtorch of international competition.

The fact of the matter was that the speed of the EIC ships was a joke. It was no longer good enough to stand by and admire the new American clippers, it was time for the British to lift their act and to charter, buy or build modern ships. The industrial revolution had pushed Britain into the forefront of international trade and commerce; it was achieved through challenging traditional notions and scientific taboos and it was only a matter of time before this same aggressive spirit of innovation coupled with the forces of change, emerged in the international trading environment.

The EIC had held its precarious position in China for more than 100 years by acknowledging the Qing dynasty rules, and it had paid a high price to keep its foot in the door. It had secured the tea market and established a permanent foreign presence. Now a new generation imbued with ideas of free trade was taking over, opposed to bureaucratic interference and restrictions at home and abroad; it had a strong voice in the corridors of power in London and following the downfall of Napoleon at Waterloo, and Nelson's victory at Trafalgar, a professional military force not to be trifled with.

Aggressive young traders were setting up business in Guangzhou, keen to bring the products of the new world to an old civilization without realizing that they were still dealing with a deeply traditional and conservative society unready for change and unprepared for the cultural, scientific and technological clash that would accompany it. The West was expecting China to leapfrog centuries of isolation to conform to the new age. They could barely communicate with one another on trade matters, but were more effective in conveying their prejudices, intolerance, frustrations and demands. It was only a matter of time before the veneer of Western impatience cracked.

Tension inevitably heightened when a foreign seaman inflicted injury on a Chinese resident. It rose to fever pitch when death resulted. But what inflamed feelings so much among the foreigners was the invariable Chinese demand for the culprit to be immediately surrendered. In complying with this in the past, the captains and traders had been surprised by the swiftness with which punishment had been meted out — and having lost three by public strangulation including one acting as a proxy for the accused, there was now a total reluctance to hand over anyone without exhaustive inquiries. There had been eight cases between 1780 and 1822 when demands had been made on the foreign community to hand over those involved for examination. A mood of defiance was growing.

A new incident occurred in 1821 involving a British warship at Lingding, the island used by Western traders to store opium. On this occasion a party of seamen from the 40-gun HMS *Topaz* was threatened by a large group of villagers. The captain ordered protective measures which included shots fired from the ship. A British landing party was later rushed to the defence of their shipmates, and in the ensuing clash two Chinese were killed and several wounded. Immediate demands were made for the assailants to be handed over for trial and when the captain of *Topaz* refused, all trade with the British was stopped at Guangzhou.

So seriously did the Select Committee view the incident that it moved all British traders from the Guangzhou factory area as well as its stock of coins and silver, while the captain of *Topaz*, sensing the danger, sailed off to India to avoid any risk of an attack on his ship, thus temporarily averting a showdown, though echoes of it would be heard for many weeks to come. There were other occasions when death by natural causes or accident occurring near a foreign ship would be blamed on some real or imagined action by a foreign seaman; the Hong merchants tried to settle these privately to avoid an official inquest. No less irksome was the continuous background of petty friction that prevailed. Letters or memorials sent to the Hoppo by the British were not read, or if read not answered, or if answered, were avuncular or condescending in tone as well as negative in detail.

When Sir George Staunton in 1811 proposed another embassy to Beijing to follow up the failed Macartney mission eighteen years earlier, the Viceroy replied petulantly: "Oh no! There is no occasion for you to send another embassy to Beijing. The Emperor knows it is a long way and does not wish you to trouble yourselves. Besides the climate does not agree with you; you may catch infectious distempers. No! Your nation must not send an embassy. I will not allow it. It is out of the question and you must not think of it."[5]

Despite this discouraging response, five years later the court agreed to another embassy, this time to be led by Lord Amherst, a leading British diplomat of less distinguished lineage than his predecessor but rated highly enough to be later appointed Governor General of India and raised to an earldom. Nor were the Chinese given as much notice of his visit, the official intimation reaching Guangzhou only six weeks before HMS *Alceste* arrived at the Leema Islands off Macau.

Six weeks' notice was hardly adequate in view of the distance separating Guangdong Province from the capital and the need to mount a series of post riders to take the news to the palace. Moreover, it was an unsettled time in Beijing. An attempt had been made to assassinate the Emperor Jiaqing only three years earlier during a serious uprising, the second in less than twenty years. The Chinese were also deeply suspicious of British manoeuvres around their coast and there were understandable misgivings about admitting an entourage from this same nation into the presence of the celestial throne. Also there was no assurance that he would perform the act of obeisance required of all tributaries from near and far. If the Dutch and French could comply, why not the stiffnecked barbarians from Europe's diminutive offshore islands? The Chinese were in no mood to receive them and made it plain.

---

5. H. B. Morse, *The East India Company Trading to China*, vol. 3.

On this inauspicious note the embassy began, proceeding from Guangzhou to Tianjin in *Alceste*, and then making a hasty 17-day overland journey to Haidien in the worst heat of summer and on roads paved at times with rough hewn rocks and at other times, left to the mercy of the elements, with deep wheel ruts and pot-holes. It was a journey Amherst and his entourage would remember for the rest of their lives. Nor were their spirits greatly revived on arriving in Beijing when told that they would be summoned at about 4 a.m. to prepare for the highly ritualized audience in the Summer Palace, complete with imperial bands, gongs, trumpets, cymbals and other dissonant musical instruments to do justice to such an occasion; in short Amherst was to get the full royal treatment complete with imperial honours suited to one of his rank. Did the Chinese smile wryly at his anticipated discomfort knowing the European aversion to the lavish display of oriental imperial pomp?

The eunuchs knew of Amherst's reluctance to perform the kowtow and hoped to manoeuvre him into a position where, fatigued from his journey and overwhelmed (or so they hoped) by the occasion, he might be forced to slump to his knees and in a dazed state be made to knock his head at least thrice on the floor of the throne room. Amherst was no fool and probably foresaw the danger; weary from prolonged travelling he pleaded that he felt ill and was unable to perform the ritual. Nor would any members of his party prostrate themselves before the Son of Heaven. In a fit of rage the Emperor ended the audience and stormed out of the room. Amherst was speedily hustled out of the chamber and packed off to Guangzhou the same day.

Staunton, Amherst's deputy, explained why later. To have performed the ceremony "would have been to purchase degradation and disgrace without even the show of an equivalent, the result of which would (in Amherst's opinion) have fatally shaken that confidence which we have with considerable success established (at Guangzhou) in the firm adherence to principle which distinguishes the British character — a confidence which is our best ally in all our differences with the Chinese and probably our only preservative against such a systematic oppression on the part of the local authorities as would necessarily terminate (in the present state of British feeling) in a rupture of the intercourse between the two countries."[6]

Jiaqing, however, made no bones about what he considered to be a calculated snub on the part of Amherst and his entourage, all the more extraordinary since he had travelled half-way around the world to present his petition. He also claimed he never entered the audience hall, and as a result he did not receive the copy of the King's letter and this was why it was sent back unopened with the embassy. In his letter to King George III, Jiaqing blamed Amherst for his "inability to communicate in your behalf with profound veneration and severe devotedness" but said he had accepted the gifts sent by Britain, namely the maps, landscape prints and portraits, and had sent back a white *ruyi* (emblem of prosperity) as well as a string of court beads, two large purses and eight small ones as a gift from the ever benevolent occupant of the dragon throne.

He then pointed out the futility of Britain sending an ambassador "such a distance over the waves of the sea" particularly when he "cannot understand and practise the rites of ceremony of the Central Nation — the subject involves a severe labour of the lips and tongue, to hear which is by no means pleasant." Furthermore, "the Celestial Empire does not value the things brought from a distance" and he commended King George to "preserve your people in peace and be attentive to strengthen the limits of your territory." He concluded: "This imperial mandate is now given that you may forever obey it."[7] Years later, the British decided to honour Amherst's memory by naming a road after him

6. H. B. Morse, *The East India Company Trading to China*, vol. 3.
7. H. B. Morse, *The East India Company Trading to China*, vol. 3.

in the international concession in Shanghai, one which the Communists promptly renamed after its liberation in 1949.

Thus foundered the last high-level attempt to open the door to dialogue and contact with the rulers of China. Even then war was not inevitable and while it proved impossible to redress the grievances over trading and living conditions at Guangzhou, the China trade may have continued to flourish for many years. Jiaqing was reminded that in spite of the aggravations at Guangzhou the EIC's trade had increased more than fourfold in the last thirty years and eighteen to twenty ships annually visited China which brought back 30 million pounds of tea. With a little sweet reason and co-operation by both sides the trade could continue indefinitely. Even the piracies now occurring with increasing frequency, were a relatively minor irritant, and corruption and extortion were accepted as an annoying but manageable expense.

The institutiton of the Chinese Co-Hong guild of merchants was recognized as a useful and at times valuable buffer between the foreigners and the Qing administrators, while individual members such as Howqua and Mowqua were considered enlightened, generous, farsighted and profoundly helpful people who often put their lives on the line to keep trade moving and to resolve arbitrary demands by the Viceroy, the Governor, the Hoppo, or some other official. On at least one occasion Mowqua was sent to prison and Ponqua, another Hong merchant, died in prison in 1811 after being committed because of a failure by other Hong merchants to settle debts owing to the foreign traders.

An event of singular importance in 1834 was the decision by the British House of Commons to dissolve the East India Company's monopoly in China and replace it with a committee of three headed by the British Chief Superintendent of Trade. On this occasion Lord Napier was nominated in preference to a more logical candidate, Sir George Staunton, who had acted as deputy to both the Macartney and Amherst missions. Lord Napier, a "tall, raw Scotchman with sandy hair," — the quintessential red-haired barbarian — immediately fell foul of the Viceroy by turning up on the coast of Guangdong without receiving the Emperor's permission. His Chinese name was immediately distorted by the Viceroy and the two characters by which he was addressed were "Laboriously Vile." For three months this so-called "Barbarian Eye" (or foreign official), was denied recognition and eventually died before taking up his duties — though not before getting his own back by pasting up deeply humiliating posters all over Guangzhou, accusing the Viceroy of "ignorance" and "obstinacy."

The Chinese suspicions about Britain's motives in ending the EIC monopoly were understandable, though it was the logical sequel to events in India following the impeachment of Warren Hastings by Edmund Burke and the supersession of the East India Company in 1773 by direct Government rule.[8] When the EIC disappeared in India it was only a matter of time before its activities in China were terminated. The Chinese, with no foreign intelligence of their own, were unable to comprehend the reasons.

To them, it appeared that out of the blue Britain had decided to abandon its major trading enterprise which had survived for over 200 years, and to replace it with a government-appointed superintendent. Whether this would lead to a forceful resolution of trade issues, or new demands for permanent diplomatic representation in Beijing, the Chinese had no idea. Nor was Britain itself much clearer, except that its frustrations had come to a head; something had to be done.

As far as Guangzhou was concerned it appeared to be something more sinister than simply a change of faces — and it was the underlying motive that worried the mandarins. For while the prospect of having a leader able to speak for, and answer to the

---

8. For a period of fifteen years prior to that, British India was run like a public company with shareholders deciding policy; the EIC trade monopoly in India ended in 1813.

entire British trading community seemed an improvement, the new superintendents were an unknown quantity. The Chinese were aware the EIC was dependable in enforcing official edicts, whether on the importation of opium or the carriage of Chinese emigrants, while the British country traders were a law unto themselves.

The Chinese soon discovered, however, that Napier and his successors had no more control over the private trade than the EIC, even when the Chinese sanctions were reinforced by a vigorous new commissioner appointed by Beijing. What the Chinese did not appreciate was that the free traders had been largely responsible for ejecting the EIC from China and having won the day in the British parliament they would strive to put this new found freedom into action in the China trading arena.

The free traders were fed up with the cynical hypocrisy of the mandarins and with the way in which edicts handed down from Beijing were treated with contempt even by local officials appointed to enforce them. W. C. Hunter, the American partner of Russell & Co., an American firm active in Guangzhou, recalled making a trip to the island of Namoa on the schooner *Rose*, where they encountered a Chinese vessel with a mandarin on board. Fearing the worst, Hunter was told the approval of the official was essential if it wished to transact its business. *Rose* carried 300 chests of opium valued at $150,000. After pleasantries between the captain and the mandarin and an exchange of cigars and wine, the captain then reported that he had been blown off course by contrary winds. Nudge, nudge, wink, wink. The mandarin read the rules about helping distressed ships and invited *Rose* to leave as soon as she had replenished supplies. The two men were then left alone and the real business of the day was transacted; money changed hands and the two finally returned to the main deck to toast each other before leaving. It was time for *Rose*, having completed her business to depart, 200 chests lighter — undertaken for the sake of adjusting the ballast, of course.

The German missionary, Gutzlaff, who travelled to North

Figure 6.3 A western merchant supervises the unloading of merchandise into a godown, by Auguste Borget.

China in 1831, 1832 and 1833 on missions for Jardine, Matheson, found the mandarins less co-operative. He reported that while Chinese merchants were keen to do business they wanted to find a way around the official edicts against importing opium and trading at ports other than at Guangzhou. Gutzlaff may not have been the ideal intermediary for Jardine, having a conscience that troubled him and only a secondary interest in contraband. Those traders with the right connections had few difficulties in selling their opium, however, given patience, persistence and prudence, for there was always a Chinese buyer willing to take the risk and pay the price.

The free traders who now occupied the key posts in the British factory in Guangzhou were men well versed in the opium trade — some like Thomas Beale had gone bankrupt owing about $400,000 to the East India Company. Others, like William Jardine, had been an EIC surgeon who also acted as agent for a Parsee firm of opium dealers in Bombay; in earlier years Jardine and Jamsetjee Jejebhoy had both been captured by the French off Sri Lanka and were later shipwrecked off South Africa, so had ample opportunity to form a durable and valuable connection in China. James Matheson, another lowland Scot, had family connections in India but found China a more promising region. He and a former EIC purser, Henry Wright, later joined Jardine to buy out the business of Charles and Hollingworth Magniac. Wright was the junior partner whose name never featured in the firm of Jardine, Matheson, but he was acknowledged to be a key figures man who did much to keep the company's accounts in order.

The Dents were also prominent in private trading in Guangzhou, both Thomas and Lancelot being partners of Thomas Dent & Co., and Thomas, though listed as a British resident, had acquired the title of Sardinian Consul from the days when private traders managed to justify their presence by assuming a diplomatic cloak. The extraordinarily large Macau consular corps also included William Jardine who was at one time the Danish Consul, a post held earlier by James Matheson, while Charles Magniac was the Prussian Consul and his brothers, Hollingworth and Daniel, Vice Consuls, while Christopher Fearon was Hanoverian Vice-Consul and A. Robertson, the Sicilian Consul. Others acted as Russian and Swedish consuls. Such a well-represented consular corps in a community of seventy-five foreign residents in Guangzhou might be hard to justify on any grounds except that it was the only point on the China coast where foreigners could live ashore for any period of time. Because China would not accept diplomatic or consular representatives, their accreditation was to Portuguese Macau.

Among others in the foreign community were missionaries, surgeons, watch-makers (two French and one English), two shopkeepers, various clerks and "a considerable number of Parsees" (not named in the EIC list of foreign residents). One of the most curious castaways was a bankrupt portrait painter who after many years of success in India, fled from his debts and his wife in 1825, and spent the rest of his life in Macau fearful that either or both might catch up with him; this was the Anglo-Irish artist, George Chinnery, who considered himself among the top six British painters of his day, a claim never seriously put to the test since he never returned to his home country. However, he managed to eke out a precarious existence painting delightful seascapes and landscapes of Macau and the Pearl River estuary, as well as the portraits of many of the leading European and Chinese traders, some of his finest being the Hong merchants, Howqua and Mowqua.

Robert Morrison was one of the two Protestant missionaries who came to China in 1807 for the London Missionary Society to learn Chinese and begin for the Protestant churches what the Roman Catholic Church had been doing for the last 300 years. Because of his skills in Chinese, both in Mandarin and Cantonese, Morrison became Chief Secretary and Translator at the British Factory in Guangzhou and also translated the Bible, a Chinese–English dictionary in three parts, and a grammar of the Chinese language, not to mention many prayers, hymns and psalms. A man of prodigious energy and literary output he established the Anglo-Chinese College in Malacca and succeeded in laying the foundations of Protestantism in China, keeping on good terms with the Jesuits and winning the admiration of the Chinese for his skills as an interpreter, particularly during Lord Amherst's embassy. His other great interest was education and his Morrison Education Society was a pioneer in the work of bridging the cultural gap between the West and China. So highly regarded was he by his peers at home and abroad that he was elected a Fellow of the Royal Society.

No less sedulous in his propagation of the gospel and an equally gifted linguist was Dr Charles Gutzlaff, a native of Pomerania who represented the Netherlands Missionary Society but who, as already noted, blotted his reputation by travelling on Jardine's opium ships as a translator.[9] There were many other gifted Europeans on the coast. One was Thomas Colledge, an English doctor in the service of the EIC, who distinguished himself as a skilled practitioner to the Chinese people, and one of the first permanent Western physicians living in China. He opened an eye hospital in Guangzhou as well as a dispensary which treated more than 6,000 patients. Colledge while in Macau met and married a Bostonian visitor, Caroline Shillaber; sadly three of their children died in Macau in infancy.[10]

Colledge was one of at least four Western doctors not just giving their services to the local people but promoting permanent hospitals. Morrison, himself a doctor by profession as well as a missionary, financially supported and helped in the running of a clinic in the city. He was assisted by an EIC surgeon named Livingstone who also gave valuable service. After Morrison's death the work was revived by Dr Peter Parker, a well-known missionary from the United States. In 1836 a Medical Missionary Society was formed in Guangzhou operating two hospitals, one of which was the eye hospital at which Colledge practised; another was a general hospital in Macau, and while Western doctors dealt with the usual run of minor ailments and diseases, the truly spectacular surgery was performed by Colledge and Parker on grotesque tumours which in some cases had grown over a period of 30 years — phenomena rarely seen by Western surgeons today.

One of Colledge's patients, with a huge tumour on his scrotum was taken to London for surgery, but in years before anaesthesia he died under the knife. Many of these hideous growths can be seen in a series of more than 100 paintings

---

9. Though it is doubtful if Karl Marx had this in mind when he asserted that religion was the opium of the people!
10. The graves are in the Old Protestant Cemetery there.

executed by a brilliant Chinese artist named Lamqua and which today survive in the Yale Medical Library in the US and in Guy's Hospital in London.

William Hunter was one of the first American residents in Macau, travelling there as a teenager and becoming expert at Chinese through his studies at Morrison's Anglo-Chinese College in Malacca. He would eventually become a partner in the leading American trading enterprise of Turner & Co. As a raconteur he was one of the most lively and colourful on the China coast. His two books of reminiscences have added flesh and blood and spirit and character to many of the old China hands then living in Guangzhou, as well as a fund of information and anecdotes which help to recapture the flavour of those times.

No less colourful was the Parsee merchant Sir Jamsetjee Jejebhoy, a prominent opium trader in Bombay who made his fortune out of exporting "foreign mud" to China. His links with Jardine have already been mentioned, but to his credit he ploughed back much of his profits into charitable projects in India, such as hospitals, schools and religious institutions. He was knighted for his services to the community and was one of the most prominent of a minority group who came to play a big part in the commercial development of the Far East under British rule in Hong Kong and in the international settlement in Shanghai.

The small expatriate community of British, American, Dutch, French, Swedish and Spanish people lived almost like castaways, albeit on a fairly comfortable scale, while members of the East India Company Select Committee enjoyed a level of opulence which justly earned them the title of merchant princes. Many were without wives, for Guangzhou strictly forbad entry to foreign women and the climate was also considered bad for health. Several wives who did attempt to join their husbands, like Robert Morrison's wife Mary, died in Macau or en route. Children brought up in Macau — such as the Colledge children — frequently succumbed to local diseases but those who survived were invariably sent back to England for schooling while most of the men spent long years in the East — at least five — before qualifying for "home leave." They entertained sumptuously and frequently, and amused themselves with cards, amateur-dramatics (men taking the female roles), horse-riding, picnicking, sailing, rowing and walking. Their recreation, however, was limited to Macau for in Guangzhou they were restricted to the strip of reclaimed land in front of the factory buildings.

While the foreign merchants employed Chinese servants, the latter would invariably go into hiding in times of tension when all food supplies would also be stopped. The Western traders learned to stockpile food and to take their turn at the stove. They also led a fairly lonely existence, news from "home" taking up to six months to reach them. Moreover, ships bringing mail from Europe rarely distributed it immediately. They would deliver letters to their own principals or to their own countrymen to ensure that any change in the market at home — say, for teas or silks — would be sighted first by their colleagues. A few days or sometimes a few weeks would pass before the rest would be distributed. For while Royal Mail might work efficiently and im-partially at one end of the long run from England to China, there was no comparable institution in China until the 1880s.

The stifling humidity of the eight summer months made life in Guangzhou/Macau miserable for all expatriates, but the European traders kept up appearances in spite of remoteness, and dressed as men of business in their own country, complete with woollen overgarments and linen or cotton shirts and blouses. The one concession they made to the climate was to install the Indian punkahs in their rooms which, for a few coppers, Chinese youngsters used to pull. They also found Chinese anti-mosquito coils highly successful in repelling the voracious insects and for greater comfort, slept under nets.

The summer months would invariably bring several tropical storms and typhoons, and humidity levels turned walls green and shoes mouldy in a few weeks. Their architecture ensured an abundance of wide, shady verandahs, sunny courtyards dominated by leafy palms and flowering bougainvillaea, and cool dark corridors inside. But the European found himself on most summer days out of his element and had to wait a long time before the electric fan, air-conditioning and light summer clothing made life more bearable.

Figure 6.4 A Guangdong market scene, by Auguste Borget.

Though not short of meat, fish, vegetables and fruit — particularly in Macau where Lisbon's modes, mores and manners were aped — the diet of the traders took in many Chinese staples such as rice and local vegetables and drew on Indian experience of serving curry at any meal, including breakfast, for a hot spice tended to cover a multitude of deficiencies. The Europeans also learned to respect Chinese medications even if they turned to their own doctors first for treatment. Some of the traders had found Indian medical practices effective where their techniques of inoculation proved helpful in warding off the evil scourge of smallpox. The Chinese practice of acupuncture, moxibustion and the use of the pulse was adopted by Western physicians from as early as the seventeenth century.

Not the least of the hazards of living in Guangzhou was the menace of fires which could sweep through the densely packed Chinese tenements on nights of high wind, not only destroying the homes of many local people but threatening the foreign factories. One such night in 1822 led to the call-out of the small hand-hauled EIC fire engine with its manual pump, but it was completely unequal to the task, so swiftly did the winds shift. A call was finally made to ships in the river to send volunteers to help remove the bales of woollen goods stored in the factories. While much was saved all the factories and many of the small Chinese shops which served them, as well as the warehouses of two of the biggest Hong merchants, were damaged or destroyed. The losses of the Chinese were said to be enormous while the East

Figure 6.5 Macau — as George Chinnery knew it in the 1830s.

India Company put its losses in the region of one million sterling, an incredibly large figure for its time.

The Opium War, shortly to break out, would radically change their lives and open up China to foreign residence and internal rebellion, ushering in powerful new influences at many levels. The sleeping giant would, in the process, be violently and angrily pitchforked into the modern world.

CHAPTER 7

The Price of Failure

China's tough new Opium Commissioner, Lin Zexu, arrived in Guangzhou at about the same time as the leading opium importer, the "iron-headed rat" (alias William Jardine) left Macau for England on retirement. Jardine, having made his fortune, may have guessed he was on Lin's "most wanted" list but it was less fear of Lin than a demand for resolute British action against China that prompted his move.

Jardine invariably takes the blame for instigating the showdown over opium; certainly he was the most prominent, but there were others such as James Innes, another Scot, dubbed the "stormy petrel of Guangzhou." His other claim to fame was that he was the seventh chieftain of the Inneses of Dunkinty, (motto: Be Firm) with a track record of almost fifteen years as a free trader in China; his substantial dealings in opium did much to exacerbate the tensions of those years, probably also contributing to his death in 1841 at the age of fifty-four. To single out two may suggest these were exceptions; they were not, and on the whole the British traders in Guangzhou were there to make big money quickly in whatever commodity was saleable.

Lin's subsequent action in seizing more than 20,000 chests of opium from mainly British traders and burning it, played into Jardine's hands. China had long ago declared opium a prohibited import but Jardine and his supporters argued that the way to stop it was within the borders of China, not by seizing foreign-owned stocks. If it was such a pernicious and immoral trade, then action must come from within.

London was ambivalent. William Wilberforce, a friend and contemporary of the Prime Minister, William Pitt, had flayed the Government and society over the shameful African slave trade; murmurs of protest over the opium trade were becoming a new point of attack by liberals and evangelicals. Palmerston, the Whig Foreign Secretary of the day, was more closely attuned to the free trade lobby, and also was well aware of the huge revenues being reaped by the Indian Government. Morality is not a strong point with any politician particularly when it conflicts with evident national or commercial interest. Florence Nightingale summed him up well: "He was a humbug and he knew it."

Besides, Palmerston was well aware of the rising tide of tension in the daily life of British traders purchasing huge quantities of tea in Guangzhou with dwindling supplies of silver. Was this — the export of opium — not an obvious way to redress the balance? Jardine could argue it was not a case of British traders forcing it upon reluctant Chinese people at the point of a gun. Chinese middlemen — indeed mandarins in some ports — were up to their necks in the trade; only the ruling bureaucracy was opposed to it and the cynical conclusion was that this was possibly because it could not find a way of cashing in on the trade. He urged its legalization.

The tension surrounding the Western traders in Guangzhou was obvious. As more and more opium found its way into the country, the incidents increased. Local villagers and bully-boys needed little inducement to make trouble and a fracas could be instigated at the drop of a mandarin's hat. When someone was killed or injured there came demands for the perpetrator to be handed over; when this met with refusal, as it invariably did, trade was stopped and servants were withdrawn from British residents, and pressure was exerted through the Hong merchants to secure compliance. Once, they came to the Western factories swathed in chains like common criminals to make their plea. Yet to hand over accused people on the demand of a mandarin would almost certainly end in a lynching after a travesty of a trial.

The Chinese Emperor, Daoguang, decided a show of strength was needed. Lin was chosen because of his seniority, experience and familiarity with southern Chinese and Western merchants. He was by birth Fujianese and had held a Governor Generalship at Hubei and Hunan where opium suppression was his chief concern. The son of a poor scholar, he was posted to Guangzhou at the age of fifty-three and in his previous post of Governor of Gansu, he had formed the view that the perfidious British were not to be trusted. He had experienced a case where the master of a trading ship tried to wangle its way into port on the pretence of being diverted by a storm while sailing to Japan. The master then gave his ship a false name so that when the case was reported to Guangzhou, the EIC could disown it.

Lin had scored successes in clamping down on salt smugglers and had turned his hand to writing a detailed paper on the opium problem. He had ideas also about how to staunch the outflow of Chinese silver — controlling the trade in tea in much the same way as the Organisation for Petroleum Exporting Countries dealt with oil exports more than 100 years later, by fixing prices and controlling supply — but the historian, Arthur Waley, felt this might only have driven the opium traders to redouble their efforts.

Lin was a remarkable man for his time; he was both zealous and incorruptible, and local worthies in Guangzhou had given him a list of sixty offenders who were flouting the imperial edict and spreading the 'foreign mud' within Guangdong Province. Most were either civil servants, soldiers or seamen, serving, retired or cashiered. But even before reaching Guangzhou he had sent out warrants for their arrest. One of his first tasks on reaching the Guangdong capital was to embark on a tour of inspection with his staff. He made it one of his cardinal rules that there would be no free lunches, no hospitality, no presents. Nor did he want to be bothered by people trying to impress him with their theories on how to solve the problem; he would punish self-seekers severely. Lin wanted not advice but action, and in the the first few months of his tenure, 70,000 opium pipes were surrendered and destroyed. He may not have scared British traders, but he certainly had the locals running for cover.

Lin's more positive measures were directed at arousing various classes of the population to the seriousness of the problem. He addressed teachers, students, civil servants, soldiers, peasants, sailors, and those on coast watch duties; finally he called for a re-examination of all who were supposed to be acting as guarantors for others to assess their effectiveness. He also applied much greater pressure on the Hong merchants whom he suspected of colluding with importers.

He was harsh in levelling blame on the people of Guangdong who, in Lin's opinion, had the worst reputation in China for their involvement with opium. Unearth a racket and you'll find a Cantonese behind it; this was his belief based on experience in other parts of China. He accepted, however, that opium was not just a problem of imports. The home-grown variety also had to be tackled though most Chinese viewed the local 'mud' as inferior in terms of potency to the foreign variety. Besides, resolute action taken in the past had only succeeded in pushing opium-growing areas to the extremities of the country where they could not be controlled.

Finally, consideration was given to sending official letters to the King (or later, Queen) of England, believing, as Macartney and Amherst did, that results were likely to be achieved only by going to the top. To attempt this level of communication, Lin would have needed a far higher calibre of writer than the linguists who were "low-grade men of not much education and able to speak only pidgin English"[1] and who were known to the

---

1. J. L. Cranmer-Byng, *Journal of the Royal Asiatic Society* (Hong Kong), vol. 4, 1964.

merchants by such names as "Old Tom," "Young Tom," Alanci and Ahi.

Lin, however, had more educated men to call upon — notably the Jesuits in Beijing. The eloquence of the letters and the force of argument was irrelevant because though written and sent through various sources they apparently never reached their destination. But there was no doubt that everyone in Britain, from the Queen downwards, was fully aware that (a) opium was being freely imported, (b) China was strongly opposed to it and (c) it had embarked on strenuous measures to suppress it. Equally clear was that the British Government would do nothing to curb it.

Apart from complying with Lin's demand to surrender all opium stocks, an action which only played into the hands of the war lobby in England, Britain's men on the spot could do nothing to curtail the trade, though for a few months it was diverted or suspended. At the same time, Britain sent naval and military units to China to protect its interests. The hypocrisy of the British reaction was compounded in the eyes of Lin and his entourage, by their profession of a superior religion and higher morality which missionaries like Morrison and Gutzlaff and the Jesuits in Beijing wished to propagate among the Chinese people. If this was Western civilization at its best, little wonder the Chinese drew strength from their own culture, traditions and beliefs and preferred to exclude these foreign influences.

Captain Charles Elliot, the other key figure in the opium dispute, acted in the capacity of Superintendent of British Trade following the death of Lord Napier; he had served earlier on Napier's staff in charge of all British ships and crews within the Pearl River, though not beyond it. From the outset, Elliot's role in Guangzhou was hindered by protocol formalities, urged on by a determined Palmerston in London who wanted direct communication, one to one, with the Viceroy of Guangdong and nothing less. Palmerston was not the Foreign Secretary of one of the strongest military and economic powers in Europe to be pushed around by any oriental potentate, particularly when Britain was paying China top dollars for a rising volume of tea and silk.

Moreover, Palmerston's brief to Elliot was far from specific in its failure to spell out alternative courses of action or likely consequences. Elliot's concern was not with the opium trade, which was under the counter, but with the tea and silk trade which was over the counter. What Palmerston ignored was that one branch of the trade impacted on the other, and when Chinese officials banned all trade and demanded the surrender of all the opium stocks held by the British, Elliot was the one who was expected to respond. While, in his own words, he had a "quarter-deck education and knew how to duck his head in a storm."[2] He was given no course or bearing to enable him to find a way out of the storm. The smuggling by British traders became more brazen as Lin became more strident and shrill in his denunciations; as Elliot could not ignore what was happening to private British traders, as his East India Company predecessors might have done, he was thrust into the central role, with Palmerston half a world away.

Elliot was isolated and marooned. He might as well have been on a desert island; not even smoke signals to a passing ship could help him. The eastern telegraph was still decades away. The Suez Canal would not be completed until 1869. The means of international communication were still archaic in spite of the Industrial Revolution. Elliot had no more idea of what was going on in England, much less in Palmerston's mind, than the last letter of instruction written months earlier. In a situation changing with the speed of light, Elliot was left floundering in the dark. The evident deterioration, gleaned from rumour and scuttlebutt in the Admiralty, prompted Palmerston to send a large battleship to the scene, HMS *Wellesley*, and while this helped to steady the nerve of

---

2. Clagette Blake, *Charles Elliot, RN, 1801–1875* (London: Cleaver-Hume Press, 1960).

the British traders when a riotous mob invaded the foreign factories, it did not impress the Chinese who had seen British gunboats often in the past and recognized them as the harbingers of
trouble, but biting insects rather than ravenous tigers.

Figure 7.1 Chinese soldiers in training, witnessed by Auguste Borget.

When Lin turned up the heat he made an interesting discovery. This conscientious, diligent but somewhat cautious naval
officer felt obliged to extend his authority to the trade going on
outside the river as well as inside. This was what Lin wanted and
he was then able to throw down his trump card, demanding not
just a token handover but a complete surrender of all opium
stocks held by British traders. At the same time he placed them all
under house arrest, stopped all food supplies, withdrew all
Chinese servants, and had every intention of starving them into
submission. Elliot, who had bravely sailed in his pinnace to the
factories to remain with the merchants during the showdown,
became a virtual prisoner and he had no alternative but to comply. By turning off the supply of food and water, Lin was able to
exert pressure at the slightest sign of delay or hesitation. Calling

for deliveries of opium stocks in four consignments he agreed to minor relaxations of the ban on food with each compliance. Confident of success he sent back boasting reports to his Emperor. Alas they were not always truthful and Daoguang was lulled into a sense of optimism, bordering on chest-beating triumph. At last the wretched barbarians were being forced into line; at last Chinese tactics were paying off.

In the tense weeks during which this drama was being played out, the merchants and seamen from nearby ships amused themselves with scarcely a thought for the hapless Elliot who agonized in silence. Drake may have bowled as the Spanish armada sailed up the English Channel, Nelson may have written billets-doux to Lady Hamilton as he waited for Villeneuve off Cadiz, but Elliot was left to contemplate the ever more depressing scene unfolding outside his window. There were moments of light relief: at the British factory one intrepid sailor climbed the flagpole right to the very top, to the loud hurrahs of his shipmates; another leapt upon a horse and rode it full pelt around the recreation ground to the cheers of Chinese and European on-lookers; on another day it was a game of cricket (scores not available) and on another, a game of leapfrog — "much to the amusement of the Chinese," wrote W. C. Hunter. "The sailors, of whom there are thirty-eight here, afford us the most fun by their queer games."[3] They were also useful in being able to help the merchants in such mundane tasks as boiling rice, milking the cow, sweeping the floors and doing the washing-up.

In London, Palmerston came under immediate pressure from not just the British traders in China, but the opium industry in India, caught with as many cases awaiting shipment, demanding compensation and support. Jardine alone had more than 7,000 chests on the wharfside in Calcutta. Palmerston was under their

---

3. W. C. Hunter, "Journal of Occurances at Canton," *Royal Asiatic Society Journal* (Hong Kong), vol. 4, 1964.

thumb. Horrified at the bill the British Government was being asked to foot, he urged Elliot to demand compensation for the action taken against the traders held under Lin's house arrest. In these instructions he also called on Elliot to demand the cession of "one or more sufficiently large and properly situated islands" on which British traders could live. He also sought reparations for the cost of the British military expedition sent to safeguard British trade.

Meanwhile, back at his *yamen* (office), Lin was tightening the screws on Elliot each day; he not only demanded the surrender of all the opium but wanted a bond from merchants on future trade. At this point, negotiations broke down, and although some merchants signed, others refused, as did Elliot, realizing it would be a dead letter, achieving nothing. Already, British trade was finding its way past Lin's embargo in neutral ships (particularly Americans who made a fortune) and there was no doubt in Elliot's mind that however many signed such a bond, with or without the seal of his approval, the traffic would resume immediately — as it did after the surrender of all 20,291 chests costing over $10 million.

To make matters worse, another Chinese resident was killed in a clash with British sailors near Kowloon Bay where British ships were sheltering — a clear sign of where the British were thinking of hoisting their flag if things got too hot in Guangzhou. When Lin heard of the killing he demanded the instant surrender of the person responsible, threatening to send troops to Macau to exert pressure on British people still living there during the summer when the trade was in abeyance. The Portuguese Governor has been accused of spineless compliance with China, but Lisbon had long ceased to be a great imperial power and was in any case unable to offer protection to the British. The Governor sensibly preferred neutrality to jeopardizing the security of his 30,000 people.

The remaining British, mainly families, were forced to evacuate Macau and boarded ships which took refuge in Hong

Figure 7.2 Chinese military camp on the outskirts of Macau, as seen by Auguste Borget.

Kong waters. The Portuguese Governor was given a demonstration of Lin's military muscle when the Commissioner sent 1,000 Chinese bannermen and tiger-troops (so-called because of the tiger-striped leotard uniform they wore) in a procession through the streets of Macau. Lin warned the Governor never to allow the British to return. If anything demonstrated to the British the futility of using Macau as a base or even an alternate place of residence, the events of the summer of 1839 removed all doubt. Some British families did move back to Macau, though unobtrusively, because the Macau Governor felt that any open defiance of Lin would provoke a showdown. Lin, of course, knew of their return but chose to ignore it. Nothing happened without his knowledge.

Those who decided to tough it out on the ships formed a miserable impression of Hong Kong with its hot, sticky weather, overshadowed by a towering cloud-shrouded peak of the kind Moses must have climbed to receive the Ten Commandments. No commandments descended from on high, however, and no manna dropped from heaven. The mosquitoes and ever-trickling beads of humidity and fast-growing mould created tension, anxiety and frustration. To add to their misery, the local villagers either refused to supply food or water or charged so much for it that everyone was put on strict rations.

Those going ashore could be certain of being chased and pelted with stones. Some armed parties did venture ashore on foraging raids and for recreation, but for most of those on board it was an agonizing ordeal. On top of this Elliot's perceived weakness in surrendering to Lin's demands helped to strengthen a mood of hostility and belligerence among villagers. It also helped convince many British traders that only a show of force would enable them to secure a base and place of residence and achieve an environment where merchants could buy and sell, free of extortion, arbitrary regulations and crippling duties.

Looking back, the abolition of the EIC monopoly in 1833 not only achieved nothing but served to aggravate the situation and opened the door to unrestrained importation of opium and thus precipitated the 1839 crisis. British traders caught trying to revive the trade were told they would face the death penalty, the same law that was applied to Chinese perpetrators (reflected in the laws applying to drug smugglers in Thailand, Malaysia and Singapore today). Fifteen British traders, moreover, were named as notorious opium dealers who were ordered out of the country. Jardine had already left; the others would be made to follow. Innes conveniently died. Lin wished more would join him.

While Lin set about publicly destroying the surrendered opium — often with lunch and dinner parties for sympathetic foreigners to witness — the machinery of war was activated by both sides. Lin realized that Britain would not take this lying down and inspected the cannon at two of the batteries at the mouth of the Pearl River, one of which was newly erected. In Elliot's case, an armed merchant ship, the 1,080-ton *Cambridge* arrived, and was chartered for eight months' service. Others would follow until Britain had twenty ships standing off Hong

Figure 7.3 How an unknown Chinese artist portrayed the first English
       paddle steamer to sail into the China Sea.

Kong and twenty-seven transports carrying 4,000 Irish, Scottish
and Indian troops. Among the armed ships were the first four
paddle-wheeled steamers to make their way up the South China
Sea.

These would prove invaluable in towing and manoeuvring
landing boats through shallow waterways. The most highly
publicized of these steamers was the Nemesis, captained by W.
Hutcheon Hall, and designed to sail into rivers with a two-metre
draught to bombard forts and land troops. She was armed with
two 32-pounders and five six-pounders and equipped with
several revolutionary features including water-tight compartments designed to keep her afloat even if her ironsides were holed

by enemy fire. Lin described them as "cartwheel ships that put the axles in motion by means of fire, and can move rather fast." She was the first of a new breed of naval steamer which would revolutionize naval warfare and give her access to many ports protected by sand bars or shallow approaches — of which Guangzhou, Shanghai and Tianjin were typical. She was also the forerunner of merchantmen capable of carrying bigger cargoes much greater distances regardless of wind and tide. The paddle wheels, pioneered on American waterways and used in hundreds during the Civil War, were ideal for river work but would eventually give way to twin-screw propellers.

Presiding over the British fleet was Charles Elliot's cousin, Admiral George Elliot, who was also made senior plenipotentiary with new instructions from Palmerston, but again based on events four months prior to his arrival in Guangzhou. These required him to compel the Chinese to sign a treaty after British forces occupied one of the Zhoushan islands off Ningbo. Failing this, Britain would blockade China's two main northern river systems, the Yangzi and the Yellow (Huanghe). This was based on the misconception that by throttling China's external and coastal trade it would rapidly bring the country to its knees. Palmerston was almost as ignorant about China as the Chinese about Britain. China did not need sea access, with its elaborate internal waterways capable of carrying virtually all its supplies to various points in the country.

Palmerston denounced Lin's measures to seize the opium stocks, deplored the use of force to exact compliance, demanded repayment of the cost of the destroyed opium and called for the opening of five ports on the China coast (Xiamen, Fuzhou, Shanghai, Ningbo and Guangzhou) where British consuls and superintendents would live. The British also wanted to set up their own courts in the treaty ports to try any Briton accused of a crime committed in China, as well as to hear any civil cases — in short, extraterritoriality.

In these orders, the hand of the powerful China lobby

masterminded by Jardine,[4] was clearly seen and foreshadowed future British policy for the next century. Once again there was no *quid pro quo* for China to open up trading bases in Britain with consuls and trade superintendents; not that China, with its self-contained economy had asked for it, but the failure of Palmerston to offer any reciprocity demonstrated his own myopic imperial vision based on the perceived ascendancy of Britain.

As one British critic, the Quaker William Storrs Fry, had said, if France had encouraged smugglers to ship wine into England in the face of an official prohibition, this would have led to war.[5] The only sop Palmerston offered was a statement that Britain was ready to consider abandoning opium manufacture in India, but only when China was ready to free trade from the irksome restrictions placed upon it in the past. But even that offer was a worthless bargaining chip, for nothing would stop British traders seeking opium supplies elsewhere from countries such as Turkey or Persia, or indeed opening plantations in other parts of its growing empire, in order to satisfy demand in China.

Moreover, Palmerston gave little thought to the problems of enforcing a prohibition in a country as vast as India where the writ of British rule was not universal, with several large independent states within the Subcontinent beyond the pale, including Mysore, Hyderabad, Orissa, Rajputana, Baluchistan and Kashmir, not to mention the independent French and Portuguese settlements. The ultimate hypocrisy, however, was that exports of opium were not a speculative trade by a handful of spivvy salesmen; more than 80 per cent of the opium exports were prepared specifically for the Chinese market — basically "designer drugs" taking into account local preferences. Moreover, its effects,

---

4. Described in Disraeli's "Sybil" as "a dreadful man, richer than Croesus, one McDrug, fresh from Canton with a million of opium in each pocket, denouncing corruption and bellowing free trade."
5. Brian Inglis, *The Opium War* (London: Hodder & Stoughton, 1976).

far from being unknown, were well-known both in India and London. The drug had been introduced in Assam some years earlier, with devastating results on the populace.

So important did the China trade — tea and opium — become to Britain and India that one-sixth of their combined revenue depended on it. Without the income from opium, the East India Company (and later the Government of India) would have collapsed; it earned between one and two million pounds a year with profit margins of 300 to 500 per cent. And as prices of opium began to fall in China in the late 1830s, with the glut being shipped in, the Company's answer was to force up production to maintain revenue levels. As one writer remarked, the Government became as addicted to revenue as Chinese buyers to the drug.[6] In short, the British Government, ultimately responsible for India, went to war with China, not to maintain free trade or to redress the arbitrary action of Commissioner Lin, but to protect its revenue and its balance of payments.

Lin's reply to Palmerston ignored the British demands entirely and instead published a list of rewards for the seizure of British ships, members of their crews and the armed forces (not at that stage deployed in the Guangzhou area, but frequently exercising on Hong Kong island and Kowloon in preparation for landing at points on the Pearl River estuary). Admiral Elliot's response to this was to sail north to deliver his demands to a mandarin up the coast and, in passing, to occupy the island of Zhoushan and raise the British flag.

Elliot's ruse paid off because he was able to hand over his letter at the mouth of the Beihe River to a senior official in attendance to the throne, named Qishan. Surprisingly he accepted it and relayed it to Beijing. Shocked by the effrontery of the foreigners in sailing north and occupying Zhoushan, and by the contents of the letter which exposed the failure of Lin's policies to control

---

6. Brian Inglis, *The Opium War*.

the opium traffic, the disillusioned Emperor flew into a rage and sacked him on the spot. Later he recalled him to stand trial.

The sudden change in the Emperor's mood took Lin by surprise. He knew nothing of the mission to the Beihe or the seizure of Zhoushan; only weeks earlier he had been the recipient of fulsome praise by the Emperor and had been promoted to Governor General of Jiangxi and Jiangnan. He had also received a scroll of calligraphy from the Emperor wishing him good luck in his fight to suppress the opium traffic. There was Lin basking in glory and even taking time to study the question paper for candidates at the civil service examination and to attempt his own answers involving the finer points of Chinese poetical expression.

Lin was an outstanding calligrapher and endowed with a poetical skill that won him the respect of many scholars; but as he penned some rhymes of his own, sleeves rolled and brush in hand, suddenly he heard the clatter of hooves in his yamen court-yard and a courier entered and dropped the missive from Beijing on his desk with an ominous thud. Lin's position had seemed unassailable; when the foreign warships had sailed from the Pearl River estuary he believed that the Bogue forts, now bristling with cannon, had given Elliot the fright of his life, little realizing that he intended to sail north to beard the imperial dragon in his den.

Lin tripped on his path to fame not because he had failed to carry out his mandate; he succeeded only too well in bringing the opium dealers to an ignominious surrender of their stocks and in intimidating local distributors. To claim he had stamped out the evil trade, however, would be going too far; that was not humanly possible. Where the unimaginative Qing rulers failed was in their inability to capitalize on the initial success, and in their blind faith in the endurance of the ancient Han civilization.

More than two hundred years had passed since the first Western penetration through the South China Sea, but the Qing court remained aloof, oblivious and unconcerned about what was happening in the rest of the world. Their own sons, leaving the country in droves to take up residence in Southeast Asia, could have told Beijing that while there was not much that was enlightening or admirable about the foreigners, yet scientifically, technologically, industrially and even militarily, Europe had moved out of the Dark Ages into a renaissance that was beginning to change the world.

Lin was sent into exile in a distant province (but was partially rehabilitated a few years later and awarded a lower-ranking governor-generalship) to be replaced by Qishan who was no cleverer than his predecessor. Having told the two Elliots that talks would be held in Guangzhou, he succeeded in persuading the British fleet to sail from the Beihe but then failed to honour his promise. The two Elliots were split on how to deal with the Chinese, one wanting to use force and the other to hold talks, and in the meantime the casualty rate among the British soldiers stationed at Zhoushan was rising rapidly; in a matter of weeks, 10 per cent were dead as dysentery, cholera, diarrhoea and malaria decimated their ranks. Doctors reported that almost every man in uniform had attended a sick-bay muster. But with no mass media coverage to alarm the British public, the unfolding tragedy largely escaped notice at home, until much later.

Besides it was a time of universal brutality; while slavery had been brought under control, convicts shipped to Australia were dying in hundreds en route. Moreover, the British Free Traders were determined to attain their three objectives which Palmerston declared to be: redress of injuries to British subjects, satisfaction for affronts to the British Crown, and security for British property and people trading in China, regardless of the loss of lives in Zhoushan or elsewhere.

Furthermore, news was circulating in London of a growing French interest in acquiring territory in China. At the same time, Russia was beginning to needle Britain about its opium policy. London was in a prickly frame of mind while China was embarking on a dangerous course of feigned conciliation through protracted talks, a course recommended by the new

Figure 7.4　A Chinese soldier armed with a matchlock gun, seen at Zhoushan by the artist, William Alexander.

Commissioner Qishan, at the same time maintaining a determined defensive stance.

Charles Elliot pressed ahead with his own agenda; talks, yes, but backed by a menacing squadron of naval and military units, and at the top of his list of priorities was the cession of an island where the British flag would fly and British law prevail. The talks dragged on and on until even the patience of Elliot, aware of the need to give face to Qishan, expired and he ordered in two frigates, *Volage* and *Hyacinth*, to batter a fleet of Chinese junks assembled near the Chinese forts at Chuanbi (Chuenpi) and Dajuetou (Taikoktau), causing heavy casualties. The Chinese caved in.

Qishan, armed with full plenipotentiary powers, signed a

convention yielding Hong Kong to the British, agreeing to official diplomatic relations on an equal footing, an additional $6 million indemnity and a resumption of trade at Guangzhou. The Emperor suspected Elliot had bribed him to get such favourable terms. Palmerston, on the other hand, was appalled at Elliot's choice of a sparsely populated island south-east of Guangzhou; initially it was not ceded but verbally leased "like Macau." The Zhoushan group of islands, closer to the tea markets of Ningbo, Shanghai and the Yangzi delta, seemed a far better choice regardless of their unsanitary state and the growing graveyard of British occupation forces. Queen Victoria, that unamused monarch, was convinced "he had tried to get the lowest terms he could." So much for the ingratitude of powerful potentates in both countries.

Figure 7.5 The south gate of the city of Tinghai, Zhoushan, as seen by William Alexander, in 1793.

The guns of January had hardly fallen silent when a new round of fighting broke out in the following month as Qishan was slow to honour promises. Charles Elliot ordered the next line of forts at the Bogue to be taken out, and among the casualties was the highly respected and widely admired Admiral Guan Tianpei, whose courage was such that a British warship fired a salute when his body was removed.

Elliot next ordered boatloads of troops to move upriver to the walls of Guangzhou; before the assault could begin, however, a deputation led by the Hong merchant, Howqua, came out of the city and pleaded that it be spared as all the mandarins had left, including Qishan who had been relieved of his commission and sent back to the capital in chains. A truce was agreed which both the merchants and the Chinese troops used to their advantage — to get 28 million pounds of tea awaiting shipment out of the way, and to reinforce the local defences with thousands of Chinese reserves.

A major Chinese counter-attack began on 29 May, with British ships attacked by fire rafts while the foreign factories were looted and ransacked. Once again the war resumed though with dwindling forces at his command, Elliot was unwilling to send them into Guangzhou. While his reasons may have been sound it was to be his last hurrah. Less than two months later a local English language newspaper carried a report of his dismissal by an ungrateful parliament concerned that he had not acted with enough firmness and had not obtained good enough terms of surrender. His own view on events in China was that "force was requisite but forbearance was indispensable"; in England he was widely criticized for his perceived weakness and his failure to press the attack at the Yangzi estuary.

Elliot, though exiled, was spared the fate of Qishan and Lin and did not have to return home in chains. The Government sent him to Galveston where he was made Consul General to the then republic of Texas. Following this he inherited a clutch of colonial governorships including Bermuda, Trinidad and St Helena; he was also made a Knight Commander of the Bath and promoted to Admiral — in short, ceremoniously and decorously "kicked upstairs." In the light of events and the role Hong Kong would play as a thriving entrepôt serving China and Britain, he deserved better treatment from historians even if his own countrymen were unable to assess the value of his achievements.

His successor was to be a tough Indian Army veteran in the person of Sir Henry Pottinger who with Major-General Sir Hugh Gough, a rugged old soldier with several victories to his credit in Europe, completed the campaign in Guangzhou, carried it north and secured the Treaty of Nanjing. This added Xiamen, Fuzhou, Ningbo and Shanghai as "treaty ports" with extraterritorial privileges for British residents stationed there, and the indemnity was pushed up to $21 million. This time, although the idea of occupying Zhoushan was abandoned, Hong Kong would be ceded, not leased. Needless to say, trade in Guangzhou was at a standstill and for the British, would remain that way for over a year. The Chinese were determined to punish them for their aggression and to demonstrate that this was a case of *force majeure* and unwilling acceptance of an unequal treaty.

The first Opium War plays such a crucial part in the story of the China Sea trade that it has been recounted at some length. The most significant outcome was not the freeing of the opium trade or the defeat of the Chinese forces in somewhat one-sided battles, or even the cession of Hong Kong, but the acceptance by China of equality of treatment not just for British but all Western traders, for the right of residence and foreign jurisdiction and for the beginning of an interflow of two-way trade between China and the West.

Chinese officials could hardly be expected, even in later years, to consider these as significant. They were invariably clouded with pain and bitterness in the knowledge that Britain was determined to ship opium to China in defiance of the court's prohibition. Little imagination is needed to visualize the reaction if the roles had been reversed, if Chinese war junks had succeeded in sailing up the English Channel, seizing perhaps the Isle of Wight and pedalling bootleg opium or gin into the grog shops of London, and then demanding Chinese jurisdiction for the successful smugglers taking up residence. Not only was there no corresponding trading station offered to the Chinese where they might market their tea and silk, but there was no provision for Chinese consular or diplomatic equality in British cities.

The Chinese did not seek such openings but it would have at least evened the scales to have offered them. It would certainly have shown China at first hand how things were done in the West and what was happening there in terms of scientific and industrial development. By opening a window on its own society, it may possibly have spurred reform in China. As it was China remained a remote, closed and deeply resentful nation, unconvinced that the West had anything to communicate that was worth adopting. Britain's action only perpetuated Chinese hostility and antagonism.

It is worth stressing that the Opium War was a wholly British affair. Although many European countries were involved in trade with China and shared the British frustrations, either their stake was small or they had no part in pushing opium. Several shipments were made by United States traders but up to 1830 they carried far more in ginseng, quicksilver, furs, sandalwood and cotton. The pace of the opium trade picked up after 1830 but with their revolutionary experience and the war of 1812 still in mind, the Americans neither wanted to support the British nor carry on a war with China.[7]

The Portuguese also had some share of the opium trade but again shrank from a bellicose stance in Macau, ever conscious of their precarious status. Sweden also sent ships to China. But the

---

7. Notwithstanding an incident a few years later, in which the US consul in Hong Kong planted the Stars and Stripes on the walls of Guangzhou following a British assault. He was duly reprimanded.

Netherlands, with their interests in the East Indies, and Spain in the Philippines, had little or no part in the trade by that time, while France, still searching for a future following the Battle of Waterloo, was out of the picture — though came into it rapidly after the British gained Hong Kong.

Following Bonaparte's defeat, northern European states were almost wholly concerned with keeping the infectious germs of revolution out by raising a *cordon sanitaire* around France. At the Congress of Vienna which followed, there was a widespread redistribution of colonial possessions, with France the biggest loser and Britain and the Netherlands the chief beneficiaries, though mainly in the Caribbean and the Indian Ocean. The return of the East Indies to the Netherlands resulted in Britain's departure from Bencoolen in Java, and its later acquisition of Singapore. Britain claimed it had no desire to become permanent occupants of the East Indies, and had acted largely to thwart French designs. Stamford Raffles, in taking over Singapore, claimed his main concern was safeguarding the route to China.

Officially, Britain was the champion of free trade. Adam Smith had published his book *The Wealth of Nations* in 1776, and among the many deeply impressed was William Pitt (the younger) who became an ardent disciple of freeing trade from the bureaucratic shackles which had throttled it in the past. No less than sixty-eight kinds of customs duties were in force in Britain, many double and triple impositions on individual products. This was Pitt's immediate target, together with substantial tariff reforms which also helped to cut smuggling. Pitt also extended this principle to trade with France, securing tariff cuts for English cottons in return for lower duties on silks and wine. But then war cut short this admirable start.

However, the free trade ethos continued to thrive under people like Richard Cobden and John Bright resulting in the repeal of the Corn Law, and Prime Minister Robert Peel became its strongest advocate. In the 1839 crisis, however, Lord Melbourne, who was Prime Minister, and Lord Palmerston, his

Foreign Secretary, were given a virtual free hand to back British interests wherever they were challenged — even in faraway China. Europeans, on the other hand, tended to shy away from their high-handed actions. Little wonder that Britain was alone in waging war in China. Little wonder that Britain, the victor of Waterloo and convert to free trade, pressured China until it got what it wanted, oblivious of the stain it would inflict on its national character.

Opinion on the outcome in Britain was divided. While the advocates of free trade rejoiced, the many critics of the opium traffic were loud in their denunciations. *The Times* felt that Britain had been guilty of an international crime in pursuing the opium issue and then fighting a war over it. A leading Tory human-itarian, Lord Ashley wrote: "we have triumphed in one of the most lawless, unnecessary and unfair struggles in the records of history" and when the terms of the Treaty of Nanjing were made known, he added that the peace was as wicked as the war. Balzac, the French novelist, declared that "the English flaunt their per-fidiousness in the face of the whole world." Coming after the slave trade, the transportation of convicts to colonize its posses-sions, and the dispossession of native peoples, it was a reputation that would smear its name for the rest of the nineteenth century.

For China, the Treaty of Nanjing would precipitate calamity, destitution, civil war, and finally the overthrow of traditional society. While changes were inevitable if China was to become part of the modern technological world, the pace and direction were dictated by those who had no knowledge of, interest in, or sympathy for Chinese beliefs, values and attitudes. The Anglo-Chinese war in all its detail is not the main theme of this book, though a succession of internal revolts and international clashes during the next 150 years played a leading part in the tragedy that would overtake the country. These will be discussed in sub-sequent chapters.

CHAPTER 8

A Divine Curse

The Opium War of 1839–41, though initially ravaging only Guangzhou and the nearby coast, devastated the country and brought about the collapse of the ancient dynastic system. With it went its traditional economy which had served China for more than 2,000 years. The Qing rulers were admittedly a spent force before the first shots were fired, but the war exacerbated economic conditions to the point where inflation, rural dispossession, unemployment, famine and finally rebellion left the court hopelessly floundering and incapable of running the country.

Amazingly, the throne survived for another seventy years through the sheer personal tenacity of a remarkable woman regent, the Empress Dowager, named Cixi. But for her and the resistance she inspired and the xenophobia she fostered, imperial China would have collapsed years earlier. However, China's downfall came about in a slow motion domino tumble, from south to north. For what the Opium War did was firstly to undermine and destroy the traditional copper cash currency, the everyday medium of exchange of the ordinary people.

For years the people of China bought and sold, transacted business and were paid their wages in copper cash, usually strung together in bundles through a hole in the coin. The basic exchange rate prior to the war was 1,000 cash for each tael of silver. After China suffered a grievous loss of silver in paying for opium imports and after Britain imposed a $21 million war indemnity, the outflow reached a level of 20 to 30 million taels of silver a year. The shortage distorted the exchange rate so that a tael of silver rose to 1,600 cash by 1840 and 2,000 by 1850. While the average peasant or worker used cash as the daily medium of currency he was required to pay taxes in silver. The impact on food prices and basic necessities was immediate.

On top of that, the dumping of foreign imports of machine-made cotton garments and cloth, now freed of Chinese tariffs, cut heavily into local production; handcrafts made by villagers were unable to compete. This was felt particularly in the three provinces most immediately affected by the war, Guangdong, Guangxi and Hunan. In five years after the war, British exports of cotton goods and yarn doubled. To pay for the war indemnity, the local mandarins were expected to raise additional taxes from the people. The Hong merchants who once contributed significantly to the throne's demands, no longer existed as an entity; the tea trade was disrupted and for a time transactions at Guangzhou were at a standstill. The unrest this caused with the doubling of prices of many basic commodities and the shortage of food, led to a collapse of land prices as small holders sought to raise money by selling holdings; in addition there was widespread unemployment not only among rural workers but among soldiers demobilized by a treasury no longer able to support them.

Banditry, piracy and rebellion gripped the south and spread north and west to other provinces. The most coherent of the rebel movements was the Taiping (literally, "great peace") which gathered a group of men imbued with radical ideals and fired by a mishmash of christianity and socialism though encased in a traditional Chinese framework. One of the leaders, Hong Xiuquan, had been a part-time school teacher who was well-educated enough to attempt the civil service examination at Guangzhou several times, though unsuccessfully. While in the city he encountered foreign missionaries and read commentaries on the gospels by Charles Gutzlaff and Robert Morrison; claiming to be inspired by visions he visited an American missionary, Issacher Roberts, but was not accepted into his church.

This meeting, coupled with his humiliating experience of rejection, turned Hong into a rebel who set about destroying idols and attacking army posts and government offices; he was determined to project himself into the mainstream of life at any price. Superstition and authority became his two main targets, convinced, as he was, of the corruption of Chinese beliefs and authority; in the economic ferment of the times it found a ready response among the hungry and homeless.

Like a Chinese Cromwell he raised a model army, introduced an organized system of command with divisions, brigades, companies, platoons and squads and conscripted men and women in separate units all operating under strict codes of discipline. In the early years at least they fought with puritanical zeal and won stunning victories.

It was during this rebellion that the Chinese statesman, Zeng Guofan, tried to create a navy which he assembled on Lake Dongting in 1854 but the Taipings surrounded it and sent it to the bottom. Zeng then launched another, using foreign steamboats and foreign armaments, as well as junks; this was more successful in staying afloat though causing little disturbance to the Taipings. At the end of the rebellion the Yangzi fleet was manned by 12,000 seamen, and proved useful in ferrying troops to various threatened areas along the river. As a navy capable of protecting China, it served no purpose but in harnessing Western technology to a national need it demonstrated that there were lessons to be learned and advantages to be gained.

The Taipings were initially unstoppable and swarmed over eleven provinces between 1851 and 1865 and during their years of rule an estimated 10 million lost their lives. The rebels captured Nanjing where Hong declared himself to be the head of a new "Great Peace Heavenly Kingdom." He styled himself Tian Wang or Heavenly King. His rule spread over large parts of the Yangzi valley, and though they staged a march through four provinces aimed at taking Beijing they failed, and a decline in their ranks set in.

As both the Qing army and the rebels lived off the land the plight of the peasants worsened. Dissensions grew among the leaders, ammunition dwindled, Qing troops reinforced by Western mercenaries, gained the upper hand and finally in a massive assault on Nanjing the walls were breached and a wholesale slaughter of the rebels took place. Confronted by failure, Hong took his own life.

One of the Jardine family then in Guangzhou, Joseph, wrote to his cousin, Rachel, in Lockerbie, Dumfriesshire, telling her of one of the clashes which took place in September 1854. He wrote: "It is rather amusing to see how the combatants carry on the fighting which we can do quite distinctly from the tops of our houses with the aid of a glass. They generally begin work at daylight by a grand discharge of great guns which never appears, however, to do any harm, and then they advance to within a quarter of a mile of one another with no end of flags flying and drums and tom toms beating, when they call a halt. Small parties are then sent forward from the main bodies who after discharging two or three rounds at one another at a respectable distance, quietly retire and allow others to take their place and so on until 8 o'clock when by mutual consent apparently they make it break- fast time. In the evening the same farce is repeated except when it rains, when their matchlocks being rendered useless they do sometimes get to close quarters, much to their astonishment, I'll be bound." War may have been a bit of a giggle to Joseph Jardine watching from the security of a foreign enclave but to millions of Chinese the consequences were sheer misery.

The intervention of the so-called Ever Victorious Army, led by foreigners, particularly the American Frederick Ward and the British Charles Gordon (who met his death twenty-one years later from a dervish spear in besieged Khartoum), helped tip the balance against the rebels, and led to a belated attempt to work out reforms for an archaic and discredited government in Beijing. Gordon and Ward, for all their prowess in the field, proved prickly and difficult in their relations with the Chinese commanders. The Governor of Jiangsu, Li Hongzhang, complained in his memorials to Beijing of Gordon's bad temper although he acknowledged he was "brave enough"; if Li had had his way Gordon would have been sacked but British diplomatic pressure, particularly on the part of Consul General Harry Parkes, kept him in charge of the Ever Victorious Army until victory was assured.

Gordon, for his part, upset the Chinese frequently by his displays of moral and military superiority; he was scathing of the Chinese for their summary execution of the eight top henchmen of the Taiping rebels (known as the "bogus kings") after the capture of Suzhou. The "kings" had surrendered the city on condition their lives would be spared. Gordon's sense of honour was outraged by Li's action. Yet unquestionably he instilled discipline in what was little better than an armed rabble and turned them into a credible fighting force; in acknowledging his efforts the Chinese Government promoted him to Brigadier General and awarded him the high honour of the Yellow Riding Jacket.

Ward, the ever flamboyant, swashbuckling, reckless and dashing soldier of fortune, who recruited the Ever Victorious Army in the face of Allied opposition, met his death near Ningbo, killed by a rebel bullet. He was the quintessential American daredevil who led from the front, revolver in hand, under a broad-brimmed hat, with flowing locks and long moustache, epitomizing the legend of hell-bent heroes in quest of blood or glory. He was one of several Allied officers to lose their lives in action against the Taipings. Without their support, the already tottering Qing dynasty would have been overthrown. The Taipings, for their part, were merciless with foreign captives, some of whom were flayed alive with strips of leather glued to their inner thighs and ritually torn off at regular intervals until death relieved them of their agony.

The Taiping Rebellion was only one of a number of tragedies

to overtake China in the years following the Opium War. Its impact was as devastating as the Black Death on Europe 400 years earlier, and the social and economic dislocation it caused sapped its energies in years when its territory, traditions and institutions came under sustained attack not only from Western nations but the new upstart of the Orient, Japan, swift to adopt reforms under the energetic Meiji emperor after its forced opening by the American navy under Commodore Matthew Perry.

In a memorial to the throne, Li Hongzhang wrote of the terrible conditions he had encountered in the once densely populated, and thriving countryside of Jiangsu. "Now we see nothing but weeds, briars and hazels obstructing the roads; for 20 or 30 *li* there may be no inhabitants. At times, among the broken walls and ruined buildings, one or two orphan children or widows survive out of a hundred inhabitants. Their faces have no colour and they groan while waiting for death. When asked about their livelihood, they answer that they live on grass and roots to survive." Li added: "my heart grows sick when I see these terrible conditions with my own eyes." He appealed for suspension of the local grain contribution until conditions recovered.

Suicides and emigration soared in the wake of the rebellion, as did the practice of infanticide, for in conditions of poverty and hunger the unwanted child was considered better off dead. China's suicide rate was always alarming to Western observers, unable to comprehend the circumstances and reasoning that prompted so many to put an end to their misery. Rural women in particular were regarded as little more than chattels with a status barely higher than a farm animal; the widespread custom of polygamy and concubinage led to rivalries, jealousy, bitterness and despair involving other wives, mothers-in-law, parents and husbands, often ending in suicide by young women desperately trying to avoid such a fate. Equally abhorrent was the sale of young girls as domestic slaves to prosperous households, or as prostitutes.

In the case of men, poverty, unemployment, and the ever

present threat of arbitrary persecution for some real or imagined misdemeanour, and the free use of the death penalty for the accused, made suicide a preferable option for many. In the aftermath of the Opium War and the Taiping Rebellion many chose to take their lives rather than continue living in the hellish conditions of those times. In 1898, in another period of extreme tension, a writer estimated that in western China half a million people were driven to suicide, with a high probability that most would succeed if not on the first attempt then subsequently.[1] The favoured method there was an overdose of opium, easily obtainable and cheap because it was grown nearby.

On the east coast of China, a more hopeful solution presented itself when in 1848 gold was discovered in California, precipitating a rush of about 80,000 people to the west coast of America, which continued for much of the rest of the century and which in turn led to the building of the Union Pacific Railway. For Chinese people seeking a new life, there was now an alternative in the "Gold Mountain" ("Gum San") on the other side of the Pacific Ocean, and later a new Gold Mountain ("Sun Gum San") was discovered in the state of Victoria in Australia. The Chinese moved in swiftly but others had been clamouring for their services as well — the Spaniards to harvest sugar in Cuba and to work mines in Peru, and the British to work plantations in the West Indies and Malaya.

To the unemployed Chinese labourer, known as "coolies" (based on a Turkish word, *kuli*, meaning a slave) the prospect of a new life overseas and the promise of $4 a month (out of which their fares would be deducted) lured more than half a million people. But the shipping conditions and their living quarters overseas were a severe indictment of colonial policy in tolerating a variation of the Atlantic slave trade of the previous century.

---

1. See J. Dyer Ball, *Things Chinese* (Shanghai: Kelly & Walsh, 1903).

The trade was conducted from Macau and Hong Kong but in the latter case was stopped in 1855 because of a number of shocking cases of brutality and butchery at sea by ruthless captains who treated the slaves as another kind of cargo. While Hong Kong abolished the contract emigration in which men were "shanghaied" and smuggled out of China, self-paying emigrants continued to leave at the rate of 12,000 a year. In 1859 whole families were persuaded to leave for the Demerara River area in British Guiana to grow sugar, and more than 2,700 women with husbands and children sailed for Georgetown in a period of four years.

Three years later, the British West Indies emigration office was switched to Guangzhou to provide closer supervision of the method of transportation. The only positive statistic to record was that by 1863, there were as many Chinese men returning to Hong Kong as were leaving, many carrying gold they had mined, but many also the victims of hastily legislated racial exclusion laws which forced them out of their adopted home. India and Tahiti were other destinations for emigrants as well as San Francisco, Vancouver and Alaska during the years of the gold mining boom. However, in the frightful shipboard conditions many did not survive the voyage and in the 1850s it was estimated that from 15 to 45 per cent of those embarked were being buried at sea, or more bluntly, dumped overboard following illness, mutiny or starvation.

The United States Commissioner in China, William B. Reed, was particularly vigorous in trying to stamp out American involvement in the trade at Shanghai, Xiamen and Macau, as was Sir Harry Parkes, British Consul in Guangzhou; but the same cannot be said of the Spanish Consul General at Shanghai who refused to take action because he received a fee of $5 for every coolie shipped. Reed moved against two American ships in 1857, *Flora Temple*, in the waters off Macau, and *Wandering Jew*, in Shanghai. With what little powers he had, Reed threatened legal action against the captains but his success was limited; in one case the captain discharged his cargo of labourers in Shanghai only to sail down the coast to a deserted and unsupervised spot where the "nefarious gangs of crimps" had a fresh load ready to be pushed aboard.

Parkes's colleague, Rutherford Alcock, reported: "The acts of violence and fraud connected with the coolie trade at Guangzhou have lately reached such a pitch of atrocity that a general feeling of alarm spread through the population, accompanied by the degree of excitement and popular indignation which rendered it no longer possible or safe for any authority interested in the peace of the place to remain inactive. When no man could leave his own house, even in public thoroughfares and open day, without a danger of being hustled, under false pretences of debt or delinquency, and carried off a prisoner in the hands of the crimps, to be sold to the purveyors of coolies at so much a head, and carried off to sea, never to be heard of again, the whole population of the city and adjoining districts were roused to a sense of common peril."[2]

A Briton named John Gardiner Austin brought about more orderly arrangements for their dispatch overseas, in co-operation with the Guangzhou authorities; this led to the abolition of the floating hulks (formerly for storing opium) which held the coolies prior to transportation, and the establishment of a centre in the city for all who wished to leave. Parkes claimed that it was also "rigorously" watched by the Allied authorities in Guangzhou "to provide the fullest protection for the emigrants and render all coercion in their engagement or shipment impossible." Parkes acknowledged that clandestine kidnapping could not be abolished but abuses, so far as the British consular authorities were concerned, became a thing of the past.

Reed, the American Commissioner, found that despite his strenuous efforts, American captains resorted to the subterfuge of

---

2. Stanley Lane-Poole, *Harry Parkes in China* (London: Methuen, 1901).

claiming that they were carrying workers from Shanghai to Xiamen. In a report to the US Secretary of State in February 1858, he again strongly denounced the trade to the West Indies as a "traffic of the most pernicious kind, morally, socially and economically." He noted that Australia had imposed a capitation tax of ten pounds a head; he considered this action and the voyage of a few weeks as far less obnoxious than the trade to Cuba in which ships carried coolies on a voyage lasting five months "in every variety of climate and no restriction imposed on them as to numbers or discipline." One such ship of New York registry, he noted, had just entered port with a cargo of coal and would return to Cuba with 2,000 coolies on board.

In one case, Reed was able to report a minor success when his interpreter in Shanghai, Frederick Jenkins, boarded *Wandering Jew* to question 200 coolies on board. "After questioning seventy or eighty," reported Jenkins, "one old man got down on his knees and begged to be taken on shore, as he had a wife and three children at home who were almost starving; he said he had been enticed on board by the payment of $3 and if they would let him go, he would get some of his friends to refund the money."

Jenkins found that the majority were totally ignorant of their condition, and when told of their destination "many begged to be allowed to go ashore as they had families who were dependent on them for support." Jenkins concluded that of the more than 200 on board not more than thirty realized they were going abroad and all had been lured aboard with money. Most thought they were being conscripted for the Chinese army.[3]

In another case, Reed reported that a steamer had been chartered to tow a lorcha (a local sailing boat) full of coolies to the port of Shantou, where they were to be loaded aboard a slaver bound for Cuba. The steamer cast off its tow just outside the

---

3. US Congressional Papers, *Chinese Correspondence 1857–1859* (Washington DC, 1860).

entrance to the port and the coolies rose up and seized the vessel, plundered it, ran it ashore and escaped. Not so fortunate was another large batch of labourers being carried to Cuba, who rose in revolt but were forced by the crew back into the holds. They then set fire to the ship and despite strenuous efforts to extinguish it the vessel burnt to the waterline with no survivors.

For all the horrors perpetrated by the slavers, there were many successes among the emigrants, none more colourful than a young Chinese named Quong Tart who arrived in Australia in 1859 aged nine, en route to the goldfields in Braidwood, New South Wales, with "about 50 of the gentlemen of the long queue," as a local newspaper reported. Quong was adopted and brought up by a family of Scottish miners who lived with several other Scots; so it was hardly surprising that as he acquired a smattering of English, he spoke it with a distinct Aberdonian brogue. Moreover, he learnt from the miners some of the poetry of Robert Burns; his star turn at the camp social evening was to leap on to the stage in a kilt and recite the beloved Scottish bard to cheering home-sick miners.

Quong grew up a confirmed anglophile and in spite of the xenophobic feelings raging around the camps at the influx of Chinese fortune-hunters, he was accepted as a "local." Not only was he a witty speaker he danced reels to the bagpipes, played cricket and eventually made a big strike of gold — not just a nugget but a reef.

In an age when Chinese were regarded as the "Yellow Peril" (a phrase coined by Count Otto von Bismarck of Prussia) Quong brought calm and quiet dignity to the cause of racial tolerance and equality. If he failed in his attempt to raise the status of Chinese and all coloured immigrants to Australia that was because of the temper of the times. His most striking act of patriotism was to join the National Guard in Sydney when the Boer War broke out; although at the age of fifty he never contemplated serving on the veld, Quong was ready to take his part on the home front while the younger men went overseas. Married to an English woman he was a prominent tea merchant who also had a popular tea room in the city of Sydney.

He was renowned in later life as a great benefactor, and as a leader of the Chinese community he was honoured by the Qing Government and made a mandarin of the fifth class with a crystal button and peacock feather. He was the unofficial ambassador for China in Australia and the foremost representative of his people in Sydney. He campaigned against opium and mediated in the all-too-frequent tong (*tang*) wars and when he died in 1902, after a murderous attack on him in his office, 1,500 people attended his funeral, representing the cream of Sydney society.

Quong Tart was one of the few newcomers to win the respect of their adopted communities which he and hundreds of thousands of Chinese joined mainly on the Pacific fringe — notably the United States, Canada, Peru, New Zealand and Australia. For while they were valued by potential employers as cheap labour their arrival in increasing numbers threatened to undercut local wage levels, undermine trade unions, destabilize the economy and introduce racial imbalances which could prove explosive.

As the wave of emigration built up so attempts to regulate the influx were initiated in many of the host territories, which ranged from capitation charges on all Chinese landing, to strict limitation of the numbers admitted. The Australian colonial legislatures in New South Wales and Victoria, the two states convulsed by the gold rush, also gave vent to an anti-Chinese frenzy which included laws restricting their entry.

Undaunted, the Chinese took ship to Robe in South Australia and marched overland to the Victorian goldfields. This precipitated serious riots and a display of racial bigotry and hatred that would institutionalize a "White Australia" policy for another 100 years, and to which all political parties subscribed. Not for them the coloured curse of a mongrel nation. Nor was the land of the free on the other side of the Pacific much better, though it waited until 1882 for Congress to push through the first of its

Chinese Exclusion Acts, effectively prohibiting the entry of Chinese coolies for a period of ten years with extensions in 1892, and then indefinitely in 1902.

The effect was to reduce the Chinese population in the US from 107,000 in 1890 to 75,000 forty years later, the laws not being finally repealed until 1943 when China was an ally of the US in World War II. The acts were a repudiation of the Burlingame Treaty of 1868 which established free immigration between the two countries; they were also a hypocritical disavowal of the "open door" policy the United States had traditionally extended to the world's destitute, oppressed and deprived people.

They were followed by a wave of massacres, murders and racist legislation; in California, Chinese were forbidden to use pavements when shouldering a carrying pole, and high licence fees were imposed for carrying laundry in anything but a horse-drawn wagon. Tens of thousands of Chinese, however, went on living in the US, dodging officialdom, moving deeper and deeper into the backwoods and small towns of middle America, clinging desperately to any document which purported to legalize their status, frantically scraping together a fistful of dollars or a bag of gold nuggets which would allow them in their old age to return proudly to China to die in the land of their birth.

One author tells of the woman described on her gravestone as Polly Bemis, who entered America on a slave ship as Lalu Nathoy.[4] Having been reared in the Chinese countryside, she survived famine, flood and drought, was kidnapped by brigands, sold into slavery and exported to the fleshpots of the Gold Mountain. Entering through San Francisco, she was auctioned to a Chinese saloon keeper in a mining camp in Idaho. Lalu had none of the luck of Quong Tart, to be billeted to a family of friendly Scottish miners. She was the barmaid to a tough beer-swilling,

4. Ruthanne Lum McCunn, *Thousand Pieces of Gold* (San Francisco: Design Enterprises, 1981).

card-playing, cigar-smoking, gun-toting crowd of gold diggers, and the chattel of Hong King, the saloon keeper. There she would have remained until a miner named Charlie Bemis won her by gambling all he possessed in a game of poker with Hong King.

Her new owner was as loving and caring and devoted a person as any woman could want and after living together they eventually married. As Polly Bemis, this tiny Chinese woman endured a hard, often bitter, often heart-rending frontier life running her own boarding house, and died as a respected, even revered person at the age of eighty — one of thousands of castaways from Chinese society who enriched American civilization and folklore with their spirit of tenacity, dedication and humanity.

More fortunate was Lue Gim Gong who was employed by a wealthy Boston family with a large orchard. He showed an aptitude for growing new varieties of fruit and his employer bought him a property in Florida to continue his work. His green fingers turned out a succession of fruit that were sweeter, larger, earlier-ripening or able to survive longer on the tree — so much so that he won a silver medal for his new variety of orange — a veritable "plant wizard."

The Western nations on the whole, viewed the Chinese with ill-concealed contempt, happy enough to take advantage of their skills, their tireless energy and perseverance, their tolerance of low wages and long hours, yet unwilling to accord them equality with their own people. Gilbert and Sullivan and other composers could lampoon orientals in comic opera, and the vaudeville theatres of London could always be sure of a laugh when they poked fun at slant-eyed Ching Chong Chinaman, the slavish Chinese laundrymen and the inevitable dope-ridden destitutes of Limehouse, Poplar and Stepney. "John Chinaman" became an object of ridicule and the butt of jokes throughout European society, to be parodied in print, song and on stage; if it was not "Jelly Belly" the famous Weihaiwei tailor who proclaimed

"English spoken, Scotch understood," it was the Shanghai beggar child who chanted "No mama, no papa, no whisky soda."

It grew out of centuries of often abrasive contact with a nation that seemed unwilling to change and unable to compromise. Disparaged as "Chinks" (though the English were equally contemptuous of other Europeans such as "Frogs," "Dagoes" and "Huns"), the Chinese were considered "inscrutable" by ignorant foreigners unable to communicate or find common ground with them. Yet the Chinese were no more inscrutable than any other people who inhabited the globe, though perhaps a little better at sustaining a veil of mystery over their culture, language and attitudes. It was mainly Western intolerance, ignorance and fear that sealed this relationship with mistrust and suspicion, and which had its parallel in the contempt which Chinese people at many levels felt for the "foreign devils" or "fan-kwai lo," terms still commonly in use today.

The Western nations had fought a continuing war through the middle of the last century to free up the flow of trade and particularly the exports of its manufactured goods; it also demanded the right to appoint diplomats, and to enable its traders, missionaries, seamen, salesmen, bankers, insurance brokers, railway builders, tea-tasters and their families to set up in China, with the added bonus of extraterritoriality. It did not come easily. For while the Opium War ended with the signing of treaties which opened Chinese ports to trade and ceded Hong Kong as a British base, the Chinese were reluctant to ratify them. This did not stop foreigners from moving in, but the war dragged on, particularly in Guangzhou where there was strong resistance to occupation by people at every level.

What Britain had achieved in treaty concessions was soon demanded by others, notably the French and the Americans (under the renowned lawyer-diplomat Caleb Cushing) though the treaties remained unratified. The US Commissioner, William Reed, discovered later that the treaty his predecessor had negotiated had never been sent to Beijing. Part of the reason was that the American draft in Chinese was so poorly phrased that the Chinese found parts of it "scarcely intelligible."

It was at this time that the Portuguese also flexed their muscles, conscious of Macau's dubious status during the past 300 years, and forever at the whim of the Chinese mandarinate in Guangzhou. Taking advantage of the strong British military presence and the inability of China to resist, the local Governor, Ferreira de Amaral, annexed the city and turned out the Chinese customs in 1845. He paid with his life when he was murdered in 1849. Eighteen years later after long and difficult negotiations, the Lisbon Protocol Agreement was signed by the two countries granting occupation in perpetuity. Meanwhile rivalries between the British, French and Americans were emerging which the Chinese were keen to exploit. They might well have succeeded had they not dragged out negotiations to the point where they exasperated all of them and ultimately helped to push the three powers into a strong alliance. Earlier, the French had even been offering to build a modern naval fleet for the Chinese. But the Chinese realized they needed more than modern ships; they had bought a former British armed merchantmen, *Cambridge* (later *Chesapeake*), during the Opium War, but the ship had blown up when struck by a broadside fired by the British fleet.

Even more than modern ships, they needed experienced crews with skills of seamanship to match modern gunnery techniques. *Chesapeake*'s fighting men were led by sword-wielding mandarins who were cut to pieces by the rockets and shot of the British attackers. The Chinese soldiers and sailors lacked nothing in daring, bravery or flair in attacking the invaders, but war, as it was fought in the West, was a new and initially demoralizing experience.

Over the centuries, China had experienced sharp bursts of military activity from invasion by nomadic tribes, and insurrection or insurgency by rebels, followed by long periods of peace. For hundreds of years the classic approach to war was enshrined in the saying of Sun Zi: "To win a hundred victories is not the height of skill; rather it is to subdue the enemy without fighting." But this fifth century BC genius also wrote: "If you know the enemy and yourself, in a hundred battles you will never be in danger."

China, however, was now confronted with enemies of a very different kind. Not only were they able to muster overwhelming firepower, but to draw on tactics and strategies used in battlefields in many parts of the world. So closely was the tradition of overseas military and naval service woven into the fabric of British life, a Chinese emperor lamented "they always seem to be going to war with someone or other." Moreover there was in Britain a school of militarists convinced, like a renowned latter-day Chinese revolutionary, that "power comes out of the barrel of a gun." The British were also contemptuous of what one general described as a nation of "unparalleled pusillanimity" and in an era of imperial expansion they had few qualms about going to war in China. This in turn became a spur to technological advance during the industrial revolution of the nineteenth century. The quest for better guns firing more bullets or shells with greater rapidity and accuracy, carried manually, transported on wheels or mounted on ships at sea, was one of the main generators of change in the political-military equation of the eighteenth and nineteenth centuries. Not accustomed to licking their wounds, the British sought dominance wherever they were challenged and when setbacks occurred, as inevitably they did, such as over the American colonies, this was an added spur to military and technological progress.

In the mid-nineteenth century Britain had reached a peak in the imperial rat-race contested by all the European powers. However much it might protest its peaceful intentions and commercial ambitions Britain was mindful of the rivalry posed by France and Germany in Europe, following in the wake of the Spanish, Portuguese and Dutch empire builders. China on the other hand had never surrendered its place at the centre of the world which it had held for thousands of years. Why should it not survive this latest

Figure 8.1 The western sector of Hong Kong habour in the 1880s.

challenge by playing for time, absorbing the pinpricks of minor skirmishes taking place on its coast, yielding nothing of substance and offering opposition whenever possible in a hundred different ways? If the British wanted to squat on the territory of China, let them realize they were sitting on the back of a porcupine. And so it was all along the coast — Ningbo, Shanghai, Nanjing, Zhenjiang, Guangzhou — that the Chinese yielded the minimum and by stealth and evasion surrendered nothing. Even when in 1844 the Chinese agreed to allow foreign women to live at Guangzhou it was designed to "soften the barbarian nature" in readiness for the day when China might recover its ascendancy.

The one obstacle the Chinese had consistently refused to remove was the right of British entry to Guangzhou; they could continue living on their little strip of riverfront land where the factories were situated, but the city itself was out of bounds. This annoyed the British who believed that as victors of the war of 1839–1841 they had the right to enter and furthermore, speak directly to the Chinese Viceroy Ye Mingshen, who had taken over from his luckless predecessors, Lin and Qishan, banished to the far west for their failure to stem the opium trade and to exterminate the foreign devil invaders.

Additionally annoying to the British was that they had helped Ye to put down a serious Triad uprising in the city by sending a squadron of five warships to the river at Guangzhou and routing a rebel flotilla blockading the city and demanding the expulsion of all the foreigners from the factories. Ye took the view the triads were simply profiting from the turmoil of a foreign instigated war and thus he owed nothing to his helpers.

British diplomacy aimed to change all this. And the man who took on this task was a young consul, twenty-four years of age, named Harry Parkes. He was an orphan son of an English iron-master with four years of formal education following a spell in boarding school after his father's death. At the age of thirteen he went out to Macau in the fateful year of 1841 to join an elder sister, Catherine, married to the medical missionary, Dr William Lockhart. Almost immediately he was "discovered" by John Robert Morrison, son of the famous missionary.

The younger Morrison was the Chinese Secretary of the new Hong Kong Government and as a fluent speaker of Chinese saw a future for the 13-year-old Harry Parkes as a linguist. If he succeeded he would be given a job in the service of the Hong Kong Government. "We are sadly in want of interpreters and the moment he can speak a little Chinese, we shall be right glad of his services," said Morrison. Parkes made good progress, moving from the colonial to the consular service and later to the highest echelon of the diplomatic corps. He was the first of a new breed of Chinese speaking diplomats capable of conversing with Cantonese and Mandarin-speaking officials as well as reading Chinese reports.

Parkes has left us with an impression of life in Guangzhou at that time. He wrote: The city "though one of the two chief ports, is by no means the pleasantest residence ... the Chinese Government have done all in their power, as far as they could do so quietly and unobserved, to inflame the people of Guangzhou against us, and thus therefore, although we have a perfect right to take jaunts into the country and breathe fresh air away from this crowded city, few attempt to avail themselves of it on account of the risk they incur by so doing; for it is no uncommon thing here to be attacked, stoned or fired at by villagers; nay, even in the very streets of the suburbs (within the city we are not admitted) we are apt to be abused or even spat upon — in fact treated exactly in the same way as Franks, in the last century, were at Constantinople — the term 'foreign devil' taking place of 'dog of a Christian' as a general mode of abuse."[5]

The right of entrance to Guangzhou quickly became a *cause célèbre* and was called "The City Question." Twice before, in 1849 and 1854, Britain had been tempted to batter down the city gates to gain what the Treaty of Nanjing had promised; twice it had held back. Since then, the British had thrown their weight around in other ways; seamen ashore had bullied local shopkeepers and others had entered villages nearby prompting the circulation of a handbill calling for the murder of all intruders. Parkes protested but without result and a couple of foreigners on horses were stoned near the city gate.

The Chinese had also upset the French by seizing a missionary up-country who, though French, spoke fluent Chinese and dressed like one; because he had the same Chinese name as a notorious local rebel, they imprisoned the Frenchman and executed him. But what brought matters to a head was the Chinese action in seizing a small British-registered sailing boat named *Arrow*, operating between Hong Kong and Guangzhou, arresting the Chinese crew and hustling them off in a war junk. Once again, Parkes raced to their defence and for his pains, the mandarin's boatman laughed at him and slapped his face. Parkes then raised the subject with Ye by letter which resulted in nine of the twelve

---

5. Stanley Lane-Poole, *Harry Parkes in China*.

men seized being freed, though its British registration was challenged.

The affair escalated with Parkes calling for the return of all twelve men, together with an apology; he also threatened to use force in the event of delay. Strictly speaking Ye was correct in claiming that the British registry of *Arrow* had expired a few days before its seizure; the captain had said he was about to return to Hong Kong to renew it.

However when *Arrow* was taken over, the Chinese authorities were unaware the registry had expired. Moreover, Ye refused to hand over all twelve, claiming the three detained were pirates. The local British Admiral, Sir Michael Seymour, then seized a Chinese junk which he thought was a war junk. He was wrong; it was a trading junk. Ye, sensing trouble, released all twelve men, without apology. Parkes hesitated but the British naval juggernaut had been launched and the Chinese forts four miles from Guangzhou were seized. The Navy followed it up with a few shells directed at Ye's *yamen*. Ye then called for a war of extermination of the British, offering $30 a head for anyone captured.

Admiral Seymour next blew down the city walls and he and Parkes marched to the *yamen* only to find the Commissioner had left on a tour of inspection to another part of the city. Parkes stepped up the pressure but to no avail, and the British, including Parkes's wife, Fanny, watched anxiously out of the factory windows as British cannon shelled the city. On 14 December, the Chinese set fire to the foreign factories, forcing all Europeans to evacuate. Still Parkes clung to the hope that this was "no war with China but simply at Guangzhou, and that because the Commissioner chose to declare it."[6]

Having launched the attack and bombarded Ye's *yamen*, the British were in no position to press home their assault, nor were

6. Stanley Lane-Poole, *Harry Parkes in China*.

they keen to become involved in another protracted long-distance war, having only recently extricated themselves from the Crimea. But the Guangzhou question could not be left to drift again. The opium lobby strongly supported war as did the Lancashire cotton industry and although many in the British parliament were distrustful of the admirals, governors and consuls in China, and expressed this in a censure motion against Palmerston, the Prime Minister called an election and committed himself to war.

As he did so, Chinese servants and workmen walked out on their foreign employers in Hong Kong, and an attempt was made by a local baker to poison the bread supply. Fortunately it caused no deaths but there were several cases of illness. However, no one has attempted to blame (or credit) Ye for an even more sinister development in faraway India which supplied many regiments for Britain's overseas wars.

The crisis, which was soon to explode in the Subcontinent, involved sepoy troops (both Muslim and Hindu) who became restless over the real or imagined use by the Army of cow or pig fat on ammunition issued for their new Enfield rifles. The mutiny would deny Indian troops to the British Army for three long years and force England to rely on its own heavily committed regiments. Already drained by the Anglo-Sikh wars a decade earlier the British were also bogged down with troubles in Afghanistan; the one decisive change resulting from the mutiny was the final downfall of the East India Company after 160 years, and its replacement by direct Crown rule.

The distractions in India, however, caused few anxieties in England. Palmerston campaigned on a jingoistic platform which denounced the "insolent barbarian in Guangzhou" who had "violated the British flag, broken treaties, offered rewards for British heads and ushered in murder, assassination and poisons." Cartoonists had a field day depicting exquisite Chinese tortures and punishments. The "Yellow Peril" of the Australian goldfields was rearing its ugly head in London. Counter arguments that the "real object is to drug the people of China with opium and raise the price of the British cup of tea," were lost in the anti-China clamour and Palmerston won by a landslide of eighty-five seats.

Lord Elgin was sent out to lead a new attack on China, and he travelled quickly by way of the Mediterranean and then on the new railroad through Suez to the Red Sea. He arrived in the China sea in record time, and three months ahead of his French colleague, Baron Gros, who would represent France in the next phase of the Allied moves against China.

With the opening of the Suez Canal eleven years later, China would be only six weeks away from Europe, while orders could be transmitted in a day on the new Eastern Telegraph snaking its way across the world and under the sea to Asia. But Lord Elgin was well aware of the dangers he faced taking on China with the remnants of military units released from the far more serious emergency in India. He wrote in his diary: "Can I do anything to prevent England from calling down on herself God's curse for brutalities committed on another feeble oriental race? Or are all my exertions to result only in an extension of the area over which Englishmen are to exhibit how hollow and superficial are both their civilisation and their christianity."

Unlike opinion in Hong Kong that Guangzhou was the key to the China conundrum, Elgin quickly accepted the Russian view that Beijing was the answer. But the first strike had to be made in the south, and after warnings from the French plenipotentiary, Baron Gros, who had his own agenda including satisfaction for the murder of a French missionary, Elgin took aim at the southern capital. He confessed to feeling ill at ease at being within shell-shot of a great city "doomed to destruction by the folly of its rulers and the vanity and levity of ours."[7]

Public proclamations and warnings were pasted on the walls of the city and transmitted to officials calling on the people to

---

7. Jack Beeching, *The Chinese Opium Wars* (London: Hutchinson, 1975).

clear out. On Holy Innocents Day, 27 December, the Anglo-French force of more than 5,000 men stormed ashore. Behind them was a Chinese coolie corps, mostly Hakkas with no love for Manchus and not much more for the Cantonese; they moved guns and carried ammunition, recognizing it as a paying job and with no evident sense of disloyalty. A large throng of spectators stood on hills overlooking the city to watch.

In a despatch sent the next day, *The Times* correspondent, G. Wingrove Cooke marvelled at the fact that the Chinese were in no hurry to surrender, even flying kites while shell bursts hurled clouds of smoke above the city. "These strange Chinese actually seem to be getting used to it. Sampans and cargo-boats are moving down the river like London lightermen in the ordinary exercise of their calling; people are coming down to the [river] bank and watch the shot and shell fly over their heads; in a room opening upon the river a family were taking their evening meal within two hundred yards of the 'Phlegethon', which was keeping up a constant discharge of shells, all of which passed a few feet over their heads; the inmates were all eating their rice as if nothing was happening outside.

"The sampans were all day long proceeding from ship to ship selling fruit and vegetables to the sailors who were bombarding their city. Who can pretend to understand such a people as this. These curious stolid, imperturbable people seem determined to ignore our business here, and to wait until we are pleased to go away. Ye lives much as usual. He cut off four hundred Chinese heads the other morning and stuck them up in the south of the city. Our leaders seem to be puzzled by the tenacious, child-like, helpless obstinacy — the passive resistance of their enemy."[8]

When the Allies entered the city, their order of priorities became clear. The Royal Marines' first destination was the

---

8. Stanley Lane-Poole, *Harry Parkes in China*.

Treasury where they took command of the silver hoard, and with the help of Chinese coolies each paid a dollar cash, carried it off — all $300,000 — to a waiting ship. Another force, led by the young gung-ho consul, Harry Parkes, chased after Viceroy Ye; armed with a none-too-flattering portrait of the overweight mandarin, Parkes spotted his posterior as he tried to escape over a wall. Grasping his ample waist, one of the soldiers pulled him back and led him to imprisonment.

The sacking of Guangzhou was accompanied by the desecration of graves and wholesale plundering and looting — trophies of war, like banners and conical hats may be excusable, but the British and French were seasoned veterans with a good eye for value, whatever its language. Soon the old Hong merchants were turning up at Elgin's headquarters calling for law and order, while the tea merchants, foreign and Chinese, clamoured for a resumption of shipments of 21 million pounds of tea.

Fortunately, Elgin found a Chinese willing to govern — the local governor, Bekuai — and they backed up his authority with a joint Allied-Chinese police force. While the city slowly settled down to the new rulers a rash of secret edicts from Beijing, to rise up and avenge the arrest of Ye, kept the countryside simmering with opposition; many districts were declared no-go areas for Allied troops. The Chinese also devised what one visitor to Guangzhou described as "very remarkable subaqueous infernal machines for use in the river and which blew up at a given time by clockwork."[9] Though not greatly destructive they kept British matelots alert watching for these rogue torpedoes.

Ye's arrest achieved nothing and while he remained in Guangzhou he was a rallying point of Chinese opposition. Detested he may have been by the Allies but he had many fine qualities; he was loyal, abstemious, faithful to one wife, hated

9. Albert Smith, *To China and Back* (1859; reprint, Hong Kong: Hong Kong University Press, 1974).

opium and loved tea. At the same time he refused to play any part in calming the populace and in desperation the British shipped him off to Calcutta, his last sight of China coming as his ship sailed through the clusters of beautiful green islands that fringe the rocky coastline of Guangdong. In India, he rejected all literature save for translations of *The Times*, the parliamentary debates being his chief amusement. He died in Calcutta, unmourned by all except his nearest and dearest, and no doubt dreading his new abode in an underworld populated by the headless victims of his relentless reign of terror in Guangdong and earlier, during the Taiping Rebellion.

CHAPTER 9

Bounty Hunters and Pirates

If there were any benefits in the wake of the Allied attack on Guangzhou and the increased naval presence on the coast of Guangdong, two are worth mentioning. The first was the virtual eclipse of the huge piratical fleets which were laying siege to coastal shipping — foreign and Chinese — and to large parts of the coast itself; the second was that in pursuing the pirates into their lairs and into many of the bays and inlets, the Royal Navy made a thorough job of surveying and mapping the China coast.

The surveys carried out from 1840 to 1861 contain many distinguished names such as Captain Sir Edward Belcher, Commander W. T. Bate, Commander John Ward, Captain Henry Kellett and Captain Richard Collinson.[1] Between them they were responsible for 90 per cent of the surveys undertaken between Guangzhou and Wusong, the Zhoushan islands, many parts of the north China coast up to southern Korea, the entire coastline of Taiwan and the Pescadores Islands, as well as the Pearl River estuary and Hong Kong waters. The surveys were essential for the maritime trade which would develop following the Treaty of

---

1. Belcher, Kellett and Collinson would later be involved in the vain search for survivors of Sir John Franklin's 1845 Arctic expedition to find and map the North-west Passage, a possible alternative route to Asia.

Nanjing, as well as for locating and hunting down pirate lairs. They were used by merchant ships of all nationalities for more than a century and in recent years have been refined and updated with the help of satellite and aerial photography.

Piracy was endemic on the China coast and had been for centuries. But it flourished in the wake of the opium boom and was compounded by the war, after which China had no effective coastguard to patrol the river estuaries. Foreign ships were the pirates' favoured targets but anything with a sail was fair game. Strictly speaking, the Royal Navy was forbidden to go on "fishing expeditions" for pirates in inlets and bays or to storm ashore and raid villages suspected of concealing pirates though they did both in a period extending well into the twentieth century, with or without official Chinese permission. They were, however, allowed to pursue a real or suspected pirate boat and this gave them wide scope; at other times the Navy justified sailing into a bay or harbour on the grounds that it was making a survey, again with or without official Chinese permission.

The Navy's action, however, was far from altruistic. It was not doing China any favours and there were rich pickings for individual ships' crews who became bounty hunters by seizing stolen cargoes and claiming rewards for capturing pirates; and in an era when the Navy still indulged in freebooting, they were not above unofficial looting on the side.

Long gone were the days when the Navy could sail into the South China Sea and pick up a Spanish treasure ship carrying silver from the New World to the Philippines. As for Dutch, Swedish and French ships, they could put up a spirited fight and were as well armed and carried as much sail as the British. Unless Britain was at war with them, they gave these ships a wide berth. During and after the Opium War, there were between forty to seventy British naval ships on the coast and surrounding waters with 5,000 to 11,000 men aboard; safeguarding British interests was their primary task.

Anti-piracy patrols were popular with the Navy for they were mostly one-sided contests with little in the pirate boats to match the 12- to 24-pounder guns carried on a frigate or a sloop. One well-placed shot could blow a boat out of the water, but the Navy needed evidence to claim rewards and so its big guns — thirty to sixty per ship — were used sparingly and mainly to intimidate.

Figure 9.1 Captured pirates after a battle, as sketched by Auguste Borget.

The official rewards for capturing or destroying pirate ships ranged from 50 pounds to 10,000 pounds. As the Lords of the Admiralty were not known for their generosity, the evidence had to be good. The bounty was divided between captains, officers and crews and by the time the average able-bodied seaman held out his hand, he would be lucky to collect a few shillings, while the teenage "powder-monkeys" (so-called because small boys, aged twelve or thirteen, scrambled up narrow wells carrying powder from deep holds to the guns) might pocket a few pennies. But with the abysmal pay of those days, any free handout was welcome.

So poorly were British ratings paid that a few found it more lucrative to jump ship and join up with the pirates where their skills as seamen or gunners were valued, though in this cut-throat company their chances of making it home with a fortune in their pockets were slender. The penalty for desertion, moreover, ranged from 100 strokes of the cat-o'-nine-tails to execution at the yard arm. Drum head court martials were common and punishment swift. Not many deserted.

As for the Chinese pirates, the mandarins subjected them to swift justice with the mere pretence of a trial, torture if there was no immediate confession, followed by immediate punishment. Those claiming innocence, such as hostages being held for ransom, had to prove they were not involved — no easy task when the automatic presumption was guilty. Punishment for pirates ranged from a beating with a thick bamboo pole on the back of the legs and buttocks (the bastinado), severe torture, strangulation, hanging, decapitation, or for the truly wicked, burial up to their necks in quicklime or death by a thousand cuts (literally being sliced to death over a period of days, when the victim would die from loss of blood or gangrene). While awaiting trial they would be tied together by their hair queues and lashed to junk masts.

As in all societies, often the worst and most intransigent offenders would be powerful or rich enough to bargain for their lives; some were even bought off with bribes and buttons — mandarin's buttons — which meant a job for life in the upper echelons of the civil service, occasionally in the role of chief pirate exterminator — though this often ended in a truce with the pirates pooling their loot with the local mandarins. There were even cases of rich men getting proxies to suffer their punishment, by paying agreed sums to widows.

In 1810, a woman pirate leader enjoyed so much influence that she was able to travel to Guangzhou to negotiate a pardon for the worst of her band, a pirate chief named Apo Tsi. The East India Company report stated that "Apo Tsi requires for himself to retain eighty armed boats under the pretence of employing them against the pirates that remain, and thirty or forty more to be employed in the salt trade." (That was another highly lucrative business under Government monopoly and Apo Tsi demanded a share of carrying salt from the salt beds, on many parts of the coast, to the Government warehouses.)

He eventually won the approval he wanted, receiving an imperial commission and a subsidy of 18,000 taels a month. He later went on a tour of inspection to Guangzhou and Macau. The EIC report added: "It may now be assumed that the ex-poacher was fully installed in his post of gamekeeper." The Viceroy, in paying too high a price for peace, was demoted.

The pirate fleets varied in size from a few small boats to hundreds of craft of all sizes, heavily armed, fast under sail, but all equipped with oars so that in light winds they could bear down quickly on their victims or make a hasty getaway. In 1807, an EIC employee who was captured by pirates, a man named Turner, reported that the pirate gang led by Jing Yi, had a fleet of 500 ships ranging from 15 to 200 tons, including several ships captured in action, the largest of which was armed with twelve 6-pounder to 18-pounder guns. A few years later they were carrying twenty to twenty-five guns. Clearly these would have been a match for small naval ships and only the skill of the naval gunners could have swung the balance.

Jing Yi met his fate in the year Turner was freed, when his fleet was decimated by a typhoon. Then his wife took over and she distinguished herself by codifying regulations under which pirates operated. She laid down rules of behaviour, how to share the booty, fair payment for all supplies bought from farmers, and respect for women and children. So well regulated was this band that finally the pirates did not have to go to sea; they accepted tribute from all ships passing by, and escaped interference from the mandarins by paying protection money. The Viceroy eventually ended the racket when he banned all shipping movements and called on the Portuguese to put pressure on the pirate lairs.

In later years, so seriously was the pirate threat viewed that the Hong Kong Government allowed junk fleets and merchant ships to engage private armed ships to convoy them to their destinations — a practice that continued for many decades. Hong Kong authorities were unhappy about it because the guard ships were quick on the trigger when it came to dealing with any vessel that looked threatening. Cases came to court in both Shanghai and Hong Kong where innocent vessels had had holes blown in their hulls and injuries caused to crew and passengers by trigger-happy guard ships.

Moreover, Hong Kong was used by the pirates as a base for buying weapons and ammunition, for servicing and repairing their ships and, most important, for collecting intelligence on shipping movements, even to the point of bribing civil servants and police prosecutors to learn of valuable cargoes or to falsify evidence. Senior officials were suspected of taking kickbacks from pirates and one, D. R. Caldwell, was censured for his associations with a notorious pirate and resigned from his post as Registrar-General shortly before a commission of inquiry delivered judgement against him.

Nor were the pirates all Chinese; two of the most notorious in the early years of Hong Kong were an Englishman, William Fenton, and an effeminate-looking American with lily-white hands, named Eli Boggs, who though tried for murder and piracy escaped hanging. After serving a few years in prison, both were sent home. The Royal Navy built up an impressive record of "kills" over the years, but the pirates were clever enough to slip into the role of peaceful fishermen or farmers at times of intense pressure, sallying forth the next year when the Royal Navy's numbers were depleted.

Not only were pirates daring (and well-informed) in picking their targets, they were innovative in the vessels they devised. Where once they used small multi-oared "crab boats" for quick movement out of estuaries, by the 1830s they had designed a so-called mussel-shell boat with sixty or seventy men manning oars with a reinforced lid to deflect cannon balls and "stinkpots" (used by both pirates and coast guards as a kind of poison gas weapon). These craft, which must have been hellish for the oarsmen on hot sunny days, concentrated on abducting wealthy citizens for ransom, a captured EIC ship's officer once regaining his freedom at a cost of $7,654. Another ploy of the pirates was to raid the graves, steal the rich funereal clothes and even the bodies, and demand ransom for their restoration which the wealthy were only too willing to pay to ensure their loved ones of a peaceful after-life.

The British in an effort to protect their own substantial trade, brought in laws to tackle the problem which effectively paid rich prizes for the destruction of ships and the capture of pirates. But it required a massive upsurge of piracy directed at British merchant ships to sting the Navy into action.

Before Hong Kong came under British rule the island was a well-known haunt of pirates. After the Union flag was unfurled the appointment of a Harbour Master and a Chief Magistrate helped to limit the problem for a time and the pirates moved across the water to Kowloon or to Lamma Island. The courts and the prisons, however, soon filled up with pirates most of whom preferred the enlightened justice of the colony — a term of imprisonment, transportation or 100 strokes of the cane, but hanging in the worst cases — to the summary punishment meted out in China.

The pirates in any case chose to operate from Hong Kong because it became the chief opium distribution centre following its cession to Britain in 1841. A murky underworld of shady British dealers, freebooting deserters, and Chinese distributors grew up whose cut-throat tactics caused the local authorities many anxious hours trying to devise ways to suppress them. One pirate chief captured by the British was quick to twist the law to his advantage. After turning Queen's evidence in his own case, he was employed to gather information on pirates and then used it to blackmail or betray them, collecting a bounty for their arrest.

It required a major effort by the Navy to suppress the wave of

Figure 9.2 Prisoner in the stocks, a sketch by Auguste Borget.

piracy sweeping the coasts of Guangdong and Fujian. The Navy's chance came in 1849 when two big fleets, run by Shap-ng-tsai (possibly his Cantonese nickname, meaning "fifteenth child") and Chui Apoo, played havoc with South China coast shipping and extorted large sums from local merchants. Chui then killed two British officers in Hong Kong and Shap-ng-tsai plundered a British registered junk near Hainan. The Navy retaliated with several attacks on known haunts and destroyed many of their vessels. Then combining with the Admiral from Cochin China (later Vietnam), Captain John Hay in his sloop, *Columbine*, cornered the pirate chief in a narrow inlet and destroyed fifty-eight of his sixty-four vessels, claiming 1,700 lives, without loss to the attackers. Assisting were five other vessels, including the East India Company steamer, *Phlegethon*. The foreign merchants of Hong Kong and Guangzhou in gratitude presented the two captains (the other being Capt George Neblett) with a handsome silver trophy (recently in the possession of Jardine, Matheson Ltd.) to commemorate the occasion.

From the Admiralty, the six naval vessels' crews were awarded a bounty totalling 42,425 pounds. However, neither Chui nor the Fifteenth Child were among those taken prisoner. Chui was later abducted by the British and sent for trial in Hong Kong, but took his own life before sentence could be passed. Shap-ng-tsai made a deal with the Viceroy of Guangdong and rose to eminence with the award of a mandarin's button. All this exercise achieved was to force the Admiralty to look more carefully at the amounts paid out in bounty and ultimately, drastically to reduce its rewards; while pirate hunts continued they never succeeded in eliminating the problem as will be revealed in a later chapter.

The ships taking part in the piracy raids, though vastly superior in speed and armament to the junks they were pursuing, were the last of the era of sail for the Royal Navy. Propeller-driven ironclads were entering the service and one writer noted that a complete revolution in the structure of warships occurred between 1832 and 1869.[2] The fleet of 1832 consisted of 572 ships with twenty ironclad paddle-steamers. Thirty-seven years later there were 735 vessels, only sixty-four of which were sail-powered.

The new vessels were aptly described as "ironclads" for they were initially hybrids — built of wood as before but with an iron cladding or armour plating. Gun ports lined the hull as before. Even the sails remained, but forward of the mainmast was the funnel. The ships still had bowsprits and were steered from the stern, and their single shaft propeller plus full sail could give them a speed of fourteen to fifteen knots. Tonnage could be up to 10,000 deadweight. It was not long, however, before the hulls were made completely of steel.

The biggest change came with gunnery and armaments and as the ordnance developed leading to large guns firing heavier shells over greater distances, so this influenced naval architecture to accommodate the creations of Sir Joseph Whitworth (amongst other things the developer of the modern torpedo) and Sir W. G. Armstrong (responsible for modern rifled multi-turret guns). Similar vessels had begun to emerge in other leading navies, notably that of the United States which in the Civil War witnessed the remarkable "drawn duel" between the Confederate steam frigate, *Merrimack* and the Union warship, *Monitor*. No longer could cannon be mounted on wheels firing through gunports; so forceful was their recoil that they had to be fixed on steel decks with protective casing.

Partly it was rivalry with the French, who gained a headstart with steam, that dictated the pace of change in the Royal Navy. The American Civil War showed how solidly these iron ships stood up to a heavy bombardment and how much fire power in turn they were able to concentrate on a given target. Britain, first

2. Grace Fox, *British Admirals and Chinese Pirates* (London: Kegan Paul, 1940).

for so long, was not about to drop into third place in the international naval league; besides, when France started to rebuild and rearm its navy, Germany, Austria, Italy, Spain and Russia followed. There could be no second-guessing the outcome; the age of the dreadnought had dawned. Coal-powered, steam-driven ships with twin propellers would soon cruise the oceans of the world. Thanks to the reforms earlier in the century by Prime Minister William Pitt, the Navy no longer had to live by ancient tradition.

At that stage, no thought was given to the impact on Japan, opened by Commodore Perry's naval squadron in 1853; yet within fifty years, Japanese warships would rank first in the Yellow and South China seas after annihilating China and Russia in epic sea battles. Harry Parkes, the British Consul, welcomed Perry when he called in at Guangzhou, but his only comment on the "old" Commodore was that he was "slowly eating his way through a phalanx of dinners, one of which it fell to my lot to give yesterday." Perry was then fifty-nine, Parkes a mere twenty-five; anyone the other side of forty must have seemed geriatric by comparison. It would have been enlightening to have heard Perry's comments on Japan's or China's potential, but if he expressed them Parkes did not record them.

While the Royal Navy was moving swiftly into a new age of fast steam-powered ships capable of crossing the world's oceans to meet imperial commitments, the merchant marine was in no hurry to follow. From 1850 to 1873, the age of the tea clippers reached their zenith and achieved a romantic brilliance that still inspires a sense of admiration and awe. Who is not drawn to the sight of a parade of tall ships under full sail through some of the world's great harbours? Yet there are few authentic survivors of the majestic age of sail.

It was the Americans who initiated this revolution in the latter years of the eighteenth century after cutting their ties with Britain in the revolutionary war. The Royal Navy, the victors of Trafalgar and a host of sea battles in many parts of the world, were still ensnarled in centuries-old red-tape where marine architecture was concerned. The Americans designed a superb frigate in 1797 named *Constitution* which was credited with many victories; in the war of 1812 it disgraced a Royal Navy frigate whose close-range shots bounced off its adversary's side.[3]

No less successful was the Baltimore clipper, with sharp bows though not yet the sleek waterlines of its successor. She was however longer and slimmer and had ample sail power to push her through the water at greater speeds. The clippers that followed improved on these changes and the most innovative ship to come off the slipway in 1853, all wooden, was *Great Republic*, with three square-rigged masts and an aft-spanker mast, huge areas of sail canvas and a future that held great promise. She was built by one of the world's finest shipbuilders, Donald Mackay of Boston. Alas, she caught fire before her maiden voyage and had to be extensively remodelled.

One of the new breed of ships to visit the South China Sea was the Confederate warship, *Alabama*, of about 1,000 tons. She was a steam-powered bark with a speed of fourteen knots. Helped by a good spread of canvas, she created terror in the South China Sea among Yankee ships homeward bound via Singapore and the Strait of Malacca. As the Civil War raged at home, she sank several ships in the Strait. These were both American and British, because when owners — many of whom were Bostonians — became aware of *Alabama*'s presence they swiftly changed names and flags and re-registered their vessels in neutral ports.

American clippers, however, played a decreasing part in the China trade after 1855, other than as slavers. The gold rush, the Civil War and the railway boom drained both its energies and its capital for the next fifty years. The British private or country traders operating between India and China had been quick to follow the American lead and the opium and tea clippers of the

---

3. This earned *Constitution* the name of "Old Ironsides," and a permanent home in Boston harbour.

mid-nineteenth century were a new breed based on racing lines. Firms like Jardine, Dent, and Russell & Co., needed fast small ships which would not only give them the edge over the pirates but enable them to beat to windward as they sailed against the prevailing monsoon in the South China seas. These firms understood that their business was a year-round affair and that with the high turnover of opium, their storage ships needed constant replenishment.

The design of the American clippers answered this need ideally. One of these early acquisitions was the two-masted schooner, *Hellas*, built in 1832 at Waterford, Ireland, only 200 tons, but ninety-one feet long and twenty-three feet wide, and with a depth of only fourteen feet. Another was *Anonyma*, with two raked masts, square-rigged, and built as a racing yacht in Gosport in 1839. She had a large crew of seventy-four but with a great spread of sail and an armoury of weapons to fight off pirates she was a superb performer on the South China Sea.

With the Americans out, the British tea clippers dominated the oceans between China and Europe, and with a premium of ten shillings a ton paid for the first to land her cargo in London, the race from Fuzhou, Shanghai and Hong Kong to the River Thames was an even bigger event than the Derby, the Melbourne Cup or the Whitbread round-the-world yacht race.

Loaded with more than a million pounds of tea, three of these splendid sailing ships, *Ariel*, *Taeping* and *Serica*, left the Min River, Fuzhou, in 1866 on the same tide and docked on the same tide together in London, ninety-nine days later. Two other ships, *Fiery Cross* and *Taitsing*, which left at the same time, arrived two days later. Two other names to achieve immortality in the annals of the clippers were *Thermopylae* and *Cutty Sark* (the latter now preserved at Greenwich Maritime Museum in London), though both came at the end of an era when the newly opened Suez Canal was inviting steamers to take the short cut home instead of the long loop around the Cape of Good Hope.

Moreover, the China tea trade had begun to decline with the

arrival of Indian tea on the British market. The designs of the British engineering genius, Isambard Kingdom Brunel, were revolutionizing shipbuilding in a way which signalled the end of the sailing ship long before it achieved its spectacular apogee. Brunel's three ships, *Great Western*, *Great Britain* and *Great Eastern* (1837–1858) were the largest and fastest in the world employing steam-driven paddles and propellers, and the first to carry passengers across the Atlantic as well as to lay the first transatlantic cable. His ships — one of which was the first to use a double iron hull (under restoration at Bristol) — were never seen in the China Sea; indeed, they were quickly overtaken by multi propeller-driven, steel-hulled ships.

The tea clippers were not just things of beauty and grace in full sail, their economy in performance was outstanding. On each journey they carried almost their own value in tea and profits of 2,000 pounds a voyage were not unusual. Displacing 600 to 1,000 tons, they were the product mainly of Scottish yards, based on the Aberdeen clipper model of Alexander Hall, and carried up to 40,000 square feet of sail. With their long sharp bows they could log up to thirteen knots in a good breeze with all sails billowing (one skipper claimed a record of seventeen knots) and could outsail the fastest that the Royal Navy, with all their seamanship and discipline, could muster. *Thermopylae* in 1869 took ninety-one days from Fuzhou to London, though she was beaten that year by *Sir Lancelot* which took two days less on the same voyage.

The tea ships sailed mainly from Pagoda Anchorage on the River Min, about twenty kilometres downstream from the walled city of Fuzhou because it was closer to the tea growing centres of China; Guangzhou and Shanghai were less favoured as tea export centres. The Anchorage was named after a tall pagoda on the north side of the Min and during the height of the season, many of the finest British and American clippers would lie in its deep waters, with cargo junks alongside and gangs of sweating coolies hauling matted chests of black tea into the holds, under the eyes

Figure 9.3 Tea clippers loading a cargo for London, a drawing by Paul Sharp.

of masters or mates dressed in white linen or pongee silk, sucking on clay pipes or a Manila cheroot.

The choice of more northerly ports resulted from the opening of the treaty ports of which there were fifteen in 1870 and another five six years later. Fuzhou was preferred as much because of its location as because of Guangzhou's war-ravaged and depressed condition. Shanghai had come into its own as a budding metropolis serving the Yangzi estuary and the rich rice-growing provinces adjoining it. The modern city of Shanghai rose from the mud flats adjoining the Chinese city after 1842; initially there were three settlements, British, American and French but ultimately all but the French joined in a single international concession, governed by the autonomous Shanghai Municipal Council, with its own administration and police force. Hong Kong, a full-fledged colony under its own Governor and colonial legislature, was developing as an entrepôt drawing produce from northern Guangdong, Fujian and Guangxi.

Following the burning of the factories in Guangzhou in 1857, the foreign merchants were no longer confined to the one strip of riverfront as they were before the Opium War; as trade picked up the new treaty ports nibbled away at its monopoly. Reporting on a visit he made to that city in February 1858, William Reed, the American Commissioner to China, said he felt that "everything was done during the British attack to confine the inevitable suffering within the narrowest limits. Sad as is the appearance of Guangzhou, once a great mart of commerce, with its deserted and ruined suburbs and houses, it is well understood that the loss of life among the beseiged was relatively small, the estimate varying from 500 to 3,000 and that the discipline of the assailants, though the town was taken by actual assault, was very strict.

"That portion of the ruin which strikes the eye as most complete is the site of the foreign factories. They seem to have been rooted out, not a vestige remaining but a portion of the flight of stone steps at the landing, from which the foreign merchants embarked in January last year. This was the thorough devastation of the Chinese."[4]

The British and French were determined to rebuild their presence in the city, though no longer could it be on the old factory site. British official archives at Kew show that the two nations began searching for a fresh site which took years of wrangling. Three sites were considered and the pros and cons were bandied about at meetings between the British merchants waiting to return to Guangzhou.

Finally, Lord Elgin made an inspection of the area and strongly favoured the site at Shameen, a sandy tidal area west of the old factory site. He rejected a return to the former factory site because it was less than 13 acres in area (whereas the new foreign quarter in Shanghai was 270 acres with an additional 300 acres as a recreational ground.)

---

4. US Congressional Papers, *Chinese Correspondence, 1857–1859* (Washington DC, 1860).

The difference between Guangzhou and Shanghai, however, was that in the former city, the Western merchants wanted a prime riverside site adjoining an already well-established city, whereas in Shanghai, the Chinese city was far smaller and the new concession offered better opportunity for expansion. Consul General Harry Parkes finally persuaded the British merchants to accept the Shameen site and negotiated a tender to reclaim an area of 55.41 acres with the city's Governor. The Chinese Government agreed to build the site for $260,296, to be completed in 18 months. (The final price was $280,000.)

The official Naval surveyors' report of the area considered that "the position of the site is one so admirably suited for trade in consequence of the wide expanse of the river and also its depth, rendering it suitable for the reception of merchant vessels." It would also receive the prevailing breeze in summer — important in a city where for eight months of the year the temperature would rarely drop below 30 degrees with humidity no less than 80 per cent.

It was also decided to leave a canal at the rear of the site to allow lighters to land goods on either the Guangzhou or Shameen side, and the two would be connected with iron bridges. A lease was later signed between the British Consul, D. B. Robertson, and a Chinese mandarin identified only as Lao Tsung-kwang.[5] This piece of land was granted to the "British authorities" to be held in perpetuity for a yearly rent of 1,500 copper cash per *mu* (which was equivalent to 7,260 square feet), or 396,000 cash in total.

The "authorities" were the British Consulate, and Shameen would be given the same extraterritorial status as other treaty ports and would be described as the British Concession; adjoining it would be a smaller French concession, approximately one-fifth

---

5. A typed copy in English of which was found in the records of Deacon & Co. Ltd., a British firm then operating in Guangzhou, and the subject of a history by the author.

of the area, in recognition of the part France played in the attack against Guangzhou. The local residents were left to set up a municipal council to run the territory and land was divided into residential lots to be sold at auction.

Parkes later reported that on the day of the sale (8 September 1859) "all the merchants came trooping up from Hong Kong, and more or less in a grumbling mood — a sign to my mind they were going to buy as it is a peculiarity of John Bull to growl when he is about to pay out money."[6] Eighty-two lots were offered, with six held back for the Consulate and one for a church. Thanks to spirited bidding by Parsee merchants for waterfront lots, the prices soared above reserves, some even doubling at $8,000 each, but rear lots were unwanted. By the second day of the sale, fifty-five lots had brought in $248,000, or just $32,000 short of the cost of the site, with twenty lots in hand which were later sold off, giving clear signs that prime real estate would always be a valued commodity in China.

Prior to completion of the new concession, the foreign merchants took up residence across the river in the region of Honam in conditions which were far from peaceful. Consul-General Parkes threatened in June 1858, to hang any "braves" (Chinese terrorists) found in the streets or anyone "blowing conch shells" and to cut off any queues of those who could not give a good account of themselves (rendering them liable to punishment by the mandarins since the queue was a universal sign of submission to the Manchu regime).

It was an era of megaphone diplomacy when both sides resorted to firing words rather than bullets and shells. The Chinese condemned the war-like practices of the British, blaming them for the destruction of the factories and the stoppage of trade for the last two years. "If they will repent of their misdeeds, some

---

6. Stanley Lane-Poole, *Harry Parkes in China*.

small portion of imperial benevolence is still in reserve for them. But if they persist in their vicious course they shall be called to account for their crimes and our people shall exterminate them before their morning meal," thundered an official proclamation from the new Commissioner Huang Zungan. It was a message calculated to stir up both foreigners and Chinese. Remembering the poisoned bread incident in Hong Kong a year earlier, the reference to an untimely end "before their morning meal" did not go down well. Among the Chinese, it aroused mass opposition and caused a walk-out of domestic staff.

It also prompted the British to station a gunboat in the river to reassure nervous merchants ashore that help was close at hand. This would become policy on the China Station for the next eighty years, for with Hong Kong under the British flag and treaty ports up and down the coast to protect, the Royal Navy now had multiple responsibilities including anti-piracy work, protection of local foreign communities, safeguarding of trade and British ships, showing the flag and representing British authority, as well as providing a floating residence for the British Consul until Shameen was built.

While the gunboat policy helped to promote confidence among the British it also ensured a resumption of the tea trade and Parkes was able to report that "trade has thriven fairly well since the port was reopened." Business commenced on 11 March 1858. He went on to say that the Chinese authorities "are quite ready to entertain a scheme for the legalisation of opium and they have been trying to sound me lately on the subject of the collection of duties in which matter I think they would not be averse to foreign assistance — indeed they have almost asked me for mine."[7]

Not only was the current tea situation thriving but the Hong

---

7. Stanley Lane-Poole, *Harry Parkes in China*.

merchant, Howqua, still playing a key role in trade despite the abolition of the Co-Hong, had told Parkes that orders for eight million pounds of tea had gone to the tea districts. "This would appear to indicate that they do not anticipate political trouble," added Parkes. "However they followed the same course last year even after Guangzhou had been abandoned. The Chinese are always an enigma." His optimism was shortlived, however, for there was a renewed trade stoppage which caused serious inconvenience and which in 1859 and 1860 led to problems with adulterated tea being supplied; this was thought to have been caused by the Taiping Rebellion affecting production and disrupting supplies, rather than an overt act of sabotage.

Parkes found that the Chinese merchants "have become adept at taking advantage of every opening for pushing (trade). In fact they have become accustomed to trade in the midst of hostilities with foreigners. The Guangzhou Chinese see clearly their opportunity and are using strenuous exertions to take advantage of it."[8] Moreover, when Shanghai encountered difficulties in ordering and shipping tea during the Taiping Rebellion, Guangzhou traders were happy to step into the breach.

In between emergencies, Parkes would pluck up enough courage to show the flag and walk through the city. "It is not an easy task to be able to find one's way through such an intricate labyrinth of streets as Guangzhou presents but by the aid of my maps and my tongue I can do this now without difficulty," he noted. While Parkes and the French plenipotentiary, Baron Gros, were keen to restore order, the Americans, under orders from President Buchanan, were anxiously sitting on the fence and assuring the Chinese they were not at war with them.

During the invasion of Guangzhou, however, three flags were at one time flying on the ramparts of the city, the third being that

---

8. Stanley Lane-Poole, *Harry Parkes in China*.

of the United States. The State Department wanted to know who put it there, rumours having circulated that it was the intemperate action of the US Consul in Hong Kong, present at the scene of the action — a former army general. They also sent a stern letter to their acting Commissioner, Dr Peter Parker, to ensure there was no repetition, though there was every desire to support the Allies short of making war, even if it meant taking cover behind British men-of-war in midstream in times of tension.

The Americans had concluded their first treaty with China in 1844 following the Treaty of Nanjing and American traders thereafter had conducted trade "peacefully and courteously," according to Commissioner William Reed. Though due for revision after twelve years, Reed at first saw no need to change it, but with Britain and France raising the stakes and pressing for redress after the *Arrow* affair, he now saw the need "to induce the Government of China to consent to such arrangements as may obviate future misunderstandings." He would therefore follow Lord Elgin and Baron Gros to North China to try to gain satisfaction from Beijing.

Reed was of a complex nature, unsure of his real mission in life. The descendant of Irish immigrants, he grew up in Philadelphia and launched into a legal career with a leaning towards politics; his only success was a six-year stint as District Attorney where he specialized in criminal prosecution. His attempts to climb out of state politics and into the Federal sphere and his support for the election of President James Buchanan earned him the job of Commissioner to China. Coming from a political background where he was a member of the "Know-nothing Party" (because of its profession of knowing nothing even when asked what it stood for!), Reed was probably well cast for a diplomatic role.

An austere but able intellectual, given to "foolish impulses," he managed to restrain himself while in the China seas where his correspondence showed him to be a man earnestly concerned as much for America's future relations with China as China's emergence as a respected independent power. He was certainly a better diplomat than a politician or author (which he became in his later years) but soured his relations with his colleagues in Washington by his bitter opposition to the Civil War. That marked his political, diplomatic and legal demise. It was in China he made his mark.

In response to their latest letter to the "supreme council of state in Beijing" Reed and other allied commissioners had received a reply "with the same tone of apparent courtesy, the same unmeaning profession, the same dextrous sophistry, and what is more material, the same passive resistance, the same stolid refusal to yield any point of substance." This lead Reed to believe that in pressing on to Tianjin he should take with him "all the available force I have if it be only to show the Chinese that it is not the want of means which compels the United States to abstain from measures of hostility." By this time, the court in Beijing had formally sacked Ye and appointed the new commissioner, Huang, in Guangzhou, and the court gave this as their excuse for refusing to conduct negotiations with the foreign plenipotentiaries in Shanghai or Suzhou. In short, the old practice of passing the buck to Guangzhou was still in force.

When Elgin arrived off Dagu at the outskirts to Tianjin he again addressed a communication to the throne only to be told that the Governor General of Zhili, Commissioner Dao, would be appointed to meet them, though Elgin suspected this was yet another delaying tactic by the throne. So it proved, and the meeting fell through though Reed now was in conflict with Elgin for he believed in making the most of every opportunity. His steam frigate, *Mississipi*, was anchored off the Beihe and Reed clearly did not relish a long drawn-out standoff in the estuary. But his mind was made up that the United States would not get involved in a new round of fighting; he deplored the Anglo-French gunboat diplomacy and if the war resumed, he would leave.

Reed even broke ranks by going ashore to meet the Chinese commissioners and experienced the same rebuff as other Western plenipotentiaries because it was "inconsistent with the established rules of the [Chinese] empire." He reported on his impressions ashore, remarkable for their depth and penetration after such a brief visit. "The symptoms patent to every eye are those of a disintegrated community, official authority perverted and corrupted and a vast and morally inert population submitting patiently to wrong, and in its decrepitude awakening no sympathy."[9]

The flotilla of British, French and American ships in the shallow waters off Dagu Bar had been pitching and tossing for five weeks waiting for diplomacy to take its course. The Beihe Gulf was never a hospitable stretch of water and to be confined to ship for such a long period would have sapped morale; on a diet of biscuits and dried meat the health of the crew must have suffered. When the Americans broke ranks and signed a treaty with the newly appointed envoys from Beijing, Elgin decided to put an end to Chinese prevarications and with the French, forced their way in small ships over the bar into the river, blasting the forts on either side, and moving into Tianjin.

Still the Chinese envoys hesitated to agree to two of Elgin's main terms, the right of foreigners to travel through inland China and to station diplomats in the Chinese capital. Stepping up the pressure with a threat to march on Beijing, Elgin at last forced a capitulation and the Treaty of Tianjin was virtually completed, with the addition of three more cities (Hankou, Tianjin and Nanjing) as treaty ports. At the same time the treaty provided for foreign access to Chinese rivers, reduced tonnage dues, enabling foreign ships to enter the coastal trade, religious toleration, revised tariffs and the legalized sale of opium. But the trouble was far from over, and ratification was still two years away.

Elgin, having achieved his objectives, sailed away leaving his deputies to finalize the small print of the treaty and to have it

9. US Congressional Papers, *Chinese Correspondence 1857–1859* (Washington DC, 1860).

signed, sealed and ratified. The Chinese had other ideas. Smarting at the punishing blows inflicted by the Allied invasion fleet, the Manchu generals set a trap into which the British Rear Admiral James Hope obligingly fell, resulting in the greatest disaster for the Royal Navy in the China seas. Hope had planned to sail into Tianjin to have the treaties ratified. Had he sailed the way intended up the Beihe he may well have arrived unscathed. But the Manchu general, Prince Seng Ko-ling-ching (nicknamed "Sam Collinson" by the British troops) suggested an alternative approach by the port of Peitang, eight miles up the coast. Hope agreed, and believing that any attack from the Chinese forts would be quickly silenced, he sailed in to the narrow river with the booms obligingly opened.

Waiting for the line of Royal Navy ships to come broadside on to the forts, the Chinese defenders opened fire with a deafening roar from forty guns. The bombardment blew six of Hope's eleven gunboats out of the water, with heavy casualties. Four were driven ashore on the mudbanks by a falling tide and were left as sitting ducks for the Chinese gunners. The British forces found there was no chance of them establishing a beachhead on the sticky estuary mudbank. Under withering Chinese fire the British were dropping in hundreds, and of 1,100 who set off to capture the forts, one in three perished in the mud. Even the Americans, holding back as neutrals, felt compelled to rush in and help extricate the survivors.

Nor was this the end of the British tale of woe. Down south in Guangzhou, a month earlier, 700 Royal Marines taking part in a raid on an insurgent hideout in the hills were caught in an ambush and severely mauled. Its pride severely dented in China and smarting from the effects of a lacklustre campaign in the Crimea against the Russians at Sebastopol, the British Parliament decided there was only one course left; it would declare war, which it did in April 1859. The Government stressed that hostilities were directed against the Manchu rulers and would hopefully not affect the tea and opium trades in the south. This time not only would the Allies force the ratification of the Treaty in Tianjin but would press for even greater indemnities, the opening of more treaty ports, a permanent legation in the Chinese capital and the cession of more territory.

Those who governed Hong Kong had long been irritated by the Chinese presence in the Kowloon peninsula and the exposed position of British ships in the harbour. Now was the chance to make a new land grab, the sooner the better since the French were also sending a large military force to take part in the war in the north. The terrible thought crossed the mind of the British Governor that the French might consider the Kowloon peninsula an ideal place to use as a staging ground for its ambitions. Mindful of the prickly nature of Anglo-French relations in Quebec, no British statesman wanted another close encounter with the French — the idea of a French Kowloon and a British Hong Kong, mon Dieu! the thought horrified all right-thinking Englishmen.

Harry Parkes was determined to get in first. He reported later to the British Government that he had visited Guangzhou and held an audience with the Governor of Guangdong Province on 12 March 1860, indicating his concerns about French intentions and expressing his wish to occupy the peninsula. He told London that the mandarin "had no objection" to this proposal, but qualified this later by saying that he had inferred this from the fact that the Chinese official had made no response. Harry Parkes thereupon put in a bid for two square miles at 500 silver taels a year in perpetuity, and arranged for the 13,000 strong British expeditionary force to camp there, armed with the latest Armstrong 24-pounder field guns and the new Lee Enfield rifles — the same rifles which had caused all the bother in India.

Kowloon had not even been formally ceded when the British army put its stamp of ownership on the peninsula and a battle royal developed between the General, Sir Hope Grant, and the Governor, Sir Hercules Robinson, over ownership. The War Office backed the General who promptly grabbed the choicest and highest ground, leaving the Governor protesting vehemently to the Colonial Office; how else, he asked, could he keep the Chinese at a distance from the European community to preserve them from "the injury and inconvenience of intermixture with the Chinese residents?" The row dragged on until 1864 when the issue was settled by a compromise which confirmed the Army's occupation of its large central cantonment and left the Government and the Navy to argue over the rest.

An Army artist has left a water-colour sketch of rows of white tents spread over the high ground of the Kowloon peninsula, presumably once common land enjoyed by the villagers, who of course were not consulted either by the British Army, the Governor of Hong Kong, the Governor of Guangdong or the Emperor in Beijing. The Army clung to its title for more than a century when the land was finally turned into parks and recreation areas and "returned" to the people.

The demands of the armed services have always commanded greater attention in Whitehall than the wishes of the Colonial Office; their belated surrender of barracks land in the final years of British occupation was partly because they no longer needed it, partly the chance to take a tidy profit (such as the sale of central dockyard land to the Hong Kong Government for HK$112 million in the late 1950s), and partly an attempt to keep out the People's Liberation Army from the central residential and business districts of Hong Kong and Kowloon after 1997.[10]

---

10. The Chinese occupants of a nearby walled village, known as "Kowloon City," proved a lot more stubborn when it came to surrendering title to the British thirty-eight years later with the leasing of the New Territories. Unplanned, over-developed, unpoliced and unregulated, it remained for many years a festering sore as a centre of drug distribution and racketeering. Eventually, an agreement with China was concluded in the last years of the lease to demolish the high-rise buildings and narrow alleys and turn it into a public park.

In taking possession of Kowloon, Britain sent Elgin back to finish the job which had ended so disastrously on the banks of the Beihe. With him would go Harry Parkes as the main Chinese-speaking diplomatic intermediary and of course Baron Gros, the French plenipotentiary, and the dashing General Cousin de Montauban to lead the 7,500 all volunteer French force. Also there would be a Cantonese "coolie corps" to do the manual work, these men recruited in Hong Kong and including many who at other times had served as pirates.

Planning their attack with much greater care this time, the Allies targeted the Dagu forts first and with devastating fire silenced them; at the same time they turned back the threat from a large cavalry force led by Prince Seng who was waiting in the wings to cut down the invasion troops. Once again the British and French took heavy casualties in attacking across the muddy approaches to the forts, but this time the greater loss was felt by the defenders.

So confident was Parkes and thirty-nine other members of the British expedition that a number of them passed through Chinese lines on a tour of inspection during a truce. Never a favourite of the Chinese because of his harsh, hectoring and arrogant manner, Parkes was seized and taken back to Beijing and thrown into a filthy dungeon; he was lucky to survive when nineteen others in his party died of mistreatment and illness. When the Allies pressed their advance to the gates of Beijing and were ready to batter them down, Parkes was set free and Elgin was later carried in triumph in a sedan chair through the streets of the capital where he dictated the peace treaty to Prince Gong, including a substantially increased indemnity.

Parkes was duly honoured for his role in the march on Beijing by being made ambassador in Japan, a country he greatly admired and whose cause he did much to promote. As his respect for Japan grew, his contempt for China intensified. When he was later asked to return to the Legation in Beijing as Minister Plenipotentiary he felt as if he were "shackled to a corpse" and held out little prospect of its emergence as a major Asian power, putting his faith in Japan.

The tragedy in Parkes's case was that he had become a proficient linguist and was a courageous, hard-working if intolerant diplomat, but never had the patience or the temperament to understand the Chinese as they struggled to respond to the Western challenge. His opinions were formed as an adolescent when China was the butt of universal scorn and disdain, and his view never changed. Nor did the slap on the face from the Chinese boatman during the *Arrow* affair, sweeten his impression of the country.

The Americans clinging to their favoured course of neutrality, chose to go it alone and signed a separate peace with the Chinese, though if they expected any appreciation for their neutrality it was not apparent. Their new commissioner, John Ward, was hustled into Beijing on the back of an unsprung cart and almost dragged before the Emperor Xianfeng; he declined, however, to perform the kowtow. At the last moment the Emperor refused to meet him and Ward peeled off his uniform to begin the long, bumpy trek over cobblestone roads to Peitang. For trying to play the neutrality card, Ward ended up being the joker in the Allied pack.

Still that was not the end. There followed the episode of the looting and burning of the Summer Palace, a reprisal for the deaths of the nineteen Allied prisoners, which remains one of the blackest pages in the history of the British Army in modern times. The breakdown in discipline was sanctioned, if not encouraged, by the officers; the looting by both the French and British armies of the treasures of Chinese culture turned one of the most beautifully designed and decorated buildings in China into a disgraceful shambles. Anything portable, such as garments, jewellery, paintings, ceramics or decorations, was seized and pocketed, and most of what could not be taken was ravaged in a systematic campaign of destruction. Playing as spirited a part in this orgy of looting, raping and desecration was the Cantonese Coolie Corps who saw for themselves the rich pickings of the despised Manchu monarchy scattered about, and gleefully pocketed their share.

The full weight of opprobrium, however, falls on Lord Elgin who apparently of his own volition, decided to compound this extraordinary act of vandalism by torching what was left of the buildings. Coming from a man who earlier distinguished himself by bringing cabinet government to Canada and who established a reputation for enlightened liberal reforms, his actions in China were out of character.

During the campaign he professed to be frequently sickened by the action he initiated but the looting and burning of the palace was an amazing lapse. He tried much later to justify it by telling a Royal Academy dinner in London that it was directed against the Manchu rulers rather than the people of China. Besides, he continued, "I do not think in matters of art we have much to learn from that country. The most cynical representations of the grotesque have been the principal products of Chinese

Figure 9.4 Cixi, the Empress Dowager, preferred this stone boat to a full-fledged navy.

conceptions of the sublime and beautiful." He added: "No one regretted more sincerely than I did the destruction of that collection of summer houses and kiosks."[11]

Few in the audience could ever have seen the Summer Palace or known its contents and so perhaps the inevitable "hear, hear!" and the shuffling of empty port glasses and puffs of cigar smoke provided the final epitaph for the old peer before he set sail for India to take up his due reward — his appointment as Governor-General.

No act of war has left such a bitter legacy of hatred as this pointless and wanton act of spite for which there could be no redress or forgiveness by Chinese trying to come to terms with the Western impact and its claims of a superior civilization. Among the items of loot presented to Queen Victoria — Montauban had himself suggested the souvenirs for the French Emperor and English Queen — was a jade and gold sceptre, three enamel bowls and a Pekingese lap dog, named Lootie.

The Empress Dowager, Cixi, hit upon a brilliant idea to restore the burnt-out palace. Her advisers told her that China would never defeat the Western barbarians until it had a navy capable of matching the warships of the allies. She agreed and decided that the national priority was so high the Imperial household must itself closely supervise the work. Somehow the signals got mixed. The only ship that was ever built with the funds allocated was the stone boat on the edge of the palace lake where the Empress could entertain her courtiers. It remains there to this day. The rest of the naval vote went into rebuilding the burnt-out palace.

---

11. Jack Beeching, *The Chinese Opium Wars*.

CHAPTER 10

Reformers and Reactionaries

The Allied invasion of Beijing made the Manchu rulers realize that the Western powers had China in a stranglehold. So great was the shock that when the opium-addicted emperor, Xianfeng, died in his summer hideaway in Rehe a year later, a *coup d'état* took place in the palace that was brutal, swift and bloody. The designated heir-apparent was five years old and two powerful women, one of whom was his mother and chief concubine, and the other the consort of the dead emperor, made a grab for the throne. Rarely have women ruled China; those who succeeded were usurpers, aided and abetted by ambitious and scheming eunuchs. In this case, Ci'an and Cixi assumed the titles of Empress Dowager. They would initially share power with the designated regent, a power they won by theft, trickery and daring.

On his death bed, the last emperor, Xianfeng, had dictated that on no account should Cixi be given any authority; preferably she should be given a silken cord — an invitation to go and hang herself. This declaration was entrusted to a eunuch to be handed on his death to his designated regent Sushun; in the meantime it was hidden with the Emperor's personal documents and his official seal of office. Cixi, also known as Yehenala, her Manchu name, had her own coterie of eunuchs anxious to win favours; from them she found out about the letter and discovered the hiding place. She grabbed it and at the same time confiscated the seal moments after the emperor's demise. Without the seal,

Sushun and his two co-regents, also designated by the dead emperor, were powerless to act in any legal framework.

Trusting that the missing seal would turn up somehow in time for them to assume their duties the three men dutifully took their places in the funeral procession from Rehe to Beijing. Cixi and Ci'an took another route to the capital, escaping a murder plot in the process, and arrived in the Forbidden City ahead of the slow-moving procession. There they enlisted a powerful ally, Prince Gong, to become "Prince Counsellor." When the three nominated regents arrived in the capital, Cixi then met them and demanded they give proof of the dead Emperor's transfer of power and their seal of office. They had neither, and with the help of her group of eunuchs, Cixi then played her ace by displaying the seal and proclaiming her succession. The silken cords were sent to the two co-regents and Sushun was condemned as a usurper to be beheaded. With the help of Prince Gong, Cixi would strive to regain the ascendancy over the Western powers.

Surrounded by reform-minded officials, Cixi was told that the only way to beat the Western powers was with more powerful weapons and well-trained armies. The reformers advised her to build a series of arsenals in different provinces and to make guns and munitions for the army and a modern navy. Events had proved the inadequacies of the coastal forts and even the barricades and booms laid across the river failed to deter the invaders. There was a belated recognition by the rulers that the greatest threat came not from internal revolt — for the Taipings still posed a danger — but from the China Sea.

It was not only ships of war that China needed but ships to carry its produce and manufactures. China could, of course, buy these guns and ships from Western industrial powers but despite Western aid during the Taiping Rebellion, its leaders were deeply suspicious of their motives and believed they would be tricked or fobbed off with inferior or obsolete products; there would be no peace of mind until China could build its own weapons and construct its own fleet and man them with Chinese seamen and gunners, China remembered that in 1841 it had bought a second-hand man-of-war from Britain which had not survived its first engagement. Also, it was humiliating that Western (mainly British) ships were carrying the bulk of China's cargoes not only to overseas customers but to Chinese ports and along the length of its rivers.

Serious enough were the attacks by the Western allies on China but as the nineteenth century wore on rebellions began breaking out in many other parts of the country, while pirates swarmed along the coastline and triad societies began battling for control of the provinces. Between 1860 and 1870 there were fifty different anti-Manchu movements in various parts of China, and another fifty-five between 1870 and 1885; some were on a small scale, but others like the Taiping and Nian revolts removed large areas from central control. Then there was the Miao Rebellion in Guizhou and the Muslim rising in the north-west.

While all this was going on inside the country the Chinese were losing their traditional support from neighbouring tribute states as colonial powers (including France and Japan) took over in Vietnam, Korea and Taiwan. The cruellest cut came from France in 1884 following several bloody encounters with the Chinese Black Flag irregulars barring their invasion path in Indo-China where the French Army was trying to gain a foothold. To convey its displeasure at what it perceived to be Chinese interference with its plans, the French bombarded one of the new Chinese arsenals and sank a fleet of new Chinese naval vessels which French technicians had helped build. On top of that, piqued by British territorial claims in Hong Kong and Kowloon, France took over bases in Taiwan and the Pescadores islands.

Up to that time France had played a minor role in China. Sulking after its defeat at Waterloo, it had regained its self-esteem with the restoration of the monarchy in the second empire of Louis-Napoleon and was ready to stamp its name on the world scene once again; where better to begin than in that great imperialist kicking ground, China. France had recently restored its military fortunes in the Crimea under General Pelissier at Sebastopol. It had built up a formidable steam-powered navy that even worried Britain. France's Ferdinand de Lesseps had persuaded Egypt to allow him to build a canal at Suez and self-esteem was rapidly turning to arrogance. France had joined forces with Britain in the *Arrow* affair of 1858–1860, following the murder of one of its missionaries in inland China, and had become intoxicated with the prospects of La Gloire en Chine.

Surveying the scene, France saw that Britain was already several jumps ahead of her, but still managed to carve out small concessions for herself in Hankou, Guangzhou and Shanghai. In the latter the French were squeezed uncomfortably between the international settlement and the Chinese city, but at least the tricolor flew unchallenged. Now France wanted its own sphere of influence in the Far East and surveying the scene, saw that the Red River in Tongking would give her access through the back door to the vast interior of south-west China; at the same time it would give her control of the territories of Vietnam, Laos and Cambodia.

Territorially, France was aiming at a land grab to rival that of Britain in the Indian subcontinent 200 years earlier where its own ambitions had been thwarted, as they had also been in the Americas. The development rights this would give to French industrialists — notably railway and shipbuilders — would gain for the country a sizeable share of the expanding international economy then unfolding. The French saw the Red River as a new unexploited point of infiltration into China — unconventional perhaps but when its European neighbours were battling to enter China by the front door, it took a special stroke of genius to find a back door with exclusive access.

The problem confronting the French was how to force their way in. A band of dedicated Black Flag terrorists barred their way, making the French fight for every square foot of territory they occupied. The missionaries were quick to follow in the footsteps of those who planted the colonial flag. The treaties of

1858–1860 re-established the right of Roman Catholics to start up missions in China closed by the Qing rulers in the previous century and France became not only the major source of missionaries both to Vietnam and China but also their official protector — at least of the Catholics.

When, as happened, the missionaries based in the interior took a lot of the punishment for the humiliations France inflicted in the coastal provinces, the most demanding voice for stricter safeguards and new indemnities was that of France. The most prominent Roman Catholic cathedrals — those in Guangzhou and in Tianjin — were provocatively built on sensitive sites, in the case of Guangzhou on the site of Commissioner Ye's headquarters and in the case of Tianjin, on a Confucian temple. In Shanghai, the French also bulldozed a temple and cemetery which got in the way of development.

The protestant missionaries, less numerous, were equally disliked by a populace that saw little appeal in the contradictory doctrines of the multi-denominational Western Christians. The teaching they introduced, the schools and universities they set up, the new knowledge of science and medicine they ushered in, were cautiously embraced. But the Chinese continued to believe in the superiority of their own system which had stood them in good stead for centuries.

Foreigners themselves were baffled at China's ability to survive, particularly after the shocks it experienced in the nineteenth-century collision with the West. The correspondent of *The Times*, J. O. P. Bland, could not help marvelling "that a machine apparently so clumsy and defective should preserve such astonishing vitality and cohesion." He believed that in Europe such a system could not have lasted a week. "At no point of its unwieldy bulk can you find evidence of definite purpose, intercommunication or method; everywhere you come upon rule-of-thumb makeshifts, compromises and gaping voids. No written law runs through the land, nor any code; edicts are meaningless except where they voice local opinion; even precedents, the unwritten foundation of rough-and-ready justice, are at the mercy of every Yamen clerk. Yet the thing holds together and does its work for a third of humanity without any great jolting or creaking. The explanation lies in the patient docility — up to a certain limit — of the Chinese people, and the wisdom of rulers who have learned to a nicety where that limit is and who seldom transgress it."[1] That was his view in 1909, just before the revolution.

Where culture and tradition were concerned, moreover, the Chinese clung tenaciously to their familiar folklore and traditional superstitition; let the newcomers prove the superiority of their industry and science; let the missionaries prove the potency of their god; let the biblical miracles they preached unfold on the sceptical ground of China. The Chinese people would then adopt and graft to their culture what was worthwhile, practical, profitable and useful. But the great wall of scepticism and doubt remained their first defence against the wise men from the West.

One of the first steps taken by Prince Gong following Cixi's *coup d'état* was the establishment in 1861 of a foreign ministry, long demanded by the West, to be known as the Zongli Geguo Shiwu Yamen, or more simply, the Zongli Yamen. This was essential if only to avoid the disasters that had engulfed China in the past whenever foreigners wanted to present petitions to the authorities. Previously there was no recognized channel of access; before the Opium War the only method of approach was through the Hong merchants to the Hoppo and the Viceroy. If that failed it was left to gunboat diplomacy.

Cixi preferred the less provocative approach if only because it allowed her to play for time. She believed that within a few months China could virtually buy her way out of trouble with

---

1. J. O. P. Bland, *Houseboat Days in China* (London: Heinemann, 1919).

sufficient armaments and ships to confront the Europeans and beat them at their own game; in this way she would also ensure her own survival and the life of the dynasty.

There are conflicting views on the role of Cixi, some believing she was under the influence of the "Iron Hat" faction of Prince Duan, the conservative element in Beijing, which dictated hardline policies she was obliged to follow. But it is hard to see her in any other light than as a reactionary product of the Qing dynasty with very firm views on maintaining an absolute rule as her predecessors had done. Cixi had definite ideas about the place of the rulers and the ruled; as long as she kept her place and they kept theirs, reform was a matter for debate rather than hasty action. Many Chinese people of that era also believed that reform could be confined to a few superficial changes; others who had been exposed to a full Western education or who had lived overseas, realized that basic restructuring was urgent and essential.

To trace the impact of Western learning on China it is necessary to go back to when the first missionaries arrived in the sixteenth century, and who as well as proselytizing their faith took on a teaching role. Those who wished to follow a religious life — and they were few in those early years — were sent to seminaries in Italy. But the Jesuits realized that so many concepts taken for granted in Europe were foreign to Chinese students; thus, all who came under their influence were first given a full Western education in the Italian or Portuguese language. However well versed they were in the Chinese classics, they needed to understand European science, philosophy, history, literature — even geography. Words could not adequately convey meaning; ideas had to be explained; names and places needed elaboration if they were to bridge the cultural gulf. The Protestants entered the field much later, notably through the efforts of Dr Robert Morrison and Dr William Milne in the Anglo-Chinese College in Malacca in 1815, and continued by the American, The Revd Samuel Brown.

One of their outstanding students was a young Chinese

named Yung Wing who, though a child of a poor farmer, mastered English so well that he was able to attend Yale University and eventually to launch the Chinese Educational Mission which did valued service in sending young Chinese overseas for further studies (120 between 1872 and 1881). These would later return to serve their country.

Another of these first graduates from the Morrison Education Society was Wong Fun, the first Chinese to graduate from a Western medical school. Another was Tong A-chick, later to join the China Merchants Steam Navigation Company, while Wong Shing was one of the first Chinese writers and publishers of the modern era, having served in the Chinese legation in Washington before running the printing house of the missionary, Dr James Legge. He later served on Hong Kong's Legislative Council. Not all, however, were an unqualified success. Tong A-chick later recalled that when the school was formed "it had five boys. Afterwards the eldest, whose name was Aling, went home because he did a very bad thing and committed a great sin against God, as in the law of Moses and the prophets."[2] Alas, we are not told more about this heinous act by Aling but in a country in which English-speaking students were all too rare it is hard to believe he did not find a way of putting his language skills to profitable use.

Other schools were founded in Guangzhou and in Tianjin while academies to provide special instruction in naval and military skills, at least one to train doctors and another teaching telegraphy, were opened in various parts of China in the 1880s. In Hong Kong a number of schools were opened for secondary education. A Board of Education was established in the colony in 1860 on the advice of Dr James Legge, and the following year saw the inauguration of the Government Central School, later to become Queen's College, while the Roman Catholics set up schools

---

2. Carl T. Smith, *Chinese Christians* (Hong Kong: Oxford University Press, 1985).

to equip students (mainly Portuguese) with a knowledge of English to help them secure jobs in local trading and business firms.

So well established and successful were these schools that twenty years later Hong Kong had its first medical graduates practising in the colony, and by 1880 Ng Choy (educated in England) was appointed to the Legislative Council. Ng Choy (in mandarin, Wu Tingfang) not only served as a stipendiary magistrate but following his term in Legislative Council, rose to the position of Chinese Ambassador to the United States in 1896 and 1897 before being appointed to cabinet posts in the Chinese republic.

Other notable "local" members of Legislative Council included Emanuel Belilios who not only provided scholarships at Queen's College and the Hong Kong Medical College but founded a school in his name; there was also Wong Shing, his son-in-law Wei Yuk (son of a comprador of a leading bank and educated at Scotland's Dollar Academy and later knighted) and the legendary Paul Catchick Chater, though he received most of his education before arriving in Hong Kong. Sir Paul, an Armenian from Bombay, was one of the most significant businessmen in Hongkong's history and the counterpart of Cecil Rhodes in Africa (without the imperial ambitions), responsible for much of the city's early development and business growth.

This expansion of Western education in Hong Kong was important because the scheme to send promising young students to the United States fell on stony ground when Chinese immigration to that country was stopped in 1880. Students thereafter were brought back and educated in new schools in Guangzhou, Shanghai and Tianjin. China needed the language experts not only to staff its Zongli Yamen but to act as intermediaries at the commercial level and to keep the rising crop of Chinese statesmen and entrepreneurs informed of the procedures, practices and policies of Western diplomats and businessmen setting up in China.

Initially, China wanted the minimum from the West — just

enough to beat it at its own game. A veneer of Western technology was thought by many to be sufficient to balance the scales. But the more deeply China became involved in setting up railways, arsenals, steamship companies, coal mines, cotton and silk mills and even steel works, the more its scholars realized that universal knowledge transcended the narrow nationalistic aims of those who only wanted to defend the dynasty. This was the dawning of the reform movement.

One of the most perceptive and articulate advocates of change was Zeng Guofan who recognized that following the Treaty of Tianjin China could not return to isolation. It was now caught up in the international political world, like it or not. To avoid a further deterioration in the country's position, he argued the need to study Western ways and institutions so that positive and beneficial negotiations could take place. The present dependence on uneducated interpreters was senseless. China also needed a modern army and navy equipped with the latest weapons built by its own arsenals and shipyards. "Only in this way can we play a leading part in world affairs and restore our strength and overcome former humilitations," he wrote.[3] China needed to study Western science and mathematics. He also emphasized the growing gulf between the throne and the people but he wanted to maintain Confucianism and traditional Chinese ethics. His ideas eventually were to emerge in an accepted policy known as Ziqiang (or, self-strengthening) and led to an era of industrial reform.

Dragging her feet, however, was the Empress Dowager, Cixi, who by now had discarded Ci'an and had reduced Prince Gong to a tolerated figurehead. Cixi believed in the ultimate triumph of Chinese culture, tradition and civilization. Shrewd and calculating she unquestionably was, but so blinkered in her vision that

---

3. Jean Chesnaux, M. Bastid and M-C Bergers, *China From the Opium Wars to the 1911 Revolution* (New York: Pantheon, 1972).

she could not look beyond her survival as head of the Qing dynasty. Fortunately for China she was surrounded by men who knew (or thought they knew) how to manipulate the old lady and profit from the changes then taking place.

One of the more unpalatable changes which Cixi had to accept was surrendering control of the Customs Service to a foreigner — one of the results of the Treaty of Nanjing. The service began in Shanghai as a temporary expedient during a local rebellion when customs duties could only be collected by the British consul; not wanting to become the permanent collector and finding the Chinese customs office riddled with rackets and corruption, it was decided to set up an independent authority. In 1861, the inspector-general in the city, H. N. Lay, became head of the national service. Two years later, Lay, son of an old China hand, and never an admirer of the people, although fluent in their language, applied to buy and manage a fleet of ships for China, only to find after sailing them from England that it was to be run by a Chinese director. He resigned and the ships were sent back to England. It was a blessing for China that Lay left for he was hectoring and truculent in negotiations with Chinese statesmen and was typical of the arrogant, intolerant Englishmen who gained such a deplorable reputation in the colonial era to follow.

He was succeeded by a man who brought more credit to the British presence in China than any other before or since. He was an Irishman, Robert Hart, who like Lay was a fluent Chinese speaker, having started his career in the consular service. When the Imperial Maritime Customs Service was transferred to Beijing in 1865, Hart introduced reforms which while keeping all the senior posts under Europeans, nonetheless turned the Service into the most dependable source of revenue available to the Government. He was, moreover, scrupulously loyal to China and acted as an intermediary with Western governments on several occasions, by whom he was also greatly respected.

Hart launched a school for Chinese customs officers and so high was its reputation that after the Boxer Rebellion it was

merged into Beijing University. Hart was incorruptible and instilled this ethic in his staff; in a land where bribery was common,
a man of his ability and character was almost unique. Where in
the pre–Opium War days, much of the tax had ended up lining
the pockets of a variety of regional officials, under Hart the collected duty was scrupulously accounted for, and remitted to the
Treasury. At the same time, the Chinese Postal Service was
launched in 1878 when the official courier service was merged
with the Native Post Office, using customs offices as distribution
and reception points.

Shipping lines were quick to move into inland waterways,
particularly the Yangzi River. Among them were those belonging
to British firms such as Jardine, Matheson and later, Butterfield &
Swire. The Chinese were irked by the fact that junks, which had
handled the coastal and river trade for centuries, were now losing
out to foreign vessels which carried goods faster and more cheap-
ly. Reformers had urged the establishment of a Chinese shipping
line to combat the alarming decline in the coastal junk numbers
from 2,000 in 1850 to 400 in a matter of twenty years. In 1872, a
Ningbo junk owner with a contract for carrying grain to the
capital launched a company with three steam ships. It had seven
times the number five years later and ran profitably within three
years. Government loans were invested in the company and one
of the leading reformers, Li Hongzhang, showed acumen in head-
hunting a Jardine Matheson comprador, Tang Dingshu, to become a director.

Another notable achievement was the establishment of
China's first modern iron and steel works at Hanyang in 1894 —
two years before the Japanese launched their Yawata steel works.
The Hanyeping Coal and Iron Company managed to keep pace
with Yawata's output for the first fifteen years of existence but
with the turmoil following the 1911 Revolution it slipped back.
Ironically it was the Chinese company that helped Yawata to
become a success by supplying iron ore to Japan. The Chinese
company declined because of its inability to develop a strong local

market and to modernize its plant, whereas Yawata thrived with its vigorous shipbuilding and armaments industry.

Railways took longer to become accepted. Not only was the Government unimpressed with them but *fengshui* problems caused the first 16-km line built from Shanghai to Wusong at the Yangzi estuary, to be torn up by angry peasants. But Li Hongzhang, who had initially opposed their construction, now decided to support railways and devised a plan to link the capital with the main trading ports such as Shanghai, Hankou, Guangzhou and inland to Lanzhou; these began in the 1880s.

It was not until ten years later that the first officially sponsored textile mill — the Shanghai Cotton Cloth Mill — got into production after a series of mishaps in trying to raise capital. Others launched in the 1860s by private enterprise had a fitful history before they became established and the first all-Chinese factory took advantage of the abundance of local silk to concentrate on that fabric, though it aroused strong Luddite opposition from local artisans who in one case attacked and destroyed a plant responsible for undermining their livelihood. No more successful were semi-mechanized flour mills, rice husking, paper-making and match-making factories.

On the whole, Government sponsored industries fared better than private enterprise in the early years with the latter finding it difficult to raise capital from a sceptical merchant community unsure of China's ability to handle modern technology. Furthermore, private local factories found it hard to compete with the far wealthier and more experienced foreigners in setting up competititive industries. The Chinese economy had been founded on agriculture with handcrafts as a sideline in off-seasons to supplement rural incomes. The advent of factories came later during the Government's campaign to promote self-strengthening. However, the impact of unrestricted Western trade would kill off many of the small handcraft makers who were unable to compete with cheap mass produced goods. Others simply made goods for themselves and opted out of trying to sell their surplus.

When Western exports increased, as they did following the development in the United States of the cotton gin (which separated the seeds from the fibre mechanically), the prices fell even further. When the Civil War ended in America, freeing exports, the Chinese were faced with the prospect of abandoning hand-made garments entirely and starting their own factories. The change was slow, reluctant and bitter. Weaving fared slightly better because Chinese domestic weavers used imported yarns to produce cheaper and higher quality goods, particularly in towns out of reach of ships and railways. This would become the basis of the spinning and weaving industry, one of the biggest in the world.

China also developed its own mining industry to support the arsenals at Hanyang, Fuzhou, Nanjing and Tianjin making armaments and building shipyards. One of the early successes was the Kaiping Mining Company producing coal and iron for the China Merchants Steam Navigation Company and the arsenal at Tianjin, while the Fuzhou arsenal obtained its coal from a mine developed by a British engineer in Taiwan.

The huge coal deposits at Tangshan quickly attracted investment capital and its supplies went into launching China's first industrial complex in North China. The greatest drawback was

Figure 10.1 The first arsenal to be built in China was at Nanjing, as this picture by John Thompson in the 1860s shows.

lack of proper equipment to achieve the productivity needed by industry. Many of the mines were so small that they were worked by hand, but while industrial technology was primitive and worker skills rudimentary, China's first major capitalists began to emerge and it was notable that many were from Guangdong where huge profits had been made from opium, tea and banditry, in that order.

While China struggled with industrial development, Hong Kong and the treaty ports had more success in introducing new industries, confident that public utilities and companies could find a ready market for their products, either internally or in the growing consumer markets outside. These included gas works, ferries, tram services and electricity generators, as well as flour and sugar mills, rope-making, soap-making, shipbuilding, cigarette-making and brewing factories.

Major local and overseas banking and insurance firms emerged in the concessions to handle the upsurge in trade, investment and industry. Many hotels under European management were quick to appear in Hong Kong, Shanghai, Guangzhou and other treaty ports, following the influx of tourists brought in by the big international shipping lines such as Peninsular & Oriental, British India, Blue Funnel (all of Britain), Messageries Maritimes (French), Java, China, Japan Line (Dutch), Nor-Deutscher Lloyd (German) and eventually Nippon Yusen Kaisha (Japan).

Peninsular & Oriental, which came into existence as early as 1837 with the advent of iron-clad paddle steamers, was running services to Singapore and Hong Kong by 1845, despite the fact that the Suez Canal would not be completed for another twenty-four years. The company split the UK–Far East run with one service undertaking the Mediterranean leg and another operating from India to the Orient. Nor were passengers its only interest for the 533-ton *Lady Mary Wood* carried opium and on one voyage, bunker coal had to be stored on deck because there was no space in her holds. But P & O ships were also the mail carrier and that was an important and profitable contract.

Napoleon Bonaparte had in the late eighteenth century, recognized that the way to control Britain was to cut off its links with India and the Far East. This led him to invade Egypt and take control of Cairo, capturing Malta on the way; in this way, the Mediterranean became a "French lake." Only his eviction by Nelson in the Battle of the Nile ended his imperial dreams. Increasingly thereafter, the isthmus was used as a transit link between Europe and Asia, and eventually a Frenchman would build the Suez Canal open to ships of all nations, transforming East–West trade and drastically cutting travelling time between Europe and Asia.

The exotic Far East had exerted a strong pull on Western imaginations and the descriptions of travels by writers such as William Thackeray, Rudyard Kipling, Joseph Conrad, Jules Verne and others spurred interest in voyages to the mysterious and exciting countries of the Middle East, India, Ceylon (Sri Lanka), Malaya, Singapore, the Netherlands East Indies, Vietnam, China and Japan. And when Puccini, Verdi and Gilbert and Sullivan added Egypt, Japan and China to their repertoire of opera the fascination with the Orient became intense.

Images of the China Sea and the South Pacific from the latter years of the eighteenth century and the early years of the nineteenth century came in paintings and sculpture, but the artists who visited the East were on the whole less prominent and therefore largely unnoticed by the world's major galleries and museums. Artists such as John Zoffany, and Thomas and William Daniell did well in India; the Daniells also produced some striking scenes of China, as did William Alexander, who accompanied the Macartney mission in 1793. John Webber did much to highlight the voyages of Captain Cook, and Augustus Earle and Conrad Martens were prolific in their output as the artists accompanying Charles Darwin on HMS *Beagle*. But they were not to be compared with the great artists of their day such as Reynolds, Gainsborough, Constable, Lawrence, Turner, Whistler,

David, Gerricault, Goya and Delacroix who found enough to employ their talents in Europe.

Before this generation of artists visited the East, the Western world took its pictures of life in the Orient from the vogue of chinoiserie which found a place on furniture, dinnerware, pottery, textiles and garden design. In a fanciful world of pagodas, tranquil lakes, misty mountains, curtained waterfalls, stately pine-trees, remote and isolated temples and becalmed junks, Western decorators created a fanciful landscape forever slumbering in idle reverie — a Shangri-La where unreal people lived in an unreal world. The fashion caught on when the style was adopted by Louis XIV at Versailles, followed by the German emperors and eventually the court in England. Thus it filtered down into popular imagination that here was a land untouched by time or tide, by greed or gain, by labour or industry. The rude awakening in the violence of the Opium Wars, the march on Beijing and the burning of the Summer Palace, did much to dispel these myths without, however, extinguishing the interest of the West.

China was no longer as innocent as the willow pattern motif on blue-and-white porcelain but it remained a destination for visitors, traders, salesmen, bankers, missionaries, diplomats — the whole gamut of grubby, grasping, greedy Western pioneers who saw new openings, new opportunities, new markets, and above all new profits, in this quaint old land that had cherished and defended its antiquity for too long.

As the great steamship lines took over from the tea clippers travelling through the Canal, the time, hazard and distance barriers that had served to bar all but the intrepid adventurer, merchant, soldier or sailor, collapsed. Those with the money also enjoyed taking the regular sailings now being advertised in the British and Continental Press to a region where the sights and smells of the exotic East beckoned and beguiled. Kipling romanticized it in verse. "Ship me somewhere East of Suez, where the best is like the worst, where there aren't no Ten Commandments, and a man can raise a thirst. For the temple bells are calling, and it's there that I would be, by the old Moulmein pagoda, looking lazy at the sea."

It became the great adventure for growing numbers of well-to-do people while there was a steady demand for cabins from army and naval officers, civil servants, entrepreneurs and commercial functionaries, school teachers, missionaries and doctors; those who could afford first-class would travel "port out, starboard home," while the rest slummed it in second-class, and the poorest suffered silently in steerage. Scenes of shipboard life by an artist more than 100 years ago recapture the easy elegance of the way in which the early first class passengers travelled. The contrast with the ships carrying convicts in the lower latitudes to Australia could not have been more stark.

As for the cargoes, mention has been made of teas, silk and opium but in time these gave way to manufactured goods such as cottons and yarns, paints, oils, chemicals, machinery, boilers, furnaces and heavy industrial goods as China became engulfed by the trappings of the West. By the middle of the nineteenth century, the East was contributing bales of rubber, ingots of tin, bags of copra, bundles of jute, and a growing list of oriental produce that had suddenly become indispensable in the West. Tea was by far the biggest item on the homeward journey but as steam took over from sail, and as Robert Fortune's tea plants took root in Indian and Ceylonese soil, so the massive exports of China tea began to dwindle.

The extensive damage to Chinese tea estates during the Taiping Rebellion and the heavier taxes imposed by provincial authorities turned British interest away from the delicate flavours of China blends to the stronger, tangier teas of the Subcontinent. Soon to develop major tea industries were the East Indies and East Africa, which also contributed their share of exports to the British market. To replace these lost exports of tea, China offered spices, ginger, cotton, hides and skins, furs, bamboo, poles, mats, lacework, chinaware, pig bristles, oil seed, lace, lacquer, *cloisonné* and embroidery.

To smell the aroma of an open hold on a freighter loading in an Eastern port was one of the most sensual memories of foreign passengers. In the decade following 1885, both imports and exports doubled in value and though there was a 10 per cent trade deficit in China's accounts with the West the figures reflected the growing diversity of China's secondary industry, mines and agriculture.

In 1894, there were about ninety foreign firms in China engaged in manufacturing; these ranged from shipbuilding and repairing, textiles, silk-spinning and various kinds of food processing, leather tanning and tobacco curing, coal mining and oil-distribution. Slowly, China was being drawn into the world trading network, albeit a reluctant, unconvinced partner, but welcoming the increasing employment it gave to people in the treaty ports and the opportunity for investment in Chinese enterprises.

Some of these firms were established by principals in the United Kingdom, Germany, France, the Netherlands and the United States — these included Imperial Chemical Industries, Shell Oil (which operated in China as the Asiatic Petroleum Company before World War II), the Chartered Bank of India, Australia and China (now Standard Chartered Bank), the Standard Oil Company of America; other companies were launched as a result of local initiatives by major firms such as Jardine, Matheson (responsible for some of the first textile and silk mills in China, as well as Indo-China Steamship Co. Ltd.), Butterfield & Swire (which launched China Navigation Co. Ltd. and Taikoo Sugar Refinery among others). The family of Sir Elly Kadoorie were involved in Hongkong & Shanghai Hotels, and later China Light & Power Co. Ltd.

Other firms were established by overseas investors and entrepreneurs trying their luck in Hong Kong or China — such as the Hongkong & China Gas Co. Ltd., the North China Daily News and the South China Morning Post Ltd., while in the case of others, local businessmen, foreign and Chinese, were the moving spirits. Foremost among them in Hong Kong was Sir Paul Chater, without whose vision its commercial expansion at the turn of the century would have been stillborn.

One of the strangest accidents was responsible for the birth of what is today the biggest business enterprise in the Far East — the Hongkong & Shanghai Banking Corporation. This was launched in 1864 as a result of the initiative of Mr (later Sir) Thomas Sutherland, head of the P & O Steamship Company in China. Sutherland recalls that he had never had a bank account in his life but while travelling from Hong Kong to Fuzhou on the P & O ship, *Manila*, he read an article in *Blackwood's Magazine* extolling the virtues of banking. Sutherland said: "It occurred to me that if a suitable opportunity arose, one of the very simplest things in the world would be to start a bank in China, more or less founded on Scottish principles."

He did not act on this inspiration immediately but when he heard that a group of leading businessmen in Bombay were planning to start a Royal Bank of China "I reflected a good deal on the subject and I thought we ought to endeavour to create a bank of our own on the same principles." He pulled out an envelope and on the back wrote out the prospectus of the Hongkong & Shanghai Banking Corporation, with a capital of $5 million in 20,000 shares valued at $250 each.

He then approached a number of leading companies to take a subscription; all agreed, the only major exception being Jardine, Matheson, which was then running a substantial banking department of its own — and was not yet convinced that it would be "the simplest thing in the world."[4] However, Jardine's main rival, Dent & Company, though similarly involved, considered it essential to launch a major independent locally-controlled bank. By the time the Bombay-based Royal Bank of China was ready to issue

---

4. Maurice Collis, *Wayfoong* (London: Faber, 1965).

its prospectus, the Hongkong & Shanghai Bank was up and running and the rival from the Subcontinent realized it had missed the boat.

The Bank's successful float was all the more remarkable because in 1865 and 1866 a world-wide financial crisis effectively wiped out six of the eleven international banks then operating in Hong Kong and China, as well as a number of leading mercantile houses, the most prominent being the firm of Dent & Company. Coming at the end of the Taiping Rebellion, Shanghai experienced a major economic crisis, particularly in real estate speculation, and the disruption of trade with the United States following the conclusion of the Civil War.

Among the casualties was one of the biggest exchange banks in Hong Kong, the Agra and Masterman's Bank; together with another leading British bank, the Chartered Bank of India, Australia and China, it had begun issuing notes which were legal tender in Hong Kong and the treaty ports. The Chartered Bank was lucky to survive; only a few years earlier both it and the Agra Bank had lost heavily — in excess of 100,000 pounds between them — when opium, which had been pledged as security for a loan, was fraudulently sold, stolen or sidetracked. The owners were unable to make good the loss. The money, literally and figuratively, went up in smoke.

These were risky days for new banks, wrestling with new forces in uncertain times following the extension of the international telegraph and the opening of the Suez Canal which called for far more immediate and urgent decisions involving large sums of money. Moreover, the outbreak of the Franco-Prussian War in 1870 had badly disrupted trade in Europe. The Hongkong & Shanghai Bank itself ran into difficulties and had to sack its first Manager, Victor Kresser, who in his enthusiasm for new business ventures made several bad decisions in regional investments, notably in sugar.

The second major blow was the failure of Dent & Co. and the Bank had to make provisions for its loss out of profits. There was worse to come eight years later when two other pillars of the bank, both big agency houses from Guangzhou, namely the American firm of Augustine Heard & Co. and the British firm of Fearon & Co., crumbled under the weight of losses. A second Chief Manager, James Greig, was given his marching orders; only a few years earlier its London manager, W. H. Vacher, had made disastrous speculations in South American railways, and had lost both on his own and the bank's account. He too was forced to leave. Thereafter it began to recover and to open branches in the region and play a leading part in financing foreign trade as its competitors dropped out one by one.

Commercial infiltration was the main priority of Western business houses in China but inevitably as the dynasty began to crumble and the bandwagon of reform gathered momentum, Chinese scholars inevitably turned to Western political philosophy for help in devising an ideology more appropriate to the times. They also wanted to examine how these ideas had influenced social conditions and spurred technological advances in the West. By the year 1900, with the outbreak of rebellion and the siege of the foreign legations by the Boxers (so-called because of their membership of the Society of Harmonious Fists) and yet another invasion of the national capital by foreign armies, China's reformers had come to accept the demise of the dynasty. But what would take its place?

Many looked hopefully at the Guangdong scholar Kang Youwei who had twice memorialized the throne with 10,000-character petitions to reform the country, urging the relocation of the capital from Beijing to a less vulnerable area — such as Xi'an, headquarters of the first Qin Emperor, Shihuangdi. Every self-respecting reformer had his long list of priorities, beginning with the armed forces, the monetary, banking and postal systems, the building of more schools, universities and libraries, changes to the examination system and the creation of elected consultative councils at the local and national level. It is doubtful whether the Empress Dowager gave them any more than a passing glance or a contemptuous sniff, and the Emperor, now of age and anxious to assert himself, was bypassed. This only increased the frustration of the scholars who realized the urgency of change and the futility of delay.

Kang and a group of scholars realized that the real stumbling block was the Empress Dowager herself and their petitions addressed the need for abolition of the absolute monarchy and its replacement by a constitutional monarchy. Another reformer, Liang Qichao, believed that overall modernization had to be brought in and that piecemeal solutions would achieve nothing, while Chen Duxiu believed that science, liberal democracy and individualism would yield the best results. Kang Youwei was then only forty, a candidate for the official examination and a far-sighted man who was also in the forefront of the movement to end the cruel crippling practice of binding the feet of young girls, beginning with his own daughters.

This provoked a family crisis among his traditional and conservative relations, but he succeeded to the point where an Anti-Footbinding Society was formed and this spread to major cities like Tianjin and Shanghai. Originally instituted by a royal concubine, this practice was widely adopted by socially prominent families. While it was intended to enhance the elegance and femininity of their daughters, essentially it was a form of domestic confinement to ensure premarital virtue and chastity. Curiously, the practice survived in the British colony of Hong Kong and so deeply was it ingrained that it lingered on until the outbreak of the 1911 Revolution, while female slavery, known as the *mui-tsai* system, and concubinage persisted until after 1945.

Kang Youwei may have succeeded in liberating women's feet but failed to achieve a top place in the national examination, dashing his hopes of preferment to high office. But he remained an articulate spokesman for reform and refused to be silenced. When his memorial to the throne was suppressed he leaked copies to the newspapers and eventually was called to the Zongli

Figure 10.2 Bound feet were common among women from well-to-do families in imperial China, as this painting by William Alexander shows.

Yamen (or Foreign Ministry) where he met ministers of state and the senior statesman, Li Hongzhang. Word of the meeting got back to the young Emperor who then conspired to bypass the Empress Dowager by using the now sickly and ageing Prince Gong as an intermediary. Believing he had at last found a sympathetic ear in the Forbidden City, Kang stepped up the pressure for reform and in China's parlous state there was widespread and growing support for his ideas.

Suddenly the old Prince collapsed and died and the young Emperor, Guangxu, freed from any restraining hands, decreed a programme of reform after a meeting with Kang and his fellow memorialists. He plunged into a frenzy of decrees, one of which dismissed Li Hongzhang from the Foreign Ministry. Choosing his advisers and supporters unwisely the young Emperor decided to stage a *coup* and lock up Cixi in the Summer Palace. One of his confidants was an ambitious general named Yuan Shikai who tipped off the old lady.

Exactly 103 days after the first reform edict was issued, Cixi swooped like an avanging angel, imprisoning the young Emperor and seizing his reformist advisers. Kang Youwei, by good luck, had left Beijing only a day earlier. His supporters survived only long enough to be hustled off to the execution ground, there to lose their heads at the hands of the swordsman, without even seeking a judicial nod. But as William Shakespeare could have told them, they had scotched the snake, not killed it.

---------------------------- CHAPTER 11 ----------------------------

The Great Land Grab

The reformers lost their heads, but the far more horrifying form of execution reserved for traitors and rebels was known as *lingchi* — death by a thousand cuts. This was death by dismemberment; it involved slicing, partitioning and finally beheading the victim in an excruciatingly slow, agonizingly painful and exquisitely Chinese form of torture. This was the fate awaiting China as the foreign powers began to scramble for concessions (or "slicing up the melon" as the Chinese described it) at first in the neighbouring tributary states and later in a revolt-racked China itself. France (in Vietnam), Britain (in Burma), Russia (in the northern province of Ili) and Japan (in Korea and the Ryukyu Islands, now Okinawa), did their utmost to strip the territorial insulation surrounding the Central Kingdom. The West used various pretexts, such as the murder of missionaries, diplomats, surveyors or other intruders, but these were thinly veiled excuses for colonial extension.

Again, China's greatest weakness was exposed in the sea approaches because it was unable to confront the foreign navies ranged against it. Its first encounter would be with a new imperialist — its quick-learning neighbour, Japan, forced open by the Americans less than fifty years earlier. The Chinese fleet of ironclads had taken on a smaller contingent of Japanese ships off the Yalu River in North Korea. Despite the presence of British gunners, the Chinese ships performed abysmally, largely because of misunderstandings due to language difficulties.

When the Chinese tried to reinforce its garrison in Korea it chartered three foreign ships to transport more than 3,000 fully armed and equipped soldiers. Leading the convoy was the Jardine, Matheson ship, *Kow Shing*; two days out of Dagu in North China, she encountered four Japanese warships. Captain Heihachiro Togo (later Admiral, who masterminded the defeat of the Russian fleet at Tsushima in 1904) ordered the skipper of *Kow Shing* to follow his vessels into a Japanese occupied port on the Korean coast. The British captain refused because of a near revolt on his ship by the Chinese soldiers. When the captain of *Kow Shing* ignored another order to abandon ship, the Japanese Navy opened fire with shells and torpedoes, sinking it.

To their credit, the Chinese soldiers on board returned fire as their ship sank beneath them, while the officers of *Kow Shing* (a Captain Galsworthy and Chief Officer Lewis Tamplin) took to the boats and rowed to the Japanese naval ships where they were rescued and later released. The Chinese perished in their hundreds, many after jumping into the sea where they were machine-gunned by Japanese sailors; the survivors were taken prisoner in Korea.

The result was that Japan took over Korea and for good measure moved into Port Arthur on the Liaodong Peninsula to safeguard its new acquisition. To ensure Chinese compliance Japanese troops occupied Weihaiwei for three years. In the Treaty of Shimonoseki which followed, the avaricious Japanese not only demanded an indemnity of $200 million and the opening of four more treaty ports, including Chongqing, but it took Taiwan and the Pescadores Islands as well in perpetuity, and to make doubly sure that there was no Chinese attempt to forestall the takeover, the Japanese Army moved in first. What Japan took by force, the Western powers took by example. The French, not satisfied with Vietnam, wanted to make the provinces of Guangdong, Guangxi and Yunnan their own spheres of influence, not to be granted to any other power. France, smarting over an incident in Tianjin in which twenty French priests and nuns were butchered by an angry mob, was obviously unhappy that with Britain ensconced in Hong Kong and now nibbling into Yunnan through its newly acquired territory of Burma, and with Japan now masters of Taiwan and the Pescadores, it would be left out in the cold.

Once again, France did not wait for a reply but moved into Guangzhou Bay, south of Hong Kong. Japan, a little miffed that it had only a foothold on the Liaodong Peninsula and the island of

Figure 11.1 A Chinese naval deputation seen on the steps of Government House, with the Governor, Sir Frederick Lugard, shortly before the 1911 revolution.

Taiwan, saw Fujian as another tempting area for Japanese development and put in a claim for that part of the coast. This effectively gave the Japanese Navy command of the Taiwan Strait, though it was not yet ready to challenge the Royal Navy on rights of passage. Britain now wanted to put its seal on the Yangzi valley, which prompted Germany (on the pretext of avenging the murder of a couple of missionaries) to make a grab for the coast of Shandong, with Jiaozhou (Kiaochow) Bay and eventually the whole peninsula, as its objective. With a slight twist of the screwdriver, Germany obtained a lease for ninety-nine years, as well as the rights to build railways.

Germany did this in rather a sneaky way, sending three cruisers from Shanghai to Qingdao on the pretext of carrying out manoeuvres. The Chinese Admiral consented to their presence and the German ships then disembarked 660 marines ostensibly to carry out drill ashore. Once again the unsuspecting admiral agreed and subsequently was informed that he had three hours to leave his city; the Germans had come to stay. Other Western powers were no less acquisitive. Britain had, by that time, raised the White Ensign on its new naval base at Weihaiwei (formerly occupied by Japan), just up the coast from Jiaozhou; far more significantly, it occupied the large hinterland behind Kowloon, known as the New Territories, leasing it for ninety-nine years. Russia then clamoured for its share of real estate and came up with occupancy rights to Port Arthur and Dalian. Next it was Belgium's turn to press for development rights, and Italy demanded Zhejiang, but courageously was rebuffed by China.

It was like a game of Chinese checkers, with each power taking its pound of flesh out of the body of China as it jumped in. If the United States missed its chance that was simply because it was too heavily committed squeezing Spain out of the Philippines. And then, having surveyed the China scene and seeing no opportunity to acquire a province, it decided to adopt the British suggestion of the "open-door policy." This meant that if American businessmen could offer better terms for railway building projects or other forms of development, regardless of which country claimed hegemony in that province, the contract would go to the best bidder. As a Chinese commentator noted: "It meant that all the spheres should be open to the United States, giving US capital more opportunities to plunder all China." The virtue of the US declaration was that while it was bound to cause friction, argument and resentment, it involved no blatant land grab and stressed the principles of free trade and open competition instead of closed shop capitalism and colonialism.

While an open door was in America's best interests in China it practised a different policy in the Philippines. The execution (by Spain) of Filipino nationalist leader, Dr Jose Rizal, brought tensions with Spanish colonials to a head. Two years later, with the two countries at war over the sinking of the battleship *Maine* in mysterious circumstances in Havana, the American Pacific fleet defeated Spanish warships in Manila Bay, thus ending more than 300 years of Spanish rule. Having watched the demise of their Spanish masters, Filipino revolutionaries might well have believed that independence was at last in sight. They proceeded to set up their first republic under Emilio Aguinaldo, but then American troops marched in.

The subsequent Treaty of Paris simply changed the flag at the Malacanang Palace from Spanish to American and a new colonial power took over. Filipino revolutionaries bitterly opposed the decision and a war lasting seven years followed, punctuated by bloody massacres by both sides, in one case of such severity that the American general responsible was court-martialled and sent home on retirement. Filipinos would have to wait another forty years before they were offered the open door to independence.

The great prize in China at that time was the right to develop railways, mines and factories. Of course, China would pay the full market price for whatever work was done, either by hypothecating part of its official revenue to the developers, or else contracting loans at interest rates dictated by the lender and of course guaranteeing repayment on the basis of taxes, such as the *lijin*, an inland tax on the transit of goods initially introduced to finance the suppression of the Taiping Rebellion. At the end of the era, China acquired a fairly extensive network of railways which with its canal system, provided the basic lines of communication still in use today, but it had to pay a ruinous price. It would have taken years to pay them off, but for the fortunes of war and the reversal of roles during the following century.

But there was a limit to the humiliations China could take. From being at the centre of the world, Chinese people at every level experienced the pain of foreign occupation and cultural oppression and degradation. The Western nations brought in not just the new technology, religion, values and their way of life but a contempt and disdain for almost everything they encountered in China. The Qing dynasty's future hung by a thread, yet while Chinese people despised the ruling house that had allowed this tragedy to engulf the country, there was no obvious alternative. Cixi may have been in her dotage, her son a prisoner in the palace; there may have been minor rebellions here and there; and a young Cantonese doctor, Sun Yat-sen, was beginning to raise his voice in the south calling for a republic. But it was too early for a change, too soon for a groundswell of countrywide support in favour of a new form of government or even a new dynasty. China would have to taste the bitter fruits of anarchy and chaos for many years to come.

A new shock galvanized the country in the closing years of the century; this was a "kung fu rebellion" in the north known as Boxerism. For many years a sect known as the Society of Harmonious Fists (Yihequan) had flared into activity at various times employing martial arts techniques combined with swords and bare fists but had been bloodily suppressed by the Qing rulers. Brain-washed by a mixture of mysticism, superstition and magic incantations, and wearing loose-fitting pantaloons and blouses tied with a red sash, these fighters from Shandong Province exploded onto the scene with a violence never previously experienced.

Three foreign powers had occupied parts of the province at various times: Japan, Germany and Britain. Railways were built by Western developers in complete defiance of local *fengshui* taboos; land was confiscated by the authorities causing rural dislocation; surveyors were trampling over ancestral graves and disrupting village life; work gangs, rail layers and eventually the dreaded ironmongery of railway lines, signals, stations, huffing and puffing steam engines and rolling stock began spreading through the countryside. Local superstitions were brushed aside in the name of progress. Taxes were raised to help pay for the lines; there was also widespread unemployment resulting from trade and industrial dislocation because of the dumping of foreign imports, while new coastal shipping services took over the carriage of freight and rice, displacing bargemen on the Grand Canal.

To make matters worse, flooding of the Yellow River added to the general misery of 1898 inundating large parts of the surrounding province while other districts were hit by drought. Plague had broken out in the south, particularly Guangzhou and Hong Kong, killing thousands. Though very much an endemic disease, plague was a recurring nightmare for Chinese administrators. Like leprosy, smallpox and tuberculosis, plague had been known for hundreds of years. Many forms of cure had been attempted. One, noted in 1896, consisted of the local headman drawing up his troops in the courtyard of his *yamen* and firing rifles in all directions "to frighten off the plague demons."

In the case of smallpox, Chinese doctors had practised inoculation since the Song dynasty. One of the earliest methods involved pulverizing smallpox scabs, mixing them with water and inhaling or rubbing them on the body. This practice may well have spread to the West through the Turks living on the western borders of China, though the most effective vaccination devised by the British scientist, Edward Jenner, involved use of the cowpox virus to combat smallpox.

Horrifying mortality rates were recorded century after

Figure 11.2 The plague hospital in Hong Kong, a photograph taken in the
last decade of the nineteenth century.

century, and as living conditions deteriorated in crowded cities
and as dirt, squalor and poverty intensified, the outbreaks grew in
intensity. Male survivors considered themselves lucky to be let off
with shocking disfigurement — and an immunization for life.
Many women survivors felt they would have been better off dead
than to endure the brutal nicknames and ridicule to which they
were exposed.

Hong Kong's impoverished Chinese quarter was the breeding
ground for several major outbreaks of plague in the last decade of
the nineteenth century leading to stringent reforms in sanitation
and hygiene, the building of modern sewerage systems, the
segregation of people from farm animals in urban areas and the
wider use of vaccination and inoculation, as perfected by Jenner
in 1796 and used to stem an outbreak in Macau nine years later. In
China, however, its use was limited; so superstitious were the
people and so suspicious of foreign innovations that in the interior the epidemic swept over whole provinces wiping out Chinese
and foreigners indiscriminately.

On the whole, Western missionaries did much to alleviate suffering but on many occasions they were overwhelmed and ill-equipped to tackle hundreds of thousands of cases. At small outlying missions they performed heroic work but nearer the major cities and towns they would often resort to pulling strings to gain favours and advantages. In one case, a German bishop, who had links with both the Kaiser at home and the Qing rulers in Beijing, used both to gain advantages for his flock or to protest against local abuses. In the Kaiser, a rabid xenophobe with outspoken views on the "yellow peril," the German missionaries found a sympathetic supporter. In other areas, British, European and American missionaries were the most visible representatives of the foreign powers and were easy targets for opposition, particularly when demands for indemnities were made following their murder.

When the Boxer Rebellion broke out, the fighters were quick to exploit local grudges against the Europeans, and in this way won the support not only of local people but Government troops ordered to suppress them. The Yihequan society thus attracted many young people, including women, with its appeal to mysticism and magic, and by the use of hypnotism and the casting of spells they persuaded many they were invulnerable to bullets. The Harmonious Fists were not the only grassroots insurgents; another was the Big Sword Society (Dadaohui). There were militant women's groups — the younger calling themselves Red Lanterns, and the older, the Blue Lanterns. Overall their aim was to stamp out Western religion and foreigners, but they also had little time for the Qing rulers who were in any case powerless to control them.

The Qing court's answer to the rising tide of discontent was to call in a trusted old retainer, General Yuan Shikai, with a reputation for brutal suppression, whose first order was to ban the Boxers; before long, with a large army in front of him, he forced them to take refuge in the adjoining province of Hubei. Gradually, however, they infiltrated back into the capital and began to terrorize the foreigners with placards and posters threatening to exterminate them. The guards at the gates were too terrified to stop them and soon the city was alive with red turbaned insurgents carrying broad swords and long spears.

Believing themselves to be immune to foreign bullets, they took over the palaces, Government offices and the homes of high officials, forcing the foreign community into the Legation Quarter and terrorizing the populace with noisy rallies, campaigns to boycott foreign goods and imported kerosene. Similar scenes occurred in Tianjin where they also set fire to churches, cut down electricity poles and stormed the offices of the Inspector-General of Customs, Robert Hart; soon, both cities were under the control of the rebels. Their depredations against churches and other foreign institutions, particularly railway lines, spread to neighbouring provinces but the full weight of the Boxers' wrath fell upon the missionaries because of the perceived or imagined grievances they had inflicted on the people.

Foreign intervention to defend their nationals in Tianjin and particularly the Legation Quarter in Beijing was inevitable. The siege of the Legations had started and it was feared that unless relief came swiftly the foreign residents would be put to the sword. Crowded into the British Legation were 473 civilians, a garrison of 400 men, 2,700 Chinese converts and 400 servants, while in the Peitang Cathedral area were four thousand converts under the leadership of the French Bishop Favier, helped by forty French and German marines. The Empress Dowager, Cixi, had decided to turn a blind eye to the Boxers when one of the royal princes became their leader, and in any case there was no Chinese or Manchu official capable of exercising control. Massacres were taking place in many parts of the country and even Yuan Shikai gave up.

With the British involved in the Boer War in South Africa it needed a composite force to relieve the Legations. The Western allies had been warned long before the attack began that this was the primary objective of the Boxers, but they ignored the warning.

At first they also seriously underestimated the strength of the Boxers; a mixed force of 1,800 men under Britain's Admiral E. H. Seymour, tried to fight its way to the capital, but twenty-five miles short of his goal his train was surrounded and forced to turn back and seek reinforcements. The desperate defenders at the Legations waiting daily for his relief christened him Admiral "See No More." With the murder of two diplomats — one the German Minister, Baron von Kettler and one Japanese, the Chancellor named Sugiyama — the Qing rulers abandoned all pretence of a hands-off stance, the Empress Dowager describing the foreigners in the Legations as being "like fish in the stewpan." What tipped the balance was the Allied demand to station 10,000 troops in Beijing to restore order. She reportedly exclaimed: "The insults of these foreigners pass all bounds. Let us exterminate them before we eat our morning meal."[1]

In outlying areas and in other provinces, Western missionaries and Chinese converts suffered grievously as the Boxers and their supporters imposed a reign of terror, killing hundreds, though others managed to escape into nearby hills and mountains and survived until the frenzy subsided. Not only did Cixi condone war against the foreigners in Beijing but ordered her subordinates in the provinces to take up arms. Several including Yuan Shikai and Li Hongzhang in Guangzhou ignored the edict and in fact offered to help mediate a settlement, fair proof that they had numbered the days of the Qing dynasty and were jockeying for places in the China which would survive the inevitable drubbing by the Western armies.

The 55-day siege of the Legations, reminiscent of the ordeal of the Lucknow Residency in the Indian Mutiny, was a traumatic affair for the residents. They were cut off from all contact with the

---

1. J. O. P. Bland and E. Backhouse, *China Under the Empress Dowager* (London: Heinemann, 1910).

outside world as the Allied eight-nation force of 16,000 men bat-
tled its way to Beijing under the command of the German Field
Marshal Count von Waldersee. The choice of a German was unpopular with the French (who had fought against the same
general in their 1870 war) but as the assassination of Baron von
Kettler was one of the main provocations, and as the Russians did
not want to be led by the Japanese and as Britain's Lord Elgin had
commanded the last expedition to Beijing, the Germans got the
vote. Curiously, however, its force was the smallest contingent —
just 100 men — and eventually they had to return to Tianjin
without pulling a trigger, together with the Italian and Austrian
forces, because of insoluble transport problems.

The brunt of the fighting was born by the 10,000 Japanese
troops who by all accounts showed extraordinary courage in the
face of withering rifle and artillery fire, though all members of the
five-power force reached the gates of the capital in the sweltering
heat of August, which took more casualties than enemy bullets.
The Russians had a miserable time. Earlier their force had set off
with a full load of shells but forgot to bring the guns to fire them.
With minimum food supplies they were forced to live off the
country and in doing so endeared themselves to no one. At the
same time, they were paranoiacally suspicious of the Japanese
(who led the attack) and the British (who made up the rearguard),
not wanting either to steal a march on their own contingent. They
finally pulled off a *coup* by being the first to breach one of the
gates, though they paid a high price in casualties, including their
general, Vassilievski, who was seriously wounded but who had
the honour of being the first to enter the city.

The relief of the Legations has been well documented elsewhere but its sequel, when arson, looting, pillage and rape broke
out among the Allied force, blackened its reputation and led to
wholesale destruction within the city. Wagon-loads of treasures
from royal palaces in Beijing's Forbidden City were removed, and
the Summer Palace, somewhat restored after its burning thirty
years earlier, was again raided. According to a Chinese source the

contents were removed by camel trains to the foreign concessions in Tianjin over a period of several months.

The great *Yong Le Encyclopaedia* (amounting to more than 300 volumes, compiled during the reign of the Ming emperor of that name) was seized and 46,000 rare books removed; the Hanlin Academy had been fired during the seige and at least part of its contents lost. Even Waldersee admitted: "The amount of damage done to the country by plunder will never be calculable but it must be immense. A big trade is being carried on here with the proceeds of the looting. Dealers, especially from America, have taken up their position and are making big profits." Which country was worse? Waldersee said: "Every nation accords the palm to some other in respect to the art of plundering, but it remains the fact that each and all of them went in hot and strong for loot." Even Lady Macdonald, wife of the British Minister, Sir Claude Macdonald, and the hero of the seige, "was out with a small force and devoted herself to looting."[2]

A curious footnote was added to the looting a year later when a young British diplomat discovered in the home formerly occupied by Macdonald a beautiful blue tablet inscribed with four golden Chinese characters — *huang tian shang di*, meaning "The King of Heaven." It should have been in the Temple of Heaven but a Chinese official politely acknowledged that it had been missing for about a year. The young diplomat offered to return it to him — only to be greeted by a horrified refusal when the official told him that he would have to kowtow twenty-seven times every time he passed it. The British Legation had it stored in the Hongkong & Shanghai Bank vaults until an auspicious day for its return to the Temple of Heaven.

The sequel was predictable. Britain and the Allies were calling for exemplary punishment for the ringleaders of the rebellion,

---

2. Peter Fleming, *The Siege at Peking* (1959; reprint, Hong Kong: Oxford University Press, 1983).

with little concern for the judicial process they had always espoused when their own nationals were involved in incidents in the past. War crimes trials would have to wait another fifty years before being instituted. Ultimately the Qing Court condemned two to beheading, sent two more the silken cord, and exiled others in the royal ranks who had supported the Boxers. One took his own life by stuffing mud into his throat until he choked.

China's total liability following this orgy of bloodletting — sixty foreigners died in the Legation seige and hundreds, both Chinese and foreigners, outside — was assessed at 67.5 million pounds. The damage inflicted by the Allied troops in retaliation and the loot removed from Beijing's palaces was never calculated. America wanted to reduce the Chinese liability by a third but Beijing agreed to pay the lot. America and Britain eventually returned their share (amounting to just under 20 per cent) to be spent under joint supervision on scientific research, medical services and education, and this policy was followed by others. One outcome was the establishment by American missionaries of the Yale Medical School in China.

Britain had already taken the New Territories in a 99-year lease and seemed content with the addition of this lush green belt and a screen of islands around Hong Kong and the Kowloon peninsula gained in earlier wars. In other respects, apologies were to be made by the Chinese Government to the Germans and the Japanese for the murder of their diplomats; arms imports were forbidden; the Dagu forts, which had hammered Russian ironclads at the outset of the Allied invasion, were to be razed, anti-foreign societies were proscribed and the Legation Quarter was to be placed under foreign control.

Meanwhile Russian troops moved into China's north-east provinces in an attempt to occupy hundreds of thousands of acres of territory to match what the other powers had acquired. There was strong Anglo-Japanese opposition, and when the Chinese resisted Russia blinked, but for the time being held on to the Liaoning peninsula and three north-eastern provinces (three times the size of France) which Japan claimed were hers by victory in the 1895 war.

This was no more than a temporary expedient and the Japanese were determined to consolidate their position. Checkmating Russia became their obsession. The opportunity came in 1902 when after nine months of secret, painstaking negotiations, Japan and Britain announced the conclusion of an alliance. Both nations had imperial ambitions — Britain to thwart Russia and France, and Japan to subdue Korea and China; it would mark the turning-point in the history of foreign penetration of the China–Yellow Seas, signalling the decline of Britain and the rise of Japan to become the dominant imperial power in the Far East. This new power-sharing arrangement would be seen as the most momentous development since Britain decided to challenge Portugal and the Netherlands for control of the sea lanes to the Far East in the seventeenth century. Only forty years earlier, the Japanese Navy's first attempt to sail across the Pacific in a Dutch-built schooner nearly ended in disaster when all the Japanese crew were seasick and home-going American passengers took over its running.

While the military pressures from the Western allies were causing serious problems to the Chinese throne, a new threat was looming in the south, posing an equally momentous change to more than 2,000 years of dynastic rule. A young Cantonese doctor who had studied medicine in Hong Kong and had spent some years in Hawaii, was stirring the pot of rebellion and using Hong Kong and Macau as a sanctuary in which to rally support and raise funds. Although Sun Yat-sen, a peasant's son, had been educated in the British colony he had been born in Zhongshan, Guangdong, and was forbidden to live in Hong Kong.

In fact, a letter was written to him in 1897 by the Colonial Secretary, Stewart Lockhart, advising him that the local Government had no intention of allowing the colony "to be used as an asylum for persons engaged in plots and dangerous conspiracies against a friendly neighbouring empire." Lockhart's letter continued: "In view of the part taken by you in such transactions

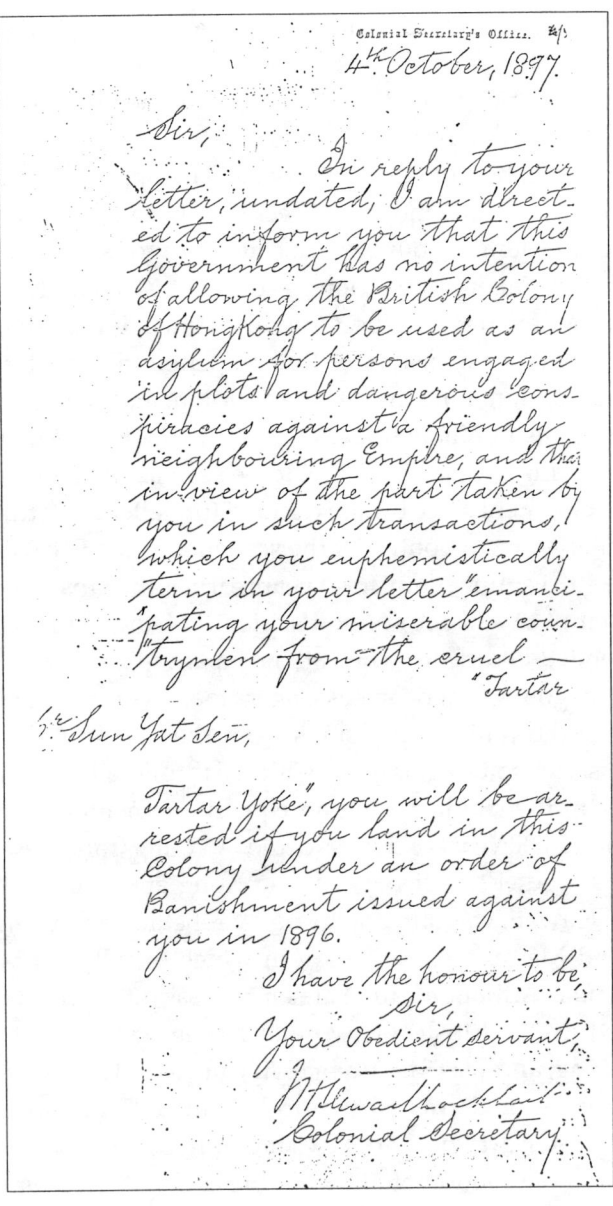

Figure 11.3   This letter from Stewart Lockhart, the Colonial Secretary, warns Sun Yat-sen of dire consequences if he ignores an order of banishment.

which you euphemistically term in your letter 'emancipating your miserable countrymen from the cruel Tartar yoke' you will be arrested if you land in this colony under an order of banishment issued against you in 1896."

This order was the payback to Qing officials in Guangdong who were trying to maintain stability in the province when the rest of the country was sliding into chaos. Almost exactly a year earlier, Sun had been seized by Manchu henchmen in London while on a visit to the British capital on a fund-raising mission. He was dragged to the Chinese Legation and held in a locked room on an upper floor pending his return to China to stand trial.

Sun tried desperately to escape knowing that instant death awaited him in China. He told a European servant in the Legation of his plight and asked him to take a message to Dr James Cantlie who was practising in London; Sun had studied under him, and worked with him in Hong Kong and Macau. That at least is the more probable story, though W. H. Donald, a close confidante, recalled being told by Sun that in desperation, while imprisoned in an upper room he wrote a note explaining his predicament, wrapped it around a stone and threw it out of the window into the street below. The stone clattered to the feet of a passerby who picked it up, read it and delivered it to the authorities. With the help of Dr Cantlie, who applied for a writ of habeas corpus, Sun was released from custody and set free.

Sun immediately resumed his calls for reform and the overthrow of the Qing rulers. There followed several attempts to assassinate senior officials in Guangdong; on one occasion a bomb was thrown at a passing sedan chair but although it killed several carriers and injured the occupant, the south was not yet ready to repudiate the Qing rulers mainly because they retained a high degree of autonomy under the very independent minded mandarin, Li Hongzhang. He was the first of a new breed of provincial leaders who would be remembered in history as the warlords.

Li paid lip-service to the Manchu rulers but was himself a Han Chinese who knew how to acquire power and great wealth and play off enemies against one another and remain comfortably on top. Controlling a local arsenal and with troops loyal to him, he had played a variety of roles in serving the Qing Government. A genial, affable Chinese gentleman, he was also shrewd, calculating and resourceful. He rose to heights of imperial honour after helping to defeat the Taiping rebels, and later helped the young Emperor Guangxu to usher in his era of reforms.

He did well to help launch the China Merchants Steam Navigation Company; he miscalculated with the French over their actions in Tongking and brought on the French naval action at Fuzhou. Having been downgraded by the Empress Dowager he was then told to sue for peace in the war with Japan. After a world tour which did much for his image but little for China, he died in 1901 at the age of seventy-eight, a spent force in Chinese politics with little chance of controlling events as the country staggered drunkenly to the end of the dynasty and the dawn of republicanism.

The international power play continued to eclipse local posturings in the early years of the twentieth century. Not yet strong enough to overthrow the dynasty, Sun Yat-sen and his rebels operated mainly from outside the country in their bid to gain control. With a price of 100,000 pounds on his head he had to move quickly and though a philosopher-dreamer in the style of India's Mahatma Gandhi he had led the life of a fugitive since the bungled Guangzhou *coup* of 1895 when many of his collaborators were caught and beheaded.

Ever a practical joker, he saved his life by escaping to Macau in a bridal sedan chair. But for all his fumbling ways, Sun touched a resonant chord in overseas Chinese communities from whom he raised hundreds of thousands of dollars. He also succeeded in enlisting the support of anti-Qing movements, particularly triad societies, ever-ready for a night of chopping to make life miserable for the mandarins of Guangzhou.

Indeed, the heart of Sun's philosophy was to mobilize the talents, skills and intelligence of the people to revive and save the country. He claimed descent from the lowest rungs of society: "I am a coolie and the son of a coolie," he once said. From his peasant upbringing he was able to discern the deep yearnings of the people. He was later to expound the "Three People's Principles" — nationalism, democracy and livelihood — in a treatise known as Sanminzhuyi. While this was strong on rhetoric and theory it fell short of a practical blueprint for the regeneration of China politically or economically.

Given a political vacuum in which to work, Sun may have turned China into a model society; but his indifference to the realities of life in the country due to his long absence overseas and his misunderstanding of the predatory intentions of the foreign powers reduced him to the role of a benevolent and respected figurehead. In the end, he showed himself to be a man without the ability to manipulate the reins of military, political and economic power — and thus a failure.

Little has been written so far of that uniquely Chinese phenomenon, the secret society, though fleeting glimpses have occurred at various times; through the centuries they have played a significant part in rallying the people to causes great and small. There was and there is no one society but they exist in hundreds and have been both makers and breakers of dynasties and their influence has been profound. Basically they were fraternal groups of men (mainly) who banded together for a common objective, usually political. Intensely nationalistic they opposed the Mongols and helped usher in the Ming dynasty, and were equally contemptuous of the Qing dynasty, as well as being strongly opposed to Western influence and particularly the Japanese. Archly conservative and traditional, the societies stressed Chinese culture and values, often appealing to mysticism, superstition and folklore as a means of building support and patriotism.

The Taiping Rebellion was an outgrowth of secret society activity which very nearly succeeded in toppling the Qing; the Boxer Rebellion was another; and the Guomindang, formed by

Sun Yat-sen, owed much of its success in its formative years to secret societies abroad and at home; in the years of anti-Japanese agitation, the societies were again active and were a back-up to more recognizable national movements — such as the May 4 Movement.

In 1936, even Mao Zedong felt compelled to address a special appeal to the societies whom he considered represented "resolute men and the broad masses of peasants and toilers" and argued that "our views and our positions are quite close." He then went on to appeal for "a close and intimate alliance of brothers to ... defend righteousness and come to the aid of our country in need." He even offered to allow them to exist legally under a soviet-style government. But after 1949, with his objectives achieved and all but a few fleeing to Taiwan with the Guomindang, Mao's mood changed.

When the Communists no longer needed their support the gangs fell back to their alternative interest — crime — and in the postwar years were prominent in Shanghai (up to 1949), Hong Kong and Chinatowns overseas. Of the many who rose to leadership, the Shanghai street-urchin turned gang leader, Du Yuesheng, challenged for the supreme accolade of evil. He enjoyed a perverse taste for sending ears and fingers through the mail to intimidate his opposition or speed up tardy ransom payments.

"Big-eared Du," as he was nicknamed, also held a seat on the nation's Currency Reserve Board, and was not averse to indulging in what is today condemned as "insider trading." On one occasion he lost US$250,000 on a foreign exchange deal that he bungled, and demanded of H. H. Kung, the Finance Minister to be reimbursed. When Kung declined, a prominent undertaker was asked to deposit a coffin on his doorstep. The next day, wiser counsels prevailed and Kung persuaded the Board that Du should be reimbursed as befitting a patriotic citizen.

The triads are commonly regarded as the major movers in the drug trade, but this is only one of their many interests;

racketeering, extortion, piracy, protection and prostitution are just some of the many ways in which they earn big money. In early years they stressed ceremonials and regalia — like a masonic movement — and gave lip-service to ancient beliefs and muttered obscure ritualistic incantations which were said to confer mystic superhuman powers on the initiated. If this seemed a strange coalition for a deeply conscientious patriot and thinker like Sun Yat-sen, he was aware of the strong hold the societies exercised over people in China and particularly overseas. He needed not only their moral but their financial support and to have spurned them would have been political suicide.

Galvanizing the support of the masses was his chief concern and another opportunity occurred to show up the impotence of the Qing dynasty when war broke out between Japan and Russia in which the occupation of Chinese territory was the issue. Japan had long smarted over Russia's aggressive takeover of the Liaodong Peninsula and the north-eastern provinces, coveting both itself so that it could exploit the rich mineral resources of the area. Japan was already occupying Korea but feared that unless it took decisive action Russia would get in ahead with the annexation of Manchuria, having already put its stamp on administration of the area's maritime and frontier customs, as well as railway concessions and a 25-year lease of the Liaodong territory of Port Arthur (Lushun) and Dalian.

Japan invaded Manchuria through Korea and though militarily inferior in numbers, its army was highly trained, deeply imbued with the principles of Clausewitz, and strongly, even fanatically disciplined. Having swept aside the Chinese army earlier the Japanese went on to attain all their military objectives in southern Manchuria including the capture of Port Arthur; the crowning achievement came in a decisive naval battle in the Strait of Tsushima.

The Russian Baltic Fleet had sailed with great secrecy halfway around the world, coaling en route at pre-arranged destinations, its final stop at Camranh Bay in Indo-China (spotted there by the Australian reporter, W. H. Donald, and exposed in a scoop to the London *Daily Telegraph*). Later it steamed north to meet the Japanese fleet (several of which were built in Britain and carried British advisers) in the narrow waters between Kyushu and South Korea.

The Japanese had no difficulty picking out the black hulled Russian battleships with their canary yellow funnels which helped the gunners to find their range. In the engagement that followed (27 May 1904) the Russian ships were outgunned, out-manoeuvred and comprehensively defeated, with thirty-four ships lost or scuttled at a cost of 4,830 lives. The Japanese lost three torpedo boats and 110 men. It was a battle that would establish Japan's supremacy as the most significant naval power not only in the China–Yellow Sea area but the North Pacific, for the next forty years.

The Treaty of Portsmouth (New Hampshire) which ended the war, resecured the Japanese foothold in Port Arthur and in southern Manchuria even if, at the same time, it put a knife in relations between the two countries that survives to this day. Russia has never forgotten or forgiven the Japanese, and the loss of its Baltic Fleet caused deeper wounds of national pride than the Pearl Harbour attack on the American Pacific Fleet in 1941.

It also spurred Japanese territorial ambitions in China. As the strongest Asian power capable of thumping the Russians, Japanese militarists became obsessed for the first time in their history with dreams of imperial conquest. If the British, French, German and even the Americans could stretch their boundaries by flexing their military muscle, why should Japan not take over the ascendancy in Asia, traditionally filled by China? Japan, moreover, had curbed the absolute power of its reform-minded emperor and become a constitutional monarchy like that in Britain, the Netherlands, Belgium, Norway and other European powers.

As they watched these developments it began to dawn on the Chinese reformers that constitutionalism might well be the path to follow, caught as the country was in a tug-of-war between the still all-powerful Empress Dowager willing to listen to everyone but heed no one, and those preaching republicanism. A high-powered group of Chinese leaders, including a royal prince, left on a study mission to Europe to learn all they could about constitutional change, notwithstanding a bomb thrown by a student activist as they left Beijing station, injuring two of them. They returned a year later convinced "there is no other way of preventing the danger of revolution than by introducing a constitution."

Agreed, said Cixi, but then announced her own agenda on how China should proceed; her inspiration might have come from England's Charles I rather than Queen Victoria whom she was at any rate determined to outlive as well as outreign — and she did both. Her determination to have the final say in all matters of state and her faint wave at reform played into the hands of her critics and swelled the ranks of opposition. She had to go, they decided. But how?

Trying to penetrate the surrounding screen of emasculated falsetto courtiers was futile. And then out of the blue the ideal solution presented itself. The Emperor Guangxu had been ailing for some months; poisoning was suspected. On 14 November 1908 he finally succumbed to his mystery illness and a small boy, Puyi, was named to succeed his uncle, with his father as regent. Cixi hardly had time to smile in triumph when she suffered a stroke and while uttering her final decree that the regent should answer to the next dowager, her niece, she gave up the ghost.

Her deathbed wish was ignored and while Puyi's father grappled with saving the dynasty he found that possession of the royal seals was not enough to save him or his son. He set up a council of princes and made tentative constitutional reforms in the provinces. Meanwhile the new Chinese industrialists and their investors were gaining an increasingly stronger voice as Western ideas took root and as educated Chinese began to absorb the works of Adam Smith, Karl Marx, John Stuart Mill, Jean Jacques Rousseau, Leo Tolstoy, Georg Hegel, Arthur

Schopenhauer, Charles Darwin and Thomas Huxley. In other cases, Chinese students, helped by overseas scholarships, returned with new ideas on reform and a wider understanding of China's predicament and the need for urgent change.

These were also years of stark tragedy for millions of Chinese as floods and drought took their toll of lives and crops in many parts of the country. It was clear the Qing dynasty had lost the mandate to rule and the widespread suffering convinced many of the reformers that they could not sit back and let events take their course. It was time to act decisively. Their pleas were answered on a significant date in Chinese politics — the Double Tenth (the tenth day of the tenth month, or 10 October).

A revolt broke out in the Yangzi city of Wuchang. A group of conspirators was discovered together with a cache of weapons; but these were not discontented youths or returned students or even frustrated reformers, but mainly military officers. They had experienced at first hand the bitterness of defeat at the hands of the Japanese, the French and other Allied nations, and felt more strongly than most that their country needed someone with courage and spirit to take charge, with authority based on the will of the country.

The prospect of continued rule by anachronistic Manchu princes, out of step with the times and isolated from the people, and yet another ghastly era of submission to Japanese and Western overlords, was too much to take. With no coherent ideas of who should replace the Qing rulers they nevertheless set up military governments in all but three of the provinces. In the Yangzi river port of Wuchang, after an accidental explosion of a bomb in a basement factory, the conspirators dragged their commanding officer from under his bed and gave him an ultimatum: "Lead us or die," and in this way Colonel Li Yuanhong became the reluctant hero who lit the fuse to revolution.

Having lit it he then conveniently handed on the spluttering torch to others in many parts of the country who followed his example; it was a case of spontaneous combustion with the nation in a state of revolutionary ferment but with no one to lead them. Dr Sun Yat-sen, the figurehead of the movement, was out of the country and his whereabouts unknown. For several weeks the republicans were in a state of confusion as they attempted to cobble together a semblance of order in the ramshackle chaos of a disintegrating empire. Their co-ordinator was a former Australian journalist, William Henry Donald, who worked from his Shanghai bunker. Some wanted to declare a new dynasty based on Chinese leadership; others wanted a republic. The council of princes, having recently sacked their old retainer, Yuan Shikai, now had to grovel to get him back again to stamp out the revolt and restore order.

Yuan, a closet dictator with imperial aspirations, chose to negotiate with the rebels, confident they would turn to him as the saviour of the country. The result was the establishment of a republic. Hardly had this been accomplished when Sun Yat-sen returned, bronzed and beaming from yet another visit abroad. Within a few days he was made temporary President of the Republic in Nanjing, by popular acclaim. But the Manchu princes were not about to hand over the seal of office to this lowly southern commoner; believing they could still rescue the country, they handed the task to Yuan.

Was it a revolution China was witnessing, or just another rebellion? Would Sun the dreamer prevail, or the man of action, Yuan? Or would little Puyi grow up to take the reins of a revived Qing dynasty under the tutelage of a dowager aunt? The old China hands in the treaty ports were not worried. Always a rebellion, never a revolution, went the old Chinese saying. They were sure things would remain the same. As the leading article in *The Times* would tell them, there were widespread doubts "whether a form of government so utterly alien to Oriental conceptions and to Oriental traditions as a republic can be suddenly substituted for a monarchy with semi-divine attributes [and] which have ruled since the first dim twilight of history."

In South China there were joyous reactions to the news of the republic. Men immediately cut off their long plaits of hair which they wore as a symbol of subjection to the Qing dynasty. Bombs were thrown at the Tartar general in Guangzhou killing him, and in Fuzhou, the Tartar general was captured by revolutionaries and decapitated. A few days later Beijing itself had fallen and the Prince Regent and his son had to flee, taking with them their hopes of reviving the dynasty.

In Hong Kong, Chinese people let off fireworks, and cheers sounded as each new burst split the night sky in a brilliant cascade of showering sparks. Trams were commandeered and swathed in banners proclaiming "10,000 years to the new Han dynasty." Chinese workers walked out of British-owned factories and industries, and riots and demonstrations broke out in various parts of the colony, with mobs calling out "Strike the foreign devils."

The Government had to arm the police and call out the troops with fixed bayonets during this wave of hysteria and jubilation, for Chinese everywhere saw it as the beginning of their country's deliverance from foreign domination, marking a new start in a new world where China would once again resume its place in the centre. The fact that Hong Kong showed such fervour in the republican cause was not surprising, being the major focus of foreign power and wealth, and relying heavily on the sweat and labour of Chinese workers drawn in from neighbouring provinces.

Inchoate they may have been, yet touched by the vision of a new, dynamic and rejuvenated China, that was a notion even the simplest could grasp, even if they could not see too far beyond it. A year later, an attempt was made on the life of the colony's new Governor, Sir Henry May. With piracy raging on the sea lanes around Hong Kong, including the burning of the vessel, *Tai On*, with the loss of 200 lives, he adopted emergency powers, freely deporting criminals and flogging persistent rioters. Similar outbreaks occurred in treaty ports, notably in Shanghai's international concession.

With a war looming in Europe, many Chinese believed their hour of deliverance had come when they could expect a loosening of the grip of Western nations on their land, and greater opportunities to control their own affairs. They were soon to discover that while the European war brought advantages and ushered in the rapid decline of the West it would establish the ascendancy of Japan and place their country in greater peril than ever before.

CHAPTER 12

The Reluctant Republic

Yuan Shikai was determined to have one more fling. He wanted to lead the country, not as a constitutional president — even as China's first — but as a regular old-fashioned emperor in a dynasty of his own making. He was neither clever, efficient, imaginative nor an inspiring leader, but a man of action; he could have headed a secret society or a band of pirates or bandits, but he chose an army career as the best way to make his mark in life. Having managed to win a few battles in various parts of the country and having crushed the Wuchang Uprising in 1911 before republicanism had got on its feet, he won the favour of the council of princes after a long lay-off in compulsory retirement.

Yuan's strongest card was the army group he led, called the North Sea Army, which was probably the best armed and trained military unit in China. With the muscle of this group of soldiers he was able to dictate terms to anyone. When on 12 February 1912, the Empress Longyu signed the abdication on behalf of Puyi, Yuan was given the task of setting up a republican government.

Working with the provisional government in Nanjing headed by Dr Sun, he persuaded the latter to hand over the reins of power to him. Sun's reasons for agreeing were hardly convincing though he probably believed that if he tried to hang on to office Yuan was ruthless enough to have him assassinated. Another point at issue was where the capital of the republic should be located. Yuan wanted Beijing. Sun's party preferred Nanjing. Yuan again got his way.

After a year of trying to work with a national assembly Yuan was tired of the politicking and resented the carping criticism; nor could he tolerate the way in which tax revenue was distributed to the provinces rather than the central government, for he had his own priorities. When he tried to sidestep the assembly by negotiating a loan with Britain, France and Germany, using the salt tax as security, the move caused an outcry from the national assembly. To instil some respect for the office of President, he resorted to assassination of one of the main party leaders resulting in armed uprisings in various parts of the country which Yuan's North Sea Army put down ruthlessly.

But crises did not come singly in China and the next shock to confront Yuan was Japan's draconian Twenty-one Demands which would have turned China into a virtual colony or protectorate of Tokyo. Yuan was clever enough to leak details of the demands to the Press and Parliament. The ensuing outcry helped to bring about a modification of the demands and Yuan was cast in a heroic light for the strength of his opposition. Then he tried to exploit both the public anger and the new demands by Japan, by requesting absolute powers — in short, becoming the next emperor of China. In a referendum, undoubtedly rigged, the Chinese people agreed to his wish. But it provoked rebellions in the provinces in what was to become a familiar feature of the Chinese political landscape — the Warlord Era.

Overwhelmed by Japan's demands and by insuperable financial problems Yuan realized he could not win popular support. The crowning indignity came when he could not even appease his three wives for whom he arranged three thrones alongside his own on descending levels. The first wife was happy enough with hers, but trouble started when the Korean second wife remonstrated over the lower position of her throne — for in the course of pillow talk Yuan, a great lover, had promised her equality with No. 1. When she heard this, No. 1 wife jumped down and attacked No. 2 with her long-nailed fingers, and it required Yuan himself to separate the warring consorts since the courtiers were too scared to lay hands on them. Yuan, an old-style autocrat, decided that the monarchy idea would not succeed and called off the restoration plan. Two months later, worn down by quarrelling wives, bickering politicians, scheming warlords, financial woes, the cares of office and ill health, he died at the age of fifty-seven, largely unmourned and universally despised.

A committed Anglophile, Yuan swung on British coat-tails to bolster his position in China, and in turn Britain admired his style and despised Sun — "the windbag." An historian and biographer, Jerome Chen, wrote that Yuan's ascendancy between 1911 and 1913 taught the Guomindang that major political issues could only be solved by force — a party without a strong armed force could play no part in Chinese politics. Chen concedes, however, that Yuan's defeat might be attributed to the lack of a well-organized party to carry out his political programmes. One other lesson was that China should never fight against a foreign power — in this case, Japan — and Chen believed that this was accepted by both Chiang Kai-shek and Mao Zedong in later years.

The Japanese demands hung around China's neck like a punishment cangue. For with the outbreak of World War I Japan saw and seized the opportunity to squeeze out the European powers and become the dominant force in China. The Genro who controlled the country had in the course of sixty years turned Japan from an isolationist feudal state into an internationalist imperial power, mapping out a strategy for the domination of Asia, and in doing so, sewed the seeds of its subsequent conquest in the 1930s and 1940s.

Japan cleverly exploited its alliance with Britain to enter World War I a few days after London's declaration against Germany, although it became apparent immediately that this posed serious problems for all allied countries with interests in China. As its price for declaring war, Japan next demanded the surrender of German interests in Shandong Province which Japanese forces and industrialists would take over. China's protests were virtually brushed aside, and when the scope of Tokyo's Twenty-one Demands were made clear the dismemberment of China was obvious. For Japan's demands for control and veto power went far beyond the one province of Shandong; they included Manchuria (Heilongjiang) and Fujian in the south and, moreover, no concession could be made to any other country anywhere in China, without Japanese approval. So much for the American "open door."

Not only did Japan insist on taking over German interests in the nominated provinces, extending a 25-year lease to ninety-nine years in southern Manchuria and gaining special priorities to develop railways and harbours in Fujian, but it demanded control of 2,000 small islands in the Western Pacific, including the Marianas, the Carolines and the Marshalls. Japan shrewdly pointed out that the only other Allied Pacific nation to declare war — Australia — had taken over all the German territories south of the Equator. What could be more reasonable than that Japan should do likewise north of the Equator?

The Western powers were too preoccupied with the war in Europe that was steadily draining their lifeblood. America, still neutral, was the only power able to resist. It opposed the wholesale Japanese takeover but supinely agreed that "territorial contiguity creates special relations between Japan and these districts." Thus Japan cleverly struck the first blow in its campaign to control China and eventually conquer all the lands bordering the China–Yellow Seas.

China, defeated in the war of 1895 and with no effective national government, was powerless to resist. The age of Western influence in China, though it would drag on for another twenty years, was at an end. By 1919, the Europeans were bled white by a war in which all the combatants were reduced to shadows, and the strongest survivor, the United States under President Woodrow Wilson, wanted no part in policing the post-war world. Japan could thus proceed to a slow methodical takeover of the richest parts of China like a boa constrictor throttling its trapped prey.

With Yuan dead, China was paralysed politically and there was no effective voice to express the national fury over what had been meekly and tamely accepted. Where newly formed political bodies wrangled with military leaders for control at provincial level, foreshadowing the era of the warlords, Sun Yat-sen and a few followers had formed the Chinese Revolutionary Party in 1914; this was reorganized and renamed National People's Party (or Guomindang) in Guangzhou shortly before Japan's Twenty-one Demands; Sun shared control with two military strongmen but was clearly the dominant political figure and engineered his election as President of the Chinese Republic while another President ruled from Beijing — in many ways similar to the north–south split that occurred in the United States seventy years earlier, and again it would finally be resolved by protracted military struggle.

In retrospect, it was surprising that China seemed so helpless in the face of the political and technological challenge of the West when Japan had in the same time span wholeheartedly embraced reform without sacrificing national character and identity. Japan had done so voluntarily, without being conquered or even coerced, under the influence of a committed leader in the person of the Emperor Meiji and his entourage. On the other hand, Chinese traditions and character worked against swift change. Its system of education emphasized rote learning rather than the application of ideas; its traditional, time-honoured, scholar-hallowed written language hampered the introduction of new thoughts and principles; its insular attitudes prevented the teaching of the Chinese language to outsiders and the learning of foreign languages. This in turn inhibited progress and development as well as the ability of scholars to come to terms with scientific and mathematical notions, concepts and formulae. The superiority of Confucian teaching, proven over thousands of years, needed no fundamental change; this view persisted generally until after the twentieth century, for its national examination was not abandoned until 1905. Officials educated under this system still ran the country.

It took an overseas Chinese like Sun, though born in China, to work out principles that would be needed to help the country to make the transition into the twentieth century and provide a basis for reform at every level. Communist writers have said that Sun was influenced by the years he spent in Hawaii "when the Hawaiians fought against American occupation and domination," though it is hard to find this as a consistent theme in Sun's writings.

He was, however, influenced by the leader of the Taiping Rebellion, Hong Xiuquan, and even vowed to become his political successor. This may be dismissed as boyish enthusiasm and hero-worship, but Sun was a romantic and later made his plans with the help of a triad leader in Guangzhou, Zheng Xiliang. At the Guangzhou hospital where they both studied and plotted is a stone monument to what was described as "the birthplace of the Chinese national revolution."

In 1923, Sun spoke of another major influence when he returned to Hong Kong to visit the university which he described as his "intellectual birthplace" where he developed his revolutionary ideas; for in the British colony he experienced and appreciated the order, the progress of the economy and the layout of the city, and he wondered how all this could have happened within seventy or eighty years. He found also that in Hong Kong corruption was the exception, and "purity" the rule. Things were quite the reverse in China, he said, where corruption was the rule. He eventually realized that he had to give up curing sick people and start treating the nation.

No doubt Sun's flattering, if somewhat sycophantic comments were designed to win support among potential backers in Hong Kong. But while this city and its university was his Alma Mater, he would not have forgotten that he was asked to leave the territory in the years before the revolution. However, he bore no

grudge. He revealed that two books which had profoundly impressed him during his student years were a history of the French
Revolution, and Charles Darwin's *The Origin of Species*, and as a
Christian he was familiar with the teachings of Jesus Christ. As for
his political ideals, Sun based his three principles of nationalism,
democracy and livelihood on Lincoln's dictum of "government of
the people, for the people and by the people."

Figure 12.1   Hong Kong harbour at the turn of the century.

Sun's readings were similar to those of many educated
Chinese who studied Western writers like Adam Smith, Thomas
Huxley, Jean Jacques Rousseau, and Karl Marx, translated into
Chinese. For Europeans, the Chinese classics such as *Confucian
Analects*, *The Great Learning* and *Doctrine of the Mean* had been
translated into English fifty years earlier by a protestant missionary, Dr James Legge. He had collaborated with the great
missionary/scholar Robert Morrison, both pioneers in the education of Chinese students in English. These gave Western scholars

an insight into Chinese thinking and helped bridge the intellectual gap between East and West.

Sun, however, was not just a reader of English books; among his prized possessions was a complete set of the histories of the twenty-four dynasties of China — not there for decoration because one of his fellow students pulled out a volume at random and questioned him. Sun knew the answers. But for all his failures of leadership, administration and political manoeuvring none can question his patriotism, his sincerity of purpose and his personal integrity; he was the father of the Chinese republic, recognized by both the Guomindang and the Communists. He set the country on a fundamentally new course which saw massive change at every level of society without destroying the underlying Chinese character and culture. When China was staggering under the oppressive weight of European and Japanese domination and unable to match these powers militarily, Sun Yat-sen provided the revolutionary impetus to achieve the downfall of the Qing dynasty and become the focal point of the revolution.

China heaved and shuddered in its bid to regain national unity. With many powerful militarists jostling for control of the provinces there was little hope of China attaining that goal. The two republics continued to claim the legitimate succession to the dynasty but this only served to underline its lack of unity on other questions including the response to Japan's demands and the extent of reform needed to modernize the country.

China's immediate aims in the World War I years, however, were to prise itself loose from the Japanese stranglehold. The first step towards this objective was to declare war on Germany in 1917 though this was undertaken in a period of political farce at home when at one time, even the boy emperor was restored to the throne, though quickly deposed by the warlords ganging up on the politicians when they tried to bring back the dynasty. China's political scene was a shambles at the time. In most provinces, effective power was held by the warlords while provincial factions jockeyed for power in Beijing. However, the Guangzhou administration was gaining increasing strength and stature in the south.

The personality and character of the various warlords such as the "Old Marshal" Zhang Zuolin in Manchuria, and his son the "Young Marshal," Zhang Xueliang, the "Christian General" Feng Yuxiang, and his on-off ally Sun Chuanfang, warlord of Zhili Province General Wu Peifu, and their colourful foreign minders, advisers, power brokers and arms dealers such as William Donald and his Australian journalist colleague, George Ernest Morrison (for many years correspondent of *The Times*), Maurice "Two-Gun" Cohen, and Frank "One Armed" Sutton, make fascinating reading; but their hold on power was tenuous and their influence short-lived. These were the "walking shadows that strut and fret their hour upon the stage and then are heard no more." Nor in the long run did they play any significant role in China's relations with the West, though Premier Duan Qirui, also head of the Anhui Group, was responsible for the declaration of war on Germany while Sun Yat-sen opposed it.

There was no real advantage to be gained from declaring war other than the hope that it might yield some dividends in the division of spoils afterwards. The United States helped to prod the Chinese into action with offers of a $10 million loan for military purposes but only after it was belatedly drawn into the war itself. China was given a pretext for action when a German submarine torpedoed a French ship carrying Chinese labourers to work behind the battlefields, resulting in the drowning of 543 people.

Both France and Britain hired Chinese coolies, Britain alone transporting almost 100,000 to France; at least 2,000 died of illness or shelling. Ironically most of these were recruited in the former German colony of Qingdao because the Shandong men, brought up on a diet of wheat, were perceived to be bigger and stronger than their rice-eating counterparts from Guangdong. Also there was less trouble feeding them. A robust physique was important because, in an age before earth-moving equipment, trench digging, sandbag filling, barracks building, weapon hauling and road repairing required willing hands and strong bodies. Officially none took part in the fighting.

Serious thought was given to raising a 300,000-man British officered force to fight in the Dardanelles (although shipped under the guise of coolies) — on the suggestion of a Chinese official; much as Britain would have welcomed it after the heavy losses suffered in the first months of the war, it came to nothing. Indeed there were not enough Allied ships to carry them and the Allied powers had reservations about using Chinese as cannon fodder, though of course Indian troops (considered a "warrior race") and *kukri*-wielding Gurkhas ("ideal mercenaries") took part in many actions in various theatres of war, notably the Dardanelles, and acquitted themselves well. The Chinese "coolie corps," however, served with distinction and was universally admired; but at war's end they were quickly sent home.

An even more bizarre plan was Britain's bid to import 200,000 German and Austrian rifles and 30 million rounds of ammunition from a China awash with arms and bought by the new republican government. So convinced was the British Government of carrying through the deal that it remitted two million pounds to the Legation in Beijing; luckily it was not paid out to the shadowy negotiators, and the deal fell through, when Germany, smarting from the Japanese takeover of "its" province of Shandong, brought strong pressure to bear on China.

World War I put Japan in the saddle in the Pacific. Not only was West–East trade drastically reduced because of the war, but Europe's first priority was to rebuild its own battered economy. Though Britain was on the winning side the cost in manpower, shipping and resources was enormous and inevitably its stature as an imperial power was drastically reduced. It continued to maintain a significant naval presence in China, both in Hong Kong and in the Shandong port of Weihaiwei where it maintained a naval base on Liugong Island (Liugongdao). Britain was still an ally of Japan, was grateful for the limited help it gave in convoying Australian troops to war theatres in the Middle East and France, but was in no position to confront Japan in Asia or counter its ambitions in China.

One of the first initiatives of the United States was to persuade Britain to end its alliance with Japan, and in its place Japan accepted a tripartite treaty to respect one another's rights in the Pacific; effectively this meant that Washington gave its blessing to the wholesale Japanese takeover of German islands in the Pacific — a concession that would cost thousands of American lives in the Pacific war twenty years later. Coupled with this treaty was another limiting naval rearmament in the Pacific and restricting further military or naval bases in the area. Japan, Britain and the United States had ended the war as the biggest naval powers. The naval treaty which appeared to favour Britain and the United States in battleship construction at the expense of Japan, actually favoured the latter. This was because its 5:5:3 ratio did not take account of the world-wide commitments of Britain and the three fleet navy of the United States (Pacific, Caribbean and Atlantic) whereas Japan had only one ocean which interested her. And as aircraft were then a relatively minor arm of warfare the great potential of fleet aircraft carriers lay open to Japan (and the US and Britain) as an option. Japan therefore emerged in an impregnable position since even if it had wanted to, Britain could do no more than strengthen its bases in Singapore, Hong Kong and Weihaiwei. Other than building a base in Singapore for docking and repair work, little was done.

About the only gain American diplomacy achieved was to sign an "open door" treaty with nine other powers to give equal opportunity to all foreign nations in dealings with China, with a restriction on further territorial concessions but without any dilution of existing rights. Following this, China asked for independence in rewriting the internationally-fixed tariff schedule which favoured exports from the West while keeping duties on imports from China as low as possible. China wanted to fix its own tariffs and import duties, for while its trade had risen roughly fourfold between 1900 and 1922 much of the benefit went to the new foreign-owned industries in China, and particularly the Japanese owned factories in Manchuria. Tea exports had fallen from almost half total exports in 1881 to 2.5 per cent in 1922. Silk, another main staple in the last century, fell away sharply, as did opium. The big boost in imports came in raw cotton rather than cotton cloth, reflecting the growing output of mainly foreign-owned textile mills using cheap Chinese labour.

The only real benefit China could claim was in internal trade, thanks to the growth of railways and steamships, enabling local farmers to reach more distant markets with their output. The nine powers, all with a keen interest in Chinese trade and development, refused to allow China to raise tariffs, but permitted higher customs duties in some cases. Speciously the foreign powers argued that higher tariffs would not benefit the people but only the rising power of the warlords.

The Versailles peace treaty and the subsequent Western agreements only served to antagonize Chinese people and did nothing to address the harsh imposition of the series of unequal treaties forced upon a prostrate China in the closing years of the nineteenth century. And while reformers and scholars were eloquent in their denunciations of the West, and students staged strikes, intellectuals at all levels of society felt disillusioned, betrayed and abandoned. Chinese communists look back to this period — known as the May 4 Movement — as the ignition which fired their party into life.

Not only the Communists gained inspiration from it but it was a moment of self-discovery for intellectuals at all levels. What happened on 4 May 1919 specifically was a student demonstration in Beijing against China's capitulation to Japanese pressure and the resolution at the Versailles peace conference confirming Japanese economic rights in Shandong. Nor was it a token gesture by a few students indulging in a "rent-a-crowd" demonstration but the start of a period of profound intellectual debate and questioning of China's current state of helplessness.

At Versailles, the magnificent royal estate of every king of France since Louis XIV, China managed to bury its internal feuds and put together the best and most skilled team of diplomats to argue not just its case against Japan but against the retention of Western privileges in China. Hoping to touch a sympathetic chord in US President Woodrow Wilson, the eloquent Dr Wellington Koo spoke persuasively but to little avail. Wilson was troubled, felt concern for China but was outnumbered and out-manoeuvred by the major European participants who had borne the brunt of the war.

China, at the end of the day, had every reason to feel cheated. The main target of its campaign was, of course, Japan; but it was the self-questioning that occurred simultaneously at home during the May 4 Movement which served to make this an on-going two-year seminar into the pros and cons of Chinese philosophy, social and political institutions, as well as Confucian ethics, ancient customs and indeed every aspect of civilization. In short, coming under intense scrutiny were all those qualities that had served the Chinese people so well for so many centuries but were now manifestly inadequate to meet the needs of the present. It was a movement that evoked responses at every level of Chinese society, and indeed in many ways the argument continues to this day.

It was the beginning of an era of political evolution that forced Chinese people to look not only at themselves and their society but at their place in the world to see how and where changes should be made. Out of it came a "united front" of many disparate groups; on the political level it persuaded people in different walks of life to clear up the confusion and mess in their own backyard by uniting to get rid of the warlords in Beijing and the provinces.

Sun Yat-sen was no Abraham Lincoln. He was, however, the greatest modern Chinese political thinker and was also pragmatic enough to realize that if China was to take its part successfully in the modern world it would have to learn from the West. While convinced that the European nations had much to pass on to China in an intellectual and technological sense Sun became increasingly disillusioned with Britain, France and the United States over their refusal to check Japan's predatory activities, or to offer tariff concessions.

Though realizing China played only a minor role in the Great War, Sun believed that its concerns were completely disregarded. Apart from the issue of tariff concessions Sun had approached Britain to release money from the British-controlled customs revenue to allow him to pay loyal troops. The appeal met with a flat refusal, and when he subsequently threatened to seize the funds in Guangzhou, the Allied navies mounted a show of force of seventeen ships on the city's waterfront. This was the last straw. He announced he would turn for help to the Russians who had similarly overthrown an autocratic monarchy and embarked on revolution. What attracted Sun and his followers was that not only were the Russians sympathetic to his ideals but the new Soviet Government renounced the special rights and interests gained by the former Tsarist government in China. This gave Soviet Russia a moral advantage over the West even though its intentions, as events were to show, were anything but benevolent. Sun, however, turned to Russia for advice on how to strengthen the republican cause; he admired Lenin's reliance on mass political organization for he considered China to be "a loose sheet of sand," needing to be galvanized into a coherent national entity.

Sun met the roving Soviet agent, Adolph Joffe, in Shanghai in 1923. This laid the basis of future co-operation, but specifically excluded the introduction of Communism. As a result of this, another top Soviet functionary, Michael Borodin, arrived in Guangzhou to reorganize the Guomindang on a more rigid Soviet pattern, and the Soviet Communist Party became the model for the Chinese movement. At the same time, a Chinese Communist Party was formed and joined up with the Guomindang. This was seen as a desperate measure but Sun was transfixed by the need to build a strong and representative central government embracing all shades of opinion; it also offered a way of trying to water down and eventually abolish the unequal treaties with the West and Japan.

The Communist Party came into existence in China not out of Soviet Russian intrigues, however, but as a result of a meeting between two academics, both of whom were active in the May 4 Movement, one of whom, Chen Duxiu, was imprisoned. The other, Li Dazhao, had an inkling of where the party's appeal might ultimately be directed when he urged students to get to know peasants and become familiar with their way of life. The party swiftly developed and expanded and in 1921 held its first congress; one of its first acts was to set up a Chinese labour union secretariat in Shanghai.

The first major strike with some suspected Communist involvement, however, occurred not in Shanghai but in Hong Kong in 1922, and was a significant portent of what was to come. Seamen struck over a demand for a 30–40 per cent wage increase. Their claim was rejected and later the Government banned the union. This in turn led to a strike and boycott by all workmen in the colony which lasted eight weeks, together with a suspension of all coastal steamer services in the Pearl River area, causing considerable dislocation to trade between Hong Kong and Guangzhou.

The strike that followed, again not instigated by the Communists, was not an industrial action but rather a political response to the killing of a Chinese workman by a Japanese foreman in a Shanghai textile mill. This brought out student demonstrators in force into the streets of the international concession; moving through one area the students approached a police barricade and strongpoint. Uncertain of the demonstrators' intentions, a British police officer panicked and ordered his Chinese and Sikh policemen to open fire. Twelve demonstrators were killed and many more injured.

This led to a wave of sympathetic strikes in other ports, notably in Hong Kong in 1925, and in the British concession in

Figure 12.2 Overlooking the British Consulate in Shanghai. This photo, taken in the 1920s, shows the Garden Bridge and the river beyond to the north.

Guangzhou a mass walkout followed lasting sixteen months; it severely dislocated trade and disrupted business in both cities. The trade boycott cost Hong Kong about a million dollars in lost revenue and hit the local economy so badly that Britain had to pump in three million pounds to shore up local merchants.

Even more seriously, it lead to a procession in Guangzhou by students, trade unionists and cadres from the Huangpu Military Academy to demonstrate against the Shanghai killings. Communists were said to be involved in organizing the procession, though it was representative of a wide band of opinion — merchants, students, peasants and soldiers. Sadly the Shanghai tragedy was repeated when British and French sailors guarding the foreign concessions, heard shots and, believing they had come under attack, opened fire as the procession passed. In the ensuing battle, between thirty and sixty were killed while between seventy and two hundred were injured. The true toll will never be known because the two sides issued conflicting figures. The massacre outraged Chinese feelings not only in Guangzhou but all over the country and exacerbated the trade boycott. Mercifully for all involved, when a similar show of force by demonstrators was staged in Hankou, it passed without incident, with both sides showing commendable patience and restraint.

It was a year of disasters for China for it also recorded the death of Dr Sun Yat-sen before he had a chance to preside over a unified country. It would also precipitate a sharp clash between the left and right wings of the Guomindang causing a split which persists to this day. The author, S. I. Hsiung, wrote that had it not been for the Shanghai and Guangzhou massacres, Sun Yat-sen and his military commander, Chiang Kai-shek, would have broken off relations with their Russian advisers and the Chinese Communists much earlier, Sun having cooled in his admiration for the Soviet system.

Much of modern Chinese history might have been different, as well, at least in terms of timing, but it is difficult to believe that the essentials would have altered. In the aftermath of Sun's death the inevitable polarization of the Guomindang occurred, the right wing falling under the sway of Chiang Kai-shek and the left wing forming an alliance with the Communists, now a political-military force of increasing stature and credibility.

Chiang Kai-shek provided the military muscle for the Guomindang during the next two decades and was as influential as Sun in the first two decades. Chiang was the first modern soldier to emerge in the post-dynastic years for he had trained not just in Chinese military schools but in Japan with its far more disciplined approach to theory and tactics. He was later appointed to set up the Huangpu Military Academy and became its first President. He also visited Russia in the days of the Sino-Soviet honeymoon in the early 1920s and there learned the value of political indoctrination of troops, a lesson the Communists were quick to instil in the regiments they controlled. Until then Chinese soldiers were mercenaries employed on the promise of a wage, a uniform, sustenance and not much more, with booty as a bonus if they succeeded in their objectives. For this reason, the various warlord armies could not be combined to form an effective national force, lacking discipline, training, motivation and cohesion.

Moreover, there was a profound difference between Sun and Chiang in their views on the political reform of China. Sun clung to the hope of a mass political reawakening led by dedicated intellectuals. With "good government" the Chinese people would respond and rally around the leaders. He believed that China had been misgoverned for many centuries and it was now necessary to replace the old values and ideals and the widespread corruption with those that would evoke a positive response and support of the people and bring about China's renaissance. Chiang was more cynical. While paying lip-service to Sun's ideals he understood that China would make no progress as long as the self-serving, corrupt warlords perpetuated the fragmentation of China. National unity by force was the only solution which he as a soldier could instil; political reform would follow in a society where like-minded officials would work for the regeneration of the country. But initially it needed firm, strong leadership rather than theories and principles. The time to apply these would come after a unified government was achieved.

By 1927, the simmering tension between the left and right wings of the Guomindang came to a head. The left wing was located in Hankou and the right in Nanjing. A year earlier the Comintern in Moscow had instructed its advisers to support the left wing of the party. Chiang suspected he was being out-manoeuvred and that through Russian support of the left wing they might gain control of the party with the help of large numbers of sympathetic industrial workers in Shanghai.

A rising star in the ranks of the Communist Party, with a political-military background, Zhou Enlai orchestrated three revolts in the city; the first two failed and the third succeeded, but was shortly after struck down in a lightning counter-*coup* by Chiang Kai-shek who formed an alliance with the triad societies to eliminate the Communists and the leftists. A bloodbath followed. Zhou, with a $200,000 price on his head, somehow managed to escape after being arrested.

The *coup* by Chiang ended the alliance and caused a panic in the ranks of the Comintern which began to see the China prize slipping away. A complicating issue was that the "Old Marshal" in Manchuria, Zhang Zuolin, had ordered raids on the Soviet embassy in Beijing where it was found that Michael Borodin, the Soviet adviser to the Hankou regime, was under direct orders from Marshal Josef Stalin, the Soviet dictator, who believed China was ripe for revolution; moreover, a timetable for the takeover of China by Communists was being drawn up.

In December of that year, Chinese Red Guards assisted by most of the cadet training regiment at the Huangpu Military Academy, under Ye Jianying (later Marshal), seized control in Guangzhou and set up a commune, freeing 700 prisoners. About 3,000 diehards took part in the operation, but 300,000 trade unionists who were expected to rally to the *putsch* failed to turn up. While large parts of the city came under Red Guard control, the island of Honam opposite Guangzhou, remained in Guomindang hands and a screen of foreign gunboats blocked the Communists. Also the Anglo-French concession was spared.

Taking part in the revolt were members of the Soviet consulate, five of whom were later accused of collusion; eleven Russians were killed in the uprising. More than 1,000 houses were set ablaze and a Royal Naval gunboat, HMS *Moorhen*, was used to rescue twenty-six Britons and Americans and fifty-five Germans living in the city; it was fired on by Communist guns as it sailed down the river but there were no casualties. After three days of bitter fighting in which thousands died, the Guomindang regained control and a systematic extermination of Communists began as China broke off relations with Russia.

A proud, prickly, temperamental martinet, Chiang Kai-shek next launched the Guomindang army, which he had trained with the help of Russian advisers, on a campaign intended to reclaim the whole of China from the warlords and eventually to sweep out the Japanese and the Western occupants of the treaty ports. He planned the Northern Expedition carefully, convinced that with his own well-trained troops spearheading the action, he would win over dissident forces on his way north, gradually amalgamating them to create a formidable adversary to any who stood in his way. It also became his springboard for the presidency of China.

The remnants of the Communists fled into the countryside ending Moscow's hegemony in the Chinese Communist Party and opening the leadership to new men with new ideas on how to win power. But this also created new problems for Chiang Kai-shek as he tried to consolidate power from his capital in Nanjing. With the help of Shanghai bankers, Sun Yat-sen's name, and diplomatic recognition by the Western powers China looked as if it might be heading for a prolonged period of stability and firm government. The Japanese had performed a small service for the Guomindang by ejecting Zhang Zuolin from Beijing and for a short period Chiang looked as if he might be able to bring most of the major dissidents and warlords to heel.

Certainly foreign merchants and businessmen in China were delighted with the turn of events, one British taipan in Guangzhou exulting over the fact that great strides had been made to improve trading conditions — "the Chinese New Year settlement passed without a single bankruptcy." But then the horrid thought dawned on them that while stable conditions were good for business, a strong China might seek to abrogate the treaties of extraterritoriality depriving them of their privileged position — made more than a theoretical possibility by what had happened in Hankou, Jiujiang and other riverine treaty ports which were returned to Chinese control. So concerned was Britain by the turn of events in 1927 that it sent a 20,000-strong military contingent to Shanghai to bolster sagging morale and to discourage any Guomindang adventures.

In the case of Weihaiwei, the British gave back 95 per cent of the territory, but the naval anchorage and certain buildings on the island of Liugongdao were reserved for the summer visits of Royal naval ships; they continued to use these facilities until the outbreak of World War II. Weihaiwei had never been a colony like Hong Kong but was designated a "territory" headed by a commissioner; its first was the very able James Stewart Lockhart who held the post for nineteen years — a Shangri-La for any civil servant.

Arnold Toynbee in his *Journey to China* in 1931 described it as an "unreal world that was just nowhere" — secluded from China and caught between "a tempestuous sea and the crescent of mountains rising in ever higher tiers towards the spine of Shandong." Because of the ideal climate and its dominating strategic position as one of the "twin gates" to Tianjin (and hence Beijing), its superb beaches and rolling surf, it was a favourite summer resort for China residents, and second only to nearby Qingdao or Beidaihe.

Weihaiwei, according to a temple stone, was built in the Ming dynasty in 1388 as one of fifty-nine fortified ports to protect China from the repeated depredations of Japanese pirates. Whatever its former glory, by the twentieth century it was little more than a quiet, picturesque village, curiously ill-named with three characters meaning "Majestic Protector of the Sea."

Incidentally, Qingdao, in the years between the two world wars, became the summer station for the United States submarine flotilla, while the US Asiatic fleet took its recreation in the languid sea of Chefoo (Yantai) harbour. This made for a lively social season for the foreign community with many eligible young bachelors ready to join picnics, tennis parties, riding groups and dances that filled the calendar in the hot summer months of July and August.

Not only were some of the treaty ports returned and rights revoked in other parts of the country but 1 January 1930 was the date on which the Allies agreed to scale down extraterritoriality "in principle" though China wanted abolition completely and immediately. No such luck. However, it was more successful in securing tariff autonomy, subject to most favoured nation treatment, initially from the United States and ultimately from the other foreign powers; after a good deal of haggling for Japanese troop withdrawals from Shandong and assuring security for Japanese loans, even Tokyo fell into line.

Britain and the European powers were at that time wholly preoccupied with the depression which had overtaken the Western world. Events in Asia were of little consequence, and though suspicious of Japan, Britain was in no mood to voice its concerns. Its only major overseas dockyard east of Gibraltar was at Malta. Twice, attempts to build up Singapore were stopped on the grounds of economy and its decline was not halted until 1933. Even then it became a responsibility of the Royal Navy, its coastal guns pointing seaward against the only perceived threat; neither the Fleet Air Arm nor the Royal Air Force had any major part in its resurgence.

Hong Kong was likewise left to languish in much the same state when work finished on the 40-acre dockyard reclamation with its 550-ft graving dock in 1908. It was never a massively fortified base and its imperial role ended with the Boxer Rebellion; thereafter it provided a shore-based administrative station with limited workshop facilities for the squadron of cruisers and destroyers and the occasional aircraft carrier assigned to patrolling the China seas. Most ships spent their time anchored in midstream close to the fleshpots of Hong Kong and Kowloon. They made a grand spectacle for the taipans and their taitais, the bankers and contractors, the bartenders and the barmaids and the pimps and the prostitutes, all of whom lived off their dollars. But the Japanese spies who knew every square mile of the colony had rightly dismissed them as paper tigers. The British Empire was a spent force.

On this bright prospect, China looked to a new era of relations with the West, coupled with stable government over most of the country. There were still pockets of opposition in some parts of

China and the Communists had set up liberated areas in others. Chiang Kai-shek and the Guomindang were not completely out of the woods and neither were the Western powers yet ready to return what they had taken ninety years earlier. But China was in its most bullish mood since before the Opium War. Chiang even had a plan to squeeze out the Communists with a grand encircling move, using some of the best strategists seconded from the German army. With the reds out of the way China could then concentrate on Japan.

Much maligned as a group were the foreign missionaries in China but they composed a significant lobby working for the removal of the unequal treaties imposed after the Opium War. If the missionaries had had their way, the foreign powers would have relinquished these privileges at this time. Particularly vociferous was the American missionary group which could count about 8,000 Protestants and another 4,000 Roman Catholics. Their submissions to Washington gained strong support in Congress and amongst the more liberal elements in the American and foreign press. The missionaries saw the unequal treaties in the same light as the colonial bonds which their ancestors had rejected in 1776. They saw Chinese leaders, notably Sun Yat-sen and Chiang, as Christians who needed the support and encouragement of the West, and were strongly critical of businessmen who defended the *status quo* and the retention of extraterritoriality.

Nor was this action confined to missionaries in China. In the United States, 20 million people represented in the Federal Council of the Churches of Christ pleaded with Congress to abandon the treaties. Their plea was taken up by some of the most respected and prominent men and women in the land, one of whom was John Leighton Stuart, a future ambassador to China. The US Government was strongly sympathetic, but Europe was cynical, seeing this posturing as yet another manifestation of American "sour grapes," having failed to gain advantages from the "open door" policy of the last century, and having little to lose by abandoning the treaty ports other than risking a few commercial assets.

But before the US Government was prepared to rock the boat with its allies, it wanted to see firm evidence that China had a viable administration capable of taking nation-wide control. The closest Britain and the United States came to revising the treaties was to issue statements calling on treaty powers to recognize the "essential justice" of the Chinese claim to meet the legitimate aspirations of the people. While this created something of a frenzy in the foreign press in China, the only concrete changes were the addition of Chinese members to the Shanghai Municipal Council and an agreement to restore tariff autonomy to China by 1929.

Overt pressure was needed to budge the treaty powers. This happened when one member of the Guomindang — Eugene Chen in Hankou — decided to take matters into his own hands, seize control of the city and declare the end of extraterritoriality. To everyone's surprise he succeeded. No foreign gunboats, no soldiers, no diplomatic offensive appeared. As Barbara Tuchman wrote, "If in the past [the West] had not been prepared to yield their privileges, neither were they now prepared to use force to preserve them."[1] If only Eugene Chen and Chiang Kai-shek had seen eye to eye, the history of China in the 1930s might have been different.

---

1. Barbara Tuchman, *Sand Against the Wind* (London: Macmillan, 1970).

CHAPTER 13

Roughshod Riders

Expatriate communities of all nationalities were grateful for the presence of, and protection given by the Royal Navy in China between World Wars I and II. For they lived in constant fear of civil wars, piracies, brigandage, warlordery and other forms of violence which were all too frequently a feature of life in the East. In doing so, the Navy was seldom troubled by the finer points of international law; decisions were often made on the spot by junior officers or by young consular officials, suddenly confronted with a plea for help. Nor did they feel bound by the restraints that are mandatory for the commanders of ships today sailing in other countries' waters. In most cases, "the Navy" was either a small river gunboat, a destroyer or a light cruiser commanded by a young lieutenant or lieutenant commander whose job was to rescue civilians caught up in a dangerous situation, and if possible to enforce treaty rights.

The Navy on at least one occasion rescued Dr Sun Yat-sen and Chiang Kai-shek from Guangzhou when their lives were threatened by a sudden revolt — the rescuer, a small river gunboat, HMS *Moorhen*, the same vessel that picked up more than eighty Europeans caught in the Communist *coup* in the same city in 1927. On another occasion the small fleet of river gunboats was sent to rescue the crew of a British steamer seized by rebel troops in the upper reaches of the Yangzi River.

The gunboats were given the role of "watchdogs" but had

more bark than bite. The fleet varied in size from ten to twelve and came under the Rear Admiral Yangzi, which was an adjunct to the ocean-going Navy. These small flat-bottomed vessels were built for service on the Tigris and Euphrates Rivers to fight the Turks in World War I.

They were ideal river boats, each with a mixed Chinese and British crew of twenty-five to fifty and ideal for navigation in narrow, shallow channels. They were painted white and the older (insect-class) vessels carried two tall yellow funnels abreast and were so low on the waterline that above the protective dikes only their funnels and mast-top were visible. Later versions were given an extra deck and had a single funnel; their main weapons ranged from six pounders to six-inch guns.

In 1910, a young British consul, Meyrick Hewlett, stationed in the riverport of Changsha saved thirty-three foreigners — mainly missionaries — from a frenzied mob shouting "Sha, sha" (Kill, kill) outraged over the use of labour from outside the province to carry out building work on the new British consulate. Hewlett ordered them all on to a British steamer until the arrival of a gunboat, HMS *Thistle*, helped to calm down the agitation. Hewlett, who spoke fluent Chinese, was warned of the impending riot and acted quickly to protect the small group, including Americans, Dutch, Germans, Italians, Norwegians, Swedish, Swiss and British. An old Harrovian and a former schoolmaster, he was always ready to act decisively and firmly; twice, he took a cane to his Chinese staff for minor misdemeanours, forcing them to bend over his desk, and remove their trousers for a ritual six strokes. When the problem grew too large, however, a gunboat was more dependable and reassuring.

In 1926, a Sichuanese warlord tried to seize a ship owned by the China Navigation Company, on its way down the Yangzi to Yichang. The master refused to stop and a small sampan manned by troops who tried to swarm on board capsized in its wake as the river steamer brushed past, causing several to drown. The warlord demanded compensation for the dead and claimed the sampan was carrying money to pay his troops. The shipping line refused and the warlord seized two other steamers of the China Navigation Company. The Navy was ordered to rescue the crew and if possible retrieve the ships.

In the subsequent action by HMS *Cockchafer*, assisted by other ships requisitioned and armed by the Rear Admiral Yangzi, the Navy ran alongside one of the seized river steamers, by now packed with the warlords' troops, boarded her and helped the officers escape. However, in the heavy firefight that followed, seven British naval personnel were killed though eventually all the captured vessels were recovered and the town of Wanxian (in which the warlord was based) was shelled, with unknown casualties. To have attempted to retrieve the ships by diplomatic means would have taken months even if the central government was able to persuade the warlord to comply, for this action took place more than 1,200 kilometres from the coast, high up in the Gorges. At that time, Guomindang rule was split and it is very doubtful if the left faction operating in that area would have heeded a request from a British diplomat or Chiang Kai-shek himself.

Eight years later, the China Navigation Company steamer, *Shuntien*, en route from Tianjin to Shanghai, was seized by pirates off the mouth of the Huanghe or Yellow River, beached and ransacked by twenty brigands. They had been travelling as steerage passengers on the ship. They were admitted into the main cabin area through security gates by their Japanese leader travelling as a first-class passenger, who had held up a guard and taken his keys.

All passengers' baggage was thoroughly looted and all women and children confined to cabins and segregated from their menfolk. The pirates then made the rounds of each cabin, demanding the surrender of valuables and threatening to cut off a finger when a wedding or engagement ring proved difficult to move. Happily, no amputations were necessary and having ransacked the ship they loaded their booty together with twenty-six male hostages into five junks and made off up river.

When radio control was restored, the Royal Navy came to the rescue. A patrolling aircraft carrier, HMS *Eagle*, sent up three fighter biplanes to chase the pirates, while two destroyers (one British, one American) came to assist the passengers injured in the skirmish and to escort the vessel back to the nearest port. But the Navy's concerns did not end there. Recovery of the hostages was their main priority and while Chinese troops were also on the lookout, HMS *Eagle*'s aircraft found the escaping junks. The pirates gave themselves away by opening fire on the low-flying aircraft which then attacked them with strafing runs and bombs, forcing them to beach their vessels and abandon their hostages (one of whom was injured) and the loot, most of which was recovered.[1]

This was only one of more than sixty piracies which occurred on the coast of China during the 1920s and 1930s and the Navy was driven to a frenzy trying to counter them. At one stage between 1928 and 1930 military guards were posted on all British-owned passenger vessels; although the incidence of piracies was drastically reduced the experiment proved so costly the guards were withdrawn. Piracies resumed immediately, in many cases based on knowledge of the ships' movements, cargo and passenger manifests.

Returning Chinese from the United States were always considered prime targets, also a wealthy compradore and his family who could be held for ransom. One piracy in 1935 involved the British vessel *Tungchow* with seventy British children aboard returning to their school in Chefoo from summer holidays in Shanghai; the children were well treated but one Russian guard

---

1. The writer and his family were travelling on this ship. Their losses included a portable gramophone, later recovered but subsequently auctioned for a few dollars. Never recovered was his mother's engagement ring. The writer, aged seven, offered his bag of marbles, but after inspection, they were declined.

who resisted was riddled with bullets and his body thrown overboard. The children and the ship were eventually rescued after planes from the carrier, HMS *Hermes*, found the ship, forcing the pirates to flee in one of the ship's lifeboats.

Many were the ruses devised by pirates to get aboard, the most common being to travel as first-, second- or steerage-class passengers; they then commandeered the ship and ran her aground. One innovative gang took over two small junks and stretched a steel cable across the path of an oncoming ship until it became entangled in the propeller. Nor were the pirates all Chinese or Japanese. In 1933, four Germans were sentenced to death by the Japanese Supreme Court in Port Arthur after a particularly vicious piracy in which ten people were murdered on board the steamer *Sheng-An*.

One of the few piracies that ended disastrously for the pirates was that involving the 2,555-tonne British steamer *Sunning* which in 1926 was seized en route from Xiamen to Hong Kong. Two officers, Thomas Beatty and Joseph Hurst, bravely counterattacked with revolvers, regaining possession of the bridge even when pirates tried to turn the chief engineer, George McCormack, into a human shield. Beatty and Hurst however rescued him, though wounding him in the process, and fought the pirates to the point where they decided to abandon ship and set fire to it. Two groups of escaping pirates perished in heavy seas, and others tried to mingle with passengers in a bid to escape detection when a Royal Naval gunboat, HMS *Bluebell*, pulled alongside. The ship was towed to Hong Kong, a virtual wreck, but the pirates were identified by passengers and eight were found guilty after trial and hanged.

In another incident in 1927, the Royal Navy's attempts to frustrate a piracy ended with the shelling of the China Merchants's *Irene*, which when sailing under pirate control into Bias Bay without lights, refused to obey an order to stop. The Navy later rescued 234 of the 258 people aboard but their shells sent the ship to the bottom. The owners sued the Navy for

$530,000 but lost the action when it was held that the rescuers had used only "reasonable force" to attack the pirates.

The British authorities finally took the law into their own hands, launching anti-piracy patrols, while shipping lines engaged private security guards, usually Sikhs or White Russians, and enclosed passenger areas in protective cages. Still the pirates managed to penetrate them, as the *Shuntien* piracy proved, and the commander of the naval vessel sent to the rescue was often faced with a dilemma in deciding how to recover passengers and ship without causing casualties.

In an attempt to forestall piracies, and on the suggestion of the then Guomindang Foreign Minister, Eugene Chen, the Royal Navy and later the Japanese Navy targeted areas known to be pirate lairs; and although they were not authorized to put men ashore in pursuit of pirates, they did so on several occasions, particularly in the Bias Bay area, well known as a pirate haunt north of Hong Kong. On one occasion, to achieve surprise, the Navy used a submarine to land a party of sailors who attacked and burnt the alleged pirate villages.

One of the biggest Naval raids on this area took place on 23 March 1937, when a task force comprising the aircraft carrier *Hermes*, the heavy cruiser *Frobisher*, light-cruiser *Delhi* and two smaller ships, sailed into Bias Bay with a landing force of 300 marines and sailors. They stormed ashore destroying 130 huts and burning forty junks. The villages concerned were described as being beyond the writ of Guangzhou law and the raid either had the tacit or official consent of the provincial authorities. The action achieved nothing in terms of curbing piracies and they continued until the arrival of the Japanese invaders a year later; with the sharp decline in river and coastal traffic between Hong Kong and Guangzhou, they then moved south in search of richer pickings.

Piracies were only one menace to shipping in the China seas. Even more damaging were typhoons and other natural disasters. In China, the vast river systems, bloated by the spring thaw, frequently inundated thousands of square miles of countryside leading to heavy loss of life and property, and decimating crops which in turn created famine on a massive scale. The traditional practice of building dikes along river banks was a puny defence against raging torrents of swirling muddy water. On the surrounding ricelands, flood waters would immerse everything, killing people and livestock and washing away villages, homes and valuable topsoil. Few if any dams existed before 1950 to control and conserve the discharge of flood waters, and with rudimentary flood alerts, farmers were left to decide for themselves when to evacuate. An upturned sampan was often a family home or pig shed which could be pressed into service in emergencies.

Tropical cyclones occur frequently each year, savaging the economies of countries like the Philippines, Taiwan, Vietnam, China, Thailand and occasionally Japan and Korea. Spawned in the warm waters of the Pacific Ocean or the South China Sea they travel either west or north-west through the Bashi Channel separating the island of Taiwan from the Philippines, or across the Philippines, causing widespread damage and a heavy death toll. With the advent of international shipping in Asian waters, the loss of vessels, crews, cargoes and bullion assumed massive proportions which severely strained insurers and owners.

In the 1920s and 1930s, meteorologists devised more effective ways of detecting and tracking storms, yet their unpredictable movements made it impossible to know when and where they would strike. Radio reports from shipping (and later aircraft) added greatly to the information available at tracking centres in Hong Kong, Shanghai, Manila and along the China coast; today meteorologists assisted by satellite photographs are able to provide more accurate predictions as they approach land.

The cost of damage to Chinese ports and to Hong Kong and Macau ran into thousands of millions of dollars and the toll of lives into hundreds of thousands killed either by high winds, flying debris, floods or storm surges. Attempts have been made by meteorologists to "tame" typhoons by seeding storm clouds with silver iodide or dry ice, though experiments conducted in the Caribbean have shown no promise of worthwhile results. It is estimated the toll of damage in the Pacific–South China Sea area exceeds five to ten billion dollars a year, with the Philippines, China and Taiwan taking the brunt of the storms.

Each year a number of cyclones devastate the coast of South China. Hong Kong has regularly received "direct hits" or near misses, its first coming only months after Britain took possession in 1841, flattening a matshed hospital in which 300 soldiers, injured in the Opium War, were recuperating. The storm drove many ships ashore and scattered others about the harbour.

Several typhoons narrowly missed the port in the next thirty years but another direct hit occurred in 1874 driving sailing ships

Figure 13.1   High and dry after the 1937 typhoon, this steamer was washed ashore by a giant wave in Hong Kong harbour.

ashore at Hong Kong and Macau, stranding some in rice fields, and killing about 2,000 people, as well as causing millions of dollars of damage. In the 1880s, the Jesuit priests at the Ziccawei Observatory in Shanghai established a rudimentary tracking and forecasting system which gained widespread respect from the maritime community. Hong Kong's observatory and tracking station, manned by meteorologists, followed soon after, though shipping continued to suffer high casualties in the typhoons of 1906 and 1923 when several sinkings occurred in the harbour with heavy loss of life.

The storm that struck the greatest terror, however, was that of September 1937 when the harbour of Hong Kong, containing a number of large ocean liners, was devastated, leaving several ships under water or beached on the shores, and with more than 200 villagers drowned in a storm surge. Part of the reason for the heavy damage was that in days before radar the typhoon swept largely undetected through the Balintang Channel, north of the Philippines, and then intensified in open sea during the next four days before turning up on the coast of South China. The big liners were unable to put to sea to ride out the storm and were grounded by wind gusts exceeding 150 knots.

One of the liners stranded was the Japanese NYK flagship, *Asama Maru*. Malcolm Goldfinch, a young Australian pilot, newly licensed and keen on photography, recalls flying low over the stricken liner and watching the crew scurry for safety, two falling into the sea, believing it to be a Nationalist Chinese warplane bent on revenge for the Japanese air raids on Guangzhou. George Scott, whose father was a senior Kowloon Dockyard engineer, also recalls how another of the liners was salvaged with the help of specially built tanks, which were immersed on each side with cables slung under the keel. They were then pumped with air to lift it off the rocks. It was a significant achievement which won high praise in the profession.

A similar calamity occurred in 1962 when the eye of typhoon Wanda, with winds in excess of 180 knots, swept through the territory, grounding scores of ships and pleasure craft in various parts of the harbour, with the loss of many lives. What occurred in Hong Kong occasionally was repeated each summer on many parts of the China coast and stoically endured by the hundreds of thousands who suffered losses and injuries.

Figure 13.2   The British-India steamer, *Talamba*, down by the bows in Hong Kong habour after the disastrous 1937 typhoon.

By far the most destructive acts of nature, however, were earthquakes. Hundreds of thousands of people in China have been killed through the centuries, one of the worst destroying the mining city of Tangshan in 1976 with casualties exceeding 240,000. Two earlier earthquakes in 1920 and 1932 took a total of 270,000 lives in Gansu province. Even worse were the tragedies experienced in Japan due to the presence of subterranean plates impacting on one another; the deadly 1923 earthquake claimed more than 100,000 lives in the Tokyo–Yokohama area. Another major earthquake destroyed Kobe in 1995, with more than 5,000 casualties and a damage bill of over US$100 billion.

The impact of natural calamities is relatively swift and recovery a matter of time. The harrowing effect of war and continuous aggression leaves deeper scars, and for China the decade of the 1930s was no passing storm or natural calamity but a period of sustained brutality still vivid in the minds of survivors sixty years later. For in 1931, the Japanese Guandong Army engineered the so-called Mukden (Shenyang) Incident in response to an influential faction in the Japanese cabinet; this involved seizing and taking over the province of Heilongjiang, which Japan renamed Manchukuo, and setting up a puppet government. Japan at that time had a weak and feckless Prime Minister, Reijira Wakatsuki, who pandered to the Army because it had direct access to the Emperor. Thus any cabinet decision was theoretically subject to challenge by the Army and the veto of the Emperor — for he was also dominated by the militarists.

Hirohito has been blamed for subsequent events. Whether he himself encouraged the Army's machinations, or was powerless to resist it, is uncertain. There is, however, nothing to prove his opposition and as the all-powerful Son of Heaven he could have publicly denounced the venture from the outset. In doing so he would have upset the Army but faced no greater risk. The Army needed his patronage and support, and got the next best, his qualified acquiescence. What happened in Mukden was not an isolated incident, a reprisal for the killing of a Japanese agent as Tokyo claimed, but a calculated act of aggression to strengthen its grip on China; thus a defiant challenge was thrown down to the West and particularly its concessions in the seaboard provinces.

Japan for years had been surveying China's economic resources. In 1917 a commissioned report detailed China's mineral wealth and subsequently the Yangzi valley was described as "a limitless treasure trove."[2] In 1923, a defence plan noted that "China's abundant natural resources are an indispensable element in both our economic development and defence."[3] War was thus no sudden impulse, no aberration of a manic faction within the army. Japan Inc. had targetted China as the rich source of minerals on which it would draw to realize its imperial ambitions. Little thought was given to the repercussions in terms of international response, though by building a strong army and a large navy and air force its position was assumed to be unassailable. In 1931 Japan was ready to take the next step in its plan for its "Greater Asian Co-prosperity Sphere."

A report commissioned by the League of Nations and written by Lord Lytton of the United Kingdom, and his fellow Western commissioners, verbally rebuked Japan for forcibly seizing Chinese territory and occupying it. Not satisfied with military occupation, the Japanese declared it to be the new republic of Manchukuo, and the League decided to accept it as a *fait accompli*. The self-concerned West could do no more than deliver a tame rebuke and a slap on the wrists, but China itself offered no resistance to the restoration of the young Emperor, Puyi in Manchukuo, and within a few months the province was under Tokyo's control.

Japan had warned that it might leave the League of Nations if the League's criticism was "too strong" but the Japanese army knew there was nothing to stop it, and it lost no sleep when it was announced that the American Pacific Fleet would hold exercises with units of the Atlantic Fleet. On the diplomatic front, Washington was anxious to support China — if only to appease the influential missionary movement — but steered clear of taking a direct role against Japan. If the League were willing to do

---

2. See Kenneth Latourette, *A Short History of the Far East* (New York: Macmillan, 1952).
3. See Paul Clyde, *The Far East* (New York: Prentice-Hall, 1952).

it — and that meant all the powers co-operating and putting their weight behind some form of sanction — so be it, but in an era when President Roosevelt was too involved with the great depression and his New Deal, Secretary of State Henry Stimson was not prepared for a showdown: in short, he was keen to avert trouble, not tackle it. Japan took that as a green light to tighten its grip on China convinced that the West had no stomach for a quarrel even at the diplomatic level. So pleased was it with its success that Japan moved to take over the neighbouring region of Rehe, once the favoured summer residence of Chinese emperors.

While events in Manchuria held the spotlight, Chiang Kai-shek's armies were concentrating on what he considered a more insidious enemy; unless the Communists were evicted from their "Soviet" strongholds in the southern central province of Jiangxi, the objectives of his Northern Expedition would be in jeopardy. Indeed, Japan exploited the Nationalist–Communist civil war to cloak its own grab for territory in the north. Faced with this crisis, the politicians temporarily sank their differences and Chiang was forced to yield his role as Head of State but clung to his post of Commander-in-chief. He continued to be a dominant figure in the ranks of the Guomindang, however, and had no intention of giving up. Chinese political leaders invariably tend to absolutism regardless of ideology. Western democracy has never been favoured except by those seeking a popular power base; once achieved, national interest soon demands either a suspension or severe dilution of constitutional and civil liberties.

In the 1930s, with the Communists snapping at their heels in Central China and with the Japanese army spreading over the northern provinces, Chiang was in no mood to share power with anyone whatever his political hue, much less experiment with imported political ideas. Besides, he had experienced Soviet Communism at first hand and hated it. Chinese leaders were quick to point out to British critics that the growth of democracy in their country had taken over 700 years (from the time of Magna Carta) and China had no intention of adopting instant constitutional reforms in such an impoverished, backward and traditional society, particularly in an era of international crisis.

Through contacts at home and overseas, however, China's ancient culture took on new dimensions in literature, art, music, drama and architecture. Films and radio made an appearance at first in the treaty ports and in later years became potent factors in shaping opinion. The major stumbling blocks in the spread of mass communications were illiteracy among large numbers of the population, coupled with language barriers, for where some form of Mandarin or Potunghua was understood by two-thirds of the population, about eight main dialects and many sub-dialects and minority languages were used in other parts, particularly outer provinces. Another major stumbling block was the lack of a national electricity grid.

Two treaty ports, using the Shanghai and Cantonese dialects, took the lead in radio and films but Mandarin speakers were quickly drawn in. Shanghai, as the most westernized city in China and with the most talented directors, actors and the most enterprising investors, made the greatest impact. Hong Kong and Guangzhou were quick to follow. But where Hollywood enjoyed large and often lavish budgets for its films, drawing from a rich heritage of literature and folklore, the Chinese film makers operated on a shoestring and took their themes initially from contemporary events which touched the lives of ordinary people, suffering from war, poverty, oppression, drought and flood.

Historical and literary themes took centre stage in live operatic performances, which had always been a popular medium of artistic and cultural expression in China and which were relatively untouched by Western influences. Long before Punch-and-Judy shows made their debut in the West, Chinese puppets were widely admired and appreciated, all the more because they required one voice, a pair of cymbals, a drum and a musical instrument or two. Films quickly gained popularity as they moved about the country with battery-powered projectors set up in village halls, and with a running commentary in the local dialect.

As with movies, sports like swimming, baseball, basketball, volleyball, badminton, fencing and table tennis gained entry through the treaty ports and in missionary-run schools and universities. Equally popular were tennis and soccer, though physical contact sports favoured in Western communities such as boxing, wrestling, and rugby were shunned. Ever practical and resourceful, the Chinese chose sports needing little space and minimum equipment, as well as ones appropriate to people with nimble bodies, quick eyes, clever footwork and exceptional co-ordination, as found in traditional pastimes such as *taiji* (*tai-chi*), unarmed combat and swordplay.

With its own popular traditional games like mah-jong, cards, and chess, China borrowed little from outside, though local people in the treaty ports were quick converts to horse-racing, particularly *pari mutuel* each-way betting. The first races in Hong Kong saw imported Arab horses (used to pull expatriate carriages) in the starting line-up, with jockeys wearing the colours of the major British trading firms. However, Mongolian ponies, fast, short-legged and ungainly animals, were the basic racing stock for many years. Later, colonial horses bred in the Australian outback came on the scene and their fame stretched from Melbourne to Madras, Cairns to Calcutta and Sydney to Singapore.

In the early days, the ever-pragmatic punter cared little about the shape or bloodline of the animal, the skill of the rider and the experience of the trainer; what counted most was who had the fastest legs. One of the most prized animals was a small equine eccentric from the Philippines, named Tetoy (or, Little Chap), twelve hands high, who in spite of big handicaps, was a regular winner in Shanghai and Hong Kong for many years. He was the toast of governors, taipans and the punting public whom he rarely disappointed.

Horses were for centuries the favoured individual form of transport throughout China for those able to afford them. They also constituted the basic official courier service for the administration and enabled the Government in Beijing to keep contact with provincial authorities with remarkable speed and regularity bearing in mind the vast distances covered by teams of riders. The noble Tang dynasty horse survives in sculptured ceramic and bronze, and the flying horse (*feima*) which galloped on the back of a swallow was the steed of mythology admired by many generations of Chinese people just as the winged horse Pegasus was the creature of Western myth.

Technological innovations introduced by the West in the shape of trains and cars offered obvious advantages over the traditional wheelbarrows, ox carts, sedan chairs or horse-drawn carriages, but trains ran into spirited opposition from superstitious locals worried about the disturbance to *fengshui*, while cars were a luxury for the rich and out of reach to the majority until recent times.

Of all the Western forms of personal transport, the bicycle (invented by the Frenchman, Pierre Michaux in 1861) was the most widely adopted in a country that must today number close on a billion owners at all social levels, sexes, and ages (now giving way to motor bicycles and small locally-built cars in urban areas). Even the rickshaw, a familiar sight on Chinese streets in the 1920s and 1930s, was an import from Japan in the nineteenth century, and said to have been invented by a foreign missionary. These ranged from luxury private rainproof models with pneumatic tyres, used by the rich and famous, to the humble wooden seat on solid wheels, and pulled by ragged drug addicts. A few pathetic relics survive in Hong Kong for tourists but are shunned by all but the innocent.

As with all forms of Western technology, the Chinese were sceptical about aviation, though in the realm of myth, the idea of flight had been around for 2,000 years when a legendary emperor made swift tours of inspections in winged chariots. Since the previous century, Chinese visionaries had been fascinated by the prospect of flight and one writer in the 1890s had marvelled at the advent of a "flying boat based on the principles of a balloon ...

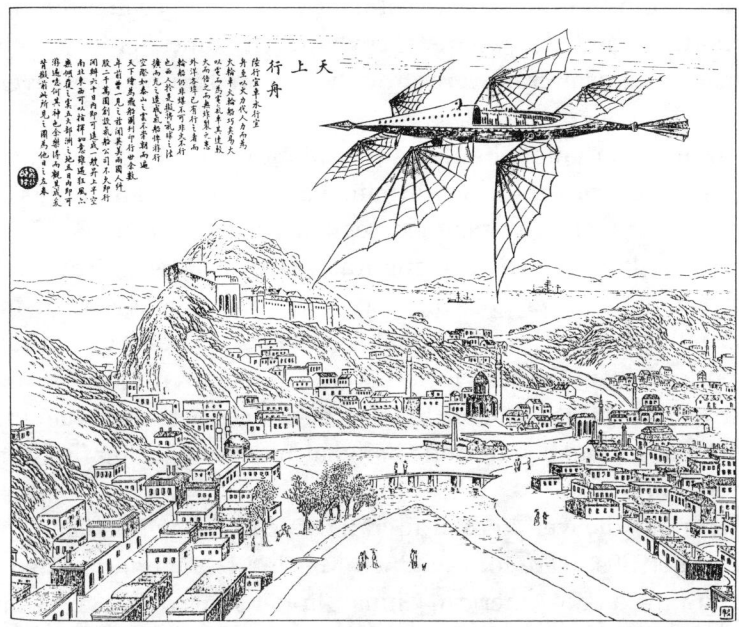

天上行舟

Figure 13.3 The imaginative Chinese artist had his own ideas on how airliners of the future would evolve.

travelling through the sky … like the clouds hovering over Mt Tai … and able to travel over all the five continents within a period of five days."[4] A man of more practical mind was a Mr Tse Tsan-tai, of Hong Kong, who was described as a "Chinese Galileo" in the designs he prepared for a dirigible before the turn of the twentieth century.

Real aeroplanes took longer to get off the ground. The first made its debut in Hong Kong in 1911 and four years later a Chinese aviator named Tom Gunn flew a hydroplane in the New Territories. Thanks to two far-sighted Chinese real estate investors, Ho Kai and Au Tak, their reclamation in Kowloon was chosen as the site of the Hong Kong Flying Club, and the land

4. Don J. Cohn, *Vignettes from the Chinese* (Hong Kong: The Chinese University Press, 1987).

rented from the Kai Tak Investment Company became the first airport. To cover the vast distances between Chinese cities and the outside world, aircraft were strongly favoured for mail and eventually passenger services.

With international airlines spreading their wings across the world, Imperial Airways of Britain, Pan American, and Eurasian Airways of Germany planned regular services to the Far East. China itself prepared to inaugurate its own internal routes to supplement its ever growing network of railways criss-crossing the country. The China National Aviation Corporation was more American than Chinese in terms of capital, aircraft, pilots and instructors, but it was able to launch services between Shanghai and Guangzhou, Beijing and Shanghai and more distant flights to Chongqing.

Among the well-known aircraft flying to and within China by the mid-1930s, were four-engined Martin M-130 flying boats inaugurating a Pan-American China Clipper service on 22 November 1935. An even larger clipper — the Boeing 314 — made the flight three years later. By that time, Douglas DC-2s and DC-3s were in service, together with Lockheeds from the United States, De Havilland 86s and "Empire" flying boats from Britain[5] and Dorniers and Junkers from Germany.

The Chinese air force, however, was in its infancy in the 1930s and Chiang Kai-shek put his faith in conventional ground forces when he lauched his carefully planned attack on Communist enclaves, with the help of German military advisers blooded in the trenches of World War I. Chiang concentrated all his energies, with a million troops taking part in the giant encircling moves.

Five campaigns were mounted in central and southern China

---

5. Imperial Airways in 1936 launched a twice weekly service to Australia, involving four different aircraft and a train trip between Paris and Brindisi, with a connecting 10-seat DH 86 service from Penang to Hong Kong, taking ten hours.

but though severely mauled by the massive firepower of the Guomindang, the main body of the Communist armies managed to slip through the cordons. Moving westward, the long trail of 100,000 escaping Communist soldiers, living off the land but under strict rules of conduct, traversed 10,000 kilometres through western China — twice the width of the American continent — before reaching a new haven in Yan'an. Though reduced to rags and an assortment of primitive firearms, the 30,000 survivors formed the basis of a new political force that within ten years would challenge the Guomindang for the control of China. The Long March, which also saw Mao Zedong's rise to supreme control of the Communist Party, was an epic with few parallels in human history. It owed something to Marxist ideology but a lot more to sheer Chinese tenacity.

Chiang Kai-shek's failure was that he could not mobilize the country behind him and in the face of continued Japanese invasion, he chose the wrong priority. Cleverly, the Communists orchestrated popular sentiment from Yan'an by calling on the people to identify foreign aggression as the greatest menace; they did this by highlighting their own role in combat against the Japanese — notably the spirited defence by the Communist Nineteenth Route Army in the Japanese attack on Shanghai in 1932. This proved that with strong leadership and effective weapons Chinese soldiers were able to match their enemy in every way. This eventually prompted widespread demands for Chiang to form a united front with the Communists to expel the Japanese.

So stubbornly did Chiang resist that his warlord ally, the "Young Marshal" Zhang Xueliang, engineered a *coup* in 1936 in the Qin emperors' old capital of Xi'an. Caught by surprise, Chiang was sleeping in the hotsprings resort of Lintong when the Young Marshal's troops raided his headquarters. After a short sharp fight Chiang's bodyguard was silenced. Wakened by the noise, Chiang slipped out of a rear door with only a robe over him and without his false teeth. He climbed into a cave in a rocky hill behind his quarters where he was later found injured and shivering in the cold of an early December morning. He was detained by the Young Marshal until he agreed with the Communist leader, Zhou Enlai, to form a united front. Sadly for China this was to be repudiated by Chiang shortly after, though both armies claimed victories in various parts of the country against the Japanese.

Zhang Xueliang, though an ally of the Guomindang, nursed a bitter hatred against the Japanese for assassinating his father, the "Old Marshal," Zhang Zuolin. At the same time he had a profound respect for the tactical skills of the Red Army which had been vindicated in many battles with the Guomindang as it fought its long rearguard actions in escaping to Yan'an. So impressed was he that he invited Red Army officers to train his own soldiers rather than Guomindang officers educated at the Huangpu Military Academy. It was his possible defection to the Communists that forced Chiang to confront him in Xi'an and into this clever Communist propaganda trap Chiang conveniently and obligingly fell.

Mao Zedong played no direct part in the Xi'an *coup*. He had regained his authority only a year earlier and although he headed the revolutionary military committee and the party secretariat, he left the manoeuvrings with the Guomindang to his able colleague, Zhou Enlai. Mao himself was distrustful and deeply suspicious of an alliance with those who had been striving to destroy him for the last nine years, but publicly parroted the united front line because it was good politics.

The Xi'an *coup* solved nothing other than to expose the fragility of Chiang's rule and the tenuous and superficial support he commanded. He was never keen to fight the Japanese, always argued that he was no match militarily and considered the Communists his most dangerous adversary. But when forced publicly to declare his priorities as a prisoner in Xi'an he had to endorse the ideal of unity of all Chinese factions, including the Communists, against Japan.

In a state of remorse after the event, the Young Marshal

submitted himself for trial by a Guomindang military court and effectively remained under house arrest for the rest of his life. Chiang made a half-hearted effort to blunt the Japanese advance but in 1938, following Tokyo's representations to Berlin, Germany withdrew the 140-man military mission to China, the same team which had helped squeeze the Communists out of their Jiangxi Soviet in 1934.

The Japanese, alarmed by the evident improvement in the Chinese economy, currency and military preparedness and with sizeable loans from Western nations, decided to force the pace of aggression in China. The Japanese Guandong Army, following a

Figure 13.4 The French Concession in Shanghai in the late 1920s.

Figure 13.5 The Bund, with its impressive skyline of waterfront buildings, in the early 1930s.

staged incident at the Lugou Bridge (Lugouqiao) on the outskirts of Beijing, broke out of the northern provinces and advanced down the eastern seaboard towards Shanghai, and in doing so alerted the world to an inevitable Pacific War.

There were occasional displays of heroism as in 1937, when the Japanese invaded Shanghai, they ran into Chiang's veterans, and despite mounting a force of 35,000 men the invaders were unable to make headway. After five days they had to be reinforced with a fresh division, making five in all. Still the resistance was impenetrable.

The Japanese air force also hammered the Chinese defences but found the 300 small Chinese combat planes, with pilots trained by Americans, disruptive. Tragically, two of the Chinese planes dropped bombs on the city hitting the international concession and killing about forty people, though for the most part the foreign residents experienced nothing worse than a bad dose of nerves. Thousands of refugees had swarmed into the city and they camped on the already crowded streets, begging, stealing and scavenging to stay alive. Several were killed by the bombs. Many more fortunate people — both Chinese and European — took ships to Hong Kong and spent the summer there.

Two months later, the Japanese were still fighting it out street by street in the Chinese city and had to revise their plans to outflank the Chinese defenders and push through to Nanjing and Hankou. They launched a seaborn invasion with 60,000 men, landing them at Hangzhou Bay about forty miles south of Shanghai, and caught the defenders unaware in a heavy November fog. At the same time another force landed on the Yangzi estuary, just north of the city. Fighting with brutality the Japanese achieved their objectives within days, slaughtering civilians who stood in their way with savage indifference. Chiang Kai-shek later said that almost 400,000 lost their lives in the advance of two Japanese divisions toward Nanjing. The Japanese lost about 110,000 but it was the sheer horror of their bloody revenge on the Chinese capital that shocked the world — a genocidal holocaust to rival the tragedy of the Jews at the hands of Hitler a few years later.

Typical of the brutality was the case of two Japanese sub-lieutenants, who in a "friendly contest" vied to be first to single-handedly slash to death 100 Chinese people — a goal extended to 150 a week later because the referees "had lost count." General Baron von Falkenhausen, the head of the German military mission to Chiang Kai-shek, said the behaviour of the Japanese was "almost indescribable." Tillman Durdin of the *New York Times* watched 200 men being executed on the bund — "then a number of Japanese, armed with pistols, trod nonchalantly about the crumpled bodies pumping bullets into any that were still kicking." The International Military Tribunal which investigated the city's conquest after World War II, gave the number of women raped at 20,000, many multiple victims, and more than 200,000 murdered, at least a quarter civilians.

A significant footnote to the events at Nanjing on 12 December 1937, was the deliberate Japanese bombing of the American gunboat, *Panay*, and two American tankers, lying in the river near the city but too far away to have been hit by a stray bomb or shell. The Japanese in any case were advised of the position of the vessel which also carried American flags painted on her decks visible from the air. Nor was she bombed once but strafed as well by a Japanese patrol boat. The gunboat sank, and the British gunboat, *Ladybird*, lying nearby, was damaged by shellfire, killing a seaman. President Roosevelt expressed "shock and concern" and the Japanese timed their apology nicely for Christmas eve — a gesture which brought a smile of gratitude to the American ambassador in Tokyo, Joseph C. Grew. But Japanese forces in China were like a mad bull in a china shop, answerable to no one. Britain and America considered joint action, but when they realized this meant going to war they promptly backpedalled. The British Ambassador, Sir Hughe Knatchbull-Huguessen, travelling in a car flying embassy flags from Nanjing to Shanghai, was shot at by Japanese planes, wounding him.

In 1938, as the Japanese advance continued, a group of foreign residents (among them, this writer and his family) were evacuated from Hankou, then under daily bombing attack. They were transported in a British cruiser and sailed 700 kilometres through a swirling Yangzi River strewn with barriers of sunken junks, packed with explosives. HMS *Capetown* had to negotiate these obstacles — "like threading a needle with a shaky hand" — while Japanese planes lurked overhead. Unlike *Panay*, *Capetown* was not attacked. Captain Cuthbert Coppinger kept his crew at action stations all the way downstream to Shanghai while the evacuees huddled below decks, coming out only at nights to refresh themselves.

Having overrun the Yangzi valley, the Japanese offered peace terms to China, concerned that they had failed to bring about a swift capitulation. After several overtures were rebuffed, the Japanese turned south where their next target was Guangzhou, and in 1937 came the long delayed declaration of open war. While horrified at the ferocity of Japanese aggression in China, the European powers were also concerned at the growth of Chinese nationalism and the continuing demands for an end to extraterritoriality and a lifting of European controls on Chinese commercial, financial and economic activities. They saw their position diminishing and prestige slipping day by day.

It is necessary at this point to recall China's age-old dependence on silver as the basis of its currency. The use of taels, or silver ingots, and later Spanish silver dollars was the one enduring feature of the Chinese financial system (These became Mexican dollars after the 1824 overthrow of Spanish colonial rule, hence the use of $Mex until well into the 1930s). Attempts to mint its own silver dollars met with mixed results, largely because of public suspicions that the silver would be debased — the Mexican dollars minted overseas never suffered from that stigma. The Chinese, however, did mint two silver coins which held their reputation — one bearing the effigy of Yuan Shikai in 1912, and another with the effigy of

Sun Yat-sen in 1928 after Chiang Kai-shek had consolidated himself in power.

China, however, discovered that while it was possible to base its currency on the value of silver and maintain stability when its economy was wholly self-sufficient, problems arose when international trade developed. First it was the British who ran into foreign exchange difficulties paying for tea imports with silver dollars, and later it was China's turn when opium began pouring in. These problems were exacerbated following the Opium War when demand and supply for silver sent prices alternately soaring and crashing on the international market.

The silver base lingered on fitfully for almost 100 years. In 1935 China was forced to act when heavy American and European buying in the post-Depression era caused a run on silver, and dangerous instability rocked the Chinese internal and external economy. A duty on silver exports failed to staunch a massive haemorrhage, aggravated by Chinese smugglers and Japanese skulduggery. In one year, 112 million ounces disappeared.

It is alleged that Britain pushed China into abandoning the silver standard and adopting a paper currency and that British officials helped draft the orders to British banks in China which were being used as channels for the remittances of Chinese silver. A British currency expert, Sir Frederick Leith Ross, was in fact asked to advise Nanjing but he was overtaken by events. He stressed the need for adequate safeguards and international support as an essential part of any overall scheme, as well as an end to instability caused by Japanese aggression. But there was no time to work out a long-term solution, and it was the Hongkong & Shanghai Bank which was given the Herculean task of propping up the Chinese dollar in the interim before convertibility was ended. Renewed Japanese aggression, however, coupled with local speculation and profiteering, did more to destabilize and erode the Chinese economy than anything else; thus inflation grew steadily undermining the value of the Chinese dollar and savaging the Chinese way of life.

At the same time, Germany's new chancellor, Adolf Hitler, and Italy's dictator, Benito Mussolini, began redrawing the borders of Europe while civil war raged in Spain, aided and abetted by Germany and Russia. This was yet another incentive to the invading Japanese armies in China and in the next three years they drove west and south to the borders of Hong Kong, as well as occupying Guangzhou and stopping all trade between the two cities.

In Guangzhou, the pattern of Japanese attack was similar to that used in other major cities, with air raids beginning in July of 1938 and ending with its occupation three months later. The Guomindang had only regained possession of the city from a local warlord two years earlier and its economic recovery was swift, with Europe beginning to emerge from the worst depression in modern times. Having lost every major city on the east coast at a high cost in civilians, troops and weapons, the Guomindang decided against a stubborn and prolonged defence of Guangzhou which would only add to the misery and distress of the people.

The rape of Nanjing was uppermost in the minds of the people and a steady flow of evacuees moved to Hong Kong, still giving refuge to many from Shanghai who had fled before or during the invasion of that city. Many Chinese businessmen thereafter came to regard Hong Kong not just as a temporary haven but a place which would be their permanent home and centre of business or investment. Later generations would see this period as the beginning of Hong Kong's emergence as the leading trade, business and investment centre of China.

In leaving Guangzhou the Nationalists set fire to many buildings including power plants, factories and offices, as well as blowing up the main railway station. The blast was so violent that a man living at the top of the Hongkong Bank building in the British concession was awakened by a lump of metal weighing 50 kilos sailing through his window. The destruction was described by a British businessman as "the biggest folly of the Canton government." He continued: "It was evident the city had been surrendered or sold. We heard that the Japanese were themselves surprised at the easy and rapid advance." Local Chinese, however, felt bitter and betrayed, having for months been pressured to pour donations into the Guomindang's war chest.

After their first encounter with Japanese toops, Western businessmen said they appeared to be well disciplined "with none of your Nanjing or Shanghai rough stuff." The Anglo-French concession was left untouched and unoccupied and serenely well ordered with its manicured lawns and the air of an upper class English garden suburb. When flames from burning buildings nearby threatened to spread, foreign volunteers from all over the city and from locally-stationed warships raced in to help bring them under control. It was the firing of the city by looters and saboteurs that caused widespread hardship and distress. Japanese troops made short work of bayonetting or shooting those caught, whom British and French police helped round up. "The general wish of most foreigners is the sooner [the Japanese] clear out all the riff-raff who are now doing the incendiarism and looting, the better for all concerned," was one Englishman's comment.

With the closure of Guangdong, many British and Chinese firms moved to Hong Kong to continue exporting, but because it was now difficult to obtain Chinese products and manufactured goods, new industries were set up in the colony. A busy trade in smuggling developed between Hong Kong and the Japanese occupied mainland but effectively foreign business operations in Guangzhou closed down and from 1939 the foreign trade area established almost sixty years earlier was unable to function.

Many transferred their operations to Hong Kong. Partly due to the Japanese invasion of China and partly to the depressed demand for China products, the British colony took considerably longer to recover from the world-wide depression. The outbreak of war in Europe, however, brought about a change. As British industry geared itself for war, the country had to replace goods supplied by local factories or imported from Europe. In an era when Empire preference was being widely trumpeted, Hong Kong, with its refugee-swollen labour supply, became a welcome alternative. A wide range of cheap, light industrial goods found favour, from canvas shoes, Wellington boots, vacuum flasks, torches, oil lamps, textiles, garments, rope, kitchenware, minor medications and a range of bakelite products (the forerunner to plastics).

Hong Kong had traditionally filled an entrepôt role, importing, exporting and re-exporting; it enjoyed a secure legal system, dependable banks, a free port status, an efficient bureaucracy and a deep-water harbour with good wharf facilities and an industrious work force. Its industry included dockyards capable of building everything from local ferries to ocean-going ships up to 10,000 tonnes, as well as a range of factories capable of milling flour, refining sugar, making concrete, processing food and dairy products. But in an age when Europe was still the major producer of consumer goods and when Lancashire ruled the textiles roost, the scope for expanding its industrial base was limited. The outbreak of war in Europe brought the first glimpse of a new potential for Hong Kong. As the U-boat war began to take its toll, even local shipyards were busy with orders for British freighters.

With the fall of France to German forces in 1940, European rule in Asia began to crumble. Only Hong Kong, Malaya, Singapore, North Borneo and the Philippines, kept the colonial flags flying while the Netherlands East Indies did its best to maintain a semi-independent status under a Dutch colonial regime. The French empire in Indo-China immediately came under Japanese pressure and ultimately control following the fall of France and the creation of the pro-Nazi Vichy regime. Chiang retired to the far west of the country and established a new capital at Chongqing.

However invincible the Japanese army seemed in China, it met with one serious reverse, from an unexpected quarter. Lying to its north were the Russian forces under General Georgi Zhukov and when a skirmish on the border of outer Mongolia in May 1939 got out of hand, the Japanese Guandong Army sent up a large punitive expedition to deal with the trouble-makers. Much to Tokyo's surprise, the Russians overwhelmed them and gave them a sound beating, using far swifter, more manoeuvrable tanks with skill on the open steppes; also the Soviet artillery proved devastating in fire power and range. Zhukov would later be put in charge of the defence of Moscow and Stalingrad from the Nazi invasion, and of capturing Berlin in the last stages of the war. However, he first demonstrated his skills as a great commander against the Japanese in a sobering and demoralizing encounter; it could have turned into a débâcle but was saved from this fate by the conclusion of the Soviet-German non-aggression pact. It led to the fall of the Japanese government and the strengthening of the army's hand before the attack on Pearl Harbour and its strike south.

Not only were all the sea approaches to China closed, but the Japanese invasion effectively blocked about 80 per cent of the Western trade reaching Chiang Kai-shek's "Free China." Sensing its encirclement and imminent strangulation, the Chinese began building in 1937 a winding, tortuous 1200-kilometre roadway through rugged, mountainous country from Lashio in eastern Burma to Kunming in Yunnan Province, and a further 1500 kilometre extension north-west to Chongqing. Two years later it was in use.

As a feat of civil engineering, experts have compared it to the building of the Great Wall, thousands of labourers hammering, drilling and digging it out of bare rock. The vision was grand but it was no more successful in bringing aid in than the Great Wall was in keeping invaders out. The United States promptly stepped in with generous multi-million dollar loans, and for three years American supplies, routed via Rangoon, found a precarious and severely limited access to the Guomindang heartland. The road quickly attracted most of the old China seas pirates and a good many new recruits to brigandry and highway robbery. What the robbers missed was diverted or hijacked by racketeers. Precious little reached its destination. Ultimately Japan collected a large consignment of stockpiled US aid when it marched into Rangoon in 1942.

Thailand also became a reluctant ally of Japan after having signed a non-aggression pact; as a payoff, it pressed for the recovery of territory which France had absorbed when it took control of Laos and Cambodia. The Japanese obliged but with a hidden price tag — the use of southern Thailand when the time came to invade Malaya with the China-blooded Fifth Division, in December 1941. Through Thailand, the Japanese also swept west into Burma, finally cutting off the Burma Road. Otherwise there was little interference in the daily life of Thailand which was exploited rather than occupied; this served the Japanese cause admirably.

From 1937 American sanctions were gradually imposed, first with aircraft and a year later with a wide range of capital and consumer goods. In July 1941, Japanese troops moved into Indo-China, and sanctions by the Western allies were intensified. Oil, rubber, tin and aluminium shipments were stopped by the United States, Britain and the Netherlands East Indies. Many believed this was the culminating provocation which tipped the balance and forced Japan to go to war — a war in which the seizure of the East Indies oil wells would be high on its agenda.

The only question exercising Japanese planners was whether its armed forces could deliver a fatal blow at American naval power, forcing its capitulation or crippling it so seriously that it would be unable to retaliate. It had adequate oil and mineral resources to ensure a penetrating first strike which took its forces to within fifty kilometres of Port Moresby. The Western oil embargo was a futile eleventh hour gesture of despair which changed nothing in Japan's plans.

At this stage, Japan realized that it had Asia at its feet, with only the British to evict from Hong Kong and Southeast Asia. With its back to the wall in Europe, and its Spitfires and Hurricanes desperately trying to keep out German bombers, Britain had no hope of a long-term defence of its Asian territories. The warnings and portents of earlier years had gone unheeded. In the event, when the Japanese bombed Pearl Harbour they took only another three months to sweep out an unprepared Britain, the United States and the Netherlands from Asia.

In doing so they exposed Singapore's alleged impregnability as a sham; the Royal Navy's prestige took the heaviest knock when two great battleships, *Prince of Wales* and *Repulse*, sent by the Admiralty to revive British morale, fell victims to eighty-four Japanese torpedo-bombers off the Malayan east coast. Without air cover the mission was suicidal and futile. The Japanese navy despatched the pride of the British fleet as completely as it had sunk the Russian men-of-war in the Battle of the Tsushima Strait thirty-seven years earlier. A thousand men were lost as well as Admiral Tom Phillips. Four bombers was the price paid by Japan, one of the cheapest victories of the war.

One by one, the British dominoes tumbled ingloriously before the onslaught of Japanese military, naval and air power, blooded by four years' campaigning in China, its staging ground for war with the West. First was Hong Kong. With its five antiquated aircraft wiped out in a dawn raid and with virtually no navy, Hong Kong's small garrison fought a brave but futile 18-day battle before surrendering. Singapore, with its big guns all pointing seaward and 90,000 defenders (twice the size of the invading force), survived for only a week after Japanese forces overran Malaya.

It was the ultimate humiliation for Britain after ruling the waves of the South China Sea for more than 300 years — though it was not yet the end. The 350-year-old Dutch empire — the islands of the Netherlands East Indies — succumbed to Japanese invasion shortly after, with the new rulers promising eventual independence for the Indonesian nationalists under Achmed Sukarno. Burma fell a few months later. Next it was the turn of the American-ruled Philippine Islands, Borneo, Sarawak, the Celebes, Portuguese East Timor, the Solomons and the cluster of islands which passed from German to Australian administration after World War I — New Britain and Bougainville. Methodically Japan collected every coconut it shook from the South Pacific tree, for each had a use, each had a purpose, each had a destiny which would be modified by the occupation. At war's end, nothing would be the same.

In Shanghai, the Japanese had an easier time; two Allied warships — USS *Wake* and HMS *Peterel* — were lying in the Huangpu River opposite the Bund. The Japanese called on both to surrender. Under instructions from its consulate, USS *Wake* put up a white flag. The commander of HMS *Peterel* and its twenty-one crew, refused and the ship was promptly sunk by the guns of the nearby Japanese cruiser, *Izumo*. The only other Allied servicemen in Shanghai were the US Marine guards at the consulate, and the Shanghai Volunteer Corps. But the Japanese army which had surrounded the concession for the last three years, was swiftly in control — before breakfast on 8 December — and the Volunteers and the Marines had no time to fire a shot.

Many Europeans had left the city already but its 3.2 million population of all nationalities (with 70,000 non-Chinese) had been swollen by refugees from other parts of China, as well as 18,000 Jews who had been lucky to escape from Austria, Poland and other parts of Europe occupied by the Nazis. The 2,764 British and 404 American residents were assigned to internment camps in various parts of the city for the next three and a half years — a vivid fictionalized account of which was given by J. G. Ballard, in his novel and film *Empire of the Sun*. The inmates undoubtedly suffered privations and hardship, but by comparison with life in other Japanese camps (particularly for prisoners-of-war) they were, with some exceptions, treated reasonably and humanely. The former international concession of Shanghai came under the rule of the former Guomindang leader, Wang Jingwei who threw in his lot with the Japanese in 1938.

In Hong Kong, while prisoners-of-war were marched off to camps in various parts of Kowloon, the 1,800 civilian internees were taken to the civilian jail at Stanley and incarcerated there for the duration, administered by a "shadow government" of British civil servants. Stanley peninsula, on the south of Hong Kong island, was where the British garrison had put up its last gallant stand before capitulating to Japan on Christmas Day, 1941. A particularly horrible hospital massacre and rape of nurses had taken place there shortly before. Apart from the arrest and execution of a spy network at Stanley in 1943, and the torture and

Figure 13.6 George Chinnery's sketch of the steps leading to the ruins of St. Paul's Church, Macau.

execution of several civilian internees, including the Chief Manager of the Hong Kong and Shanghai Bank, Sir Vandleur Grayburn, the ordeal of Hong Kong's European internees was relatively mild.

The Chinese residents suffered much more. In addition to severe food shortages many who had escaped from Guangdong to Hong Kong during the height of the Sino-Japanese War were forced to return to their native villages. For those who remained, the privations of living in the steadily decaying and repeatedly bombed city were harsh. The more fortunate escaped to the neighbouring neutral territory of Portuguese Macau, which became an open city. There Western consular officials, Hong Kong Eurasians, White Russians, European Jews, Irish "third nationals" and many British naturalized Chinese lived out the war in varying degrees of discomfort and stringency, rubbing shoulders with Japanese officers on rest and recreation visits from Guangzhou and Hong Kong.

For many years Macau was considered the capital of "lechery, robbery, treachery, gambling, drunkenness, brawling, wrangling, cheating and other vices" — a reputation bestowed by a visiting Franciscan friar in the eighteenth century. With the outbreak of World War II, it found a new vocation as a benevolent, caring, protecting, supporting haven for refugees for the next three and a half years.

CHAPTER 14

The East is Red

The Japanese attack on the United States in December 1941, brought relief to both the Guomindang and the Communists. For both realized that having failed to deliver the knockout blow at Pearl Harbour and that by its rapid advance through Southeast Asia and the Southwest Pacific, Japan had over-reached itself. Despite stunning initial successes it was apparent as 1942 wore on that not only had Japan not succeeded in delivering a knockout punch but it would not be able to hold its gains in the inevitable Allied counter-attack. Chiang Kai-shek virtually gave up the fight against the Japanese, convinced, wrongly, that Japan had pushed its advance in China to the limit. Henceforward, he would concentrate on undermining and destroying the Communists, which he did with a rancour that perplexed his allies and angered his people.

But in 1942 and even 1943, Japan was far from finished; indeed Chiang would be forced to prove his commitment to the war effort and show how he was deploying the American aid that was being flown in from India over "the Hump." Under the leadership of US General "Vinegar Joe" Stilwell, Chinese troops helped the British slow the Japanese advance through northern Burma to the borders of India. America had sent Stilwell to kindle a fighting spirit in the reluctant Guomindang. Chiang Kai-shek always had a long shopping list of weapons and loans — big ones — to cover his needs. How much of those funds went into the war effort remains a mystery for there were many private war chests that benefited together with the Guomindang's. Stilwell conducted a running feud with Chiang, whom he scathingly dismissed as "peanut," and the British generals whom he considered inept, irresolute and defeatist. He was not far wrong. An excess of colonial comfort and a lack of challenge had sapped their martial spirit in the aftermath of the bloody trench-fighting of World War I and they were no match for the invaders.

Far from putting muscle into Chiang's army to defeat the Japanese, Stilwell saw his country's aid frittered away in side-shows, with the Guomindang squaring off against old rivals, particularly the Communists. Not only did Chiang spurn co-operation with Mao Zedong but committed himself to the in-evitable showdown with him. In the event it was the Japanese who launched a strong offensive in 1944 to strengthen its position in Central China, to wipe out American air bases and Communist guerilla bands and to force Chiang's surrender. The air bases moved back, the guerillas moved away and Chiang did nothing but blame America's failure to divert Japanese pressure. He also denounced Stilwell's carping criticisms of his leadership, so at odds with what President Roosevelt proclaimed publicly. No less critical was Chiang of the diminishing volume of American aid, restricted as it was to a hazardous air corridor over the Himalayas from India.

It was, however, one of the most arduous ventures of the Pacific War in which hundreds of American pilots flew Dakota (C-47, or DC-3) aircraft over "the Hump" of the world's highest mountains taking aid to Kunming and Chongqing. These twin-engined all metal aircraft had a range of only 2,500 kilometres, a speed of 370 kilometres an hour and could carry 4,000 kilograms compared with the 4,000 kilometres range of today's Lockheed C-136 with a capacity three times as large and twice the speed. But the economics of the almost daily flights (weather-permitting) show that it took the DC-3s one gallon of fuel for every gallon delivered, while every ton of bombs dropped on the Japanese required a total of eighteen tons of supplies.[1] In short it was ruinously costly and after three years of operation the Americans lost almost 500 planes, or about one every two days, not to mention the attrition of young pilots. Needing about 5,000 tons a month to supply Chiang's reluctant forces the Americans struggled to get a tenth of that amount to its destination. For all the undoubted heroics of the pilots of the US Air Transport Command, and before them the American Volunteer Group, the mission must be seen in retrospect as a costly failure. With the British advance into Burma in 1944 and the reopening of the Burma Road, the supply bottleneck was broken but by this time Chiang could sniff Allied victory in the air and his own post-war recovery was uppermost in his priorities.

The Pacific War had its full share of tragedy and triumph on land and at sea, but it was the suffering of civilians, native and expatriate, during enemy occupation that characterized this as one of the harshest. This was particularly so in many prisoner-of-war camps and on the infamous Burma-Siam Railway where prisoners laboured as slaves to build a track through fetid, mosquito-ridden, dysentery-infected jungle — conditions as inhuman as only human beings could devise. The hatred of Japan towards the Western powers wreaked a terrible vengeance on those who came under its control as evidence in subsequent war crimes trials showed. This was a pitiless war which scarred people at many levels — civilians and soldiers, men and women and children — not in thousands but in millions.

Official estimates of those who died in the Nazi holocaust in the death camps of Europe range to 5.75 million. In Soviet Russia the figure of civilian deaths was 7.7 million. In China conservative estimates are in the region of 20 million. Mere figures do not tell the whole story and even in retrospect there is no point in trying

---

1. Barbara Tuchman, *Sand Against the Wind.*

to answer the question of which nation or people suffered most. Horrifying as the death ovens of Auschwitz, Belsen and Treblinka were, the inhuman butchery of hapless civilians in Nanjing, many killed in "sporting contests" of a kind that might make an entry in the Guinness Book of Records, demonstrates the universality of human decadence and depravity.

Despite more than half its army being tied down in operations in China, the Japanese advance through South Asia reached as far west as the Indian border town of Imphal, where it was turned back by General William Slim's Anglo-Indian forces, as far south as fifty kilometres from Port Moresby in New Guinea, where it was blunted by General Edmond Herring's Australian troops, and in the east in the Philippine Islands, which were retaken by General Douglas, MacArthur's American forces. The long, hard, grinding, island-hopping campaign by Allied forces to recover the myriad islands occupied by the Japanese claimed thousands of lives in the next three years, none more bloody than Guadalcanal, or more fiercely contested than the Owen Stanley ranges in New Guinea, Iwo Jima and Okinawa, before the defeat of Japan could be assured. China, the first to be attacked, was also the last to be liberated — after an occupation lasting thirteen years in some parts.

Long before the war ended with the atomic bombing of Hiroshima and Nagasaki, however, President Franklin Delano Roosevelt was keen to redraw the map of Asia. The French, he believed, did not deserve to recover Indo-China, so he offered Chiang Kai-shek the chance to move in; the Generalissimo, with his eyes firmly focused on North China, politely declined. Roosevelt next proposed a three-power commission to determine its future. Again Chiang was apathetic. Roosevelt wanted Chiang to liberate Hong Kong and raise the Chinese flag there — a view which prompted Winston Churchill's memorable remark that he was not about to preside over the liquidation of the British Empire. Churchill managed to hang on to Hong Kong and Singapore but the subcontinent of India and Burma were quick to turn partial self-government into full independence. Dearer to China's heart and closer to its immediate interest was the declaration at the 1943 Cairo Conference of the Big Four powers that he was assured of the return of Manchuria and Taiwan following Japan's defeat.

To be promised the return of captured territory was one thing; Chiang's more immediate task was to restore Guomindang control there. The Communists in Yan'an were convinced that as Japanese military power weakened they were well placed to recover all of North China and the heavy industrial base in Manchuria and Liaodong Peninsula. Of the two parties vying for control the Communists proved to be the more committed and had hundreds of Japanese prisoners to prove it. Chiang had hardly any except a token few he paraded whenever war correspondents questioned his claims.

Repeated efforts were made by Stilwell to forge a united front but Chiang was adamant. "The Japanese are a disease of the skin, the Communists a disease of the heart," was his reply. Moreover he refused to allow US aid to be sent to Yan'an even though the Americans wanted to give it if only to help bring about an early defeat of Japan. So scared were unit commanders in the Guomindang of joining forces with the Red Army that they believed if only 20 per cent of their troops consisted of Communists all would be converted in a fortnight.

Many Americans at that time naively believed the Communists to be "agrarian reformers" and were seen by some as a reincarnation of the Taiping rebels of the mid-nineteenth century, this time influenced by Marx. They were impressed with their fighting skills, particularly the battle at the Pingxingguan pass at the Great Wall in 1937 when under the leadership of General Lin Biao Communist guerillas ambushed and destroyed a large Japanese force. Stilwell, good soldier that he was, admired their tactical skill and courage as much as their ability to get results.

It was the successful action of the Communist Eighth Route Army in Hubei and Shanxi several years later that prompted the

Japanese to wreak a terrible vengeance on local people in their infamous "three all" principle — kill all, destroy all, burn all — to deter further guerilla attacks. Nor did Chiang care to be upstaged by the Communists, launching a vicious attack on them when the New Fourth Army was slow to respond to an order to leave an area south of the Yangzi River. There was no love lost between them, and Stilwell's hopes of a united front dwindled as the war progressed.

In spite of Japanese pressure, by 1944 the Communists had expanded from a base of 35,000 square miles to four times that area and the population they controlled had risen from 1.5 million to 55 million; their armies had grown fivefold and Communist enclaves were flourishing in many parts of China behind Japanese lines, from as far south as Hainan Island, Guangdong (just north of Hong Kong), Gansu and Hubei.

The biggest plus for China to come out of the Pacific War was President Roosevelt's success in persuading Britain to renounce extraterritoriality in all its concessions — Hong Kong, as ceded territory, was the only exception. Roosevelt had a personal interest in the China treaties. His great uncle, Warren Delano Jr, had lived and worked in Guangzhou in the years before the Opium War. He had served as a partner of Russell & Co. which established a reputation as a leading American trading firm. Its trim, fast clippers carried everything from opium to ginseng, tea, silk, furs and bullion. Roosevelt was proud of the connection but it offended his Yankee pride that the unequal treaties of that era were still binding over 100 years later while waging a war to restore freedom to occupied territories. Their abrogation effectively meant that all foreigners living in any of the treaty ports or concessions would be subject to local jurisdiction and would pay all rates, levies and taxes as decreed by the Chinese Government and the local municipal authorities.

All would have vivid memories of what was virtually the swan-song of the old Shanghai Municipal Council when in January 1941 — ten months before Pearl Harbour — a prominent

Japanese ratepayer had approached W. J. (Tony) Keswick, chairman of the Council and head of Jardine, Matheson, and shot him at point blank range, the second shooting of a council functionary in a year. One bullet passed through his chest, above the heart, and another through his arm. Keswick, wearing a heavy overcoat, survived — and even succeeded in jumping on his assailant and wrestling him to the ground; a Japanese man standing nearby sustained injuries. The meeting broke up in chaos. It was a portent of what would happen to the international concession itself.

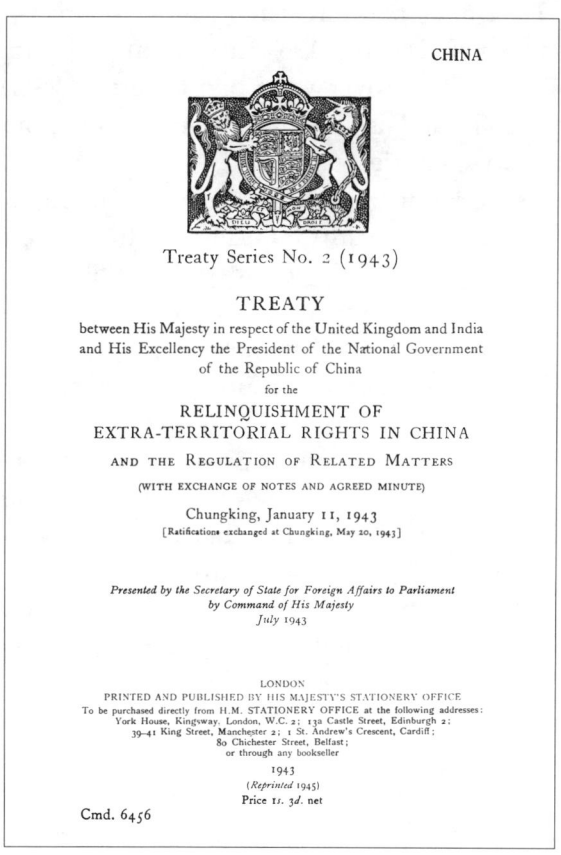

CHINA

Treaty Series No. 2 (1943)

TREATY

between His Majesty in respect of the United Kingdom and India and His Excellency the President of the National Government of the Republic of China

for the

RELINQUISHMENT OF
EXTRA-TERRITORIAL RIGHTS IN CHINA

AND THE REGULATION OF RELATED MATTERS

(WITH EXCHANGE OF NOTES AND AGREED MINUTE)

Chungking, January 11, 1943
[Ratifications exchanged at Chungking, May 20, 1943]

*Presented by the Secretary of State for Foreign Affairs to Parliament
by Command of His Majesty
July 1943*

LONDON
PRINTED AND PUBLISHED BY HIS MAJESTY'S STATIONERY OFFICE
To be purchased directly from H.M. STATIONERY OFFICE at the following addresses:
York House, Kingsway, London, W.C. 2; 13a Castle Street, Edinburgh 2;
39–41 King Street, Manchester 2; 1 St. Andrew's Crescent, Cardiff;
80 Chichester Street, Belfast;
or through any bookseller

1943
(*Reprinted* 1945)
Price 1s. 3d. net

Cmd. 6456

Figure 14.1 The front cover of the Treaty ending British extraterritoriality in China.

It was Japanese aggression that was responsible for the ending of the treaties, for while China had been pressing for their revocation as early as 1930, Britain was not keen to make any more than token changes. It was all very well for Roosevelt to elevate Chiang Kai-shek to one of the Big Four but Britain, for its own imperial reasons, had no intention of lowering the flag in Hong Kong, Singapore, Malaya or North Borneo. India and Burma were quick to stress to the newly elected Labour government of Clement Attlee that they wanted to quit the empire. But wartime Britain under Churchill saw a strong China reasserting claims to Tibet and thus threatening India — which is exactly what happened in October 1962, in the bitter argument (and equally bitter fighting) over what one historian described as a "difficult, desolate and useless" tract on the northernmost border between the two countries.

Britain's Foreign Secretary, Anthony Eden, once told Roosevelt that he did not care for the idea "of the Chinese running up and down the Pacific." He admitted that civil war was likely, but considered this an advantage because it would leave the country weak and divided. Thus Britain saw a continuing justification for legal safeguards for foreign nationals living and working in China.

As for Hong Kong, Churchill saw Roosevelt not as a friendly ally but a committed opponent, and made his own plans for the recovery of the colony. Realizing that America's first priority would be to get Chiang back into the driving seat in Nanjing, and Guomindang authority restored throughout the country, he gave orders to Lord Louis Mountbatten as Supreme Commander in charge of the Southeast Asian region, to raise the flag in Britain's former territories.

The Americans ridiculed the idea and insisted that Mountbatten's task was first and foremost to reopen the Burma Road to China. Mountbatten pursued his role singlemindedly and while it was the job of the British forces to retake Burma, Malaya and Singapore, it was his job to ensure that civil authority was restored under British rule. British troops were also used to recover the East Indies until Dutch troops could be rushed to the scene. Even surrendered Japanese troops were used to help keep order in the interim. His political role as divorce broker in India would come later as the last viceroy.

Hong Kong's liberation had a high priority and within days of the Japanese surrender, a fleet of Royal Naval, Australian and Canadian ships, including the battleship HMS *Anson*, several cruisers and a contingent of Royal Marines under Rear Admiral Cecil Harcourt, sailed into the harbour. Two Australian corvettes swept the Lyemun pass for mines. The liberators discovered that a feisty pre-war Colonial Secretary named Franklin Gimson had walked out of Stanley internment camp, hauled up the Union flag at Government House, and installed himself as officer administering the Government.

Figure 14.2 Rear Admiral Cecil Harcourt scrutinizes the surrender document signed by a senior Japanese officer in September 1945.

Harcourt's acceptance of the Japanese surrender was not nearly as splendid as MacArthur's ceremony on the deck of USS *Missouri* in Tokyo Bay, but it signalled Britain's intention to hang on to the colony for as long as possible. Few in Hong Kong would have quarrelled with that. Mountbatten noted in his diaries: "All the richer Chinese are most anxious that Hong Kong should remain British since it is the one stable place in which they can invest their money and put up houses." This was long before the outbreak of civil war in China.

In the last stages of the Pacific War, an even more crucial meeting occurred at Yalta between Roosevelt, Churchill and Stalin; Chiang Kai-shek was missing even though one of the main subjects was the future of China. Roosevelt was dying and no match for the wily Stalin who dictated his own terms for agreeing to enter the war against Japan — between the two atomic bombings of Hiroshima and Nagasaki.[2] Possibly Roosevelt was influenced by the horrendous casualties and sufferings of the Russians during Hitler's invasion — but these paled into insignificance compared with China's. For what Yalta did was to restore sovereignty to China in Manchuria on the one hand, but take it away with the other and hand it to Russia, with Port Arthur to be leased as a naval base and Dalian as a port, while the railways were to come under a Sino-Soviet company. Russia was also to get a clutch of northern islands including the Kuriles. These they seized in the last days of the war; they remain under its control to this day with no sign of surrender.

---

2. It is a telling reflection on human conscience that fifty years after the end of the war, while some Western commentators are obsessively guilt-ridden about the atomic atrocities inflicted upon Japan, the Japanese are largely dismissive and unrepentant about their own wartime atrocities on civilians and prisoners. Were the atomic bombs really necessary? Would Japan have fought on, inflicting hundreds and thousands of casualties on invading Allied troops, or would the Emperor have conceded that the nation was at the end of its tether, with the armed forces all but defeated and his throne at risk? The atomic bombs may not have been the only factor, but they must have exerted a crucially persuasive influence in the equation of self-survival of the nation in the late summer of 1945.

The Yalta Agreement was a godsend to Russia and the Communists in China. When Chiang heard the terms he must have known he would lose at least North China in the post-war grab for territory. The Russians realized that unless they became involved in Manchuria, they would have no say in the distribution of spoils at the conclusion of peace. With old scores to settle from 1905 the Soviets swept across the country in a few days, reminiscent of the Zhukov victory in 1939. Ostensibly the Russians were doing for the Chinese Communists what the Americans were doing for the Guomindang. In fact, the Russians were primarily acting for themselves. And while they were not opposed to a Communist takeover of China, Moscow was determined to replace the Western powers as the dominant influence in northern Asia, with its control over North Korea already sealed. Stalin also had a team of ideologically friendly Chinese Communists ready to administer the north-east provinces in Russia's interest.

Mao Zedong had no illusions about the Russians but was firmly opposed to foreign domination of the country, regardless of ideological hue. He doubted the ability of Chiang to survive the post-war era, even with American help, but he had told the Americans he would join forces with Chiang Kai-shek only if a national government of all parties was formed. Chiang would have none of it, knowing that to give an inch to the Communists would mean surrendering thousands of square miles to their control. So when the mushroom clouds rose over Japan and the war ended it was a race to see which side could claim the most territory.

The Communists were swift to follow up the Soviet advance into Manchuria, led by 38-year-old General Lin Biao, later to be appointed Marshal and a key man in the Chinese military hierarchy. They accepted the surrender of the notorious Japanese Guandong Army and into their laps fell a huge cache of weapons. These the Chinese Communists would use to hold on to the northern provinces. Their task might have been made easier if Moscow had also passed over the 900 planes and 350 tanks seized from the Japanese, but these Russia claimed as its own war booty. Lin's strategy was to mount his offensive before the Guomindang had a chance to strike north. However, with some ports already in Guomindang hands, he concentrated on tightening his grip on the Manchurian countryside and building support among the peasants until he was ready to renew his attack.

The Russians remained in occupation for a year largely to cement claims to the spoils of war. In the process they looted Manchuria of much of the machinery Japan installed during its occupation. They also served as a useful rearguard to the Chinese Communists who, as a result, were able to commit fewer men to an occupation role and more to frontline action against the Guomindang. On their way south the People's Liberation Army scored a series of stunning victories, swallowing up Chinese armies serving the Manchukuo puppet regime of Emperor Puyi, who was himself seized by the Russians and taken to Moscow as the one tangible token of its week-long war effort. (Later he would be returned to China to work out his days as a prison gardener.)

In the year after the Japanese surrender, the US Air Force moved almost half a million Chinese troops to the coastal cities, in the process recovering Yan'an for the first time since the Long March in 1935. At the same time, 50,000 US Marines, originally intended to form the invasion bridgehead on the Japanese coast, were dropped into rail centres, coal mines and ports to ensure they were not grabbed by Communits, looted by Chinese freebooters, or fired by arsonists. Mao Zedong was furious, but the Americans argued that armed Japanese were capable of causing a security problem; when US forces discovered Communist troops already in place in Chefoo in the Shandong peninsula, however, they kept away to avoid a showdown. Both Russia and the US were helping their surrogates in a similar way but the Communists were strategically far better placed. Chiang Kai-shek would rue his dog-in-the-manger retreat to Chongqing, sulking away the war in the far west of China and feuding endlessly with Roosevelt's acerbic General Stilwell.

Generous and unstinted though American post-war aid was, Chiang's men could only reach a few major cities on the eastern seaboard and on the Yangzi River. The Americans could see the danger and their concerns about the Communists grew. Ideologically, they now seemed far more committed Marxists and their political indoctrination not just of the army but the people in the areas they controlled, demonstrated they were a formidable opposition to Chiang Kai-shek whose reputation was increasingly being tarnished by inflation, a tumbling currency and widespread corruption.

The corruption issue had been a festering sore throughout the 1940s, even in Chongqing. One noted American journalist, Theodore White, then head of *Time Magazine*'s China bureau, noted that when the Sino-Japanese War broke out in 1937 the currency was stable at three Chinese dollars to the US dollar. Two years later it was six to one and by December, 1941 it was up to twenty to one. Three years later it was 200 to one. By that time, said White, "the friction between Americans and Chinese over the dollar rate of exchange … was critical to the breach that was approaching between the two." It was a fictitious rate which Americans knew was being rigged to extort their country for dollars. Nor would the Chinese admit the existence of inflation. Dr H. H. Kung, the Finance Minister, declared: "There's no inflation in China. If people want to pay $20,000 for a fountain pen that's their business, it's not inflation. They're crazy, that's all."

As a result, the distribution of American aid became an issue of acute and increasing importance to both the Guomindang and the Communists. Chiang got the lion's share for one reason only; his troops held the ports through which the aid was funnelled. However, it soon became obvious to the US Administration that China was slipping from its grasp once more. Over the past 100 years America had moved from being a casual trader to a reluctant participant in the country's subjugation by the West. Though concerned that it should be seen to be dealing fairly with the Chinese before and immediately after the Opium War, it was torn between its strong anti-colonial sentiments on the one hand, and frustration over China's vacillating response to reform on the other. On the horns of this dilemma it swung uneasily.

The Americans had actually created a "settlement" in Shanghai soon after its opening as a treaty port even though it had not been officially approved, and the first US Consul had his residence there. But apart from harbouring a few missionaries, the area was not popular with the merchants, and when large numbers of Chinese moved in during the Taiping Rebellion the Americans joined with the British in 1863 and formed the International Settlement. Its conscience absolved, the Americans next argued for an "open door," and as the civil war in the US ended and industry returned to a peacetime role, the opportunities in China beckoned.

As reform began to rear its head in China, far-sighted Americans realized its huge market potential with its then population of 350 million, and as an aggressive railroad builder and shipbuilder it saw the rich pickings that China offered, particularly in Shanghai, Wuhan and Tianjin. The American firm, Russell & Co., had in fact helped China establish its first shipping company, the Shanghai Steam Navigation Company, but put up less than a third of the capital, and though enjoying a large share of the business on attractive routes, lost its monopoly to a British firm, Butterfield & Swire. With Jardine, Matheson also active the Americans were squeezed out and their assets were bought out by the China Merchants Steam Navigation Company.

In between the two world wars, the Americans were relatively minor players in the shipping industry in China and while active in tobacco, petroleum, mining and railways the opportunity to play a significant part in the Chinese economy did not open up until the defeat of Japan. With Britain seriously distracted by wartime losses and the defection of Burma and India from the empire, America as the new super-power of the Pacific alone had the resources to help China recover. Significant US aid was offered as a backup to the work of the United Nations, successor to the pre-war League of Nations, and in Washington's (alas, mistaken) view Chiang Kai-shek was the only credible leader. The Communists were viewed as a danger but not yet as an alternative to the Guomindang.

Roosevelt and his successor, Harry Truman, had no trouble in swallowing the blandishments of the very persuasive, attractive American-educated wife of the Generalissimo, Madame Chiang Kai-shek, who in many war-time speeches in the US had helped project China as a great power. She was also the healer in the many wartime rifts between the intolerant Stilwell and her equally stubborn husband. In the process she won hearts throughout the country. Moreover not only had she been educated at an American Methodist college (Wellesley) but Chiang himself was nominally Christian. Little wonder that America's response after the war was unstinted.

Huge quantities of arms, ammunition, Chevrolet lorries, jeeps, armoured vehicles, landing craft, fuel and much of the backup for the planned invasion of Japan ended up in China under the Lend-Lease programme. Most of the civilian aid was diverted to private hands before it reached the people. American Red Cross blood plasma quickly went on sale at up to US$25 a unit, and with the American greenback now commanding 10 million Chinese dollars in the hyper-inflation of the day, few impoverished Chinese felt American blood coursing through their veins. Moreover, large quantities of aid provided by the UN Relief and Rehabilitation Agency (UNRRA) failed to reach its intended objectives, thanks to widespread racketeering; it found its way to the black market instead. Chiang refused to accept any advice from his American allies or colleagues at home on what his priorities should be. As a result the stricken country tottered from crisis to crisis. An effort to put value back into the currency with a gold backing, backfired when the Premier, T. V. Soong, was accused of sparking a gold rush before the reform had been announced.

Another American mediator, Major-General Patrick Hurley,

was no more successful in uniting the factions, and indeed was one of the first to push America into its new post-war anti-Communist orbit. On his resignation from China, this committed Republican fired a broadside at the misguided Democrats under Truman who were "soft on Communists." A growing sense of betrayal, induced as much by domestic espionage as by strident anti-capitalist rhetoric overseas, would give rise to an era of witch-hunts and domestic hysteria that convulsed America following the fall of the iron curtain.

General George Marshall, the new American power broker in China, now realized the Communists were militarily superior and Chiang's only hope of survival was to negotiate a peace. Stubbornly Chiang refused. Marshall stopped the US arms supply but it made no difference. Then, confronted with the choice of leaving Chiang in the lurch or continuing support, Washington despatched another $400 million worth of arms. Not only did it not change the course of the civil war but helped convince the Communists that this was the new face of Western imperialism with which it had to contend. Marshall had more than fifty private meetings with Zhou Enlai but failed to bring the two sides together. Curiously, the Russians, with their own political agenda, were trying to delay a Communist takeover. Mao Zedong told the Tenth Plenum in 1962 that Stalin "tried to prevent the Chinese revolution by saying that we must collaborate with Chiang Kai-shek." Mao ignored the advice.

Marshall sent gift-wrapped candies to Madame Mao, but the aid continued to flow to the discredited Guomindang. The Communists were the ultimate beneficiaries because most of the American equipment was still in crates on the wharfside when overrun by the southwards-driving People's Liberation Army. By 1949 they had crossed the Yangzi — trapping a British naval frigate, HMS *Amethyst*, en route to Nanjing with supplies for the Embassy — and were pushing hard for Shanghai which they took in May. The frigate ran the gauntlet of Guomindang and Red Army guns and escaped, its funnel, bridge and upper deck a shambles of twisted metal. It would be the Royal Navy's last hurrah in China.

Chiang Kai-shek now realized there was no stopping the Communist juggernaut sweeping from north to south. After flying from Nanjing to Chengdu and Chongqing, his wartime capital, he concluded there was no chance of a "long march" for the Nationalists to a remote refuge on the mainland; even if the Americans were prepared to fly in supplies there was no as- surance that India or Burma would allow their ports to be used as entry points. Nor was there any certainty the Burma Road could be his lifeline as it was during the Pacific War.

Chiang was now desperate. Advisers convinced him the only security was on the island of Taiwan, with a stretch of sea be- tween him and Mao Zedong on the mainland. The island had been liberated from fifty years of Japanese rule at the end of World War II. The Americans were still active in the area, with major naval bases in Japan and in the newly independent Philip- pines under its first President Manuel Roxas. Following the obliteration of the Japanese navy, America had the biggest con- centration of naval ships of any Western power in the Pacific. With this as his buffer, he could survive indefinitely.

In escaping to Taiwan, Chiang Kai-shek took with him much of the artistic wealth of China — the priceless porcelain, bronze and jade antiques from the National Museum in Beijing, many of which had been stored in western China during the war to protect them from looting by the Japanese. Among them were some of the masterpieces created by Chinese potters at the imperial kilns at Jingdezhen in Jiangxi Province, dating back to the sixth century. Immaculately shaped bowls with flawless celadon glazes, stun- ning blue and white vases, complex famille rose jars, intricately designed bronzes and exquisitely carved jades of translucent green and mauve, were among the thousands of items hidden by Chiang Kai-shek; all were loaded aboard C-47s and flown to Taipei, where the Guomindang set up its new capital. These have since been displayed at the National Palace Museum, where there are said to be enough exhibits to enable a complete change every three months for ten years. It is the world's finest collection of Chinese antiques.

Following the Generalissimo and his treasures was the bulk of his defeated army, said to number about two million, and transported to the island by American ships and planes. With the powerful American Seventh Fleet patrolling the Taiwan Strait, and with the Communists unable to mount a challenge or a pursuit due to lack of shipping, the Guomindang escaped largely intact and even clung to two offshore islands within a few miles of the Fujian coast. Another large island in the South China Sea, Hainan, was under Communist control well before the civil war and Chiang mounted no challenge there.

In Taiwan, the resumption of Guomindang control provoked opposition which culminated in rebellion in March 1947 and was brutally crushed. The Taiwanese, after fifty years of Japanese rule, were not about to welcome a new invader, even one of Chinese descent. Centuries of virtual freedom from mainland rule had bred a strong streak of independence both among native Taiwanese and Han immigrants, which continues to this day. Given the choice of Chiang or Mao Zedong, the islanders sullenly and resentfully bowed to *force majeure* and the defensive umbrella offered by the Americans.

The only other part of Chinese territory not recovered by the Communist steamroller was the British colony of Hong Kong. No one knows why the People's Liberation Army stopped at the New Territories border in 1949. American officials had thrown out veiled warnings against invasion, but coming so soon after the same officials had been trying to persuade Britain to hand it back to Chiang Kai-shek the Communists could hardly have taken this seriously. Long before any American intervention could have been mounted, the momentum of an invasion by the People's Liberation Army would have been unstoppable.

Hong Kong was then filled with refugees from the mainland, including Guomindang soldiers who had sought asylum, and the

Chinese civil aviation fleet of seventy planes had flown into Kai Tak Airport. The Communists exerted strong pressure, including legal action in the Hong Kong courts, to have them returned but this was unsuccessful.

The Communists could well have followed up with military threats on the border. For not only was Hong Kong harbouring rebellious troops but many leading capitalists, including industrialists, with skills and equipment badly needed by the new regime. China also had many old scores to settle with British imperialism. With few aircraft of its own, however, and dependent on Soviet aid to build up its air force — not at that stage available — the new People's Government recognized its limitations. Besides, the far more urgent priority was to establish its authority throughout the country. In 1949, with Mao assuming chairmanship of the People's Republic in Tian'anmen Square, the future of Hong Kong was put on the back burner.

China may have also realized it needed an outlet to a world that had not yet made up its mind about Mao or his ideology. Hong Kong, filling an entrepôt role in trade, might provide that access. As a source of hard currency the Hong Kong banking/financial structure could be useful, with the local branch of the Bank of China handling hundreds of millions of dollars in trade finance and foreign exchange. The Chinese commercial structure in Hong Kong, with its excellent contacts with overseas Chinese communities, could be useful. Moreover, if China was to be treated as a pariah, it would be helpful to have a window on the world and a meeting point on neutral territory. Also, Russia was still a doubtful ally and a grudging aid-giver.

Following Zhou Enlai's invitation to all countries to open diplomatic relations, Britain was one of the first in the Western world to do so, arguing that recognition did not imply approval but simply the reality of the change of government. With many assets in China, such as mining ventures, banks, commercial operations, and shipping lines Britain had no choice but to keep open its communications with Beijing — though following the

Communist takeover all its assets and investments in the former treaty ports were confiscated.

Mindful that Chiang had survived under American patronage, Britain also decided to maintain a consulate in Tamsui, accredited to the regional authorities, but keeping an ear close to the ground on developments in Taipei itself. Following Britain's move, Norway, the Netherlands, Sweden, Denmark, Switzerland, Sri Lanka and India joined in recognizing the People's Republic. The old East India Companies of Europe had long been defunct but the desire of these countries to re-establish effective links with the new rulers — regardless of political hue — was soon rekindled.

Elsewhere in Asia, the old colonial regimes began to collapse. For a few more years, Britain would hold on to Malaya, Borneo, Brunei, Singapore and the old Straits Settlements; the French similarly clung to Indo-China. The post-war map of Asia would take several more years to unravel and then only after bitter wars of liberation. But the winds of change, signalling the end of the colonial era, began to blow first in Asia, as much a recognition of Britain's economically and politically bankrupt status as an acceptance of the political and economic maturity of what Rudyard Kipling had once described as "lesser breeds without a law."

Under both Britain's Labour administration of Clement Attlee and the Conservative Harold Macmillan, decolonization was the order of the day. However, the Americans geared themselves to take on a new role as guardians of the "free world" against Communist infiltration — in Europe and Asia — where before the war it had espoused "open door" liberalism. With Stalin ruling over the conquered states of Eastern Europe, the emergence of the North Atlantic Treaty Organization and the outbreak of the cold war, the Berlin blockade, and the era of atomic brinkmanship, Washington led a Western crusade against the threat of aggressive Communism both in Europe and Asia. In fact, it would be another twenty-two years before the United States recognized "Red China" and a further year before Beijing gained its seat in the United Nations. In the meantime, Taiwan (representing 2 per cent of the Chinese people) held one of the permanent Big Five UN seats, together with the power of veto in the Security Council.

One of Mao Zedong's first diplomatic initiatives was to visit Moscow where he remained for two months sparring defensively with Josef Stalin on trade, aid, treaty revisions and other sensitive issues. Mao thought it more important in 1950 to persuade Russia to give up rights in Manchuria than to reclaim Hong Kong from the British. It was widely recognized, moreover, that when Mao wanted to reclaim the colony all he had to do was undermine its morale and trigger its collapse — a single phone call would achieve the object. That he did not once utter disapproval — other than the familiar line that "all capitalists are paper tigers" — was proof of the value that Beijing saw in its survival.

In choosing to go to Moscow, his first ever visit outside the country, Mao needed a credible package of loans, credits and trade deals which none in the Western world was prepared to offer. The Russians surprisingly played tough. Far from showering a fraternal state with largess, Stalin offered US$300 million over five years which was just enough to satisfy Beijing without provoking a clamour for similar treatment from other members of the Soviet bloc in Europe. Why it took so long to draw Soviet blood from a stone; why the official photograph looked like a funeral service; why most senior Chinese officials were missing from the talks almost until the last day, no one knows.

Subsequent events, however, would show that Stalin and Mao were at odds from the outset. Not only had Stalin given Mao the wrong advice in 1946 (as he also did in 1926) about how to seize power, but Mao had his own ideas on the best way to win the hearts and minds of his people, contrary to the accepted wisdom of Marx, Lenin and Stalin. Nor did Mao want Soviet aid to be so hedged with conditions that he would forever be at Moscow's beck and call. Nor did he care for Soviet intrigues with Chinese officials in provinces bordering Russian territory (notably Gao Gang, Russia's stooge in Manchuria). China had had enough of predatory foreigners and it aimed to hold on to every bit of land which made up the old dynastic empire; that included Tibet (invaded by the People's Liberation Army in 1951, forcing the Dalai Lama to flee to India), Xinjiang and Inner Mongolia. On the other hand, Outer Mongolia could be independent (though a puppet of Moscow) and a useful buffer.

Korea also would be independent, though divided at the 38th parallel between a Soviet state in the north and an American backed fiefdom under an old autocrat named Syngman Rhee in the south. On this border, both America and China would snatch for their holsters in the first post-war showdown.

The first strike was the invasion of the south by the North Korean regime with a Nazi-style blitzkrieg which caught the world off guard. It reckoned without the resilience of the Americans and other Western allies. Unfettered by any Soviet veto in the UN Security Council, with its delegate strangely missing from the chamber, the former war-time Allies created a post-war precedent by setting up the first UN flag force to resist aggression. Squeezed into a tiny salient at the southern port of Pusan, the Americans under General Douglas MacArthur, with backup from several UN member states, unleashed a massive counter-attack. This sent the North Koreans reeling all the way back to the Yalu River on the border with China. Never an easy man to control, General MacArthur then defied his own President by threatening atomic retaliation.

China responded by sending in its own "volunteers" which sent the whole UN cavalcade rolling back to the south. Mac-Arthur was sacked by a feisty President Truman for his sabre-rattling comments and after three years of wrangling and skirmishing an armistice was finally signed on a new border close to the original 38th parallel. The armistice survives today, albeit tenuously, with the authoritarian northern regime unwilling to open up the country's nuclear facilities to international inspection. The old Soviet protégé and autocrat Kim Il-sung died in

1994; his son, Kim Jong-il, succeeded him but he remains a shadowy figure.

The Korean War, in which the Chinese effectively demonstrated the power and tactical skill of the People's Liberation Army, employing "human waves" of troops armed by Soviet weapons, soured relations with Washington, and brought them to the lowest point in the history of the two nations. Not only was the war bitterly fought out in the military arena, but the US also managed to have China declared the aggressor and to engineer an embargo under the aegis of the United Nations on all Western trade with China. So broad was the definition that little was excluded. In the early post-war years when America possessed the strongest economy in the world, it needed nothing from China but had much to offer to such a backward economy still suffering from prolonged Japanese occupation and Russian looting of industrial infrastructure. However the embargo was applied to all the UN allies in the war. None was more seriously hit than Hong Kong.

After the Communist takeover of China in 1949, Hong Kong immediately became the entrepôt funnel through which Chinese trade passed to third countries and China bought Western manufactures through Hong Kong. The United Nations' embargo killed it immediately though the Portuguese territory of Macau, more nimble-footed in tiptoeing through the small print of international restrictions, continued to do a complex side trade with Hong Kong for goods which travelled across the Chinese border. This flourished particularly during the Korean War when China was buying products such as time-expired penicillin for its wounded soldiers, believing it better to have the outdated product than none at all. Several other strategic items seeped into China through this tiny fissure.

For China, with the Russian connection now producing results, the embargo was never more than a nuisance. It never inhibited its war-making potential and served to strengthen the country's resolve to remain self-reliant and contemptuous of the wealthy West. In many ways it helped to reinforce political indoctrination as Communism tightened its grip on the economy and began the transformation of the peasant society into commune-style production of grains and produce, coupled with the launching of major state industrial and trading corporations.

British and foreign vessels were discouraged from operating in Chinese waters and were also shelled by patrolling Guomindang naval ships and bombed and strafed by its aircraft. China was forced into chartering ships and reactivating shipyards in cities like Shanghai to build its own ocean-going fleet which paid rich dividends in the long term. It also helped to develop ties with nations in Southeast Asia and the Indian Ocean — the so-called Afro-Asian or Third World group of newly emerging states — whom China was anxious to woo. China would later take a leading role in their affairs, giving Beijing an effective and often dominant voice in the politics of the region. The UN embargo helped push China in that direction and was thus counter productive to American intentions to isolate and "punish" Beijing.

The Korean War also polarized the post-war political divide between Communism and the West, pushing the United States into a more reactionary role at home and abroad. It also forced the pace of developing and testing nuclear weapons as well as persuading America to take a leading role in the councils of the North Atlantic Treaty Organisation in Europe. In this way, the so-called Iron Curtain became a fixture between the West and Eastern bloc countries and helped intensify the cold war.

An even more bizarre domestic aberration emerged in the era of anti-Communist witch-hunting of prominent academics, journalists, officials and artists during the era in which Senator Joseph McCarthy of Wisconsin occupied centre stage in Washington. In this inquisitorial climate, many were hounded from office for little more than expressing an alternative view to that favoured by the administration. In such a climate, Chiang Kai-shek was destined to hold the affections of Washington, and make increasing claims on financial support as well as the unlimited protection of the Seventh Fleet.

It also increased risks for American citizens in the Far East. Those living in Hong Kong who moved outside territorial waters were liable to be seized and held hostage by China; this happened when two correspondents, Richard Applegate and Don Dixon, went sailing with their companion, Ben Krasner, a former Isbrandtsen Line captain, and three Chinese crewmen. They endured eighteen months detention after their yacht sailed near sensitive Chinese areas. Later, a young Chinese reporter working for United Press in Hong Kong, Bill Yim, sent by his manager, Wendell Merrick, to cover the release of an American detainee in Guangzhou, was detained for several months.

One of the most severely affected territories, however, was Hong Kong. As a British dependency, it loyally complied with the terms of the UN embargo. The China entrepôt trade on which it had thrived, collapsed virtually overnight and the statistical graphs of its trade look like a leap from the roof of a tall building. With refugees pouring across the border in thousands each day, the consequences were devastating.

Most were poor, surviving on their wits and token welfare handouts and living in hastily built shelters. As a result Hong Kong had abundant labour. Several Chinese industrialists, who had seen the trend of events on the mainland, had held up shipments of new spinning and weaving machinery destined for factories in cities like Shanghai and Tianjin. These they now assembled in factories built in Hong Kong and launched into production. Refugees added to industrial output with their own backyard factories making a range of light industrial goods of the kind that helped bring prosperity to Hong Kong in the years immediately before the Pacific War.

In this way, Hong Kong discovered that while it might be locked out of the China trade for the time being, the UN embargo had nothing to say about exports, so long as the raw material did not come from Red China. The remarkable feature of this renaissance of industry was that it was for the most part self-generated. British aid was virtually non-existent and America did not want to be seen supporting a colonial regime on the doorstep of China which might at any time be forcibly absorbed. Hong Kong was well endowed with banks (mainly British, European and Chinese, after the hurried departure of one prominent American bank) and they were generous with loans. With low taxes, an adaptable commercial infrastructure and strong links wth overseas Chinese, the industrial take-off was gradual and eventually spectacular.

This digression shows how economic performance in the years of the middle 1950s and early 1960s helped create what would eventually become one of the "Four Little Asian Dragons," with one of the most dynamic economies in the region. The Hong Kong administration overseeing this growth relied on a market economy and the advice of a Legislative Council comprising bankers, businessmen, industrialists, social workers and educationists — all appointed. They succeeded in devising a sensible legislative and policy framework allowing private enterprise to take the leading role in growth and development, and building the infrastructure to match.

With the major utilities in the hands of highly motivated and far-sighted businessmen, notably Lawrence Kadoorie, chairman of China Light & Power Co. Ltd., providing power and light to the rapidly growing Kowloon and New Territories, Hong Kong was able to keep ahead of every new phase of business expansion. This enabled enterprises at many levels to boost profits, the Government to achieve balanced budgets by selling existing and newly reclaimed land, and to maintain a duty-free port on a 15 per cent standard tax rate.

Social security was provided in the form of primary education, basic health and hospital services and particularly public housing, albeit spartan in the early years; in this way, the territory achieved steady increases in GDP and standards of living. A rapidly growing population (both natural and immigrant) kept wages and production costs low which in turn generated rising output and expanding exports. From a fairly basic level, Hong Kong's industry grew in diversity and sophistication. Without the UN embargo this change would not have occurred so rapidly.

Many who made their fortunes in those years also contributed to business and real estate expansion. Liberal loans offered by a growing banking sector, with investment capital from a small but well-supported stock exchange, helped to boost Hong Kong as a finance and business centre. Enlightened management in what passed for the territory's central bank — though it had no such status in fact — was credited for much of the venture capital which fostered new industries. The Hongkong & Shanghai Bank, founded a century earlier, was in its earlier years never too comfortable in dealing with non-English-speaking business people, its senior executives all drawn from expatriate ranks. However, swallowing its colonial diffidence it recognized the opportunities and helped many big and small entrepreneurs to get started. The fact that the bank issued the bulk of the colony's banknotes and enjoyed independence from Government control gave it a unique role as a free-wheeling business developer and economic pathfinder. It grew largely without a coherent or planned policy.

Equally involved were many smaller Chinese banks. So successful was the Hong Kong textile and garment industry that British, West European and American governments felt compelled to impose restrictions and quotas on Hong Kong exports; this also met with an enlightened response. Far from becoming despondent, industrialists realized there was scope for a wide range of alternative industries, skidding dangerously close at times to the thin ice of the UN embargo, but finding imaginative ways of circumventing it.

Thus duck's feathers imported from China for quilt-making were disqualified, but not if they were plucked from ducks reared from eggs imported from China. Similarly with water chestnuts;

ineligible if they were imported from China and reprocessed in Hong Kong, but eligible if the seeds were imported and grown domestically. Likewise goods finished with imported Chinese paint were rejected where products coloured with paint locally-made from Chinese chemicals qualified. Local content was the name of the game. It was fortunate in those years that no prohibition was placed on imports of Chinese rice and foodstuffs — for on a strict cash basis they kept Hong Kong alive, as did Chinese water brought in by converted oil tankers, but later piped from a specially constructed Chinese reservoir across the border. China was in fact Hong Kong's cheap no-frills supermarket.

The embargo became a challenge and a stimulus to devise increasingly innovative solutions. To its credit, never once did China renege on its deliveries, and the foreign exchange it earned from Hong Kong was in turn welcomed by the struggling mainland economy. In this way, Hong Kong developed major textile export markets in the West — employing at one time 40 per cent of the work force and accounting for 40 per cent of total production. Later it diversified into other industries to become a significant trading territory.

Always a strong maritime community, Hong Kong's shippers moved away from China coast operations to major regional and international shipping trades. Its vessels ranged from freighters and bulk carriers owned by groups such as China Navigation (Swire) and Indo-China Steam Navigation Co. Ltd. (Jardine, Matheson) to major tanker and container ship operators, overtaking the Greek shipowners who dominated the oil-carrying trade in the 1960s and early 1970s.

Equally, aviation took off in the post-war years with Swire and Jardine, Matheson taking the initiative; DC-3s and DC-4s, survivors of the Pacific War, bounced through the humid tropical skies of Southeast Asia, picking up passengers and cargoes wherever they could. But Cathay Pacific with its team of Australian and British war-time pilots dominated the regional and international routes. With backing from Swire,[3] the private enterprise company was able to invest in the most modern airliners — highly profitably. As newly independent countries emerged, their own flag-carriers sought landing rights in Hong Kong, to make it one of the busiest in Asia.

By the early 1960s, Kai Tak Airport urgently needed space to usher in the jet age of American 707s and British Comets and Britannias. Surrounded by Kowloon's teeming multi-storey tenements, a new 2,500-metre runway had to be built on the seabed of Kowloon Bay, using eleven million tons of fill chiselled from a nearby hill — a solution since copied by many others. Hong Kong had begun to take off.

---

3. Whose chairman Jock Swire blanched at the costs, declaring "this air business is certainly terrifying and they talk the most fantastic figures."

CHAPTER 15

Three Shades of Red

Mao Zedong's 1949 visit to Moscow not only brought in useful aid to an economically beleaguered and cash-strapped country (the US having frozen all China's assets in 1950) but set up a range of joint stock companies to develop oil, minerals, railways and civil aviation. As part of the deal, China bought a fleet of Soviet airliners which, over the years, had problems getting off and on the ground and staying in the air. Fortunately Soviet MIG fighters were far better designed and under Chinese pilots performed well in the Korean War. A top American general declared: "Almost overnight China has become one of the major air powers of the world."[1]

The effect of the accords, however, was to place China politically and economically squarely in the Soviet orbit, and to make sure Soviet Russia had speedy access to Beijing the longest overland telephone line in the world — 12,000 kilometres — came into existence soon after the first Beijing–Moscow rail service. To put icing on the Sino-Soviet cake, Russia agreed to hand back all former Japanese residential and industrial properties in Manchuria taken over after the Pacific War, though machinery and equipment taken to Russia was regarded as war booty to compensate Moscow for its last minute declaration of war.

---

1. See David Rees, *Korea: The Limited War* (London: Macmillan, 1964).

Nothing was said publicly about the compensation China deserved for its protracted 14-year war with Japan.

While Soviet aid was appreciated China was determined to pull itself up the economic ladder using its one major natural asset — more than 600 million people. By intensive political indoctrination and relentless coercion the masses were organized in a way never previously attempted. Chiang Kai-shek could appeal to patriotism and the natural talents of the people, but he did not try to change their work practice or mobilize them as a work force, and life continued much as it had for hundreds of years in the rural areas. Under the Guomindang the deadweight of superstition and traditional belief, with all their accompanying evils, was left intact. With the coming of the Communists all that was changed.

Life became an endless series of meetings and political harangues, interspersed with long hours of work in the fields. Crackly amplifiers located every 100 metres blared slogans, patriotic songs and rousing cries of defiance and hatred — mainly directed against landlords and saboteurs at home and imperialists and capitalists abroad. Show trials were common and executions almost a daily spectacle. Local temples and domestic shrines were abandoned; costly celebrations of weddings and births were banned and replaced by simple ceremonies, saving poor rural workers from ruinous debt in following traditional custom. Other welcome social changes included a new marriage law which endorsed a single spouse, this to ensure that the old evils of multiple marriages would be outlawed; at the same time, arranged marriages, concubinage and polygamy were prohibited; it also laid down equal rights for men and women, though men continued to retain primacy. In theory life would be a lot better for everyone; in practice Chinese tradition proved indestructible and the old observances of ritual persisted.

Other laws prohibited corruption, tax evasion, cheating, speculation and insider trading, with harsh penalties for offenders. At the same time people were encouraged to lift education levels by studying and reading at home — though in most cases the stress was on political studies and the works of Mao and Marx, reprinted in millions of copies. A major innovation was the decree that there would be one language for all — *putonghua* — though provincial dialects survived. Today, however, an estimated 75 per cent speak variants of the official language. As for foreign run schools and universities, most of which were established by Roman Catholic and Protestant missions, these were taken over by the State.

Western missionaries were expelled — unthanked and unlamented by all but a handful of dedicated Christians who were cut off from all ties with the West and the Vatican. They were regrouped into two broad "patriotic" categories — Catholics and Protestants; yet the vestiges of the old order remain, with a former Anglican (Shenggonghui) bishop heading the Protestant church, while in other parts of the country the Lutheran influence established by German missionaries before World War I survived seventy years later in the worship of old parishioners. Christianity remains a minority religion in China though today claims a strong resurgence, with many more (smuggled) copies of the Bible in Chinese available for distribution and an upsurge of "house churches" to make up for the shortage of church buildings, many of which were requisitioned as factories and remain under state control — notably the former Anglican Holy Trinity Cathedral in Shanghai, as well as Catholic churches elsewhere.

American historian Professor John K. Fairbank, himself the son of a missionary, once wrote: "The missionaries came as spiritual reformers, soon found that material improvements were necessary, and in the end helped to foment the great revolution. Yet as foreigners they could take no part in it, much less bring it to a finish. Instead it finished them."[2] The seed they planted, nevertheless, survived.

---

2. John K. Fairbank, *The Great Chinese Revolution 1800–1985* (New York: Harper and Row, 1987).

When the new ideology of Marxism came in, the resulting social upheaval destroyed many features of traditional rural life. Landlords were ejected and "peasant ownership" came into existence. The new administrators were the communes which became the collective owners in the name of the people. Communes were widely established in the countryside in the belief that total organization on a mass scale would alone achieve the results needed to haul China out of backwardness.

In the process, communal eating became the norm and the privacy and sanctity of individual or family lives a thing of the past. Children went to a village school where the State — and specifically Chairman Mao — became the father figure, with portraits of state leaders and the Communist trinity of Marx, Lenin and Engels displayed prominently in public squares of larger towns and cities. Errant parents were often pilloried by local officials and children were taught to expose their failures and disloyalty to a state which demanded total commitment. Confucius was pensioned off, together with household deities. Christianity was given a Marxist straitjacket — better than a silken cord! — and Islam and Buddhism were asked to make ritual kowtows by putting Mao above Muhammad and Gautama.

Thus the country experienced the most radical reform ever attempted. However, it conferred a social benefit for many at the lowest and poorest level of society in return for arduous and unremitting labour. This was accompanied by a high level of political indoctrination, thought reform and cultural transformation. No longer a backward, passive, tradition-bound, superstition-riddled Confucian society, China planned to leapfrog into an era of Marxist enlightenment and social progress. Even Chinese opera, a favourite pastime, was dragged into the political arena and given an ideological message. Musicians, dramatists, and playwrights were put to work to remould the minds of the people, to extol socialist virtues and to decry the decadence and evils of the past. An essential part was to emphasize the enslaving influence of the Western capitalists and the materialistic, self-serving, hedonistic, greedy way of life they extolled. They had come to China not to benefit and help the people but to enrich themselves and dominate the country.

An important part of China's new policies thus aimed at obliterating the role of the West throughout the country. In Shanghai, the properties and facilities and stocks of giant corporations such as Shell, Standard Vacuum, Texas Oil and Cathay Oil were taken over, as well as the former British properties of Butterfield & Swire, Jardine, Matheson, Hongkong & Shanghai Bank, *North China Daily News*, Hongkong & Shanghai Hotels, the Shanghai Gas Co. Ltd., and Shanghai Water Works Co. Ltd., while in Liaoning Province, seat of China's heavy industrial area, its first large-scale electrical machinery plant was opened, also a large automatic steel rolling mill and iron-smelting furnace at Anshan and a major open-cut mine in Liaoxi.

On the trade front, China was quick to bury the hatchet with Japan and sign an agreement to exchange goods to the value of $50 million, and at the same time a similar agreement was made with Indonesia. China extended its largess to other parts of the Third World, where India would receive a shipment of 100,000 tons of rice; while small in scale these were signs of a positive resurgence of China as an influential force in the Asian region.

On the diplomatic front the Chinese were assiduous in cultivating ties with Asian neighbours (notably India and Burma) on the basis of the five principles of peaceful co-existence[3] which was to be the cornerstone of its foreign policy in the 1950s and 1960s — though it would not prevent India and China fighting a brief but bloody war in 1962 in the snowy wastes of the Himalayas over the old imperial McMahon Line dividing Tibet from India. This the

---

3. Mutual respect for sovereignty and territorial integrity; mutual non-aggression; non-interference in each other's internal affairs; equality and mutual benefit; and coexistence.

Chinese repudiated for no better reason than that it was drawn by the British, and thus bound to be unequal.

China also played a diplomatic role in patching up North Vietnam's war of liberation from French control, following the prolonged siege and capture of the Foreign Legion fort of Dien Bien Phu in May, 1954. It was an action which was not only significant in military terms, emphasizing the skills and strategy of a 40,000-man peasant army (known as the Vietminh under General Vo Nguyen Giap) against a small but well-armed professional contingent aided by US supply drops, but climactic in terms of ending French rule in Indo-China. It also plunged France into an era of soul-searching over its post-war ideals and aspirations and in consequence triggered the downfall of the Fourth Republic and the reincarnation of the wartime hero, Charles de Gaulle, as the next leader.

The Geneva Conference setting up the border between North and South Vietnam on the 17th parallel was not the end of the strife but the beginning of an even more protracted campaign that eventually drew in the United States and some of its Korean War allies (such as Australia), in a force at one time numbering half a million men. Zhou Enlai, the Chinese Premier and Foreign Minister, was an active diplomatic participant who worked hard to bring about a ceasefire and the withdrawal of France from Indo-China after seventy years' colonial domination. However, as with India, China would eventually fall out with Vietnam in a border war fought with savage ferocity in which the People's Liberation Army came off worst.

Every step of China's progress and development in these early years of Communism was taken painfully and at great human cost. Raw manpower was involved in every project whether at the rural or industrial level, and though there was widespread scepticism in the West at some of China's claims, yet at the level of basic infrastructure these were years of achievement, based on muscle, brawn and sinew, and the mobilization of millions of people, digging, dragging, manhandling and hauling, often in the most primitive way, whipped by the ever tormenting hysteria of amplified sloganeering.

The achievement of the human spirit in this torrid physical and political environment and the ability to survive and per- severe, was akin to the way in which earlier generations of Chinese workers built the Great Wall and the system of canals and waterways which crisscross the country. Here they were engaged in creating a modern infrastructure to serve the country, trying to come to terms with the twentieth century, at the painful cost of hundreds of thousands of lives.

In a bid to revive foreign trade, China staged an impressive Export Commodities Fair in Guangzhou in 1957, displaying a wide variety of native products and light manufactures. It was to be the first of an annual exposition re-emphasizing Guangzhou as the trade centre of China, as in dynastic times, to which thousands of buyers were invited from all over the world. It would stress the increasing range of exports and the rising standards of its products, albeit dominated by traditional goods such as arts and crafts, minerals, herbal medicines, musical instruments, the in- evitable bicycles and sporting goods, textiles, garments and shoes. One of its exhibits was a "Liberation" lorry, closely resem- bling those China had received from the United States during the Burma Road days, but now being turned out in thousands by Chinese assembly plants. Many other Western products which fell into Chinese hands re-emerged in Chinese colours — the dividends of peace from the spoils of war — before terms like intellectual copyright had been invoked.

The year 1958 marked the inauguration of the Second Five- Year Plan, and the Chinese ushered in the campaign known as the "Great Leap Forward." Its aim was to catch up with Britain's steel production in the next two decades — a massive undertaking which earned the scorn and ridicule of Western commentators given the primitive facilities available to China. These were the years of the backyard furnaces, when home-made ovens were set up to produce iron and steel — the lamentable quality of which destabilized the country economically and socially and caused a series of calamities all the way down the production line.

It was a case of Communist ignorance and idealism over-riding planned, methodical and inevitably gradual development. In the same year, Chinese planners launched a more cautious campaign to get rid of four pests — flies, mosquitoes, rodents and sparrows. This was based on the lessons of an earlier experiment which backfired badly when the extermination of a number of predators exacerbated insect infestation of grains, fruit and vegetables and severely affected output in many areas. The figure of "kills" did much to confirm the country's reputation as pesticide champions without however adding substantially to the quantity of food and produce grown.

On top of these and other major bungles, the years 1960 and 1961 were fraught with serious problems of another kind. Natural calamities, including floods, crop failures, typhoons, devastating drought and plagues of locusts, coincided with the extraordinary rupture with the Soviet Union. This was when the Soviet Party Secretary and Premier, Nikita Kruschev, fell out publicly and violently with Mao Zedong on differing ideological interpretations of Leninism, imperialism and war.

The rift with Kruschev, architect of de-Stalinization, went much deeper. Unhappy with Kruschev's newly proclaimed policy of coexistence with the West and his decision to withdraw Soviet missiles from Cuba (under pressure from US President John Kennedy), Mao also resented Russia's reluctance to help China build nuclear weapons and to redraw the Sino-Soviet border. In the eyes of the Maoists, the Soviet Union were "revisionists" or compromisers. So bitterly did the arguments rage that they led to the wholesale withdrawal of Soviet aid, assistance, collaboration and indeed every form of economic involvement with China.

The Soviet technicians, skilled workers, scientists, engineers and architects simply rolled up their plans at a signal from Moscow and headed home with their families. If the issues appeared childish and self-destructive to Western observers, even more baffling was the way in which senior state functionaries such as Liu Shaoqi and Deng Xiaoping visited Moscow in 1960 to celebrate the 43rd anniversary of the 1917 Bolshevik revolution, with little overt sign of rancour — like a wife turning up to celebrate the birthday of the husband she had just divorced.

The natural disasters of those years together with the disruption caused by collectivization caused famine and suffering on a huge scale, affecting every province but two, and more than half the arable land — the worst for 300 years. Many blamed the Great Leap Forward. To assist recovery Canada sold five million tons of wheat and one million tons of barley while Australia sold a million tons of wheat, 400,000 tons of flour and a million tons of barley, oats and milk powder.

These were unhappy years for China. Not only were people hungry and confused from the failure of socialist experiments — causing a massive exodus of 60,000 across the Hong Kong border in a matter of weeks — but the Chinese Communist Party made an abortive call to intellectuals to speak their minds on how to overcome the country's problems. The campaign was known as "Baihua qifang, baijia zhengming" — "Let 100 flowers bloom, let 100 schools of thought contend." To a frustrated and disillusioned middle class it was like letting a genie out of a bottle. So vociferous were the critics that the party abruptly clamped down and arrested the more outspoken — dismissed as "poisonous weeds" — for counter-revolutionary tendencies.

With the Soviet Communist Party baying at their heels, senior Chinese statesmen embarked on a series of overseas visits to friendly Afro-Asian nations following the example of their Soviet counterparts, Nikolai Bulganin and Nikita Kruschev. Zhou Enlai, Chen Yi and Liu Shaoqi were keen to stress China's increasing ascendancy as a regional power, though the emphasis was very much on equality and co-operation in the Third World. China's most spectacular aid project was the nine-year construction of the

1,860-kilometre railway line to link the copper mines of Zambia with Dar es Salaam in Tanzania. It was at this time that Deng Xiaoping, in his late fifties, came into prominence, as Acting Premier during Zhou's mission overseas.

It was an era, too, when China was developing and testing its own atomic, and later thermonuclear weapons, while denouncing America's growing arsenal of hydrogen bombs as "paper tigers." China also began to worry about an atomic attack — more from Russia than the United States; it embarked on building a massive network of tunnels and air raid shelters beneath its northern cities which would enable its citizens to avoid the fallout, though not survive a direct hit. In these tunnels were elaborate complexes of schools, hospitals, and shops to enable thousands to survive a nuclear winter, excavated by millions of workers using the most primitive tools. Chinese officials proudly displayed the under-ground cities to visitors who saw tunnels illuminated, well paved and air conditioned, far exceeding conditions above ground, dubbed by one commentator as "subterranean socialism for a population of troglodytes."

In 1965 and 1966 China suffered a series of reverses in its foreign relations, the worst being the anti-Chinese riots in In-donesia following a *coup d'état* allegedly engineered by local Com-munists; pro-Beijing Chinese were targetted because of their assumed complicity and hundreds were violently murdered whatever their political allegiance. Fidel Castro's Cuba, a close ally of Moscow, was accusing China of disrupting its economy by stopping purchases of sugar and rice. India was protesting over Chinese military works on the Sikkim border. In Africa, Dahomey and the Central African Republic broke off diplomatic relations following Taiwanese diplomatic intrigues, and in Ghana, a *coup* occurred while its President, Kwame Nkrumah was on an official visit to China. Closer to home, China was involved in a minor skirmish with the Guomindang over the offshore islands of Quemoy and Matsu, just a shell-shot away from the Fujian coast, while in Beijing there were strong protests at the escalation of

America's air war on Hanoi and Haiphong harbours where Chinese freighters, delivering supplies and aid, were among those hit by bombs.

By this time, American ground forces were deployed in hundreds of thousands in South Vietnam in an attempt to prop up the independent non-Communist puppet regime of Ngo Dinh Diem following the French withdrawal. As part of its war effort, the US was bombing targets in the north in an attempt to blunt the Vietminh attacks on the south, as well as the alleged Vietminh sanctuaries on the Cambodian border and the so-called Ho Chi Minh jungle trails. More bombs fell on Vietnam than during the Allied bombing of Germany during World War II, without however seriously impairing Hanoi's war effort. But while Vietnam's revolution was just beginning, China's, only sixteen years old, was suffering a mid-life crisis.

The darkening cloud of dementia overtaking Beijing's ageing leader would be starkly displayed in what occurred in the mid-1960s when China embarked on what was described as the Great Proletarian Cultural Revolution. This was no mere political campaign but country-wide anarchy orchestrated by Mao and his supporters; it was pursued with fanatical zeal at all levels of the party to expose backsliding officials who had lost their revolutionary roots.

Mao touched it off with his own handwritten big character poster calling on people to "Bombard the headquarters" — a one-line invocation to revolt against a complacent self-satisfied bureaucracy. Mao was a stylish calligraphist who enjoyed putting his seal on the major initiatives of the Communist Party. This poster was intended to create political chaos in the country so that cadres at all levels would perceive their own failings and rekindle the old fire of revolution which had brought the party to power, reviving the spirit of the Long March and years of tribulation in Yan'an. Instead, it backfired causing enormous disruption at every level — nowhere more than in the education system which virtually collapsed under mass truancy. Today, Chinese at every level agree it was a time of collective madness which set the country back at least a decade.

The vanguard of this new movement would be the Hongweibing (or Red Guard), mainly youthful zealots, propelled into a wave of destructive rebellion by Maoist cadres and numbering eventually several million men and women. These shock troops of the revolution were the main instruments of terror and re-enacted a "long march" from various provinces to Beijing; they published their own newspapers, wrote their own posters, and persecuted officials, wreaking their own private vengeance and settling old scores, with a frenzy reminiscent of the French Revolution.

More than 100 million people were mobilized in the country-side for political demonstrations — including frogmarching delinquent officials through streets jammed with jeering mobs, the offenders attired in grotesque dunce's caps together with a catalogue of their alleged crimes. Museums, churches, temples and homes of industrialists and businessmen were raided and ransacked and their inmates hounded by youthful Red Guards with a free hand to desecrate or destroy whatever they considered reactionary or bourgeois. Many treasured antiques were smashed, libraries pillaged and books burnt. Students were given free travel all over the country so that they could "exchange experiences"; this clogged the railways bringing the economy to a halt.

Those who suffered most were alleged "capitalist roaders" and traditionalists who were thought to be creeping back into positions of power and influence. Amazingly, so much survived in the midst of such widespread destruction — thanks to forewarned officials hiding many of the treasures which had been targetted by rampaging mobs in other cities. Even the most prominent officials in the land, including Zhou Enlai, Liu Shaoqi and Deng Xiaoping were denounced at public rallies and forced to make self-criticisms. Men and women in senior levels of the bureaucracy were driven to suicide as they watched their world crashing around them and in the Red Guard mania that was unleashed, Deng Xiaoping's eldest son, Deng Pufang, jumped from, or was pushed out of a fourth floor window at Yanjing University in Beijing, but survived as a paraplegic. His daughter, Deng Rong, was also roughed up and packed off to the country for re-education.

In this white hot political environment the British Embassy in Beijing was ransacked and burned, while the foreign staff was made to run the gauntlet of jeering Red Guards who slapped, abused and sexually molested them as they escaped. A Reuter's correspondent, Anthony Grey, was held under house arrest for two years, though under more humane conditions than the Western hostages detained in Lebanon twenty years later.

For six months in Hong Kong and Macau leftist demonstrators staged daily riots in the streets, with bombings, beatings and assassinations of Chinese who dared to denounce the events in the mainland. The Macau Governor was forced to sign a humiliating apology for the deaths of Chinese protestors killed by police bullets following the ransacking of the Senate building by Red Guards. The gates and walls of the Governor's residence in Hong Kong were smeared with political slogans and posters by demonstrators led by a prominent left-wing newspaper publisher, Fei Yiming, all brandishing "little red books" containing the thoughts of Chairman Mao. While his fellow demonstrators marched in a long line up the hill to Government House for their daily demonstrations in 30 degree temperatures, the publisher arrived in his chauffeur-driven air-conditioned Mercedes-Benz.

It was an era of megaphone diplomacy when highly amplified sloganeering from the central headquarters of the Bank of China was countered by the colonial government with multi-decibel Chinese operatic music from its nearby information office. The aural damage to those in the neighbourhood was irrelevant. There was a sharp exchange of insults in the Press; left-wing critics lampooned the Hong Kong establishment as "white skin pigs" aided by their "yellow running dogs," while "red fat cats" were the butt of the right-wing media. It was an era of derring-do, commando-style operations when helicopters dropped armed and helmeted policemen on to the roof of the high-rise head-quarters of leftist agitators, discovering a secret hospital and ar-resting many for interrogation. Bomb-makers had a field day with potent home-made cannisters stuffed with fire-cracker powder, powerful enough to blow off the legs of a police officer who tried to move one, and killing several others.

Nevertheless, food and water supplies from China continued uninterrupted throughout the six months of confrontation. Nor were there any military threats on the border against the biggest concentration of "capitalist roaders" on the China coast, indicat-ing that the People's Liberation Army retained control despite the anarchic behaviour of the Red Guards in China. In Hong Kong, leftist school children and trade unionists occupied the pivotal role and staged riots and confronted the police in repeated acts of violence amidst clouds of swirling tear gas, shrill demonstrations and exploding bombs. Throughout the six-month period, Hong Kong relied on local police to contain the riots, with the Army controlling the border.

The impact of the Cultural Revolution was felt in many parts of the world, splitting Communist parties into Maoist and pro-Soviet factions and touching off a wave of terrorism and confron-tation that convulsed several Western capitals. No city was more affected than Paris where the Red Army Faction of the Baader-Meinhoff Gang and Maoist Communists, led by high profile intel-lectuals, created chaos for French police in many running battles. The Gang was mainly active against US military installations in West Germany and formed links with terrorist groups in many parts of the world, notably the Palestinian Liberation Organiza-tion, the Irish Republican Army and Iranian Hez Bollah (Army of God). Frequent hijackings of international airliners, seizure of hostages, acts of arson and car bombings kept anti-terrorist police active in many countries through the years of the 1970s and 1980s.

Che Guevara's leftist revolutionaries were similarly inspired by the Maoist resurgence, though Che had been fighting his own battles in Africa, Cuba and other parts of Latin America years before the Cultural Revolution.

Gradually Chairman Mao lost control of the state he created and left it to fall into the hands of a group of manic Marxist anarchists, led by his scheming ex-filmstar wife, Jiang Qing, and known as the "Gang of Four." Deng Xiaoping scathingly dismissed them as "helicopters" because of their meteoric rise from inexperience, obscurity and political ineptitude, yet they remained in control until 1975, presiding over the ruins of the party and state apparatus they helped to destroy.

Their patron, Jiang Qing, was no more astute. Exploiting her privileged position as Mao's former secretary, she tried to project herself as his closest confidante and interpreter of his thoughts; her political aspirations foundered on the same grounds of shallowness, immaturity and sheer incompetence, and even Mao warned her against becoming mixed up with the Gang. Sacked from most of her earlier posts in the cultural sphere she was unable to rise above the stigma of a failed actress who had forgotten her lines. With no power base and few friends after the death of Mao, she ended in prison as a usurper caught loitering in bad company. If the author of a recent biography is to be believed,[4] the "Black Empress" was not only the most hated woman in China, but in Mao's last days the least favoured bedmate, the red lantern being repeatedly raised for a groupie named Zhang Yufeng, who was better able to cope with his sexual appetites. She alone could interpret his final incoherent ramblings, endure his halitosis and supply him with new young talent.

Increasing friction with the Soviet Union saw the outbreak of clashes on the northern Amur River border though these were

---

4. Li Zhisui, *The Private Life of Chairman Mao* (London: Chatto & Windus, 1995).

insignificant compared with the country-wide dislocation caused by the Cultural Revolution. With the decline of Mao Zedong, an attempted *coup d'état* was staged by a former trusted hero, Marshal Lin Biao, who eventually made his escape from China in his Trident jet only to crash in the grasslands of the Mongolian People's Republic. Whether it was a guided missile, a clever counter-*coup* by Mao's bodyguard or an empty fuel tank that caused his death, is open to speculation. Years later China published photographs purporting to be the remains of the aircraft; a naked body lying in the wreckage was said to be that of Lin Biao.

One of the highlights of this period was the era of "ping-pong diplomacy" which, under the guise of casual sporting encounters between Chinese and American youths, helped bring about a reconciliation between Beijing and Washington. Secret contacts were launched from Islamabad in Pakistan where the US Secretary of State, Dr Henry Kissinger, flew to an unpublicized rendezvous in China with Zhou Enlai, his absence being explained by illness. At their first meeting, the two men, in the words of historian and journalist Dick Wilson, "simply fell in love with each other."

Kissinger, an intellectual of complex attitudes, had earlier been a strong advocate of the US bombing of Cambodia, but finally switched and became a firm advocate of disengagement from the war. The contrast between Kissinger and his predecessor, the stern, inflexible anti-China hawk, John Foster Dulles, did much to allay suspicions; the success of his contacts with Zhou finally lead to the visit of US President Richard Nixon to Beijing and Shanghai, and the resumption of diplomatic relations between the two countries.

As the US President and Zhou shook hands, "one era ended and another began," Nixon was to write later. Not only were there handshakes with Mao Zedong but the final communiqué declared "all Chinese on either side of the Taiwan Strait maintain there is but one China and that Taiwan is part of China." Officially this was a climbdown by Nixon's administration which had inherited and relentlessly pursued a "two Chinas" policy; however, it continued to support Chiang Kai-shek's regime on Taiwan. To celebrate the occasion, an American musician later wrote an opera "Nixon in Shanghai" — no threat to Puccini, Wagner, Verdi, Mozart or Donizetti, but a musical testimony to a political and diplomatic turning-point in East–West relations.

Nixon promised to withdraw all American forces and military installations from Taiwan which included the removal of the defensive screen of the US Seventh Fleet and its powerful carrier force. He also lifted the ban on US ships and aircraft visiting China, sold 15 million bushels of wheat to Beijing and ten Boeing 707 airliners at a cost of $25 million — all without a single kowtow. Later that year Japan also recognized Beijing, going further than Nixon in "fully understanding and respecting China's claim to Taiwan." Quite suddenly the watchdogs of the UN embargo on trade with China lost their bark, and were returned to their kennels.

Three years later, the Americans bit the bullet of defeat in South Vietnam at the hands of the Vietcong whose tanks crashed through the gates of the American Embassy in Saigon shortly after the last US Navy helicopter took off from the roof with desperate refugees still hanging from its open doors. It marked the end of the heavily criticized American involvement in Indo-China at a high cost of civilian lives and servicemen; their sense of betrayal and abandonment by the administration left a legacy of bitterness and hatred of this "dirtiest of wars." It was a clear defeat for Washington, a decisive victory for a reunited Vietnam and brought autonomy for the adjoining states of Laos and Cambodia. The latter rapidly slid into a genocidal civil war in which Communist Khmer Rouge soldiers slaughtered hundreds of thousands of innocent citizens in a fiendish bloodbath with few parallels in world history, doing much to tarnish the Communist takeover of the three Indo-China territories.

In 1976, China lost both its leaders, Mao Zedong and Zhou

Enlai, the latter widely lamented for his sagacious leadership and greatly respected for his statesmanship, courage, and ability. But it was Mao as the leader of the revolution which brought the Communists to power, who ended up in a glass case in Tian'anmen Square; his memory was still revered 100 years after his birth, though by diminishing numbers. Zhou's remains were, at his own wish, cremated and scattered.

Succeeding them would be a political Lazarus, thrice restored from the wilderness of yesterday's men, who would lead China out of Communism into a new era of state capitalism, once a no-go area for all the party faithful. His name: Deng Xiaoping, which was also a homophone for "small bottle," but this one contained a remarkable genie whose escape will form the subject of the final chapter.

The Great Proletarian Cultural Revolution which turned China inside out and destroyed the budding careers of hundreds of thousands of adolescents and young adults caught up in the Red Guard turmoil, brought temporary trauma to Hong Kong and Macau. But with their resilient economies and independent administrations they were quick to heal their wounds and recover. Hong Kong was at that stage still one of the world's biggest producers of garments and textiles.

Chinese industrialists from Shanghai were by then per-manent fixtures in the British colony. One of the most notable had been Rong Hongyuan, eldest son of Rong Zongjing, who came to Hong Kong first in 1938 but returned to China ten years later to assess opportunities — not the most propitious of times, for the Communists were poised to cross the Yangzi and move south. Nor was the younger Rong the most diplomatic in his comments on the Guomindang Government. He was arrested for buying Hong Kong dollars to pay for a shipment of cotton, and sent to prison. But the Chinese judicial system was flexible, and with the payment of US$500,000 to some worthy or unworthy cause, Hongyuan was allowed to fly back to Hong Kong to set up a cotton mill. He was one of a number who found it hard to migrate to the United States where the Chinese Exclusion Act of 1882 and subsequent legislation restricted Chinese entry.

Several other industrialists were attracted to the low-cost regime of Hong Kong. While wages were equally low elsewhere in Asia, it was hard for them to break through anti-Chinese immigration barriers. Taiwan was an exception but when Chinese industrialists saw that it was dominated by the same corrupt officials who had presided over the liquidation of China in 1949, their interest cooled. Hong Kong was popular because of its free port status, excellent shipping connections, diverse banking and commercial network and an apolitical government.

People like P. Y. Tang, his son, Jack Tang, C. Y. Wong, V. J. Song, H. C. Tang, Alex Woo, T. K. Ann, Cha Chi-ming and Sally Leung made their fortunes in textiles; the Ningbo clan of Run Run Shaw and Raymond Chow were successful in movies and television. Equally prominent in an age before women's liberation was the executive head of the Federation of Industries, Susan Yuen. Two other notable men were the Kadoorie brothers, Lawrence and Horace, sons of Sir Elly Kadoorie of Shanghai, whose achievement in building up China Light & Power Co. Ltd. and a major hotel chain, earned Lawrence a peerage and his brother a knighthood.

It was this synergy of Chinese and foreign talent which contributed significantly to Hong Kong's economic success in the post-war years. Moreover it encouraged competition from Cantonese businessmen who made strong contributions in such diverse fields as property, banking, electronics, food, plastics, toys and garments. Men of the calibre of Li Ka-shing, a one-time plastic flower maker, industrialist S. Y. Chung, K. S. Lo and Haking Wong, bankers Arthur Morse, Q. W. Lee, Li Fook-shu and his son, David K. P. Li, entrepreneurs Fung King-hey, Lee Shau-kee, Gordon Wu, Douglas Clague, George Morden, Peter Woo and Helmet Sohmen, were all movers and shakers in turning Hong Kong into one of the Four Little Asian Dragons. Many were ranked among the world's most successful businessmen of the twentieth century — among them, Sir Y. K. Pao who became the world's biggest private tanker owner, and C. Y. Tung, the shipowner. He was remembered for having bought the former Cunard liner *Queen Elizabeth*, only to endure the tragedy of losing her in an arson-fire in Hong Kong harbour in 1972 the day before sea trials as a floating university.

Equally outstanding men and women were to be found in the professions, journalism, the law, medicine, architecture, academia, education, the civil service and the arts (Chinese and Western) — all products of a Western education in Hong Kong or overseas, or from leading Chinese universities. The superlatives were spread over the entire field of commercial and professional practice.

When containerization of cargoes brought a new style of shipping and loading to the harbours of the world, Hong Kong already one of the top 20 trading states, built facilities which would make it the second biggest container port after Amsterdam; it also achieved one of the fastest turnrounds. Ever ready to flaunt its wealth, Hong Kong established records for having more luxury cars per mile of road than any other city. At the same time, the billions of dollars passing through the tills and telephones of the Royal Hong Kong Jockey Club's two race tracks, and its network of offcourse betting shops, placed it in a category of disposable megawealth few other cities have attained. Hong Kong remains one of Asia's top three financial centres and seventy-seven of the licensed international and local trading banks operating there are among the world's top 100. With all that, it was still a city of extremes and many hundreds continued to fall through the welfare net into drug-addiction, homelessness and vagrancy.

Hong Kong's first post-war boom came in the early 1960s when the city began to sweep away its decrepit pre-war tenement buildings; it was rapidly submerged by high-rise constructions, nourished by a stock exchange and real estate boom. Continuing reclamation of land on the harbour foreshores added hundreds of acres to commercial and residential development and yielded substantial revenue for the Government. Yet despite its wealth Hong Kong's poorest languished in substandard hillside shacks, frequently battered by typhoon winds, torrential rains and massive fires which claimed hundreds of lives over the years. Only huge outlays of Government funds and the building of five new towns in the once rural New Territories helped to raise the quality of life of the urban population. A total of 70,000 units of public housing were built each year in the early 1980s and over 100,000 in later years which did much to soak up the homeless.

While the Government was anxious to create living space for its six million people on a land area of slightly more than 1,000 square kilometres, an even more pressing need was to preserve a substantial green environment for recreation. This was achieved by designating almost 40 per cent of the territory as Country Parks to add to the many beaches and bays for boating and swimming. Hong Kong at the beginning of the last decade of the twentieth century was one of the top ten richest countries as it moved towards a new destiny as a Special Administrative Region of China in 1997. Many wonder whether the quality of life can be preserved.

Hong Kong has been living under the threat of a Chinese takeover since 1949. Because of that, Hong Kong cultivated a short-term outlook. Business investment was based on a maximum five-year recovery of capital — for all but the most costly projects. In good and bad times the policy persisted, strongly influenced by pre-war events in China, the Japanese occupation, the short-lived post-war Guomindang era and the first (and worst) three decades of Communist rule; Hong Kong enjoyed short bursts of stability punctuated by long periods of uncertainty. *Sunday Times* reporter, Richard Hughes, described it as a "borrowed place [living on] borrowed time."

When China finally succeeded in winning its place in the United Nations, twenty-three years after ousting Chiang Kai-shek from the mainland, one of its first steps was to remove Hong Kong from the UN's decolonization list. Effectively this meant that where territories like Kenya, Tanganyika, Malaya, Singapore, Brunei, Bahamas, Trinidad and Malta were able to gain self-government and independence under Prime Minister Harold Macmillan's "winds of change" policy, Hong Kong would one day be returned to China. Beijing gave clear notice of its intentions but no timetable of when this would take place.

However, it was a reminder to investors and businessmen that time was running out. The Nixon visit to China did not include discussion on the future of Hong Kong, dealing mainly with Taiwan and Sino-American relations. Nor, at first, was China anxious to raise the question with Britain. The Chinese had no reason to rush, for the Hong Kong connection had proved profitable to Beijing. Time was on its side.

Embittered by Soviet Russia's stab-in-the-back in 1959 it decided never again to rely on a single country, no matter how closely allied. This was Zhou Enlai's legacy and insight. China, he argued, needed friends all over the world, and the ability to speak directly through normal diplomatic channels. A century of turmoil with the West had made that much plain. No longer could the country retreat into isolation.

To confirm the value of its open door, China was able to buy 100 million pounds worth of jet engines from Britain for new aircraft ordered from Europe, while another British firm would instal a coaxial cable between Hong Kong and Guangdong. Japan would build a three million tonnes-a-year steel rolling mill in Wuhan. Even the Vienna Philharmonic Orchestra would visit the People's Republic. The Western world was beginning to beat a path to China's door and Hong Kong welcomed the prospect of being the doormat to the influx of international bankers, investors, diplomats, businessmen, salesmen and technicians. There were several unwelcome visitors as well.

In 1975, Saigon had fallen to the Communists and all of Vietnam was now ruled by a Marxist dictatorship under President Ho

Chi Minh. The impact on the people of the south was traumatic and they began fleeing in thousands, one group of 3,500 arriving in Hong Kong harbour aboard a Danish freighter the day the Queen of England arrived on a royal visit. Tens of thousands more arrived on freighters, either picked up from sinking boats in the South China Sea, or on vessels chartered by refugees with the connivance or assistance of corrupt officials.

When Hong Kong intensified naval patrols in a bid to deter them, ships carrying thousands of refugees ran themselves aground on the shores of the British territory, even though it meant spending years in detention camps while awaiting resettlement in countries prepared to admit them.

Hundreds of thousands followed not just to Hong Kong but to Malaysia, Indonesia, the Philippines and as far south as Australia. Many fell prey to Thai pirates in the South China Sea, bent on murder, loot and rape, for many were carrying their wealth in the form of gold leaf wafers stitched into the hems of their clothing. In some cases the refugees' arrival provoked such hostility that local authorities opened fire on incoming boats in an attempt to deter them; when boats overturned in tumbling surf there was no attempt to save them.

More than half a million chose this escape route, with about 15 per cent ultimately reaching their chosen destinations in the US, Canada and Australia, 25 per cent being repatriated to Vietnam, and many thousands slipping ashore on various islands and deserted coastal areas of Southeast Asia where they remain today. At least half perished on the way, victims of storm, typhoons, pirates and hostile officials where they tried to land. But they believed the risk was worth it, particularly the thousands fleeing the blood-drenched "killing fields" of the Khmer Rouge's holocaust in Cambodia.

Twenty years after the first major exodus thousands of Vietnamese were awaiting resettlement or repatriation from Hong Kong where more than 100,000 were held in camps at various times. Not all who left Vietnam or China were considered refugees fleeing political persecution; many were self-confessed economic escapees or migrants seeking a new life in more prosperous parts of the world, unable to wait for visas or entry permits. There are still small groups of mainly Chinese boat people landing in northern Australia in the hope of gaining permanent residence, following the former Prime Minister, Robert Hawke's concession to 20,000 Chinese students to remain after the 1989 Tian'anmen Square Incident. Australia, however, was no more willing to accept queue-jumpers than other countries and threatened to return all illegal arrivals.

In 1978, with no clear idea of China's intentions on Hong Kong's future, the most pressing concern was the future of thousands of properties in Kowloon and the New Territories where 99-year leases were due to expire. Hong Kong residents and businessmen wondered whether they would be regranted or renewed and for what period and on what terms. With the New Territories lease due to expire in 1997, its future had to be clarified, amounting as it did to about three-quarters of Hong Kong's total area.

The Governor, Sir Murray MacLehose and the senior member of the Executive Council, Sir Y. K. Kan, decided to visit Beijing to test sentiment. In a top-level meeting, the Chinese leader, Deng Xiaoping, advised them to tell the people to "put their hearts at ease." But he gave no hint of what was in store. The visitors returned with their hearts anything but at ease. The future of the leases remained in doubt.

Thereafter, diplomacy between Britain and China would try to resolve the matter. Britain had no Henry Kissinger capable of charming his Chinese counterpart, and it took another four years for Deng Xiaoping to inform the Foreign Office through a visiting British Minister of State that China favoured a takeover in 1997. With this point established China agreed to talks with the "Iron Lady" of British politics, Mrs Margaret Thatcher, who for her part vowed there would be no supine surrender. The twists and turns of negotiations over the next two years in Beijing, and the hard bargaining by both sides, left Britain in no doubt that there were no alternatives to China's resumption of sovereignty.

It fell to the new Hong Kong Governor, a former top official of the Foreign Office, Sir Edward Youde, to attend talks yet give nothing away following his frequent visits to China; his sole comment after each visit was that the talks had been "useful and constructive" — a statement delivered with urbane, monotonous and bland uniformity, in a vain effort to discourage speculation by the media. The negotiations proved difficult and on several occasions verged on breakdown.

Many have described the agreement as a sell-out. It was generally agreed, however, that Hong Kong and Kowloon would not be viable without the New Territories with all its new townships, container port, airport, factories, reservoirs and recreation areas. If no extension of the lease was possible, the alternative was the creation of an autonomous region under Chinese jurisdiction, with its existing way of life guaranteed by both sides.

The Joint Declaration, signed by British and Chinese leaders in Beijing on 19 December 1984, explained what a "high degree of autonomy" entailed. There would be a continuation of Hong Kong's social, economic, legal, commercial and trading systems with existing rights and freedoms of assembly, speech, media, travel and religion untouched for fifty years after. It would not be required to adopt socialism. Deng Xiaoping described the new arrangement as "one country, two systems."

The *South China Morning Post* summed up reaction in Hong Kong the next day as "the sound of one hand clapping — for the wish to applaud the Sino-British agreement is tempered by the uncertainty of whether it will all come to pass." That uncertainty continued as the new (and last British) Governor, Mr Chris Patten, a former Conservative politician, tried to force the pace of con-stitutional change to ensure that in a formerly all-appointed Legislative Council a "large degree of autonomy" would be preserved by the introduction of a fully elected membership.

Figure 15.1 The British Prime Minister, Margaret Thatcher, and her Chinese counterpart, Zhao Ziyang, sign the Joint Declaration on the future of Hong Kong as a Special Administrative Region of China in Beijing on 19 December 1984.

His predecessor, Sir (now Lord) David Wilson, preferred to place more emphasis on "convergence" and a smooth transfer of power than on the level of elected representation in Legislative Council. Economic buoyancy and a harmonious relationship with China were considered more important for the territory and its people than the composition of the Legislative Council which could be undermined, emasculated, pushed aside or cut down by the new owner, and thus offer no guarantee of realistic autonomy.

Hong Kong's concerns about China and specifically its tolerance of opposition and criticism, were given forceful emphasis by the events at Tian'anmen Square on the night of 4 June 1989 when following the failure of highly publicized negotiations in the Chinese capital, elite troops and tanks of the People's Liberation Army burst through cordons and crushed Chinese demonstrators calling for more freedom. Indelibly etched in the memories of those present was the slight figure of a lone protestor, bag in hand, defying an oncoming tank amid the carnage and debris of the city centre. This was followed by a brutal crackdown of students in a state of martial law.

Several hundreds were killed and thousands arrested, though a full accounting may never be made. While these roundups were underway, heavily armed troops took over the city, watched by curious bystanders amidst blazing, smoking trucks fired by saboteurs and demonstrators. Weeping residents clamoured for news of their children; friendly soldiers who sat quietly at road blocks the day before listening to student activists now lined the streets, armed, sullen and unapproachable. Tanks patrolled road junctions, guns ready. Beijing's brief flirt with democracy had ended.

It was a sobering and deeply disturbing sight for the people of Hong Kong as they watched events unfold on their television screens, for it showed what their own fate could be under such a repressive and authoritarian rule. Several hundred thousand Hong Kong people joined spontaneously in a march to the official Xinhua (New China) News Agency to register their protest — a courageous outpouring of public concern, beneficial for Hong Kong's morale even if the Chinese authorities were unimpressed.

For while the Chinese Government, under the liberal decrees of Deng Xiaoping, had initiated major reforms in China to achieve a market based economy, no change has occurred at the political level. With Soviet Russia's disintegration under the reforms of "glasnost" and "perestroika" initiated by Mikhail Gorbachev, the Communists in China are certain to maintain strong control of the central political machine.

Moreover, the Tian'anmen sanction remains a threat to any would-be provincial leader who contemplates flouting Beijing's authority. The Chinese are conscious that not only has the Russian empire disintegrated and become a collection of warring states, but the "Eastern bloc" of European satellites no longer exists, several throwing in their lot with the West, some even joining the North Atlantic Treaty Organisation.

China is not prepared to run the same risks of losing control of its extensive border zones of Tibet, Xinjiang and Mongolia. The lessons of the Soviet breakaway state of Chechnya in 1995 provided a vivid illustration of the contaminating effects of the independence and freedom virus. Not the least of China's concerns is its strong desire to draw Taiwan back into a close association with the motherland, and to exert its influence in the region, particularly on the wealthy and commercially powerful overseas Chinese living in Southeast Asia.

China's relations with Moscow are never likely to be as cordial as they were in the first decade of the People's Republic — even then it was the politics of desperation and self-survival that influenced the relationship. The Russian reforms in the 1990s were viewed in Beijing with undisguised contempt, hardly improved by elections in 1993 which saw a throwback reactionary group become the largest party. The party bond has been temporarily eclipsed, though at the state level, strong trade, industrial, defence, even diplomatic links, continue.

Another compelling concern for China is control of the South China Sea and its oil and gas reserves, so far unquantified but already being exploited at several points. China is determined to ensure control of the Spratlys and Paracel Islands, and defend them with a modern, well-armed navy including nuclear submarines. For a time in the early 1990s, Beijing contemplated the purchase of an unwanted 67,500-ton Ukrainian aircraft carrier with ninety-six fighter and support aircraft. With its long coastline and extensive offshore islands, land-based aircraft provide sufficient safeguard and surveillance and the carrier option is not a top priority. Even with its existing squadrons and its already deployed medium and long-range nuclear rockets, China is the strongest air and naval power in the east China Sea, and well able to confront any challenge. The residue of rotting, rusting wrecks in Valdivostok harbour tells Beijing clearly the US Seventh Fleet remains its only rival.

CHAPTER 16

A Change of Flags

Deng Xiaoping may have ended his days as the saviour of China, but in doing so he became a robust supporter of private enterprise. While he may have been fired by the ideals of socialism in his early manhood, tempered and hardened by experiences on the Long March and at Yan'an, and forged into a loyal, obedient apparatchik and forceful leader, he became increasingly disillusioned with Maoist Communism as a means of transforming China. In 1978 he made a historic right turn in his economic thinking; this meant largely dumping hardline Marxism–Maoism for a form of market capitalism. He had, after all, experienced the personal bitterness of public humiliation during the Cultural Revolution; his eldest son had been made a permanent cripple; comrades from Long March days had been hounded and villified leading to dishonour and suicide. The Gang of Four had done its best to bury him as a political rival. The disastrous repercussions of the Cultural Revolution and the ideologically perverted Gang had to be expunged and modernization introduced. Hardline Communism had failed to deliver the goods. He chose to tap the natural qualities of the hard-working Chinese people who would respond to any call, given the right incentives and fair rewards.

The basic decisions were taken at the end of 1978 at the third plenum of the Eleventh Central Committee meeting of the party but the way ahead was uncertain. To some extent the process of change took on its own momentum. Having turned away from the collectivization of agriculture, many were freed to do other work, and by introducing market reforms and economic autonomy in the central and border regions the party gave flexibility to local administrations. Peasants were allowed to sell on the open market what they grew in excess of state needs. Immediately there was a positive and welcome response from the people.

Through this open door and in the five Special Economic Zones (SEZs) established by Beijing, provincial authorities were able to canvass investment and technology from outside the country. Patriotic Chinese living in Hong Kong and Southeast Asia were invited to investigate the prospects of the new economic zone at Shenzhen, just over the border from Hong Kong, once notorious as a "dirty weekend" getaway for wealthy layabouts in the pre-war years. Girls and gambling were the magnets then. Deng offered them a gamble of a different kind, fully backed by the Chinese Government. In China money is one of the strongest magnets.

In most cases, Chinese officials did not have to beg for favours or appeal to loyalty; the terms offered were pitched attractively and with low wage rates, coupled with good communications to Hong Kong, many investors immediately saw the potential. A few who were slower to respond and whose participation was deemed essential, were cornered and had their arms twisted by persistent mainland officials; they were asked to make donations, loans and contributions in much the same way as the Hoppo, two centuries earlier, squeezed donations from Chinese merchants. And so Shenzhen got underway.

Many and varied were the motives and responses. Sir Yuekong Pao, the multi-billionaire shipping magnate, established a US$400 million university for his home town, Ningbo, and a $10 million library at Jiaotong University, Shanghai, while his family donated clinics and welfare centres in Ningbo. He also set up a foundation to enable promising Chinese students to study at leading British universities. There was, of course, a payback in that Pao was a majority shareholder in a US$50 million joint venture with the Chinese Government and others in a company to operate and arrange charters and sales for Chinese built ships. Similarly Sir Run Run Shaw, the movie-TV tycoon, donated a large sum to his home town of Ningbo. These were just two of many substantial and spontaneous donors.

The Special Economic Zones were meant to be self-sustaining areas capable of accommodating viable industries operating at a profit; there were to be no subsidies though inducements, such as tax incentives, were offered at the outset to encourage some high profile international investors. Deng Xiaoping's swing to capitalism came when many firms in Hong Kong were looking for opportunities to diversify and lower their labour costs. The SEZs, initially in Shenzhen and later in other parts of Guangdong, Fujian and Hainan, were chosen for new industrial developments but have taken over the bulk of the highly labour-intensive work once performed by Hong Kong workers. The result was that by 1995, between three and four million Chinese in Guangdong were directly or indirectly working for Hong Kong companies, making a wide range of goods from garments to electronics, travel goods to fireworks.

As the pace of investment grew, so did the incidence of bribery and corruption as local officials saw opportunities to take advantage of the more liberal business environment. Favours were offered at a price that rose steeply month by month. Business missions from China expected red carpet treatment from prospective investors. Businessmen familiar with what happened in the closing days of the Guomindang, found their successors no less grasping. In extreme cases, demands were made for luxury apartments in Hong Kong, cars, pleasure boats, Swiss watches, gold bars, expensive jewellery and airline tickets to exotic destinations.

The "gravy train" was picking up speed and one of the most conspicuous group of passengers was the so-called "princelings" or sons and daughters of party cadres who appeared to hold the keys to many doors in China. These were people who were either businessmen in privileged institutions, influential officials or representatives of the National People's Congress. Though the intention of Deng's reforms was to liberate the country from the dead hand of Communist orthodoxy and bureaucracy, foreign and Chinese businessmen found the new power structure and the maze of regulations perplexing, obstructive, and costly to circumvent, while middle-rank bureaucrats raised administrative or legal barriers even after approval had been granted at higher levels. Every new handshake carried an implicit expectation of a handout — with a 24-carat glove. A 12-course banquet and the best French cognac was a useful introduction.

Growth was most spectacular in the rapidly modernized city of Shenzhen, on the borders of Hong Kong, where a major effort was made by Chinese authorities to plan an efficient, well-run community of 2.5 million. But the rapid rise in wages drove investors to look for other areas, notably in their own "heung ha" (home town). Many Taiwan manufacturers had a natural affinity with Fujian; others saw a big potential in Shanghai and particularly the new industrial area of Pudong, on the southern bank of the city's Huangpu River, one of the first major industrial areas following its opening as a treaty port in the last century. This became the site of shipyards, oil installations, wharves, textile mills and other industries. But it was always a grubby, run-down factory area, interspersed with market gardens, facing the opulent high-rise commercial city with its fine promenade along the Bund.

In the 1950s and 1960s, Shanghai fell under the control of left-wing elements who were strongly entrenched in its bureaucracy. They contributed a significant share of turmoil in the era of the Gang of Four. The shifting power base in Chinese politics, following the Gang's overthrow, and the ascendancy of Deng Xiaoping, as Chairman of the Central Military Commission, coupled with the evident gains in prosperity stemming from his new policies, helped to open up Shanghai to new influences. Rather than rebuild the old city, the new team of administrators envisage Pudong as a well-planned, multi-function high-tech commercial-industrial area, served by transport and communication links with the west bank.

To relieve overcrowding the city is building five million square metres of housing each year; an underground railway and a system of elevated roads have significantly eased the pressure on the over-crowded narrow city streets, giving its more than ten million residents a similar convenience to Hong Kong's Mass Transit Railway. Multi-lane bridges, such as the Nanpu, and tunnels span the mud-brown waters of the river, still one of the busiest waterways in China. Pudong will also have free-trade areas, wharves, container facilities and an airport. For this it needs large amounts of foreign capital and investment and has launched its own securities exchange to attract funds. Potentially it could rival or even surpass Hong Kong in the twenty-first century, such is the growth predicted for China as a whole.

Private enterprise and banks in Hong Kong have recognized the potential and several former Shanghai residents, once scared off by the draconian measures after the 1949 Liberation, are now returning with money in their hands. They are building residential property mainly for staff who will be employed in the city, but eventually local buyers will be encouraged to invest. Chinese property developers are adept at identifying opportunities and raising funds, and Shanghai is proving a lucrative growth area. The old 1930s waterfrontage will remain for the time being, its buildings sold to new owners, but a high-rise city will grow around it.

Other ports to be developed in South–Central China are in Guangxi Province, next to Guangdong, with the emphasis on Qinzhou serving the south-western provinces. Plans have been laid to develop Qinzhou Bay into a complex of berths for vessels up to 100,000 tons. Local authorities have been encouraged by Beijing to press on with a scheme to build as many as seventy berths which will be served by the higher-grade railway linking the provincial capital of Nanning and Kunming; in years to come it could realize the dream of Sun Yat-sen to turn this into one of the seven major ports in the country. Another Hong Kong company is pressing ahead with the Ningbo Port Authority to develop Beilun for containers, giving access to central China and transhipment facilities to other parts of the country.

Yet another major project involving Hong Kong capital will be located close to Shenzhen; a joint venture consortium is developing a port at nearby Yantian costing more than $US1 billion, with five 50,000-ton container berths and four general cargo berths. These will handle an increasing proportion of Shenzhen's own products and there is scope to build up to forty berths as output grows. Yantian has been named as one of China's four-main deepwater international ports. This was the site raided by the Royal Navy in pre-war years to stamp out piracy and is close to the site of China's first nuclear-power plant at Daya Bay, built with French and British help. A second is to be built nearby.

Not only sea ports but river ports are receiving the attention of Hong Kong investors who also are planning to extend their own container wharves on reclaimed sites at Lantau. One major Hong Kong developer will be engaged in two port projects at Chongqing, 2,250 kilometres from the East China Sea and serving south-west China. At the same time special shallow draft container vessels are being built to carry this huge volume of internal freight. This was Chiang Kai-shek's wartime capital, fed by US aid flown over "the Hump" from India; today it is rich in iron and steel mills, coal mining, and factories producing chemicals, fertilizers and farm implements as well as a range of light industries ranging from cotton to handicrafts, all of which is imposing a heavy environmental penalty.

Because of Japanese bombing, the old city has been transformed into a traffic-choked, over-populated metropolis of more than fourteen million people. Similar facilities are planned for the triple-city of Wuhan, once the former treaty port of Hankou, where many foreign companies established major branches in the last century and where the left-wing of the Guomindang broke away from Chiang Kai-shek in 1928. It was also one of the first treaty ports to be returned to Chinese administration. Like Chongqing and many other industrial cities, its murky brown haze permits only fleeting glimpse of the sun.

Yet another deepwater port for 300,000-ton tankers is planned for Daxie Island, off Ningbo, though so demanding in terms of investment capital are many of these projects that even with Hong Kong input, they will not be realized in the lifetime of the present generation of Chinese people. To the east is the Zhoushan archipelago where Britain wanted to establish its first trading post and where British soldiers died in hundreds following its occupation in 1840.

The two biggest development zones, however, are in Fujian and Guangdong, each served by the external economic powerhouses of Taiwan and Hong Kong. In Fujian, where output has been rising at the rate of 13.3 per cent a year, almost US$1 billion has been invested in the province, three quarters of which was earmarked for industry and came mainly from Taiwan. About 80 per cent of the products from these factories were exported. Moreover, Taiwanese investors are growing more confident about longer-term commitments and periods of up to fifty years are not uncommon. Industries already well-established include motor cycles, spare parts, computers, Chinese–English typewriters, electronics, opticals, fax and telex machines, both for export and to serve the needs of local businesses.

Additionally, plans are underway with the help of outside capital to establish a large sea port and industrial zone for heavy industry. Pending approval of direct trade, there is a thriving multibillion dollar indirect trade between Taiwan and China. Taiwan's investment in Guangdong (mainly Shenzhen) was more than 50 per cent higher than in Fujian but the gap will narrow as Taiwan's links with Fujian grow closer — so much so that Taiwan fears that its own industries will "desert" to China to reap the benefits of lower wages.

A strong competitor is the Special Economic Zone of Shantou

in Guangdong Province which has extended generous privileges to Taiwan investors, with some success. The special areas of Shenzhen, Dongguan and Guangzhou have been the big winners, however, largely through joint ventures with Hong Kong companies. It is all the more remarkable that China has advanced so quickly since up to 1994 the country did not have comprehensive laws on companies, securities, contract or tort; its accounting regulations and standards differed from those of the International Accounting Standards; however, the two-tier yuan, which previously operated in a managed exchange rate mechanism, was from 1994 converted into a single currency unit, and Foreign Exchange Certificates (FECs) were gradually withdrawn. Effectively this led to a 33 per cent devaluation of the yuan against the US dollar.

Two stock exchanges — in Shanghai and Shenzhen — were opened in 1990 and 1991, the former having a market capitalization of US$19.4 billion and the latter, about half that, as at the end of 1993. Only four Chinese companies had been listed at that stage on the Hong Kong Stock Exchange which, however, played a crucial role in providing capital management and other services. China was able to claim that it had about 130,000 foreign investment projects with about $170 billion in contracts.

The more disturbing feature of the Chinese economy, however, was that a wide range of economic and commercial crimes, which might attract fines or short-to-medium jail terms in most countries, were punishable by death, and a number of executions have been well publicised to discourage repetition. Nor have Chinese security officials been scrupulous about recognizing international borders or extradition treaties, in at least one case abducting a Chinese man holding an Australian passport from a Macau hotel to stand trial in China (and later sentenced to 16 years jail for alleged embezzlement).

During the 1980s, Guangdong's Pearl River Delta experienced a 20 per cent annual growth rate in industrial output, rising to 27 per cent in 1991 and its foreign investment projects in 1993 were producing more than half the province's total output and 40 per cent of hard currency earnings. Hong Kong has, moreover, invested US$45 billion in China in fifteen years (representing 61 per cent of total foreign investment in the country) while China has ploughed back US$14 billion in Hong Kong. These figures are continually changing, with the ebb and flow of the economy. Not only is Hong Kong and Taiwan capital being invested in the main southern province of China, but Hong Kong dollars are moving in at an accelerating rate and almost 30 per cent of the total currency issued in Hong Kong was circulating in China — at around US$2–$3 billion. Monetary experts expect that as investment increases the level of integration between the two areas will strengthen.

The figures for trade are even more spectacular. Total trade in 1992 had increased by 32 per cent a year (to US$80 billion) and Hong Kong accounted for 27 per cent of China's imports and in turn 45 per cent of its exports went to Hong Kong. Tourism is also booming, with Hong Kong residents spending more than US$2 billion, or 85 per cent of total tourist receipts.

Thus the economic integration between Hong Kong and China has already progressed to the point where the two are closely interlocked and the process can only continue. China and Hong Kong appreciate the economic advantages but the political implications give rise to concern in Beijing. For while Deng Xiaoping was pleased with the interlocking economic growth he warned of the dangers of "bourgeois liberalization" and "cultural pollution" that might flow from it.

Chinese officials do not have to visit Guangdong and Shenzhen to be aware of the consequences. The rapidly changing lifestyle of people in Beijing itself gives the clearest indication of how traditional values have been eroded and replaced. For the growth of wealth widens the purchasing power of the people and exposes them to new forms of entertainment and leisure, many copied from satellite television received by thousands of Chinese homes. Through this medium, as well as directly from Hong Kong and Taiwan, the pop culture has made inroads. Chinese stars, imitating cult singers like Madonna and Michael Jackson, albeit with a strong local flavour and character, are drawing growing audiences. With barely intelligible lyrics loaded with slang, innuendo and double meaning they sing in a language that defies rational translation — though most are syrupy love songs; the fear among paranoid officials, is that this may become an information highway for freedom-seekers pushing their message to youth all over the country.

In a society where political brainwashing has dwindled to token levels and where Communist ideology is barely acknowledged even at the highest level, consumerism is breeding an upsurge of hedonism and self-seeking, with a serious erosion of the values propounded in earlier years. The Chinese authorities have tried to ban satellite dishes but have found this cannot be generally enforced. The quest for wealth has widened the gulf between the affluent east-coasters and the majority of poor rural people. This has led to a massive influx of country folk into the cities, heightening overcrowding, homelessness, crime and un-employment.

Because of the demand within China for exotic jewellery, top brands of wrist watches, highly priced cars and speed boats — unavailable in local shops — thefts in Hong Kong in the early 1990s soared to record levels. Hundreds of cars were spirited from the city by armed gangs on high-powered multi-engined speed boats. Frequent gun battles broke out between smugglers and naval and customs patrols, but the speed of the hijackers resulted in few arrests. Particularly favoured were Italian speed boats and German luxury cars. Equally notorious were the military-style gangs from China which raided gold and jewellery shops, engaging in shoot-outs with police in busy streets and shopping centres. Greater co-operation between Hong Kong and Guangdong helped reduce the incidence.

Powerful triad gangs in Southeast Asia, Canada, US and Australia, involving Hong Kong and Chinese mainland emigrants, have taken part in drug trafficking on a major international scale.

No longer is it a case of China trying to keep out imported drugs, as it was before the Opium War, but First World countries struggling to control drug imports from the Far East.

More ominous is the resurgence of piracy in international waters extending from the coast of South China to the waters of Singapore, with Filipinos, Thais and Chinese bidding for a lucrative share of the greatly increased volume of shipping plying these waters. While international container ships and passenger liners have not been targetted, smaller vessels have been regularly plundered, and Chinese coastguards (or people posing as them) have been involved. Where the Royal Navy could swiftly respond in years before World War II its jurisdiction is limited today to Hong Kong's own territorial waters; even there they have had mixed success in combating smugglers.

China is awash with cash and the demand for luxury foreign-made goods cannot be satisfied with the limited import quotas permitted. This causes dissatisfaction to exporting countries which run up large deficits in their trade with China due to Chinese import barriers. Most seriously affected was the United States which in 1993 was burdened with a deficit of more than US$18 billion. Of particular concern was the extensive breach of copyright laws and trademark piracy in goods ranging from compact discs, cornflakes and soft drinks to designer fashions, manufactured in the myriad factories that the industrial boom has spawned. On the other hand, China's growth rate of almost 13 per cent was seriously straining the economy and, though later reduced to 11 per cent, the danger of overheating continued to cause serious concern to Beijing with inflation running at 15 per cent.

China's initial reaction was to impose controls, but when this proved unpopular with the provinces it relented and allowed continued growth. China's somewhat lopsided development in recent years, which has seen a massive concentration of industry in the south, has meant that the gains have been unevenly spread. Moreover, the rail system is unable to cope with the transport of minerals and chemicals from western provinces to the major industrial plants on the eastern seaboard. A Hong Kong–Beijing rail link to relieve this bottleneck is expected to be completed in 1996 at a cost of US$65 billion. One of the more spectacular communication links is a highway which runs from the Hong Kong border around the Pearl River estuary to Macau. A bridge will span the Pearl River in 1997 where the old Bogue Forts used to stand guard at the Bocca Tigris to keep out predatory foreigners.

Impressive as the performance of secondary industry has been, China for many centuries has depended on its rural production to feed the mouths of its hundreds of millions of people. Its vulnerability to floods, storms and droughts has taken a heavy toll of lives, land and crops. Where does it stand in the last decade of the twentieth century? The one area where the Deng market reforms made first and greatest impact was on the land. The Mao-era communes were replaced with small private plots and each farmer was given a state quota and then a free hand to sell the surplus. This triggered a nine per cent a year increase in output for the next six years, and was the first and most evident sign of prosperity seen by Western visitors.

The open markets were invariably rich in produce and enjoyed good business. Over the years China not only moved closer to self-sufficiency but became the world's biggest producer of food; in terms of cereals it outperformed the US. A relatively unknown bureaucrat took most of the credit. He was the Minister for Agriculture, He Kang, who brought increased prosperity for many of the 800 million people who live on and off the land. China occupies about one-seventeenth of the total land area of the world yet feeds one-fifth of its population — an achievement to inspire others searching for a bigger food bowl in the years ahead.

By the turn of the century, China's economy could exceed that of Japan's and if growth continues without interruption it will be challenging that of the United States by the middle of the twenty-first century. The economy has been growing at the rate of 12–13 per cent a year compared with the more conservative official target of 9 per cent. Whereas in 1983 China could manage only twentieth place in the world trade league, a decade later it was in tenth place and in the next fifty years could be among the top two or three.

China is understandably proud of its economic achievement which will, on current trends, give it the kind of growth in the next two decades that Japan took forty years to achieve. But it is concerned at the price it may have to pay, particularly in the environment. Capitalism has come to stay, however, and any government or party that tried to reverse this trend would encounter explosive opposition at many levels. Riding the tiger of capitalism entails a mastery of the techniques of economic management and the adoption of policies to siphon off and reinvest the substantial fortunes being made by Chinese people. The fear that people will demand an increasing say in how these funds are taxed and spent is clearly uppermost in Beijing officials.

For while in a small economy like Singapore's, a strong charismatic leader such as Lee Kuan Yew was able to exert pressure on people to comply with national policies, in a country of 1.2 billion it is almost impossible. Already there has been much decentralization of the Chinese economy, with more power being given to the provinces under the market reforms of 1978. Trying to regain control and reimpose strict regulation from Beijing could lead to the kind of internal disintegration seen in the 1920s.

Moreover, China still has a serious problem with more than 100,000 state enterprises — the dinosaurs of Communist industrial policy. All enjoyed decades of feather-bedding by indulgent party machines; all built up massive payrolls, offering employees the privilege of the "iron rice bowl," with job and social security for life. Now, more than a third are bankrupt and need to be phased out, throwing many hundreds of thousands out of work — a potentially serious source of instability. Many more need urgent modernization with large capital inputs and drastic staff cuts. Placating, relocating and gainfully employing them, together with millions of rural job-seekers, will be a massive and severely testing task.

To retain the loyalty and support of regional chiefs, Beijing will have to exercise a loose rein and give more freedom to the provinces, relying on cultural and linguistic bonds to hold the country together. The era of the warlords, earlier in this century, should be a reminder of the potential for fragmentation. China experienced a tense and difficult situation after June 1989, when widespread dislocation occurred, with employees absenting themselves from workplaces following the imposition of martial law in many cities. A fine line divides stability and turmoil in China and the loyalty of the People's Liberation Army which played a key part in 1989 in restoring order, will be crucial.

There is also the vexing question of human rights which countries like the United States are stressing, though no longer as a condition for granting tariff reductions and most-favoured nation status for imports. China has never favoured dismantling its tight control of domestic security and holds a typically Asian contempt for the individual freedoms espoused in the West. Token gestures may be offered but with responsibility for 1.2 billion people Beijing will play this card carefully. Chinese supporters of the *status quo* argue that democracy in the West is less than 200 years old, and has only been adopted in 20 per cent of the world's independent states. Why, they argue, should China be forced to plunge into a risky political experiment that is neither consistent with its traditions and culture nor widely endorsed by the world at large.

In the case of Hong Kong, Beijing sees only dangers in moving towards greater political freedoms, as envisaged by Governor Christopher Patten. Its economic record, however, is valued; for Hong Kong has the third highest GDP in Asia and is one of the ten richest territories in the world. Moreover, its phenomenal growth can only be blunted by an act of recklessness similar to Mao's Cultural Revolution in 1966. China warned of "turmoil" in Hong Kong if political reforms were introduced before 1997 and there were dark threats of "intervention." To do so, however, would totally destroy international confidence in the territory which, with its nestegg of US$45 billion in accumulated savings, has a key role to play in financing future investment.

The alternative course was to put in place the "second kitchen" — a process whereby the 150 members of the Preparatory Committee would prepare to appoint a Chief Executive and a provisional legislature in 1996.[1] They would move into operation the day Hong Kong changes flags, 1 July 1997. On that date, Patten's elected Legislative Council, together with the Urban Council and the district boards, would cease to exist. It would then be up to Beijing to decide whether the new Special Administrative Region (SAR) legislature would be fully or partially elected and when and how this would take place.

The existence of parallel competing legislatures is itself fraught with difficulties and complications and the last years of Hong Kong seem likely to be marked by confusion and uncertainty both for the administrative machine and the man in the street. The civil service, answerable only to one ruling authority — Governor Patten — cannot help but keep an eye on the deliberations and decisions of the "second kitchen" to ensure a problem-free takeover. Yet at almost every level, civil servants were discouraged from communicating, in any more than a perfunctory way, with those taking over the running of Hong Kong after the British departure. Chinese officials retailated by refusing to speak to Patten or his officials — a stand-off that proved not only a strain on individual loyalty but a divisive tension for those at a senior level. However, police, immigration and water supply

---

1. The Preparatory Committee, comprised of both local representatives and PRC officials, would set up a Selection Committee. Its key responsibilities include: firstly, to select the first Chief Executive-designate and his team-designate, and secondly, to establish the provisional legislature by the end of 1996 or early 1997.

Figure 16.1 Governor of Hong Kong, Chris Patten, exchanges toasts in Hong
Kong with Director of Xinhua News Agency (Hong Kong
Branch), Zhou Nan, at the celebration of the forty-sixth anniver-
sary of the founding of the People's Republic of China, on 1
October 1995.

problems have for many years come up for routine discussion at
a working level — harmoniously for the most part. Moreover,
with the formation of the Preparatory Committee, Britain
promised co-operation, and senior Hong Kong officials visited
Beijing for talks.

Why did Hong Kong act on political reform so late in the day?
Britain considered making constitutional reforms at the
municipal level in 1946 under the then Governor, Sir Mark Young.
The push came from London, not Hong Kong, and the British
Government was responding to the newly proclaimed UN charter
which stressed the need to develop self-government "to take
due account of the political aspirations of the peoples." Young
intended to start with an all elected Municipal Council and
believed this was in accordance with local opinion. The plan
was approved by London, but Young then retired, worn out by

wartime imprisonment in Taiwan and China. The new Governor, Sir Alexander Grantham, was less enthusiastic.

However, under London's encouragement the Government published the bills to set the process in motion. By 1949, with China going Communist, the mood began to change. David Landale, Jardine's taipan, and an appointed member of Legislative Council, voiced objections on the grounds that "a strong body of opinion does not favour this reform and would rather see a larger and more representative Legislative Council working in conjunction with a larger and more representative Urban Council." The "strong body of opinion" was not further identified. Grantham promised there would be no Government steamroller, and the Young plan fell dead in its tracks. The Legislative Council was later expanded but members were appointed, not elected. This gradual expansion continued, with minor variations, for the next thirty-five years. There was no popular demand for constitutional reform; low taxes for a few and none for the majority of bread winners minimized discontent while living standards moved up steadily. Hong Kong also enjoyed a high degree of individual freedom if not on the electoral level, certainly in pursuing life-styles, careers, recreations, entertainment, beliefs and media outlets.

The changes made in 1985 and the introduction of nine elected functional constituencies and twelve voted by electoral colleges (but still with twenty-two appointed members) were the first major step towards a more representative system for Hong Kong, though the Urban Council had been largely elected for some years. In addition to Legislative Council, Urban Council and elected district boards, there is an extensive consultative network at many levels which contributes much to current policies.

When China agreed on a "high degree of autonomy" for Hong Kong in the Joint Declaration of 1984 it is doubtful if it envisaged creating an independently self-governing state. Neither Sir David Wilson nor Sir Edward Youde was considering such a step. Sir Edward favoured introducing more functional constituencies while his successor, Sir David Wilson, endorsed the concept of "the through train" shunting Hong Kong into its new SAR status in 1997 and continuing thereafter along the same track without interruption.

In 1992, the newly elected Conservative Government in Britain made a dramatic change in Hong Kong policy. The Prime Minister, John Major, was tired of dictation by Foreign Office mandarins, and frustrated by Governor Wilson's failure to win agreement with the Chinese on building a major new airport in Hong Kong; he was also disenchanted with the provisions of the Joint Declaration, believing British officials had been out-manoeuvred by the Chinese. Terminating Wilson's appointment prematurely, he threw the governorship to a trusted high profile political ally who had however lost his own seat in the last general election. For the first time, Hong Kong had a politician as a gover-nor who was given the green light to push for democratic reforms in the territory's last years.

How much this was driven by influential Hong Kong busi-ness interests anxious to preserve a greater measure of inde-pendence and to frustrate Chinese interference in the projected Special Administrative Region, can only be guessed. Certainly there was some local pressure for democratic reform. Fears of excessive Chinese meddling and interference were articulated from the outset. The Tian'anmen Square massacre of 1989 showed how ruthlessly the Chinese leadership would intervene to defend its interests. Hong Kong needed protection — more palpably than in the promises voiced by Chinese officials or in the fine print of the Joint Declaration and the Basic Law.

Patten relished the challenge and arrived with almost a mes-sianic flourish, discarding the Victorian plumes and trappings of a model colonial Governor, and promising changes which would make autonomy a visible and quantifiable reality before the dawning of 1 July 1997. This goal he pursued doggedly, brushing aside opponents and conservatives who made up the old Hong Kong establishment. He wooed young people and careerists with a long-term stake in the territory; the old guard of conservative taipans and Chinese millionaires, by now swinging behind Beijing and anxious to preserve their stake in the post-1997 community, was sidelined. The still influential denizens of the Hong Kong Club felt affronted at their cavalier dismissal. Chinese officials in Beijing turned up their criticism to full pitch; Patten, no slouch in the debating arena, retaliated with a force that shocked his China critics and many in Hong Kong, unused to bearpit politics.

Patten could plead some justification for his reforms. The Basic Law promulgated in April 1990, envisaged a legislature half elected by functional constituencies and half by direct elections but this would not take place until the third term of the Legislative Council in 2003; ultimately it was envisaged that all Legco members would be elected by universal suffrage. Thus Patten appeared to be anticipating this eventuality. But in assuming this role his actions implied clear distrust of China's intentions and by pre-empting the Chinese timetable he offended their sensitivities and intensified suspicion about Britain's political objectives. Since then his reforms moved to a point where the directly elected element in Legco were considerably increased, with greater voting power to more than two million people.

The former British Foreign Secretary, Mr Douglas Hurd, told the House of Commons at the end of 1993 that "there is no argument between Britain and China over the principle that Hong Kong's democratic institutions should continue to develop [for] that is set out in the Sino-British Joint Declaration." He went on to say "the issue is how these principles should be turned into practical arrangements." And the underlying question was whether Britain would "bequeath to Hong Kong an open and democratic system offering the electorate a genuine choice, or … settle for a system based on small electorates open to manipulation and corruption."

Patten may plead he was both responding to a perceived

demand of the people and fulfilling an agreed commitment in pursuing electoral reform. But however necessary it is to ensure the "high degree of autonomy" as promised in the Joint Declaration, a high-flying capitalist Hong Kong also has to be grafted on to a China still struggling to reconcile a socialist past with a private enterprise future. It thus has a dual interest — its own progress and development, and China's ability to mesh comfortably with the economically volatile territory. In considering Hong Kong's needs without giving due weight to Chinese concerns, Patten alienated those in Beijing and Hong Kong whose support was crucial.

Long before the arrival of Patten, Beijing was able to dictate its own agenda for Hong Kong's return to Chinese sovereignty — a fact he initially rejected but belatedly admitted in 1995. In China's case, however, redressing unequal treaties is one thing; swallowing and digesting a freewheeling capitalist economy the size of Hong Kong's poses real and serious challenges which London has consistently minimized in the political point-scoring that has marked its last years.

At the end of Hong Kong's life as a British colony, its last chief administrator encountered much the same opprobrium as its first. Captain Elliot was rebuked by his Government for mishandling the shooting war with the Chinese, and Governor Patten was widely despised by many for mishandling the shouting war. Captain Elliot was made Consul General in Texas. Governor Patten should do better — possibly returning to a senior political role in London, or in a leading corporate, diplomatic or economic post. For many in Hong Kong, his return could not come soon enough, though this would entail a serious succession problem for London, unless it were adroitly to choose the man Beijing is eyeing as the new chief executive.

How will history judge Patten? He was both an articulate politician and a bold innovator in Hong Kong terms but a double failure, having neither assured democracy for the people, nor reconciled China to British thinking. Indeed, old antagonisms and suspicions were painfully revived. The blame, however, was not all one-sided.

For its part, Beijing insists on controlling the political evolution in Hong Kong not only because of repercussions on China but also to ensure its dominant influence in the Special Administrative Region. Time, however, is on China's side. If its economy continues to grow, Beijing may well believe that it has developed a momentum of its own, and that Hong Kong has no further need of special privileges after the year 2047. Much will depend on the future of cities like Shanghai and Guangzhou as the wealth god spreads his wings.

Already there are many features of Hong Kong life that could cause friction in the long run, notably the massive differences in salaries and benefits paid not just to civil servants but managers, executives and employees at many levels of private industry compared with the still spartan rates in China. There is also the continued employment of expatriates in the civil service and the higher levels of the judiciary, particularly in the court of final appeal. For the time being these will be tolerated but in the long run, a two-tier system — a "socialist" China and a capitalist Hong Kong — will prove difficult to justify politically, particularly as other big Chinese cities begin to take-off; in the meantime a high level of corruption will continue to bridge the gap between the Hong Kong "haves" and the Chinese "have-nots". This could seriously hamper the respected regulatory system Hong Kong has built up.

Hong Kong's success in recent years may owe little to British colonial policy since, in its first century, it did little more than offer a safe haven to foreign traders, bankers and businessmen. When the time came for change in the post-war years, it was the concentration of Chinese talent and skills and the abundance of labour which got Hong Kong started as an industrial force. The Government's contribution was to put as few physical and financial obstacles in their way as possible; it deserves credit for what an official once described as "positive non-interventionism," while creating and developing the infrastructure necessary for it to grow.

Today Hong Kong is the outcome of more than 500 years of international contacts in trade, science, technology and business that have helped push China and its people into the modern world. However much it may despise the West for the misfortunes it experienced in the last century it is doubtful if it could have achieved its position in any other way.

China may claim that Hong Kong was always part of its territory (acquired by unequal treaties) and that more than 95 per cent of the population and its assets are Chinese. It is equally true to say that these Chinese people, without any loyalty to a flag, have amply demonstrated what kind of environment they need to create and build wealth. If China now feels it knows most of the answers, putting them into practice and giving people the freedom to use, enjoy, redistribute or invest that wealth will be one of the crucial challenges of the twenty-first century.

The bigger the Chinese economy becomes, and there are new "cities" spawning like mushrooms all over the country to accommodate this growth, the more acute will be the demand for personal freedom. There will be corresponding strains on the administration and greater demands for a decentralized authority in China and greater flexibility at the provincial and regional level; this process is bound to accelerate as wealth and prosperity spread. In a country as populous as China, this will impose enormous strains on the political machine. A successful creation of "largely autonomous areas" like Hong Kong could be a valued solution for other regions.

China today has become the world's industrial powerhouse, with a wide range of consumer goods emerging from its factories. It is the world's biggest maker of toys and Christmas decorations and makes more shirts and sweaters than the rest of the world put together; that is at the simple end of its industrial technology; it is also selling AK-47s to arms dealers all over the world and its "Silkworm" missiles found their way to Iraq during the war over

Kuwait. It builds everything from hydrogen bombs and space rockets to Ninja Turtles — and the hope must be that the three never get together. It is bad enough that a maverick like North Korea has sufficient plutonium to make bombs.

For while the menacing, monolithic image of "Red China" has been absent in recent years, there are still many defence planners in the region who place China in the potentially threatening category. This reputation was sharply rekindled by the sudden upsurge of aggressive, intimidating action against Taiwan in early 1996 when the issue of independence loomed large on the island's political agenda during a presidential election campaign. China thus still has to demonstrate that it is serious about becoming a responsible political-economic power, without resorting to destablishing military means to maintain unity; only then can it gain the respect and trust of its neighbours.

China is capable of making an impact on the world in many ways other than on the economic scene. It has, for example, gained the reputation of spawning one of the most debilitating strains of influenza known to mankind, the first in 1957 which not only claimed millions of victims in China but then circled the world, infecting many more. This was followed by another, originating in Hong Kong or South China, eleven years later, which likewise followed the trade and tourist routes around the world. The advent of "Beijing A" strains in later years demonstrates that in a world which has eradicated smallpox it still has a long way to go in effectively checking the spread of minor illnesses such as flu, literal proof that when China coughs and sneezes the world catches a cold.

In the meantime, a more enlightened approach to eradication of serious illness came in 1993 with the country-wide campaign to offer anti-polio vaccine to all Chinese children, a step taken thirty years ago by many advanced countries, but essential as China attempts to stabilize its population by limiting families to one or two children. Equally damaging could be a resurgence of tuberculosis which today claims less than 4 per cent of deaths, as against 25 per cent due to heart diseases and 15 per cent to cancer. AIDS is another great concern though unlikely to be as devastating as in the West.

By far the biggest killer, however, is the noxious weed which China imported from the Philippines in the seventeenth century — tobacco — which today claims more than 300 million smokers. Tobacco-induced heart disease, cancer, strokes and respiratory disease take millions of lives yet cigarette production has trebled in sixteen years. Nor does the Government care to stop it because of the huge windfall of more than US$5 billion in duties, not to mention export earnings of more than $100 million a year. Chinese attitudes to life and death have always been cynically pragmatic, as Mao Zedong argued when dismissing the nuclear war danger as a "paper tiger," because so many would survive.

For the smaller Chinese families (with a natural increase rate of 11.2 per 1,000 population compared to a world average of 18), the expected quality of life in the next century should be considerably enhanced — not only because of the country-wide economic improvement but because of China's increasing participation as a member of the international community. Though China may have missed out on staging the year 2000 Olympic Games, its athletes promise strong performances and many gold, silver and bronze medals at the 1996 Atlanta and the 2000 Sydney Games, possibly eclipsing the traditional dominance of the United States, Russia and Eastern Europe. This is particularly likely to be the case in women's sports — even in such "un-Chinese" events as weightlifting — provided of course they can avoid the pollution of performance-enhancing drugs which marred the achievements of the grotesquely overdeveloped swimming champions of 1994.

The opportunity for more and more Chinese people to travel overseas not only for professional or business reasons, but as tourists, should make them conscious of being part of a global community — something they may perceive through their television screens at present but which relatively few can enjoy.

When the Chinese masses begin to move in significant numbers, the major aircraft builders will be inundated with orders. As it is, air travel is growing internally at 25 per cent a year with almost forty airlines taking to the skies, and this in spite of serious air traffic control problems, several crashes and many hijackings.

The prospect of mass Chinese tourism is one engaging planners at present. It has been obvious to Hong Kong for some time in its initiative to build a new airport to replace the ageing Kai Tak. The justification is crucial in the eyes of Hong Kong planners if only because there are limits to the operation of a single runway airport in a dense, hill-ringed urban situation. Admittedly China is developing several airports nearby which could take some of the pressure from Kai Tak, particularly for Chinese regional air services. Moreover, with the conclusion of formal agreements for future economic and cultural co-operation, direct flights between Taiwan and the mainland can only be a matter of time, cutting out Hong Kong as the intermediary.

Regardless of local alternatives, however, Hong Kong and Macau (with its new airport completed) will continue to be the chosen gateways to China for international tourists, flocking there in increasing numbers following the opening of many attractive mainland destinations. With some of the best hotel accommodation in the region and reliable flight schedules offered by a variety of international airlines, Hong Kong has a clear advantage over any other city. China will be hard put to offer better facilities in the forseeable future. China has however made impressive headway in building new hotels and training staff in many cities; and after Japan, Hong Kong and Singapore, is one of the top destinations in Asia for foreign visitors. Its share of the traffic will grow with increasing internal prosperity.

China may be apprehensive of the huge outlays Hong Kong is planning on its airport and other infrastructure — new roads, tunnels, bridges, reclamations and townships — but far from being a device to strip the colonial larder bare, these schemes are planned to ensure continuing expansion and modernization —

crucial in an era when it faces strong challenge from Asia's other "little dragons" — Singapore, Taiwan and Korea. None can risk stagnating.

No less urgent is the need to expand container shipping facilities for these serve not just Hong Kong but southern China as its trade grows year by year. Container tonnage handled in Hong Kong doubled between 1985 and 1989 and accounts for more than half of Hong Kong's total seaborn trade. The elaborate but costly Port and Airport Development Strategy (PADS) devised by Hong Kong in 1989 is an attempt to cater for all foreseeable growth until the year 2006. This will involve a radical change of the physical map of Hong Kong, but direct shipments are expected to double in these years (with container throughput growing by five times) and transhipments and river traffic to triple, while air cargo and passengers should more than double.

The daunting cost of US$16 billion up to 2006 might well deter the faint-hearted but the past growth of Hong Kong gives every confidence that it will take this in its stride. When it is realized, moreover, that once the new airport at Lantau is operational and when Kai Tak is surrendered for redevelopment, the liberating effect on building heights and land values in Kowloon (where a new city of 250,000 will be built) will result in a considerable windfall for the SAR Government.

Great as the changes are on land, at sea the last two decades of the twentieth century have witnessed radically new designs of vessels to carry the growing volume of trade. Most of the old international shipping lines that served the Far East with freight services in the pre-war and early post-war years no longer exist, one exception being the first international steamship company to run services to the Orient — P & O. With the heavy investment needed to build container ships in excess of 50,000-tonnes many have had to form consortia and today fly flags of other nations, mainly those of Panama and Liberia — so-called "convenience flags" because of their less onerous and less costly operating and crewing conditions.

One other old China-coast firm deserves mention — Jardine, Matheson, though today shipping is a minor activity and opium long discarded as an item of trade. One of the first to enter Hong Kong after the Opium War, it was one of the first to quit after the Joint Declaration. Jardine, of course, is not leaving "lock, stock and barrel," but it has relocated its legal domicile to Bermuda, and delisted from the Hong Kong Stock Exchange which it dominated for many years. After failing to achieve the safeguards it wanted in Hong Kong, it transferred its listing to the relative safety of Singapore where it would be less exposed to hostile takeovers. Its pointed and clumsy withdrawal, while leaving all its money-making ventures in place in Hong Kong, upset China and later evoked a guarded apology; poor public relations in explaining the move, was blamed. There have been other Jardine actions which have upset the Chinese. It was in turn "punished" by China which refused to endorse Governor Patten's award of a lucrative container terminal contract to a consortium in which Jardine was a main partner. Regardless of its future in Hong Kong, however, it will continue to be significant in the region.

As for the physical profile of the maritime trade in the China–Yellow Seas, the dominant unit is the container ship which took over the bulk of international transportation in the early 1970s carrying freight in six to twelve-metre long steel boxes. Though more numerous, these are not the biggest ships afloat. There are bulk carriers of up to 150,000 and 200,000 tonnes to carry ore and coal, even larger carriers for oil (up to 400,000 tonnes), and a wide range of special product carriers moving gas, timber, wheat and other major trades, as well as the usual assortment of coastal carriers and freighters handling either containers or break/bulk cargo. Another specialized carrier is the roll-on/roll-off car carrier travelling between Japan and Germany and their major markets. All these are familiar sights in the China and Yellow Seas and are commonly seen at Chinese ports.

As in the era of tea and opium clippers, the ships of today are highly specialized, purpose-built vessels; there are however significant differences: modern technology, radar, satellite navigation and automated engines and steering, have taken most of the hazards out of sea travel. No longer is it necessary to lash a seaman to an outsize kite to test whether a journey will be auspicious. Indoor swimming pools, gymnasiums, cinema theatres and satellite television have taken the loneliness out of life at sea. The bridge has been commandeered by the computer and old-fashioned seamanship in a stabilized, air-conditioned, speed-regulated ship no longer commands the high premium it once did.

China's merchant fleet in terms of numbers of vessels (about 1,600) is one of the ten biggest in the world, though in terms of tonnage is only a quarter of that registrered in Liberia with about the same number of vessels. Panama, with more than 5,000 vessels, has a tonnage of under 70 million, reflecting its large "flag of convenience" tanker fleets. In addition to China's merchant marine, Hong Kong had two major owners, the largest being the late Sir Y. K. Pao's World-Wide Shipping, which at its peak in the mid-1970s owned 13.5 million tonnes, while the late Mr C. Y. Tung's Overseas Orient Container Line owned 4.5 million. Under his son, Mr C. H. Tung, these have since been substantially reduced due to the vagaries of world economics, but Hong Kong can still claim to be a significant owner and operator of ships.

The shift in industrial output from the United States and Europe to the Asian region in the last twenty years is clearly evident. Japan and Korea dominate as the world's biggest builders of ships, particularly of Very Large Crude Carriers (VLCCs). Japan is also among the world's biggest makers of cars (7.8 million), trucks and buses (7.3 million), colour television receivers (13 million), electronic desk calculators (64 million), videocasette recorders (31 million), cameras (18 million), refrigerators (4.7 million) and washing machines (4.6 million).[2]

---

2. *Encyclopaedia Britannica*, 15th edition, Chicago.

These were achieved at the height of the boom in 1986 and as the world moved through recession in the 1990s the numbers fell sharply.[3] The extent to which China is moving into some of these areas of production is being closely followed by Japanese industrialists concerned about the impact on their economy in the next century. China will, however, need a major boost in transport, roads, and related infrastructure to distribute its widening range of products.

With new ports in Guizhou and nearby Guangzhou, Fujian, Daxie (near Ningbo), Shanghai, Tianjin, Dalian, and Yantian, China may well question whether Hong Kong's place in an integrated network of China coast ports will be as crucial as the present administrators now believe. Much depends on China's growth and the pace and volume of investment. China's wish to decentralize its ports to cater for all sections of its country is laudable but it is hard to imagine Hong Kong surrendering its pivotal position in at least the first half of the next century until some of these ventures come on stream, particularly railways and highways.

Indeed not only is the Hong Kong infrastructure essential but the men and women who make it work — the businessmen, industrialists, investors, salesmen, lawyers, architects, merchants, judges and civil servants, with their wide range of contacts and their understanding of foreign commercial practices, banking procedures and foreign exchange mechanisms in Hong Kong, Asia and the rest of the world. For at least the next half century these people are irreplaceable in Hong Kong and Macau (to be surrendered by Portugal to become a special administrative region two years after Hong Kong).

The Portuguese today seem an anachronism, clinging to their tiny arrowhead of land, but their contribution to the grooming of

---

3. US output was still higher in some lines, however, with 40 million TV receivers, 6 million refrigerators and 5.7 million washing machines.

China was that of a pioneer getting a foot in the door. Visitors like Marco Polo, the Jesuit priests and scholars who came as scientists, mathematicians and canon-makers, Robert Hart at the Maritime Customs, Robert Morrison and James Legge as translators and compilers of the Chinese–English dictionary, Joseph Needham as a scientific communicator, contributed significantly to China's emergence. Equally the West has been greatly enriched by the many Chinese who have opened up the treasures of their culture, tradition and civilization to Western understanding.

At the end of the last century, a distinguished Chinese scholar, Kang Youwei, called on Emperor Guangxu to initiate a complete change of China's economic and educational system. Drawing on historical precedent he pointed out that some of China's most gifted emperors in various dynasties — Han, Ming and Qing — had made important changes and adjusted to new circumstances, employing talented people from outside the mainstream of scholar/officials and setting up new institutions.

The Japanese achieved this during the Meiji era; and modern writers could point to the liberating effect of United States policy in Japan, Korea and Taiwan in the post-war era. Regrettably the Emperor Guangxu missed his opportunity. Sun Yat-sen had his chance and it slipped through his fingers. Chiang Kai-shek became obsessed with destroying his opponents, though redeemed himself in the post-war years in Taiwan. Mao Zedong was the man who moved mountains but was injudicious in relocating them; they ended up falling on his feet.

Deng Xiaoping's opening of the door in 1978 to new ideas and new influences — culminating with his heady declaration, "To get rich is glorious" — has transformed China in the space of a few years; with 750 million people under the age of thirty-five by the year 2000, it can only be a miscalculation of immense proportions that will stop China from becoming a super superpower. Increasingly China has to accept that its leading position places upon it obligations and responsibilities not only for its own people but in complying with the international agreements and protocols that have been devised to ensure fair and harmonious relations between the nations.

In the closing years of the twentieth century China will be looking to the China–Yellow Seas as the main highway for incoming investment and technology and outgoing exports. From the China Sea it hopes to bolster oil production to supplement its vast coal resources and to ensure that it is the guardian of its own seaways, without any help from the United States Seventh Fleet. Chairman Mao's declaration that the "East is Red" at last has gained some substance, except that its "redness" has undergone some degree of dilution in the case of China and Vietnam. But for as far ahead as we can see China will be master not only of its own house, but of the eastern Pacific. The concerns and fears this may engender are understandable, particularly when periodic outbreaks of tension flare up, such as in the Taiwan Strait in 1996, threatening as they do not only mainland trade and investment links with Taipei, but international commerce and investment in the region. With no likelihood of democracy taking root in this society its government will always be at the mercy of autocratic leaders relying ultimately on force, as Deng Xiaoping himself did in June 1989, with no legislative checks and balances to restrain them.

There will be other setbacks in China in future, for there is no consensus on how to manage growth and too many centres of provincial power jostling and challenging the central regime. The country is already too big for a single political entity to govern comfortably and there will be serious and possibly explosive tensions if China has to rely indefinitely on tanks and AK-47s to enforce its will.

China has so far shown little interest in complying with international standards, treaties or agreements except where its own concerns dictate. With a population as large as the combined total of North America, all Europe, the old USSR and Japan, its growing economic might could well encourage a belief that it can set its own rules, regardless of others. The world, however, will view its future with concern until it demonstrates that it wants to be a full, participating and contributing part of the international community, treating its own people and those elsewhere with the respect, rights and responsibilities that have come to be accepted as the norms of a mature, civilized society in the twentieth century.

Bibliography

Atwell, Pamella. *British Mandarins and Chinese Reformers*. London: Oxford University Press, 1985.

Ball, J. Dyer. *Things Chinese*. Shanghai: Kelly & Walsh, 1903.

Bard, Solomon. *Traders of Hong Kong: Some Foreign Merchant Houses, 1841–1899*. Hong Kong: Urban Council Publication, 1993.

Beattie, Owen, and John Geiger. *Frozen in Time*. New York: Plume Books, 1990.

Beeching, Jack. *The Chinese Opium Wars*. London: Hutchinson, 1975.

Blake, Clagette. *Charles Elliot, RN, 1801–1875*. London: Cleaver-Hume Press, 1960.

Bland, J. O. P. *Houseboat Days in China*. London: Heinemann, 1919.

Bland, J. O. P. and E. Backhouse. *China Under the Empress Dowager*. London: Heinemann, 1910.

Bloodworth, Dennis. *The Chinese Looking Glass*. New York: Dell, 1969.

Bonavia, David. *Deng*. London: Longmans, 1989.

Borg, Dorothy. *The United States and the Far Eastern Crisis, 1933–38*. Cambridge: Harvard University Press, 1964.

Boxer, Charles R. *Fidalgos in the Far East*. Hong Kong: Oxford-in-Asia, 1968.

Boxer, Charles R. *Jan Compagnie in War and Peace, 1602–1799*. Hong Kong: Heinemann, 1979.

Buchan, Alistair. *China and the Peace of Asia*. London: Chatto & Windus, 1965.

Buck, David. *Betrayer of the Republic*. Hong Kong: Orientations, 1974.

Cameron, John. *Our Tropical Possessions in Malayan India.* 1865. Reprint. Hong Kong: Oxford-in-Asia, 1965.

Chang, Hsin-pao. *Commissioner Lin and the Opium War.* Cambridge: Harvard University Press, 1964.

Cheng, J. C. *Chinese Sources for the Taiping Rebellion.* Hong Kong: Hong Kong University Press, 1963.

Chesnaux, Jean. *Secret Societies in China.* New York: Pantheon, 1971.

Chesnaux, Jean, M. Bastid and M-C. Bergere. *China from the Opium Wars to the 1911 Revolution.* New York: Pantheon, 1972.

Chin, Steve S. K. *The Gang of Four.* Hong Kong: University of Hong Kong, 1977.

China: A Geographical Sketch. Beijing: Foreign Language Press, 1974.

Chiu, T. N. *The Port of Hong Kong.* Hong Kong: Hong Kong University Press, 1973.

Chow Tse-tsung. *The May Fourth Movement.* Hong Kong: Harvard University Press, 1967.

Churchill, Winston. *The Island Race.* London: Cassell, 1964.

Clyde, Paul. *The Far East.* New York: Prentice-Hall, 1952.

Coates, Austin. *China Races.* Hong Kong: Oxford University Press, 1984.

Coates, Austin. *Prelude to Hong Kong.* London: Routledge & Kegan Paul, 1966.

Coates, Austin. *Rizal.* Hong Kong: Oxford University Press, 1968.

Cohn, Don J. *Vignettes from the Chinese.* Hong Kong: The Chinese University Press, 1987.

Collis, Maurice. *Foreign Mud.* London: Faber, 1946.

Collis, Maurice. *Wayfoong.* London: Faber, 1965.

Collis, Maurice. *The Great Within.* London: Faber, 1941.

Cottrell, Leonard. *The Tiger of Chin.* London: Evans Brothers, 1962.

Couling, Samuel. *Encyclopaedia Sinica.* 1917. Reprint. Hong Kong: Oxford University Press, 1983.

Cowan, C. D. *The Economic Development of China and Japan.* London: George Allen & Unwin, 1964.

Cranmer-Byng, J. L. *Journal of the Royal Asiatic Society* (Hong Kong), Vol. 4, 1964.

Cronin, Vincent. *Wise Men from the West*. London: Rupert Hart-Davis, 1959.

Crow, Carl. *Handbook for China*. Shanghai: Carl Crow Inc, 1925.

Crow, Carl. *400 Million Customers*. New York: Harper, 1937.

Davidson-Houston, J. V. *Russia and China*. London: Robert Hale, 1960.

Davis, Ralph. *The Rise of the Atlantic Economies*. London: Weidenfeld and Nicolson, 1973.

Dawson, Raymond. *Imperial China*. London: Hutchinson, 1972.

Day, Clive. *The Policy and Administration of the Dutch in Java*. 1904. Reprint. London: Oxford University Press, 1966.

Diez, Ernst. *The Ancient Worlds of Asia*. London: Macdonald, 1961.

Donnelly, Ivon A. *The China Coast*. Tientsin: Tientsin Press Ltd., 1921.

Drage, Charles. *General of Fortune*. London: Heinemann, 1963.

Draper, Alfred. *Dawns Like Thunder*. London: Arrow Books, 1987.

Dun, J. Li. *The Ageless Chinese*. London: J. M. Dent & Sons, 1968.

Dyson, John. *Columbus, for Gold, God and Glory*. London: Hodder & Stoughton, 1991.

Eitel, E. J. *Europe in China*. 1895. Reprint. Taipei: Ch'eng-wen Publishing Co., 1968.

Encyclopaedia Britannica. 15th edition. Chicago, 1988.

Endacott, G. B. *Government and People in Hong Kong*. Hong Kong: Hong Kong University Press, 1964.

Fairbank, John King. *The Great Chinese Revolution 1800–1985*. New York: Harper & Row, 1987.

Falkus, C. *The Life and Times of Charles II*. London: Weidenfeld & Nicolson, 1972.

Fay, Peter Ward. *The Opium War, 1840–1842*. Rainbow Bridge Book Co., 1975.

Fitzgerald, C. P. *The Southern Expansion of the Chinese People*. London: Barrie & Jenkins, 1972.

Fitzgerald, C. P. *The Third China*. Singapore: Donald Moore, 1966.

Five Essays from the History of Modern China. Beijing: Foreign Language Press, 1976.

Fleming, Peter. *The Siege at Peking*. 1959. Reprint. Hong Kong: Oxford University Press, 1983.

Fortune, Robert. *A Journey to the Tea Countries*. 1852. Reprint. London: John Murray, 1987.

Fortune, Robert. *Visits to Japan and China*. London: John Murray, 1863.

Fox, Grace. *British Admirals and Chinese Pirates*. London: Kegan Paul, 1940.

Geography of China. Beijing: Foreign Language Press, 1972.

Gernet, J. *Daily Life in China on the Eve of the Mongol Invasion*. London: George Allen & Unwin, 1962.

Gittins, Jean. *Behind Barbed Wire*. Hong Kong: Hong Kong University Press, 1982.

Gittings, John. *The World and China, 1922–1972*. London: Methuen, 1984.

Gompertz, G. H. *China in Turmoil*. London: Dent, 1967.

Gottfried, Robert. *The Black Death*. London: Robert Hale, 1984.

Guillermaz, Jacques. *A History of the Chinese Communist Party*. London: Methuen, 1968.

Gutzlaff, C. *Three Voyages along the Coast of China*. London: Westley & Davis, 1834.

Harries, Meirion & Susie. *Soldiers of the Sun*. London: Heinemann, 1991.

Hatcher, Michael. *Nanking Cargo*. London: Hamish Hamilton, 1987.

Hawks Pott, F. L. *A Short History of Shanghai*. Shanghai: Kelly & Walsh, 1928.

Hewlett, Sir Meyrick. *Forty Years in China*. London: Macmillan, 1943.

Hibbert, Christopher. *London*. London: Longman, 1969.

Hibbert, Christopher. *The Dragon Wakes*. London: Longman, 1970.

Ho Ping-ti. *The Cradle of the East*. Hong Kong: The Chinese University of Hong Kong, 1975.

Hong Kong Government Information Services. *Hong Kong Airport*. Hong Kong: Yee Tin Tong Printing Press, 1962.

Honywill, E. *At His Imperial Majesty's Pleasure*. England: Book Guild, 1986.

Hough, Richard. *A History of Fighting Ships*. London: Octopus Books, 1975.

Howarth, David, and Stephen Howarth. *The Story of P & O*. London: Weidenfeld and Nicolson, 1986.

Howarth, Stephen. *Morning Glory*. London: Arrow Books, 1985.

Hsiung, S. I. *Chiang Kai-shek*. London: Peter Davies, 1948.

Hutcheon, R. G. *First Sea Lord*. Hong Kong: The Chinese University Press, 1991.

Hutcheon, R. G. *The Merchants of Shameen*. Hong Kong: Deacon & Co., 1991.

Hunter, W. C. *Bits of Old China*. 1855. Reprint. London: Kegan Paul, Trench, 1966.

Hunter, W. C. *The Fan Kwai at Canton*. 1882. Reprint. London: Kegan Paul, Trench, 1965.

Hunter, W. C. *Journal of Occurrances at Canton*, Royal Asiatic Society, Hong Kong.

Inglis, Brian. *The Opium War*. London: Hodder & Stoughton, 1976.

Jen Yu-wen and Lindsay Ride. *Sun Yat-sen: Two Commemorative Essays*. Hong Kong: Hong Kong University Press, 1970.

Judd, Denis. *The British Raj*. London: Wayland Publishers, 1972.

Kennedy, J. *A History of Malaya*. London: Macmillan, 1962.

Keswick, M. *The Thistle and the Jade*. London: Octopus Books, 1982.

Landstrom, Bjorn. *Sailing Ships*. London: George Allen & Unwin, 1969.

Lane-Poole, Stanley. *Harry Parkes in China*. London: Methuen, 1901.

Latham, Ronald. *Marco Polo: The Travels*. London: Penguin Classics, 1958.

Latourette, Kenneth. *A Short History of the Far East*. New York: Macmillan, 1952.

Lavery, Brian. *Nelson's Navy*. London: Conway Press, 1989.

Loewe, Michael. *Imperial China*. London: George Allen & Unwin, 1966.

Lancaster, Roy. *Roy Lancaster Travels in China*. Suffolk: Antique Collectors Club, 1989.

Lloyd, W. W. *P & O Pencillings*. London: Peninsular and Oriental Steam Navigation Co. Ltd., Day and Co., 1890.

Lubbock, Basil. *The China Clippers*. 1914. Reprint. London: Century Publishing, 1966.

Matz, Erling. *Vasa*. Stockholm: Vasamuseet, 1990.

McCunn, Ruthanne Lum. *An Illustrated History of Chinese in America*. San Francisco: Design Enterprises of San Francisco, 1979.

McCunn, Ruthanne Lum. *Thousand Pieces of Gold*. San Francisco: Design Enterprises, 1981.

Mackenzie, Compton. *Realms of Silver*. London: Routledge, Kegan Paul, 1954.

Mackerras, Colin. *Modern China: A Chronology*. London: Thames & Hudson, 1982.

Malone, Dumas, ed. *Dictionary of American Biography*. New York: Charles Scribners' Sons.

Majumdar, R. C., H. C. Raychaudhuri and Kalikinkar Datta. *Modern India*. London: Macmillan, 1951.

Maxwell, Neville. *India's China War*. London: Jonathan Cape, 1970.

McAleavy, H. *Black Flags in Vietnam*. London: George Allen & Unwin, 1968.

McAleavy, H. *The Modern History of China*. London: Weidenfeld & Nicolson, 1968.

Meadows, T. T. *Desultory Notes on the Government and People of China, and the Chinese Language*. New York: Praegar, 1970.

Mirsky, Jeanette. *The Great Chinese Travellers*. London: George Allen & Unwin, 1965.

Moorehead, Alan. *Darwin and the Beagle*. London: Penguin, 1971.

Moorehead, Alan. *The Fatal Impact*. London: Hamish Hamilton, 1966.

Morse, H. B. *The East India Company Trading to China*, Vols. 1–5. 1929. Reprint. Taipei: Ch'eng-wen Publishing Co., 1975.

Morse, H. B. *Trade and Administration of the Chinese Empire*. London: Longmans Green, 1908.

Ng, Peter, Y. L. *New Peace Country*. Hong Kong: Hong Kong University Press, 1983.

Poole, Otis M. *The Death of Old Yokohama*. London: George Allen & Unwin, 1968.

Potter, John Deane. *Admiral of the Pacific*. London: Heinemann, 1965.

Rees, David. *Korea: The Limited War*. London: Macmillan, 1964.

Ride, Lindsay. *Biographical Note on James Legge*. Hong Kong: Hong Kong University Press, 1960.

Ride, Lindsay. *Robert Morrison: the Scholar and the Man*. Hong Kong: Hong Kong University Press, 1957.

Rue, John. *Mao Tse-tung in Opposition, 1927–35*. California: Stanford, 1964.

Ryan, T. F. *Jesuits in China*. Hong Kong: Catholic Truth Society, 1961.

Scott, J. M. *The White Poppy*. London: Heinemann, 1969.

Seagrave, Sterling. *Dragon Lady*. London: Macmillan, 1992.

Seagrave, Sterling. *The Soong Dynasty*. London: Sidgwick & Jackson, 1985.

Selle, Earl Albert. *Donald of China*. Sydney: Invincible Press, 1948.

Smith, Albert. *To China and Back*. 1859. Reprint. Hong Kong: Hong Kong University Press, 1974.

Smith, Carl T. *Chinese Christians*. Hong Kong: Oxford University Press, 1985.

Snow, Edgar. *Red Star Over China*. London: Pelican Books, 1972.

Spence, Jonathan. *The Gate of Heavenly Peace*. London: Penguin, 1982.

Summerskill, Michael. *China on the Western Front*. Self-published, London, 1982.

Swarup, Shanti. *A Study of the Chinese Communist Movement, 1927–1934*. London: Oxford University Press, 1966.

Travers, Robert. *Australian Mandarin*. Sydney: Kangaroo Press, 1981.

Trevelyan, G. M. *History of England*. London: Longmans Green, 1926.

Trevor-Roper, Hugh. *A Hidden Life*. London: Macmillan, 1976.

Tuchman, Barbara. *Sand Against the Wind*. London: Macmillan, 1970.

Turnbull, C. M. *The Straits Settlements 1862–67*. London: Athlone Press, 1972.

US Congressional Papers. *Chinese Correspondence 1857–1859*. Washington DC, 1860.

Vinacke, Harold. *A History of the Far East in Modern Times*. London: George Allen & Unwin, 1950.

Waley, A. *The Opium War Through Chinese Eyes*. London: George Allen & Unwin, 1958.

Watson, Francis. *The Frontiers of China*. London: Chatto & Windus, 1966.

Wei, Betty P. T. *Shanghai*. Hong Kong: Oxford University Press, 1988.

White, Theodore. *In Search of History*. New York: Warner Books, 1979.

Wilson, Dick. *Chou*. London: Hutchinson, 1984.

Wilson, Dick. *The Long March*. London: Hamish Hamilton, 1971.

Wong Siu-lun. *Emigrant Entrepreneurs*. Hong Kong: Oxford University Press, 1988.

Yao Ming-le. *The Conspiracy and Murder of Mao's Heir*. London: Collins, 1983.

Ziegler, Philip. *Personal Diary of Lord Louis Mountbatten, 1943–46*. London: William Collins, 1988.

Index